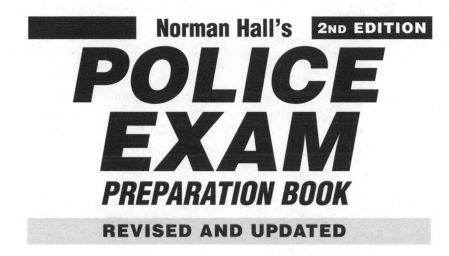

Norman Hall's **2ND EDITION**

POLICE EXAM

PREPARATION BOOK

REVISED AND UPDATED

ADAMS MEDIA CORPORATION
Avon, Massachusetts

Acknowledgments

Special thanks go to my wife, Shannon, for her patience and her help in making this manuscript possible, and to Mr. Howard Berry, Lieutenant (retired), LaHabra Police Department, LaHabra, California, for his professional expertise and editorial contributions.

Published by Adams Media, an F+W Publications Company
57 Littlefield Street, Avon, MA 02322 U.S.A.
www.adamsmedia.com

ISBN 10: 1-58062-842-7
ISBN 13: 978-1-58062-842-6

Printed in the United States of America.

20 19 18 17 16 15 14 13 12 11

This publication is designed to provide accurate and authoritative information with regard to the subject matter covered. It is sold with the understanding that the publisher is not engaged in rendering legal, accounting, or other professional advice. If legal advice or other expert assistance is required, the services of a qualified professional person should be sought.
> — From a *Declaration of Principles* jointly adopted by a Committee of the American Bar Association and a Committee of Publishers and Associations.

Many of the designations used by manufacturers and sellers to distinguish their products are claimed as trademarks. Where those designations appear in this book and Adams Media was aware of a trademark claim, the designations have been printed with initial capital letters.

The names used in this book (of suspects and victims) are fictional. Any similarities with real people is unintentional.

Illustrations ©Marnie Swenson, 2002.

Contents

Preface

CONGRATULATIONS on taking the most important step toward becoming a police officer. The fact that you purchased this study guide to prepare for the exam indicates your determination to be a successful candidate—one who gets hired.

All too often, test applicants fail to prepare themselves adequately and, as a consequence, receive just average test scores. Considering the present state of the economy, the unemployment figures in some areas, and the number of people desiring to serve as police officers, the competition for jobs is intense. Thus, Civil Service personnel have the luxury of screening only top-ranking applicants and can afford to pass up other qualified applicants.

By using this book to prepare, you have already gained a competitive edge over others. At the completion of your studies, you will know what to expect on the exam, the best way to handle difficult test questions, and common mistakes or pitfalls to avoid, and you will understand time management, preparation for the physical fitness exam, and many other techniques too numerous to include here.

You can be certain that you will be able to approach the exam with confidence and a sense of ease. This publication even takes that confidence one step further with its Guaranteed Test Results. If you do not score 80% or better on your written exam, you can return this study guide to the publisher for a complete refund. No other publication offers such an assurance. (See details on the last page of this guide.)

I am serious about helping you in your endeavors to become a police officer. I have a personal stake in your success, and as such, I will provide you with the most current, up-to-date material available. Before you begin your studies, I would like to wish you the best. Once you are hired by a police department, the rewards and job satisfactions are great and the service you provide to the community is invaluable.

— NORMAN S. HALL

Becoming a Police Officer

NATIONWIDE, THERE ARE CLOSE TO HALF A MILLION POLICE OFFICERS working in approximately 15,000 departments. Most of these jobs are concentrated in the larger municipalities (cities with populations exceeding 20,000), which have substantive tax bases to fund police protection services. The employment outlook for police officers is excellent because as populations expand, there is a corresponding need for extra personnel. Additionally, people are becoming increasingly less tolerant of crime and as a result demand more revenue be appropriated for expanded police forces.

The annual personnel turnover rate for police officers is relatively low in comparison to that for other occupations. A 10 to 15% turnover is typical for metropolitan areas. It can be significantly less (i.e., 5% or less) in police departments of smaller communities.

This rate can be attributed to promotions, transfers, retirements, disabilities, deaths, and other, unspecified, personal reasons.

Because of normal attrition and potential community growth, a police department must maintain an active register of qualified applicants to hire from as vacancies arise. The frequency of exams given to screen prospective applicants can vary. Typically, exams are given once a year; however, some departments examine two or three times annually, depending on the personnel needs of the department in question. Public announcements are made several weeks in advance of the exam in the local media (usually newspapers, radio, and even television) specifying when and where people can apply for the test. Another means of keeping abreast of exam dates is to submit a job application form at the local Police Department or Civil Service personnel office. Then, when exam dates are determined, you will be notified by mail. This option circumvents the possibility of overlooking a public test announcement.

Some states also publish a monthly or quarterly newsletter that specifies the location and time of exams being given around the state. To obtain such publications, call your state Civil Service commission and request to be placed on the mailing list for current updates. The service is free.

In addition to the written exam, there are some basic minimum requirements that job applicants must meet for employment eligibility. You must

- Provide proof of high school graduation or satisfactory completion of the GED test.
- Be at least 21 years old. (Some departments may accept applications at 18 years of age.)
- Be a United States citizen.
- Possess of a valid state drivers license and have a reasonable driving record.
- Be free of any felony convictions and of dishonorable discharge from the military.
- Have normal color vision and better than 20/100 vision in both eyes, corrected to 20/20 in the better eye and 20/30 in the lesser eye (vision requirements may vary among various departments) Contact your local Civil Service Bureau for more specifics.
- Meet minimum medical standards as set forth by Civil Service personnel.
- Have no history of excessive drug or alcohol use.

Other desirable accomplishments or abilities that would better qualify an applicant would include

- An Associate degree or course work relating to law enforcement from an accredited college.
- Good communication skills, both oral and written. Bilingual applicants are especially sought after by police departments, particularly if the non-English language known is used by local ethnic populations.
- Ability to work under pressure and maintain a collective sense of direction.
- Some knowledge of first aid and emergency medical care.
- Enjoyment of working with the public.

THE SELECTION PROCESS

Police officers are essentially the embodiment of a public trust and as such carry a wide degree of responsibility. If one were to generalize about the kind of work a police officer does, one could say that the protection of life and property is the primary goal. However, it cannot be emphasized enough that this is, at best, a vague synopsis of a police officer's job. There are a myriad of duties and responsibilities, which serve to protect life and property.

These duties can include the enforcement of laws and ordinances, maintenance of order, crime investigation, and court appearances. Community service functions can involve a degree of marriage counseling during a domestic dispute, acting as a quasi-lawyer with the respect to protecting everyone's constitutional rights, and even acting as a psychologist in knowing how best to handle suicide attempts.

The work load of a police officer can be as diverse as it is challenging. As a consequence, it is easy to understand why departments are extremely thorough in screening job applicants.

The steps that most departments follow in their selection process include the written exam, physical abilities test, oral boards, psychological evaluations, background evaluations, polygraph exams, and medical evaluations.

There may be exceptions to either the order or contents of this screening process but, by and large, this accurately reflects what is to be expected by a police applicant. A brief description of each step involved is given here, then elaborated on further in sections throughout this book.

THE WRITTEN EXAM

The police officer exam is a general aptitude test normally comprising 75–150 multiple choice questions. You are generally given $1^1/_2$ to 3 hours to complete the test. The test questions themselves will concern such areas as

- Memory
- Reading comprehension
- Situational judgment and reasoning
- Directional orientation (map reading)
- Report writing
- Grammar, vocabulary and spelling
- Basic mathematics

Although most questions relate to law enforcement, you are not expected to have the same knowledge as an experienced police officer. Instead, your grasp of general concepts, logic, and reasoning are the main focus of the exam. A passing score consists of 70% or better; however, some departments require applicants to score in the top 20-25% to be eligible for employment.

Note: Veterans who served in Vietnam between August 5, 1964, and May 7, 1975, or have received the Armed Forces Expeditionary Medal or Marine Corps and Navy Expeditionary Medal for opposed action on foreign soil (e.g., Iran, Southeast Asia, Grenada, or Lebanon), Service Medal for Operation Desert Storm, and who have not been discharged longer than eight years by the actual date of the police officer written exam, may qualify for preference points. A copy of your DD Form 214 will be required to substantiate the claim. For specifics, contact the office of personnel of the department you wish to apply to.

THE PHYSICAL ABILITY TEST

Since a police officer's job can place significant demands on his or her overall stamina, it is not hard to understand why an applicant must be physically fit. Various ability exercises are set up to test an applicant's flexibility, muscular strength/endurance, and aerobic conditioning. Exercises seen on past exams include these:

- Running an obstacle course involving short-distance sprints, weaving around traffic cones, ducking overhead obstructions, climbing stairs, and use of the balance beam.
- 165-pound Dummy Drag (simulated victim carry).
- Running a predetermined distance (e.g., $^1/_4$, $^1/_2$, or 1 mile) and climb over a 6-8 foot wall or chain link fence.
- Sit up, push-up and pull-up repetitions.
- Bench pressing, curl, and squatting with various weights using either barbells or variable-resistance weight training equipment.
- Stair climb (specifically designed to measure pulse rate).

Normally, applicants are rated on a pass/fail basis in accordance with a department's established minimum standards. Recently, however, some departments are rating how well a candidate performs in a physical abilities test in terms of percentages. Test score parameters can range from 100% for top performance to minimum acceptable standards of 70%. What's more, this test score is combined with the written test score and then averaged to determine an overall score. Departments may elect to average both scores evenly or may place a greater emphasis on the written exam score.

ORAL BOARD

Traditionally, if a vacancy in the department arises, applicants with the highest test scores are requested to appear before an oral board. This interview is conducted by a panel composed of three to five people who serve as staff officers or are involved in police personnel management. Typical questions asked of applicants are, "How do you think you are better qualified than other applicants? What do you feel are your strong and weak points? Could you use lethal force against another person?" and similar questions. These kinds of questions give panelists a means of gauging your personal characteristics, oral communication skills, and ability to respond decisively and effectively to situations. Board approval is prerequisite for further employment considerations.

Note: Discussions relating to how to prepare for both the physical abilities test and oral board are given at the back of this study guide. Guidelines, as well as hypothetical test questions for the oral board, are provided to give you the best possible insight into what to expect once you have reached this level in the screening process. After studying these questions, you should feel better prepared and subsequently more relaxed during an oral interview. Well-thought-out answers to anticipated questions not only make you appear more confident but give a favorable first impression to those conducting the interview.

PSYCHOLOGICAL EVALUATION

Since a police officer works independently most of the time, it is imperative that he or she be mentally fit to respond appropriately to any incident. The profile of a professional officer not only encompasses a thorough knowledge of police procedure; it also involves sound judgment.

When an officer is the first to respond to a crime scene, accident, or incident, his or her decisions and actions can dramatically affect the outcome. Often there is not enough time to second guess an initial response. Decisions must be made quickly and in the best interests of those involved. This is particularly relevant when a weapon is involved. Sound judgment, good sense, and basic instinct are essential elements in a good officer. However, these can be undermined by prejudices or biases. If an officer is handicapped by either, it will be impossible for that officer to live up to the professional standards expected.

Psychological evaluations are conducted with the sole purpose of ferreting out such shortcomings. This kind of exam can come either in the form of a one-on-one interview with a qualified psychologist or psychiatrist or a written exam called a *personality test*. Either way, the applicant is asked questions that can effectively discern both the sincerity of the candidate and the likelihood of behavior unbecoming a professional police officer.

These exams are not impossible to prepare for. In fact, many of the questions seen on these exams are somewhat similar to what may have been asked in the oral board. Like the oral board, a psychological exam is a prerequisite for further employment consideration.

BACKGROUND INVESTIGATION/POLYGRAPH EXAM

The information you provide on your job application form concerning personal history is subject to intense scrutiny. Typically, a detective or other qualified staff member is assigned to conduct a thorough investigation into your past. Such areas as your education, employment history, past residences, military career, driving record, personal references, and health status will be reviewed for validity and completeness. It is extremely important that you furnish accurate and complete information about your background. Information is kept confidential. Leaving portions of a personal history statement blank and/or providing information that doesn't reconcile with a background check is a mistake that has disqualified many candidates in the past. If a discrepancy is discovered, it will be difficult for you to continue in the screening process as a viable contender. Be truthful about your past. Outside of a felony conviction, other indiscretions can often be overlooked if the offender has learned a lesson and matured to become a better citizen. Denying there was a problem or placing the blame on someone else is a sure way to discredit yourself.

As mentioned earlier, background checks are very thorough. The investigators assigned to your file may not only check academic records but talk to teachers or professors whom you have studied under. Past neighbors may be consulted as well. Every detail of your past is subject to examination. Additionally, some departments may elect to go one step further in the investigation and utilize a polygraph or "lie detector" test. A standard format of questions concerning an applicant's personal history is asked by a qualified technician. The results are interpreted and forwarded to personnel. In conjunction with what was learned in the background investigation, these results can ultimately determine whether an applicant is recommended for further employment consideration. If a problem shows up in this stage, unlike the other steps of the screening process, it may be difficult for an applicant to find out why he or she didn't receive a recommendation. This can be particularly frustrating to those who have made it this far in the screening process. Filing a formal appeal at this stage of the procedure will be of no avail. Therefore, the best advice here is to be honest and forthright about your past and demonstrate a positive attitude toward any past mistakes. Remember, the police department recognizes the fact that no one is perfect. However, a person who shows sincerity and a high degree of honesty is more likely to receive a recommendation than is one who tends to have a sketchy or questionable background.

MEDICAL EVALUATION

Medical guidelines followed by departments can and do change over the years and vary among departments. What may be acceptable to one department may not be acceptable to another (e.g., in height and weight requirements, or the prospect of vision correction through either glasses or contact lenses). Thus, it is recommended that you pick up a medical standards form and medical history questionnaire from the department you intend to apply to. Going about it in this manner, you will know exactly what is required by that department. Be truthful in filling out the medical questionnaire; this is one more element subject to being cross-checked during a background investigation. False information on these forms is bound to be discovered during the course of a thorough medical exam. So be honest about any medical conditions you may have. If you have a borderline condition, such as diabetes, hernias, or the like, consult your regular physician to see what, if any, steps can be taken to improve or alleviate the problem altogether. If a candidate must take medication for a medical condition, it can be safely said that most, if not all, police departments will reject that person from further screening. The major concern is what may happen to an officer afflicted with an illness that requires regular medication if he or she is deprived of that medication in the line of duty. Will that officer become disabled as the illness manifests itself unchecked? This is a significant concern to both the department and the officer involved.

You should be made aware, too, that medical evaluations are required not only prior to appointment but periodically throughout one's career. This is particularly true as some agencies may require tests conducted intermittently at random to check for illegal substances. A clean bill of health is mandated both for the aspiring police officer and the veteran officer.

GENERAL JOB DESCRIPTION

Once a candidate is appointed as a police officer (typically a decision that rests solely with the Chief of Police), an extensive amount of training is required prior to receiving his or her first assignment. This formal training usually occurs at a basic law enforcement academy and can last for several weeks or months. Areas of study include civil rights and constitutional law; federal, state and local laws; the criminal justice system; police ethics; patrol procedures; crisis intervention; firearm training; first aid; traffic control; self-defense; and criminal investigation. In tandem, a candidate must go through rigorous physical training. Mastering the prescribed studies and meeting minimum physical standards are both required to successfully complete academy training.

Once a recruit gets to this stage, he or she works under the close supervision of either an experienced veteran or a field training officer. During a probationary period of 3 to 12 months, every facet of the recruit's performance will be reviewed. If the recruit's performance measures up to departmental standards, he or she will then be entitled to the full benefits bestowed on veteran police officers. Normally, benefits include a comprehensive medical and dental plan, life insurance, paid vacation, a liberal pension, uniform allowances, and potential for promotion as determined by written exams and on-the-job performances. Average beginning salaries for police recruits can range anywhere from $24,000 to $33,000, with annual raises over the first few years raising that range to $33,600 to $40,800. Police sergeants and lieutenants, and police chiefs can earn $43,200, $48,000, and $90,000 per year, respectively, with the larger salary packages generally going to those working in the larger jurisdictions.

Layoffs within a police department are relatively rare, and most cuts that have to be made because of budgetary constraints can be handled through early retirements and no new hiring. If, in fact, a layoff must occur, an officer would have little trouble obtaining a lateral transfer to another town in need of qualified personnel. An important consideration here is that a police department has a significant investment in your training to become a qualified police officer. It is not about to sacrifice such positions unnecessarily, nor to deprive the community of an imperative service.

The working conditions encountered by police officers can be diverse as well as challenging. A typical work week constitutes 40 to 45 hours; anything over these parameters is considered overtime, for which the officer will be compensated additionally. An officer can be assigned to one of three shifts (i.e., day, evening or graveyard) and be expected to work weekends and holidays when necessary. Activities during a shift can include directing traffic at the scene of an emergency, rendering first aid to an accident victim, patrolling various districts for the sake of crime prevention, enforcing traffic ordinances, apprehending criminal suspects, becoming involved in public relations such as implementing D.A.R.E. (Drug Awareness and Resistance Education) in the schools, rendering roadside assistance to stranded motorists, helping quell public disturbances, and the like. The list of responsibilities can be endless. Nonetheless, a police officer has to be able to respond to any of these kinds of demands at any time and in any kind of weather. The best summary of what exactly is required of a police officer is seen in the Law Enforcement Code of Ethics advanced by the International Association of Chiefs of Police. The Code of Ethics is comprehensive in the respect that it addresses four very important fundamentals: duty description, standards of performance expected in the line of duty, standards to adhere to in your personal life, and an oath of commitment to follow these guidelines.

If an officer is willing to dedicate him or herself to the principles described below and will strive for self-improvement through training programs and education, he or she will reap the personal benefits and serve to improve the community as a whole.

CODE OF ETHICS

As a Law Enforcement Officer, my fundamental duty is to serve mankind; to safeguard lives and property; to protect the innocent against deception, the weak against oppression or intimidation, and the peaceful against violence or disorder; and to respect the Constitutional rights of all men to liberty, equality, and justice.

I will keep my private life unsullied as an example to all; maintain courageous calm in the face of danger, scorn, or ridicule; develop self-restraint; and be constantly mindful of the welfare of others. Honest in thought and deed in both my personal and official life, I will be exemplary in obeying the laws of the land and the regulations of my department. Whatever I see or hear of a confidential nature or that is confided to me in my duties will remain confidential unless revelation is necessary in the performance of my duty.

I recognize the badge of my officer as a symbol of public faith, and I accept it as a public trust to be held so long as I am true to the ethics of the police service. I will constantly strive to achieve these objectives and ideals, dedicating myself before God to my chosen profession . . . law enforcement.

PREPARATION FOR THE WRITTEN EXAM

As noted earlier, the written exam can basically be broken into seven areas:

1. Memory
2. Reading comprehension
3. Situational judgment and reasoning
4. Directional orientation
5. Report writing
6. Grammar, vocabulary, and spelling
7. Basic mathematics

Each of these topics will be discussed at the beginning of this study guide, followed by sample test questions and answers. Test strategies and hints will be provided and elaborated on as they apply to each subject area. It is important to note that there can be significant variations in test content, judging by what has been seen on past exams around the country. Some tests place a stronger emphasis on one or more subject areas while having few questions, if any, relating to other topics. To prepare yourself adequately for such a test, all seven areas warrant equal consideration, Then, you will be prepared regardless of what you may encounter on your exam.

STUDY SUGGESTIONS

The police officer examination is not the kind of exam on which you can hope for a high test score after just cramming the night before. Good study habits can have a significant impact on how well you do on the exam. If you follow these few simple guidelines, you can approach the exam more relaxed and confident, two essential ingredients for top performance on any exam.

Regular study times should be established and tailored to your comfort. Each person's schedule is different. Some people prefer to study for one or two hours at a time and then take a break, while others prefer several hours of straight study. Regardless of how you study, it is important that you do it regularly; do not rely on a marathon. You will remember the subject matter more easily and comprehend it better if you establish regular study habits.

Where you study is important, too. Eliminate any distractions that can disrupt your studies. The television, the telephone, and children can hinder quality study time. I suggest you set aside one room in your home as a study place and use it to isolate yourself from distractions. If you elect to use a bedroom as a study area, avoid lying in bed while you read. Otherwise, you may find yourself more inclined to sleep than to learn. It is important to have a good desk, a comfortable chair, and adequate lighting; anything less can hamper studying. If studying in your home is not feasible, go to your local library or some other place that offers an environment conducive to study.

Again, be sure to get plenty of rest. It is counterproductive and will slow learning if you try to study when you are overly tired. It is also important not to skip meals. Your level of concentration during the exam can suffer if you lack proper nutrition. Coffee and other stimulants are not recommended.

Memory

ONE OF THE MOST IMPORTANT SKILLS a police officer uses in the line of duty is memory recall. Officers who remember specific physical descriptions of people or vehicles wanted in connection with criminal activity stand a much better chance of apprehending suspects than those who have only a partial recollection of the facts. Another prime example of the importance of memory involves directives issued by a superior. It is imperative that such directives be followed quickly, accurately, and completely without having to be repeated. Valuable time can be lost and an emergency call may be handled less effectively if directives are second-guessed, forgotten, or jumbled. Additionally, it may be necessary for a police officer to memorize the geographical layout of jurisdictional boundaries and know the quickest route to any given location. Other tasks may include memorization of the various codes and procedures on police radio networks, remembering people in your area of patrol that have the propensity to commit various crimes, and the like.

This memory section has been placed at the beginning of this study guide because memory normally is the first subject encountered on the actual exam. Test examiners prefer to arrange an exam in this manner so that the rest of the exam can be given without any further interruptions. Typically, a memory exam booklet, film, video, or key or some other form of diagram is passed out to test applicants. Applicants are allowed limited time to memorize as much of the diagram as possible, then the material is collected. The question and answer sheet for this section may be handled separately, but is likely to be an integral part of the main exam. In any case, the key or diagram will not be available for reference during the test. All your answers must be arrived at by memory alone.

From what has been encountered on past exams, memory recall sections follow one of three different formats.

The first approach may involve studying a picture or sketch of an emergency or crime scene. Virtually any detail is subject to questioning. A second approach may entail studying a portfolio of various criminals complete with composite sketches or pictures, physical descriptions, personal data, and details pertaining to the crime involved. The third involves descriptive passages. A written passage is given that pertains to an incident involving a crime or provides information regarding law enforcement policy. Questions are based on what the reading specifically said. This closely parallels reading comprehension type questions that will be seen at a later point in this study guide. However, memory recall questions ask only about specifics of what was stated in the reading and do not involve making any kind of inferences.

Whichever format is seen on your exam, you will be given anywhere from 5 to 15 minutes to study the key or passage provided. The memory test may appear simple at first, but may require you to memorize between 50 and 75 items quickly. Unless you are gifted with a photographic memory, memorizing such volumes of material in such a short time may seem impossible. Don't despair, because this study guide offers a system that will substantially help those with marginal memory skills as well as improve the skills of those who are fairly proficient. The technique employed is called *imagery and association*. Any memory task can be simplified by using this system. It requires you to form images in your mind relevant to the item to be memorized. Each of these images is then linked together in a specific order by means of association. It may sound complicated, but learning to stretch the boundaries of your imagination can be enjoyable.

A. NAMES

Street names may be among the items that need to be committed to memory for the exam. Use the following street names as examples:

Jorganson Street
Phillips Avenue
Tremont
Tricia
Edgewater Boulevard
Bloomington

Most people would approach this exercise by rote memorization, or in other words, repetition of thought until recall can be accomplished. This is a boring way of doing things, wouldn't you say?

Believe it or not, by using the imagery and association techniques, you can actually have a little fun doing memory exercises. Now, look at those same street names again and see what key word derivatives have been used and what images we can associate with them.

For example:
Jorganson Street — Jogger
Phillips Avenue — Phillips screwdriver
Tremont — Tree
Tricia — Tricycle
Edgewater — Edge
Bloomington — Blossoms

Carry the process one step further and place those key word derivatives in a bizarre context, story, or situation. Using this process, we have developed the following story:

A **JOGGER** with his pockets completely stuffed with **PHILLIPS SCREWDRIVERS** wasn't paying attention and ran into a giant **TREE**. After dusting himself off, he jumped on a child's **TRICYCLE** and pedaled it to the **EDGE** of a pool filled with flower **BLOSSOMS**.

Sounds ridiculous, doesn't it? However, because of its strong images, you will not easily forget this kind of story.

Another advantage of the imagery technique is that you can remember items in their respective order by simply reviewing where they fit in relation to the other items in the story.

Look at each of the street names below and develop a story using imagery. There are no right or wrong key word derivatives. What is important is that the images conjure up a clear picture in your mind and then interlink.

Work on each of these columns separately:

Bedford Ave.	Apple Dr.	Anderson Blvd.	Bayberry Rd.
Wellington	Constantine Way	Cannon Ave.	Hickory Ridge
Walker St.	Bristol	Foxtail Run	Ebony Ln.
Penny Ln.	Echo Ln.	Arsenal Way	Ester Ct.
Ridgemont Dr.	Darrington	Jacobson St.	Steinbald Ln.
Bowmont	Smalley St.	Prince Williams	Georgia St.

Once you have finished this exercise, cover the street names and see if you can remember all 24 items. If your four stories are bizarre enough, you certainly can have this entire list committed to memory in a short time.

B. NUMBERS

Numbers are another problem in memory recall. For most people, numbers are difficult to memorize because they are intangible. To rectify this problem, numbers can be transposed into letters so that words can be formed and associated accordingly. Below is the format for transposition. Remember this format as if it were your Social Security number because on the exam you will draw from it regularly.

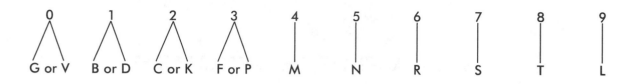

(All other letters can be incorporated into words without any significance.)

For instance, let's say you are given the number 10603328157. Memorizing this number so well that you can recall it after any length of time would be very difficult. However, by using this memory system, you could use the number to spell out a variety of memorable things. Here is your chance to use your creativity!

After you have had the chance to figure out what words can code such a number, one particular problem should become apparent; the more numbers you try to cram into one word, the harder it is to find a compatible word in the English vocabulary. To simplify matters, there are two alternative ways to form words. The first method is to take two numbers at a time, form a word, and associate it with the next word. Dealing with the number (10603328157) **DOG** could be derived from the number 10, **RUG** from 60, **PIPE** from 33, **CAT** from 28, **BONE** from 15, and **S** from 7. There are many ways you could imagine and link these words. One possibility would be a **DOG** lying on a **RUG** and smoking a **PIPE** while a **CAT** prances by carrying a **BONE** shaped like an **S**. This is just one way to memorize this long number. Other words and stories could work just as well.

The second alternative, which offers greater flexibility, is using words of any length but making only the first two significant letters of the word applicable to your story. For example, the word **DIG/GING** could represent 10 in the number 10603328157.

> **RAV/EN = RUG/BY = REV/OLVER =** 60
> **POP/ULATION = PUP/PY = PEP/PER =** 33
> **CAT/ERPILLAR = CAT/TLE = COT/TON =** 28
> **BIN/OCULAR = BEAN/S = DIN/NER =** 15

By doing this, you have a larger number of words at your disposal to put into stories. With a little originality, it can be fun to see what you can imagine for any number given.

Below are exercises to help you apply this system. The first group of numbers is meant to be used as a transposition exercise. See how many different words you can use to represent each number. The second series is for practice with transposition and story fabrication. This technique may seem difficult at first, but with practice, it will enhance your memory capabilities tenfold.

I.	44	63	86	40
	53	97	93	32
	61	10	48	26
	13	3	60	91
	12	57	35	99
	8	52	27	16
	41	11	21	68

II.   1754732115810   63211347890
          6980421569497   145344175328
          147329944710   917403218977
          8321355572119   638146119900
          488770509453   433351896487
          1530197865321   765320146991

C. PICTURES/SKETCHES

When you are presented with a picture or sketch on your exam, try to mentally walk your way through the diagram. Pay particular attention to details. For example, if there are any people, determine their relative position with respect to other landmarks in the scene. Are they initiating some kind of criminal event, being victimized, or just standing by idly serving as potential witnesses to what (if anything) is taking place? Look for locational references such as street names, numbered addresses, and store signs or logos. If any vehicles are present, what are the license numbers and general descriptions (e.g., two-door, four-door, sedan, van, truck, etc.)? If an emergency is apparent, what exactly is involved? Is a weapon present? If so, how is the perpetrator dressed and what are his or her physical characteristics (e.g., approximate height, weight, color, length of hair, etc.)? Are there any time references such as clocks or calendars? Is it day or night? Can the weather be accounted for? Being aware of such things and answering these kinds of questions will definitely sharpen your skills of observation. Now you will need to systematically develop lasting mental images of what was observed and link these into a memorable story. Look at the example below and determine a way that all the details shown can be committed to memory.

Note: Remember you are limited only by your imagination. There really is no one particular story that is correct. It is the intent here to demonstrate the mechanics of imagery and association and not to convey any absolutes. Chances are, you will develop a better story more custom-tailored for your own interpretative abilities than anyone else can develop for you.

Two students lay asleep in their bunkbed. A "Hawii" University diploma hangs directly overhead. Think of the bunkbed as two hammocks suspended between two palm trees to represent the Hawaiian association. The year 1987 on the shingle can be transposed into the letters BLT and S, which as an acronym by itself, can stand for a bacon, lettuce, and tomato sandwich.

Note: Two separate words could be transposed from 1987; however, an acronym that fits the entire number is far more convenient for memorization. So, picture "Hawii" University as the BLTS capital, much the same as McDonald's is the Big Mac capitol. As the perpetrator attempts forcible entry into the students' quarters, the clock above the window falls on his head, causing him to see stars (night association). Simultaneously, an unseen passerby outdoors asks the perpetrator what time it is. He replies "Tend to your own business" before resuming his break-in. "**TEN**" is the key word here, which refers to the time (i.e., ten o'clock). As the window is raised further, the crowbar he brought takes on a life of its own and turns into a crow. It lights upon the phonograph and uses its beak as the needle to play a record. The music played could be from the Jackson Five to represent the stereo model number JCX 221. Here again, two words could have been substituted for 221. You can see how a stretch of the imagination can come into play here. As the phonograph's rpm increase, the crow is thrown off and bounced between the two speakers before lighting on the chair in front of the desk. Only now has it become apparent to the crow that there was a cat on the bedroom floor licking his chops in anticipation of an easy dinner. The crow, now fully aware of his dire predicament, turns on the desk lamp and scribbles a last will and testament in triplicate: one copy to go to each of the drawers in the desk. The final chapter was near as the cat stalked closer. "If only I had the benefit of nine lives," said the crow. Note that the crow's final epitaph represents the number of books present in the desk.

You can see by the example given that a story can become outlandishly crazy. Perhaps it could be said that the crazier the story, the easier it becomes to memorize. More importantly, be sure all concocted images are properly linked together. Otherwise, you will be left with a collage of cute fabrications that can become somewhat meaningless when viewed independently of the main story. You should have a pretty fair idea by now of how to use this memory system to your advantage. Examine the sketch provided below for five (5) minutes. After the five minutes has elapsed, proceed to the questions on the next page and fill in the answers without looking at the diagram again. Check your answers with those provided at the end of the exercise to determine the effectiveness of your storytelling memorization skills. If you get through only part of your story development before time expires, don't despair. You will find that the more you use this system, the easier it will become to apply it to any memorization task.

SAMPLE SKETCH I

Study the sketch below for 5 minutes. *DO NOT* exceed the time allowed; if you do, you will forfeit the true sense of how an exam is actually conducted. When time is up, turn to the questions given without making further reference to the sketch. In the actual exam, the test examiner will collect the sketches when the time for studying is up, and then you will be directed to answer the related questions in your test booklet or supplement. You will not be allowed to review the sketch in the course of answering the applicable questions.

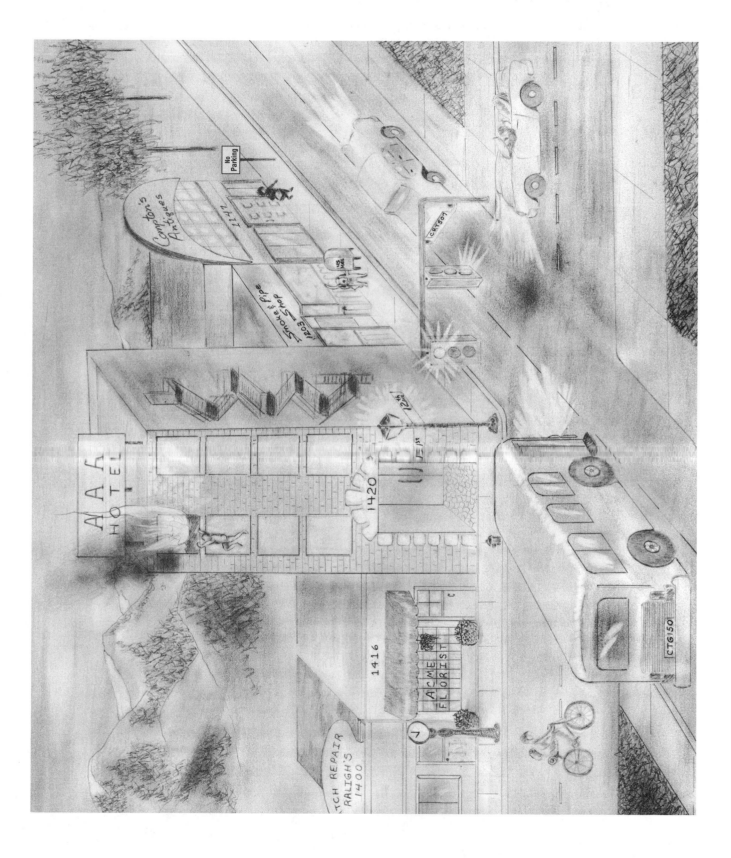

SAMPLE QUESTIONS FOR SKETCH 1

1. How many people are actually seen in this sketch?
    A. 1
    B. 2
    C. 3
    D. 4

2. Twelfth Avenue is a
    A. Two-way street
    B. Two lane, one-way street
    C. One lane, one-way street
    D. There is no 12th Avenue in the sketch.

3. 1416 151st Street is the address for
    A. ACME Florist
    B. AAA Hotel
    C. Raligh's Watch Repair
    D. Compton's Antiques

4. If any kind of emergency is depicted in the sketch, who or what is implicated?
    A. The bicyclist on 151st Street
    B. The motorist on 151st Street
    C. Someone on the third floor of AAA Hotel
    D. None of the above

5. What is the license-plate number of the bus entering the intersection?
    A. CGT 150
    B. CTR 150
    C. CTG 150
    D. CRT 051

6. What is the approximate time of day shown in the sketch?
    A. 10:00 a.m.
    B. 1:00 p.m.
    C. 5:30 p.m.
    D. 10:00 p.m.

7. The Smoke and Pipe Shop is located at
    A. 1197 12th Avenue
    B. 1420 12th Avenue
    C. 1203 12th Avenue
    D. 1400 151st Street

8. What is nearest to the person walking on the sidewalk of 12th Avenue?
    A. *NO PARKING* sign
    B. Fire hydrant
    C. Time clock
    D. Parked bus

9. Assuming that each window of the AAA Hotel above ground floor represents a room, how many rooms could be discerned in the sketch?

    A. 6   B. 8   C. 9   D. 10

10. The person who appears to be in trouble was
    A. Bent on committing suicide
    B. Forced out to the window ledge by fire
    C. Pushed out the window by an unseen assailant
    D. Robbed at gunpoint

11. Where is the fire hydrant in reference to the incident described in the previous question?
    A. Around the corner in front of Compton's Antiques.
    B. Closer to Raligh's Watch Repair than where the incident is taking place.
    C. On the 12th Avenue side of the AAA Hotel.
    D. Directly out in front.

12. According to the sketch, what individual or vehicle committed a driving infraction according to the sketch?
    A. The bicyclist pedaling down 151st Street.
    B. The lone motorist on 151st Street.
    C. The pedestrian crossing the street.
    D. The bus.

13. What is the license-plate number of the two-door sedan headed down 12th Avenue?
    A. ACT 125
    B. TAC 152
    C. CRT 507
    D. GCT 150

14. The Postal Service mail collection box is closest to what address?
    A. 1203 12th Avenue
    B. 1197 12th Street
    C. 1420 151st Avenue
    D. 1420 151st Street

15. Where is the unleashed dog located in the sketch?
    A. At the fire hydrant.
    B. At the ACME Florist shop.
    C. At the parked car on 12th Street.
    D. At the Postal Service mail collection box.

ANSWER SHEET FOR SAMPLE SKETCH 1

1.	Ⓐ Ⓑ Ⓒ Ⓓ	6.	Ⓐ Ⓑ Ⓒ Ⓓ	11.	Ⓐ Ⓑ Ⓒ Ⓓ
2.	Ⓐ Ⓑ Ⓒ Ⓓ	7.	Ⓐ Ⓑ Ⓒ Ⓓ	12.	Ⓐ Ⓑ Ⓒ Ⓓ
3.	Ⓐ Ⓑ Ⓒ Ⓓ	8.	Ⓐ Ⓑ Ⓒ Ⓓ	13.	Ⓐ Ⓑ Ⓒ Ⓓ
4.	Ⓐ Ⓑ Ⓒ Ⓓ	9.	Ⓐ Ⓑ Ⓒ Ⓓ	14.	Ⓐ Ⓑ Ⓒ Ⓓ
5.	Ⓐ Ⓑ Ⓒ Ⓓ	10.	Ⓐ Ⓑ Ⓒ Ⓓ	15.	Ⓐ Ⓑ Ⓒ Ⓓ

Answers can be found on page 41.

As mentioned earlier in the discussion of memory recall, another format seen on exams utilizes sketches of various criminals accompanied with physical descriptions and other information pertinent to the issuance of a warrant. Since there are a lot of numbers to remember, this is where the number transposition system can be very useful. Study the three sketches and associated personal data below for ten (10) minutes. Do not exceed the time allowed; if you do, you will forfeit the true sense of how an exam is actually conducted. When time is up, turn to the questions provided without making any further references to the composites just studied.

Note: Study each of the suspects for only 3 minutes each. That will leave an extra minute for quick review.

SAMPLE COMPOSITE SKETCH/FILE ONE
SUSPECT 1

Name:	Karl Scott Woodward
Alias:	Karl Paul Matthews
Date of Birth:	November 5, 1950 (Hint: look at this as 11-05-50)
Height:	6'2"
Weight:	185 pounds
Hair:	Brown
Eyes:	Hazel
Sex:	Male
Race:	White
Scar or Marks:	None
Social Security Number:	536-50-1240
	Wanted for interstate flight—murder
Criminal Record:	Second degree assault and criminal trespass
	NCIC (National Crime Information Center) file number: 23-16

SUSPECT 2

Name:	Frank Allen Anderson
Date of Birth:	January 9, 1963 (Hint: look at this as 01-09-63)
Height:	5'8"
Weight:	190 pounds
Hair:	Blonde
Eyes:	Blue
Sex:	Male
Race:	White
Scar or Marks:	Snake-like tattoo on left biceps
Social Security Number:	175-20-7531
	Wanted for interstate flight—rape and kidnapping
Criminal Record:	First degree sexual assault and parole violations
	NCIC File Number: 90-26

SUSPECT 3

Name: William Richardson

Alias: Dennis Brown, Dale Abernathy, and Wendall Cunningham

Date of Birth: February 20, 1959

Height: 6'4"

Weight: 180 pounds

Hair: Black

Eyes: Brown

Sex: Male

Race: Black/medium complexion

Scar or Marks: Scar on right outer edge of upper lip

Social Security Number: 963-44-9072

Wanted for attempted murder and possession of an unlawful weapon

Criminal Record: No priors

NCIC File Number: 40-12

SAMPLE QUESTIONS COMPOSITE SKETCH/FILE 1

1. What is the true name of Suspect 1?
   A. Karl Paul Matthews
   B. Karl Scott Woodward
   C. Karl Allen Mathews
   D. Wendall Cunningham

2. What color hair does Suspect 2 have?
   A. Red
   B. Black
   C. Blonde
   D. Grey

3. Which of the three suspects utilized multiple aliases in the commission of his crimes?
   A. Suspect 1
   B. Suspect 2
   C. Suspect 3
   D. All suspects used only one alias.

4. What height and weight is listed on the NCIC file of Suspect 3?
   A. 5'8" and 175 pounds
   B. 6'2" and 190 pounds
   C. 5'11" and 185 pounds
   D. 6'4" and 180 pounds

5. What is Frank Allen Anderson's Social Security number?
   A. 175-20-7531
   B. 936-75-3172
   C. 536-20-9072
   D. 875-30-1751

6. What does the acronym NCIC mean?
   A. National Crime Information Center
   B. National Crime Investigative Center
   C. Network for Criminal background Information Core
   D. Federal Bureau of Investigation

7. What is the date of birth of Suspect 2?
   A. February 9, 1969
   B. August 9, 1963
   C. January 9, 1963
   D. November 9, 1950

8. Which of the three suspects did not have any prior criminal record?
   A. Suspect 1
   B. Suspect 2
   C. Both suspects 2 and 3
   D. Only suspect 3

9. Which suspect used the alias Dale Abernathy?
   A. William Richardson
   B. Wendall Cunningham
   C. Karl Mathews
   D. Frank Anderson

10. According to the NCIC file, what was Karl Scott Woodward wanted for?
    A. Interstate flight—rape and kidnapping
    B. Interstate flight—murder
    C. Mail fraud
    D. Attempted murder and possession of an unlawful weapon

11. What is Frank Allen Anderson's NCIC file number?
    A. 12-40
    B. 90-26
    C. 32-26
    D. 23-16

12. The picture shown to the right is a sketch of which suspect?
    A. Dennis Brown
    B. Wayne Harper
    C. Frank Anderson
    D. Karl Woodward

13. What physical peculiarity sets Suspect 3 apart from others?
    A. Tattoo on left biceps
    B. Scar on outer edge of right lower lip
    C. Scar on outside of right wrist
    D. Scar on right outer edge of upper lip

14. What color are suspect 3's eyes?
    A. Brown
    B. Blue
    C. Hazel
    D. Unknown

15. What is Suspect 1's Social Security number?
    A. 963-50-1480
    B. 536-50-1240
    C. 175-20-5131
    D. 936-50-1240

16. According to the NCIC files provided, which of the three suspects is female?
    A. Suspect 1
    B. Suspect 2
    C. Suspect 3
    D. None of the above.

17. Who was described as having a medium complexion?
    A. Suspect 1
    B. Suspect 2
    C. Suspect 3
    D. None of the above.

18. What crime had Frank Allen Anderson been convicted of?
    A. First degree sexual assault
    B. Possession of an unlawful weapon
    C. Murder
    D. Parole violations and first degree sexual assault

19. According to the NCIC files, what is Suspect 1's weight?
    A. 185 pounds
    B. 190 pounds
    C. 195 pounds
    D. 200 pounds

20. Which of the three suspects can be considered the oldest?
    A. Suspect 1
    B. Suspect 2
    C. Suspect 3
    D. It cannot be determined from the information given.

ANSWER SHEET FOR SAMPLE COMPOSITE SKETCH/FILE I

1. (A) (B) (C) (D)
2. (A) (B) (C) (D)
3. (A) (B) (C) (D)
4. (A) (B) (C) (D)
5. (A) (B) (C) (D)
6. (A) (B) (C) (D)
7. (A) (B) (C) (D)

8. (A) (B) (C) (D)
9. (A) (B) (C) (D)
10. (A) (B) (C) (D)
11. (A) (B) (C) (D)
12. (A) (B) (C) (D)
13. (A) (B) (C) (D)
14. (A) (B) (C) (D)

15. (A) (B) (C) (D)
16. (A) (B) (C) (D)
17. (A) (B) (C) (D)
18. (A) (B) (C) (D)
19. (A) (B) (C) (D)
20. (A) (B) (C) (D)

Answers can be found on page 41.

If you are like most people, you may have felt a little rushed completing this last exercise. Since the informational format (name of suspect, date of birth (DOB), height, weight, etc.) is standard on wants and warrants, a fair amount of test time can be saved by becoming thoroughly familiar with the format. Thus, your number transposition and associated stories will not have to include that information. Awareness of your stories' chronological order will enable you to correctly interpret what information is pertinent to the question at hand. You may even wish to remember this informational format in a different order and plug in the facts as they are given. However, don't vacillate between different format orders because doing so can lead to some confusion.

Once you are comfortable with a certain conformation of the facts, commit them to your long-term memory. You will find this technique to be particularly time-saving when you run across such test questions.

Study the three sketches and associated personal data below for ten minutes. Do not exceed the time allowed; if you do, you will forfeit the true sense of how an exam is actually conducted. When time is up, turn to the questions provided without making any further reference to the composites just studied.

SAMPLE COMPOSITE SKETCH/FILE TWO
SUSPECT 1

Name:	Dale Willis Winfree
Alias:	Dale Hollensworth, Chance Forsythe
Date of Birth:	December 12, 1963
Height:	5'10"
Weight:	155 pounds
Hair:	Brown
Eyes:	Brown
Sex:	Male
Race:	White
Scar or Marks:	4" scar on right hand
Social Security Number:	208-55-5212
	Wanted for mail fraud, burglary, and robbery
Criminal Record:	First-degree assault
	Considered armed and dangerous
	Case Number: 87-512

SUSPECT 2

                    Name: Carl David Youngerman
                    Alias: None
          Date of Birth: June 1, 1948
                   Height: 6'4"
                  Weight: 210 pounds
                      Hair: Brown with reddish tint
                     Eyes: Hazel
                       Sex: Male
                     Race: White
         Scar or Marks: None known
         Social Security
                  Number: 832-58-9571, 832-85-9751

                              Wanted for conspiring to distribute cocaine
                              and conspiracy to transport funds outside the U.S.

      Criminal Record: Possession of heroin
                              NCIC File Number: 48-20

SUSPECT 3

                    Name: Tammy Faye Ellington
                    Alias: Brenda McCarthy
          Date of Birth: July 15, 1970
                   Height: 5'8"
                  Weight: 135 pounds
                      Hair: Brown (greying)
                     Eyes: Blue
                       Sex: Female
                     Race: White
         Scar or Marks: C-shaped scar around the left kneecap
         Social Security
                  Number: 652-44-0431

                              Wanted for storage and concealment of stolen
                              explosives and unlawful possession of false
                              identification documents

      Criminal Record: Possession with the intent to distribute counterfeit social security cards
                              NCIC File Number: 43-10

SAMPLE QUESTIONS COMPOSITE SKETCH/FILE II

1. Which of the three suspects did not have an NCIC number assigned to his or her file?
    A. Suspect 1
    B. Suspect 2
    C. Suspect 3
    D. All suspects were assigned an NCIC file number.

2. What was Dale Willis Winfree wanted for?
    A. Robbery
    B. Storage and concealment of stolen explosives
    C. Mail fraud
    D. Both A and C

3. Tammy Faye Ellington used which one of the names given below as an alias?
    A. Brenda Youngerman
    B. Brenda Forsythe
    C. Brenda McCarthy
    D. None of the above

4. Which of the three suspects' DOB is 6-1-48?
    A. Tamy Ellington
    B. Carl Youngerman
    C. Chance Forsythe
    D. None of the above

5. In trying to further elude the authorities, which of the three suspects utilized multiple Social Security numbers?
    A. Suspect 1
    B. Suspect 2
    C. Suspect 3
    D. Only one social security number was on file for each of the three suspects.

6. What kind of distinguishing scar or marks did Suspect 3 have?
    A. C-shaped scar around the right kneecap
    B. None are known
    C. L-shaped scar around the left kneecap
    D. C-shaped scar around the left kneecap

7. What color is Suspect 2's hair?
    A. Brown with a reddish tint
    B. Red with a tint of brown
    C. Brown (greying)
    D. Blonde

8. Which suspect was assigned NCIC file number 43-10?
    A. Suspect 1
    B. Suspect 2
    C. Suspect 3
    D. No such file number was given.

9. What was on Carl David Youngerman's record for prior convictions?
   A. Possession of cocaine
   B. Possession of false documentation
   C. Possession of heroin with the intent to distribute
   D. Possession of heroin

10. Dale Hollensworth had what color hair and eyes, respectively?
    A. Brown and blue
    B. Brown and brown
    C. Blonde and hazel
    D. Brown with a reddish tint and hazel

11. Which date given below represents Tamy Faye Ellington's date of birth?
    A. 7-15-70
    B. 6-15-70
    C. 12-11-63
    D. 12-12-68

12. Which of the three suspects did not utilize an alias in the commission of his or her crimes?
    A. Dale Willis Winfree
    B. Carl David Youngerman
    C. Brenda McCarthy
    D. Each suspect has at least one alias

13. Which choice below inaccurately describes Suspect 3?
    A. Male
    B. Height: 5'8"
    C. Eyes: Blue
    D. Social Security Number: 652-44-0431

14. The picture shown to the right is a sketch of which suspect?
    A. Chance Forsythe
    B. Preston Hollensworth
    C. David Willis Winfree
    D. Carl David Youngerman

15. According to NCIC file number 48-20, the suspect described used which of the following Social Security numbers?
    A. 632-45-0162
    B. 208-55-5212
    C. 832-58-9571 and 832-85-9751
    D. 823-85-7159 and 652-44-4301

16. Which of the three suspects was described as being white with a medium complexion?
    A. Tammy Faye Ellington
    B. Carl David Youngerman
    C. Dale Hollensworth
    D. None of the suspects' files mentioned complexion.

17. Who was wanted for conspiracy to transport funds outside the U.S.?
    A. Brenda McCarthy
    B. Carl David Youngerman
    C. Dale Hollensworth
    D. Chance Foresythe

18. Who was described as armed and dangerous?
    A. Suspects 1 and 3
    B. Suspects 2 and 3
    C. Suspect 3
    D. Suspect 1

19. Which of the three suspects has a distinguishing 4" scar on the right hand?
    A. Brenda McCarthy
    B. Dale Willis Winfree
    C. Preston Hollensworth
    D. Carl David Youngerman

20. What was the case number assigned to the criminal file of Suspect 1?
    A. 87-512
    B. 43-102
    C. 82-51
    D. 48-202

ANSWER SHEET FOR SAMPLE COMPOSITE SKETCH/FILE II

1. Ⓐ Ⓑ Ⓒ Ⓓ   8. Ⓐ Ⓑ Ⓒ Ⓓ   15. Ⓐ Ⓑ Ⓒ Ⓓ
2. Ⓐ Ⓑ Ⓒ Ⓓ   9. Ⓐ Ⓑ Ⓒ Ⓓ   16. Ⓐ Ⓑ Ⓒ Ⓓ
3. Ⓐ Ⓑ Ⓒ Ⓓ   10. Ⓐ Ⓑ Ⓒ Ⓓ   17. Ⓐ Ⓑ Ⓒ Ⓓ
4. Ⓐ Ⓑ Ⓒ Ⓓ   11. Ⓐ Ⓑ Ⓒ Ⓓ   18. Ⓐ Ⓑ Ⓒ Ⓓ
5. Ⓐ Ⓑ Ⓒ Ⓓ   12. Ⓐ Ⓑ Ⓒ Ⓓ   19. Ⓐ Ⓑ Ⓒ Ⓓ
6. Ⓐ Ⓑ Ⓒ Ⓓ   13. Ⓐ Ⓑ Ⓒ Ⓓ   20. Ⓐ Ⓑ Ⓒ Ⓓ
7. Ⓐ Ⓑ Ⓒ Ⓓ   14. Ⓐ Ⓑ Ⓒ Ⓓ

Answers can be found on page 41.

D. DESCRIPTIVE PASSAGES

The third form of memory exercises seen on past exams involves descriptive passages. Such passages are designed to test an applicant's ability to remember literal details from what one reads. Normally, you will be given a reading that pertains to either a crime or emergency scene or to some kind of technical or procedural issue. This kind of test differs from reading comprehension exams in that you are not required to make deductions; rather, you are to memorize the facts only as they appear in the passage. Trivial items become just as important as main concepts.

The best advice here is to become a part of the article instead of just reading it. If the reading details how a crime scene or other emergency unfolds, think of it as if you were witnessing the events as they occur. It can be helpful to incorporate some bizarre or funny aspects into the story to facilitate better memory of the passage.

Regardless of the passage's length and content, you will be given only a specified amount of time to read. When your time is up for studying the article, the test examiner will collect the readings and then direct you to answer related questions in your test booklet or supplement. You will not be allowed to review what was read while answering the questions provided.

SAMPLE DESCRIPTIVE PASSAGE 1

Study the passage given below for ten minutes. When your time is up, answer the questions that follow without further reference to the passage.

> Chuck McGregor, Teresa Goodwill, and Mr. and Mrs. Vince Matley had just attended a monthly Economic Development Council meeting at the Sheridan Hotel. Normally, these meetings start at 7:30 p.m. and last only a couple of hours, but on this evening, important issues had to be addressed that protracted the meeting an extra 20 minutes. En route to their parked cars, the group was confronted by two juveniles and one adult, the latter of whom brandished a nickel plated .45 caliber pistol. They were told to relinquish wallets, purses, jewelry, and anything else of value or risk being shot. As the victims of the robbery were complying with the perpetrators' demands, a parking attendant witnessed the crime and immediately dialed 911. The call was made at exactly 9:55 p.m. Officer Melvin Jenkins, Shield Number 740, was on bicycle patrol in the downtown precinct one block southwest of the incident when dispatched to investigate. It was only a matter of a couple of minutes before Officer Jenkins arrived at the parking lot. However, one of the juveniles quickly spotted the officer's approach, and the trio immediately dispersed; one juvenile ran south down an adjacent alley and the other pair jumped into a 1977 two-door Monte Carlo, license plate LNT 503. It was too dark for Officer Jenkins to provide any physical descriptions of the suspects. The information he had concerning the getaway vehicle was immediately radioed to CenCom for further follow-up.
>
> Officer Jenkins obtained good physical descriptions of the suspects from the victims. Ms. Goodwill was particularly adept at remembering details. The first juvenile was a white male, approximately 17 years of age, 6', 140 pounds, black, curly shoulder-length hair, and brown eyes. He was dressed in lightly faded blue jeans with the left knee worn through, white tennis shoes, and a dark blue T-shirt that revealed an axe-like tattoo on his right biceps. The second juvenile was a white male, approximately 15 years of age, 5'6", 130 pounds, brown hair, hazel eyes, wearing dark-colored pants, black loafers, white T-shirt, and a Toronto Blue Jays baseball cap. The third suspect was a white male, approximately 30 years of age, 6'2", 190 pounds, blonde hair cut extremely short, brown eyes. This suspect was wearing acid-wash denim jeans and jacket. He had a deep scar on his left temple.
> These physical descriptions and the fact that the trio was considered armed and dangerous were radioed into CenCom.

Officer Jenkins obtained the names of the victims, their respective addresses, and a list of the personal effects that were stolen. The following information was included in Officer Jenkins' stolen property summary:

Teresa Goodwill
— lynx-trimmed dress jacket valued at $750
— silver jewelry valued at $75
— $150 cash and 2 credit cards

Chuck McGregor
— wallet containing $85

Mr. Vince Matley
— wallet containing $125
— gold Rolex watch valued at $1850
— gold wedding band

Mrs. Vince Matley
— diamond ring valued at $1300

Officer Jenkins submitted a completed report detailing the robbery to Sergeant Bruce Day, Shield Number 432. Sergeant Day signed the report and assigned report number 1561 to the record.

SAMPLE QUESTIONS ON DESCRIPTIVE PASSAGE 1

1. Where was the location of the meeting referred to in the reading?
   A. Sheriton Motel
   B. Holiday Inn
   C. Sheridan Hotel
   D. Ramada

2. What was Sergeant Day's shield number?
   A. 1516
   B. 503
   C. 470
   D. 432

3. What time did the meeting referred to in the reading actually come to a close?
   A. 9:50 p.m.
   B. 9:30 p.m.
   C. 9:55 p.m.
   D. 10:05 p.m.

4. Who alerted the authorities to the fact that a robbery was in progress?
   A. Chuck McGregor
   B. The parking attendant
   C. Melvin Jenkins
   D. Teresa Goodwill

5. What was the height and weight of the oldest suspect?
   A. 6'5", 130 pounds
   B. 6'2", 190 pounds
   C. 5'6", 140 pounds
   D. 6', 140 pounds

6. What was the license-plate number of the getaway vehicle?
   A. BVT 740
   B. NBT 911
   C. LNT 503
   D. ECD 103

7. How often did the members of the Economic Development Council meet?
   A. daily
   B. weekly
   C. monthly
   D. annually

8. Which of the four victims lost a wallet and $85 cash as a result of the robbery?
   A. Chuck McGregor
   B. Teresa Goodwill
   C. Mrs. Vince Matley
   D. Bruce Day

9. What time was it when the authorities were first notified that a robbery was taking place?
   A. 9:55 a.m.
   B. 9:52 p.m.
   C. 9:52 a.m.
   D. 9:55 p.m.

10. All of the following descriptions fit the second suspect except:
    A. 5'6"
    B. approximately 17 years of age
    C. wore a Toronto Blue Jays baseball cap
    D. white male

11. Who was described as being particularly adept in remembering details?
    A. Officer Bruce Day
    B. Vince Matley
    C. Teresa Goodwill
    D. No one in the reading was given that distinction.

12. The oldest of the three suspects was described as having:
    A. blonde, curly, shoulder-length hair
    B. brown hair
    C. blonde hair, cut extremely short
    D. black, curly hair

13. What was the year and make of the vehicle used by the suspects?
    A. 1975 two-door Monte Carlo
    B. 1977 two-door Grand Prix
    C. 1975 four-door Pontiac
    D. 1977 two-door Monte Carlo

14. Which of the four victims of the robbery had a gold Rolex watch stolen?
    A. Mr. Vince Matley
    B. Mrs. Vince Matley
    C. Chuck McGregor
    D. Teresa Goodwill

15. What kind of weapon was used by the suspects in the course of the robbery?
    A. Switchblade knife
    B. Silver-placed .44-caliber pistol
    C. 12-gauge shotgun
    D. Nickel-placed .45-caliber pistol

16. When Officer Jenkins was told by CenCom to investigate the robbery, where was he in relation to the crime scene?
    A. One block northeast
    B. One block southwest
    C. Two blocks south
    D. One block west

17. Which of the suspects was described as wearing faded blue jeans with the right knee worn through?
    A. The first juvenile suspect
    B. The second juvenile suspect
    C. The third suspect
    D. None of the suspects fit that description.

18. The superior officer that accepted Officer Jenkins' report was a:
    A. Captain
    B. Sergeant
    C. Lieutenant
    D. Chief

19. What was Officer Jenkins' shield number?
    A. 503
    B. 740
    C. 977
    D. 130

20. Which of the numbers given below was assigned to Officer Jenkins' robbery report?
    A. 432
    B. 1651
    C. 1561
    D. 1551

ANSWER SHEET FOR SAMPLE DESCRIPTIVE PASSAGE 1

1. Ⓐ Ⓑ Ⓒ Ⓓ   8. Ⓐ Ⓑ Ⓒ Ⓓ   15. Ⓐ Ⓑ Ⓒ Ⓓ

2. Ⓐ Ⓑ Ⓒ Ⓓ   9. Ⓐ Ⓑ Ⓒ Ⓓ   16. Ⓐ Ⓑ Ⓒ Ⓓ

3. Ⓐ Ⓑ Ⓒ Ⓓ   10. Ⓐ Ⓑ Ⓒ Ⓓ   17. Ⓐ Ⓑ Ⓒ Ⓓ

4. Ⓐ Ⓑ Ⓒ Ⓓ   11. Ⓐ Ⓑ Ⓒ Ⓓ   18. Ⓐ Ⓑ Ⓒ Ⓓ

5. Ⓐ Ⓑ Ⓒ Ⓓ   12. Ⓐ Ⓑ Ⓒ Ⓓ   19. Ⓐ Ⓑ Ⓒ Ⓓ

6. Ⓐ Ⓑ Ⓒ Ⓓ   13. Ⓐ Ⓑ Ⓒ Ⓓ   20. Ⓐ Ⓑ Ⓒ Ⓓ

7. Ⓐ Ⓑ Ⓒ Ⓓ   14. Ⓐ Ⓑ Ⓒ Ⓓ

Answers can be found on page 41.

SAMPLE DESCRIPTIVE PASSAGE 2

Study the passage given below for ten minutes. When your time is up, answer the questions that follow without further reference to what you just read.

On December 15, 1791, Congress ratified the first ten amendments to the U.S. Constitution, known as the "Bill of Rights." These and the 14th Amendment, which was ratified in 1868, address specific inalienable rights of an individual in this country. They have had a profound impact on law enforcement and the administration of the criminal justice system. They are as follows:

AMENDMENT I

Congress shall make no law respecting an establishment of religion, or prohibiting the free exercise thereof; or abridging the freedom of speech, or the press; or the right of the people peaceably to assemble, and to petition the Government for the redress of grievances.

AMENDMENT II

A well regulated Militia, being necessary to the security of a free State, the right of the people to keep and bear Arms, shall not be infringed.

AMENDMENT III

No Soldier shall, in the time of peace, be quartered in any house, without the consent of the Owner, nor in time of war, but in a manner to be prescribed by law.

AMENDMENT IV

The right of the people to be secure in their persons, houses, papers, and effects, against unreasonable searches and seizures, shall not be violated, and no warrants shall issue, but upon probable cause, supported by Oath or affirmation, and particularly describing the place to be searched, and the persons or things to be seized.

AMENDMENT V

No person shall be held to answer for a capital, or otherwise infamous crime, unless on a presentment or indictment of a Grand Jury, except in cases arising in the land or naval forces, or in the Militia, when in actual service in time of War or public danger; nor shall any person be subject for the same offense to be twice put in jeopardy of life or limb; nor shall he be compelled in any criminal case to be a witness against himself, nor be deprived of life, liberty, or property, without due process of law; nor shall private property be taken for public use, without just compensation.

AMENDMENT VI

In all criminal prosecutions, the accused shall enjoy the right to a speedy and public trial, by an impartial jury of the State and district wherein the crime shall have been committed, which district shall have been previously ascertained by law, and to be informed of the nature and cause of the accusation; to be confronted with the witnesses against him; to have compulsory process for obtaining witnesses in his favor and to have the assistance of counsel for his defense.

AMENDMENT VII

In suits at common law, where the value in controversy shall exceed twenty dollars, the right of trial by jury shall be preserved, and no fact tried by a jury, shall be otherwise reexamined in any Court of the United States, than according to the rules of the common law.

AMENDMENT VIII

Excessive bail shall not be required, nor excessive fines imposed, nor cruel and unusual punishments inflicted.

AMENDMENT IX

The enumeration in the Constitution, of certain rights, shall not be construed to deny or disparage others retained by the people.

AMENDMENT X

The powers not delegated to the United States by the Constitution, nor prohibited by it to the States, are reserved to the States respectively, or to the people.

AMENDMENT XIV Section 1

All persons born or naturalized in the United States, and subject to the jurisdiction thereof, are citizens of the United States and of the State wherein they reside. No State shall make or enforce any law which shall abridge the privileges or immunities of citizens of the United States; nor shall any State deprive any person of life, liberty, or property, without due process of law; nor deny to any person within its jurisdiction the equal protection of the laws.

SAMPLE QUESTIONS DESCRIPTIVE PASSAGE 2

1. Which amendment to the Constitution concerns search and seizure?
   A. Amendment II
   B. Amendment III
   C. Amendment IV
   D. Amendment XIV

2. Which amendment concerns the accused being specifically informed of the nature and cause of the accusation and to be confronted by the witnesses against them?
   A. Amendment I
   B. Amendment V
   C. Amendment VI
   D. Amendment X

3. The Bill of Rights was ratified
   A. 11-12-1791   B. 12-15-1791   C. 12-15-1868   D. 12-5-1799

4. Which amendment states, "No State shall make or enforce any law which shall abridge the privileges or immunities of citizens of the United States; nor shall any State deprive any person of life, liberty, or property without due process of law"?
   A. Amendment V
   B. Amendment VII
   C. Amendment X
   D. Amendment XIV

5. Which amendment to the Constitution concerns the right of people to keep and bear arms?
   A. Amendment II
   B. Amendment III
   C. Amendment IV
   D. Amendment V

6. Which amendment concerns the issue of excessive fines and cruel and unusual punishment?
   A. Amendment V
   B. Amendment VII
   C. Amendment VIII
   D. Amendment X

7. The first ten amendments are referred to as
   A. The Constitution
   B. The Bill of Rights
   C. English Common Law
   D. Civil Rights

8. Which amendment concerns freedom of religion and speech?
   A. Amendment I
   B. Amendment II
   C. Amendment III
   D. Amendment VII

9. "No Soldier shall, in time of peace, be quartered in any house, without the consent of the owner, nor in time of war, but in a manner to be prescribed by law." This quote reflects which of the amendments?
   A. Amendment II
   B. Amendment III
   C. Amendment IV
   D. Amendment V

10. Which amendment concerns the accused being granted the right to a speedy and public trial?
    A. Amendment I
    B. Amendment IV
    C. Amendment V
    D. Amendment VI

11. Which amendment specifies that the accused can not face a double jeopardy of life or limb for the same offense, or in other words, be tried again for the same crime if found not guilty the first time?
    A. Amendment XIV
    B. Amendment IX
    C. Amendment VI
    D. Amendment V

12. Which amendment specifies that if the value in a controversy exceeds twenty dollars, the right of a trial by jury shall be preserved?
    A. Amendment IV
    B. Amendment VII
    C. Amendment VIII
    D. None of the amendments given above contain these specifics.

13. Assistance of counsel for the accused's defense is addressed by which one of the constitutional amendments?
    A. Amendment IV
    B. Amendment V
    C. Amendment VI
    D. Both A and B

14. When was the Fourteenth Amendment ratified?
    A. 1868   B. 1791   C. 1776   D. None of the above dates.

15. Which amendment grants equal rights to all persons born or naturalized in the United States?
    A. Amendment VIII
    B. Amendment X
    C. Amendment XIV
    D. Amendment XIX

ANSWER SHEET FOR SAMPLE DESCRIPTIVE PASSAGE 2

1. Ⓐ Ⓑ Ⓒ Ⓓ   6. Ⓐ Ⓑ Ⓒ Ⓓ   11. Ⓐ Ⓑ Ⓒ Ⓓ
2. Ⓐ Ⓑ Ⓒ Ⓓ   7. Ⓐ Ⓑ Ⓒ Ⓓ   12. Ⓐ Ⓑ Ⓒ Ⓓ
3. Ⓐ Ⓑ Ⓒ Ⓓ   8. Ⓐ Ⓑ Ⓒ Ⓓ   13. Ⓐ Ⓑ Ⓒ Ⓓ
4. Ⓐ Ⓑ Ⓒ Ⓓ   9. Ⓐ Ⓑ Ⓒ Ⓓ   14. Ⓐ Ⓑ Ⓒ Ⓓ
5. Ⓐ Ⓑ Ⓒ Ⓓ   10. Ⓐ Ⓑ Ⓒ Ⓓ   15. Ⓐ Ⓑ Ⓒ Ⓓ

Answers can be found on page 41.

ANSWERS FOR MEMORY RECALL SAMPLE QUESTIONS

SAMPLE SKETCH 1

1. D	6. D	11. D
2. B	7. C	12. D
3. A	8. A	13. C
4. D	9. B	14. A
5. C	10. B	15. D

SAMPLE COMPOSITE SKETCH/FILE 1

1. B	8. D	15. B
2. C	9. A	16. D
3. C	10. B	17. C
4. D	11. B	18. D
5. A	12. C	19. A
6. A	13. D	20. A
7. C	14. A	

SAMPLE COMPOSITE SKETCH/FILE 2

1. A	8. C	15. C
2. D	9. D	16. D
3. C	10. B	17. B
4. B	11. A	18. D
5. B	12. B	19. B
6. D	13. A	20. A
7. A	14. D	

SAMPLE DESCRIPTIVE PASSAGE 1

1. C	8. A	15. D
2. D	9. D	16. B
3. A	10. B	17. D
4. B	11. C	18. B
5. B	12. C	19. B
6. C	13. D	20. C
7. C	14. A	

SAMPLE DESCRIPTIVE PASSAGE 2

1. C	6. C	11. D
2. C	7. B	12. B
3. B	8. A	13. C
4. D	9. B	14. A
5. A	10. D	15. C

Your score for the exercises would be as follows:

For the 15-question exercises:
14–15 correct, EXCELLENT
12–13 correct, GOOD
10–11 correct, FAIR
less than 10 correct, POOR

For the 20-question exercises:
18–20 correct, EXCELLENT
16–17 correct, GOOD
14–15 correct, FAIR
less than 14 correct, POOR

Reading Comprehension

FROM THE START OF ACADEMY TRAINING to the highest rank achieved, a police officer will have to study and interpret a vast amount of information and apply it to innumerable situations. How efficiently that knowledge is acquired depends largely on the officer's reading comprehension. Some people find it easier than others to comprehend written material. Some attribute this difference to inherited ability, but for the most part, it is directly related to the kind of reading habits acquired in elementary school. Of course, if bad habits are acquired, they can impede, rather than enhance, a person's ability to read, and comprehension will suffer as well.

Let's examine some reading habit facts and fallacies. One misconception is the belief that *subvocalizing*, moving your lips or other parts of your mouth or throat as you read silently, is detrimental to your comprehension. Some teachers have even gone to the extent of passing out candy in class to prevent students from subvocalizing. In truth, subvocalizing has been proven in various studies to be beneficial. Students who did subvocalize while reading were shown to have a better understanding of most material studied. This was especially true when difficult or technical information was read.

Another widespread fallacy is that a student should not read word for word. Rather, some people suggest that reading should be done by looking at several words as a unit. Some say that these units provide sufficient insight into the article's content. The idea is that time is saved and reading comprehension is improved. Studies demonstrate that exactly the opposite is true. Reading comprehension is improved only when each word is read.

Some teachers also believe that if a student does not fully understand the material presented, it is better to continue on instead of rereading. The line of reasoning here is that if a student does not learn what is read the first time, repetitive reading only proves to be unproductive and a waste of time. Many studies have disproved this theory. In fact, rereading can be a necessity when the material being studied is complicated or abstract. Articles should be reread as many times as necessary to get the full meaning of the text before continuing.

Another misguided belief is that any text can be completely and quickly comprehended if key words are discerned. This very concept has given rise to the speed reading industry. Speed reading experts claim that reading at 250 to 300 words per minute is too slow when it is possible to skim at a rate of three to six times that speed. What they fail to mention is that comprehension is sacrificed for the sake of speed. This raises the question: What is gained if a fair share of information is not fully understood, or retained?

The other major shortcoming of skim reading practices is that key words may be taken out of context and when viewed cumulatively may cause the reader to misconstrue the underlying meaning of the article. Verbs and prepositions that link nouns can dramatically alter the tenor of the material being studied. If verbs and prepositions are not given attention as key words, a passage may be read as meaning one thing when skimmed although in fact, it actually means something entirely different. You can be assured that college students studying for the L.S.A.T., V.A.T., M.C.A.T., or other professional exams do not skim their readings. Subject matter expected to be covered on these exams is closely scrutinized without regard to speed. There is no acceptable substitute for full and accurate reading comprehension.

To better hone your reading skills, practice reading as much material as possible, taking care to avoid the bad habits just discussed. You will find it is easier to do this if the articles you read are on topics of interest. Nothing will discourage reading more than a dull or boring article. Reading of any kind is beneficial; newspapers, magazines, and fiction and nonfiction books are a few possible sources.

As you read an article, try to discern the underlying meaning of the reading. What is the author trying to say? Are there ideas or other forms of information that support any conclusions? If so, which are the most important? In this respect, certain concepts can be prioritized. You will find that if you follow such an inquiry into all your reading, your comprehension and reading efficiency will improve immensely.

Another way to enhance reading efficiency is to develop a better vocabulary. Quite often, words encountered in your readings may be unfamiliar to you. Don't skip over such words. Use a dictionary to discover the meanings of unfamiliar words, then make a mental note of them. Some people find it easier to write each word on a small card as a reminder. As a challenge, try incorporating that particular word into your everyday language. A continuance of this practice is a viable way of building a strong vocabulary.

If a dictionary is not handy when you encounter an unfamiliar word, it is still possible to discern the meaning of the word. Start by looking at the word and see how it is used within the sentence. This should give you some clue as to its general meaning. For example:

The restaurant patron was extremely **vexed** when the waiter accidently spilled coffee on his lap.

Obviously, the customer would not be happy under such circumstances, so we know the word *vexed* implies a degree of dissatisfaction.

Another method that can be used to further understand or define an unfamiliar term uses basic word derivations or etymology. Word derivations can provide a partial, if not complete, meaning for a term. For example, take a look at the word *injudicious*. The first two letters, *in-*, are a prefix that means "not" or "lack of." The root of the word, *-judiei-*, means "judgment." The last portion of the word, *-ous*, is the suffix, and means "characterized by." Therefore, "injudicious" may be interpreted as a characterization of someone who lacks judgment.

The following etymology table has been provided for your convenience. This, in conjunction with viewing unfamiliar terms in context, will lend the best possible insight without the assistance of a dictionary.

COMMON PREFIXES

PREFIX	MEANING	EXAMPLE
a-	not or without	atypical—not typical
ab-	away from	abnormal—deviating from normal
ac-	to or toward	accredit—to attribute to
ad-	to or toward	adduce—to bring forward as evidence
ag-	to or toward	aggravate—to make more severe
at-	to or toward	attain—to reach to
an-	nor or without	anarchy—a society with no government
ante-	before or preceding	antenatal—referencing prior to birth
anti-	against or counter	antisocial—against being social
auto-	self or same	automatic—self-acting
bene-	good or well	benevolence—an act of kindness or goodwill
bi-	two or twice	bisect—to divide into two parts
circum-	around	circumscribe—draw a line around or encircle
com-	together or with	combine—join
con-		conciliate—united or drawn together
contra-	against or opposite	contradict—opposed or against what someone else says
de-	removal from	decongestant—relieves or removes congestion
dec-	ten	decade— a ten-year period
demi-	half	demigod—partly divine and partly human
dis-	apart, negation, or reversal	dishonest—a lack or negation of honesty
dys-	diseased, bad, difficult, faulty	dyslexia—impairment of reading ability

e-, ex-	from or out of	evoke—draw forth or bring out
extra-	beyond	extraordinary—outside or beyond the usual order
hemi-	half	hemisphere—half of the globe
hyper-	excessive or over	hyperactive—excessively active
hypo-	beneath or under	hypodermic—something introduced under the skin
im-	not	impersonal—not personal
in-	not	inaccessible—not accessible
ir-	not	irrational—not having reason or understanding
inter-	among or between	interdepartmental—between departments
intra-	inside or within	intradepartmental—between departments
kilo-	thousand	kiloton—one thousand tons
mal-	bad or ill	malcontent—dissatisfied
mis-	wrong	misinterpret—to interpret wrongly
mono-	one or single	monochromatic—having only one color
non-	not	nonresident—person who does not live in a particular place
ob-	against or opposed	object—declared opposition or disapproval
omni-	all	omnivore—an animal that eats all foods either plant or animal
per-	through or thoroughly	perennial—continuing or lasting through the years
poly-	many or much	polychromy—an artistic combination of different colors
post-	after or later	postglacial—after the glacial period
pre-	before or supporting	preexamine—an examination before another examination previous
pro-	before or supporting	proalliance—supportive of an alliance
re-	again, former state or position	reiterate—do or say repeatedly
retro-	backward or return	retrogressive—moving backwards
self-	individual or personal	self-defense—act of defending oneself
semi-	half or part	semifinal—halfway final
sub-	below or under	submarine—reference to something underwater
super-	above or over	superficial—not penetrating the surface
tele-	distance	telegraph—an instrument used for communicating at a distance
trans-	across, over or through	transparent—lets light shine through
ultra-	beyond or excessive	ultraconservative—beyond ordinary conservatism
un-	not	unaccountable—not accountable or responsible

COMMON SUFFIXES

SUFFIX	MEANING	EXAMPLE
-able, -ible	capacity of being	readable—able to be read, eligible-qualified to be chosen
-ac	like or pertaining to	maniac—like a mad person
-age	function or state of	mileage—distance in miles
-ally	in a manner that relates to	pastorally—in a manner that relates to rural life
-ance	act or fact of	cognizance—knowledge through perception or reason
-ary	doing or pertaining to	subsidiary—serving to assist or supplement
-ant	person or thing	tyrant—a ruler who is unjustly severe
-ar	of the nature or pertaining to	nuclear—pertaining to the nucleus
-ation	action	excavation—act or process of excavating
-cede, -ceed	to go or come	intercede—to go or come between; succeed-to follow
-cide	destroy or kill	homicide—the killing of a person by another
-cy	quality	decency—the state of being decent
-dy	condition or character	shoddy—pretentious condition or something poorly made

-ence, -ery	act or fact of doing or pertaining to	despondence—loss of hope confectionery—place of making or selling candies or sweets
-er	one who does	lawyer—one who practices law
-ful	abounding or full of	fretful—tending to fret or be irritable
-ic	like or pertaining to	artistic—having a talent in art
-ify	to make	magnify—to make large
-ious	full of	laborious—full of labor or requiring a lot of work
-ise	to make	devise—to create from existing ideas
-ish	like	childish—like a child
-ism	system or belief	capitalism—an economic system that revolves around private ownership
-ist	person or thing	idealist—a person with ideals
-ize	to make	idolize—to make an idol of
-less	without	penniless—without a penny
-logy	the study of	archaeology—the study of historical cultures using artifacts of past activities
-ly	in a manner	shapely—well formed
-ment	the act of	achievement—the act of achieving
-ness	state of or quality	pettiness—state of being petty or small-minded
-or	person who acts	legislator—person who enacts legislation
-ory	place	dormitory—building that provides living quarters
-ship	condition or character	censorship—overseeing or excluding items that may be objectionable to those concerned
-tude	state of or result	solitude—state of being alone or apart from society
-ty	condition or character	levity—lightness in character
-y	quality or result	hefty—moderately heavy or weighty

COMMON ROOTS

ROOT	MEANING	EXAMPLE
acou	hearing	acoustical—pertaining to sound
acro	furthest or highest point	acrophobia—fear of heights
acu	needle	acupuncture—puncturing of body tissue for relief of pain
aero	air or gas	aeronautics—study of the operation of aircraft
alt	high	altitude—a position or a region at height
ambi	both	ambidextrous—capable of using both hands equally well
anter	in front	anterior—toward the front
anthrop	human being	anthropology—science of mankind
aqueo, aqui	water	aquatic—living in water
audio	hearing	audiology—science of hearing
auto	self	autocratic—ruled by a monarch with absolute rule
avi	bird, flight	aviary—large cage for confining birds
bio	life	biography—written history of a person's life
bona	good	bonafide—in good faith
capit	head	capital—involving the forfeiture of the head or life (as in capital punishment)
carb	carbon	carboniferous—containing or producing carbon or coal
carcin	cancer	carcinogen—substance that initiates cancer
carn	flesh	carnivorous—eating flesh

cent	a hundred	centennial—pertaining to 100 years
centro, centri	center	centrifugal—movement away from the center
cepha	head	hydrocephalus—condition caused by excess fluid in the head
chron	time	synchronize—to happen at the same time
citri	fruit	citric acid—sour tasting juice from fruits
corpor, corp	body	corporate—combined into one body
crypt	covered or hidden	cryptology-an art of uncovering a hidden or coded message
culp	fault	culprit—criminal
cyclo	circular	cyclone—a storm with strong circular winds
demo	people	democracy—government ruled by the people
doc	teach	doctrine—instruction or teaching
dox	opinion	paradox—a self contradictory statement that has plausibility
duo	two	duologue—conversation involving two people
dyna	power	dynamometer—device for measuring power
eco	environment	ecosystem—community or organisms interacting with the environment
embry	early	embryonic—pertaining to an embryo or the beginning of life
equi	equal	equilibrium—balance
ethn	race, group	ethnology—study of human races or groups
exter	outside of	external—on the outside
flor	flower	florist—dealer in flowers
foli	leafy	defoliate—to strip a plant of its leaves
geo	earth	geophysics—the physics of the earth
geri	old age	geriatrics—division of medicine pertaining to old age
graphy	write	autograph—a person's own signature
gyro	spiral motion	gyroscope—rotating wheel that can spin on various planes
horti	garden	horticulture—science of cultivating plants
hydro	water	hydroplane—form of boat that glides over the water
hygi	health	hygiene—practice of preservation of health
hygro	wet	hygrometer—instrument used to measure moisture in the atmosphere
hypno	sleep	hypnology—science that treats sleep
ideo	idea	ideology—study of ideas
iso	equal	isotonic—having equal tones or tension
jur	swear	jury-body of persons sworn to tell the truth
lac, lacto	milk	lacteal—resembling milk
lamin	divided	laminate—bond together layers
lingui	tongue	linguistics—study of languages
litho	stone	lithography—art of putting design on stone with a greasy material to produce printed impressions
loco, locus	place	locomotion—act or power of moving from place to place
macro	large	macrocosm—the great world; the universe
man	hand	manual—made or operated by hand
medi	middle	mediocre—average or middle quality
mega	large	megalopolis—urban area comprising several large adjoining cities
mero, meri	part or fraction of	meroblastic—partial or incomplete cleavage
micro	small or petty	microscopic—so small as to be invisible without the aid of a microscope

mini	small	miniature—an image or representation of something on a smaller scale
moto	motion	motive—what moves someone to action
multi	many	multimillionaire—person with several million dollars
navi	ship	navigation—to direct course for a vessel on the sea or in the air
neo	new	neonatal—pertaining to the newborn
noct, nocti	night	nocturnal—occurring in the night
oct, octo, octa	eight	octagonal—having eight sides
olig, oligo	scant or few	oligarchy—a government which is controlled by a few people
oo	egg	oology—a branch of ornithology dealing with bird eggs
optic	vision or eye	optometry—profession of testing vision and examining eyes for disease
ortho	straight	orthodontics—dentistry dealing with correcting the teeth
pent, penta	five	pentagon—having five sides
phob	panic or fear	arachnophobia—fear of spiders
phon	sound	phonograph—instrument for reproducing sound
pod	foot	podiatry—the study and treatment of foot disorders
pseudo	false	pseudonym—fictitious name
psyche	mental	psychiatry—science of treating mental disorders
pyro	fire	pyrotechnics—art of making or using fireworks
quad	four	quadruped—animal having four feet
quint	five	quintuple—having five parts
sect	part or divide	bisect—divide into two equal parts
spiri	coiled	spirochete—spiral shaped bacteria
stasi	to stand still	hemostatic—serving to stop hemorrhage
techni	skill	technician—skilled person in a particular field
terri	to frighten	terrible—capable of exciting terror
tetra	four	tetrahedron—a shape with four faces
therm	heat	thermostat—device that automatically controls desired temperatures
toxi	poison	toxicology—science concerning the effects, antidotes, and detection of poisonous substances
uni	single	unilateral—involving one person, class, or nation
urb	city	suburb—outlying part of a city
uro	urine	urology—science of studying the urinary tract and its diseases
verb	word	proverb—a name, person, or thing that has become a byword
veri	truthful	verify—to prove to be truthful
vit	life	vitality—liveliness
vitri	glass or glasslike	vitreous—resembling glass
vivi	alive	viviparous—giving birth to living young
vol	wish	volunteer—to enter into or offer oneself freely
zo, zoi, zoo	animal	zoology—science of studying animal life

Vocabulary at one time constituted a major part of the police officer exam. Now, however, it is fairly common to see vocabulary test questions constitute only 5 to 10% of the entire exam. Additionally, however, some words not commonly used are incorporated into reading comprehension questions. Without some understanding of what those terms mean, your comprehension of the article can be diminished.

Most reading comprehension test questions encountered on past exams ask questions that concern three things. First, what is the basic underlying theme of the passage, or what would be a suitable title or heading that summarizes the article? In most cases, this is an inferential question. In other words, you have to assimilate all the information given and select the one of four possible options which best encompasses the meaning of the article. There will not be a sentence taken directly out of the article to serve as a potential option. These questions require more judgment on your part.

Secondly, some questions may concern literal reading comprehension. In other words, questions about certain details, ideas, or facts will be asked. If the answer is not immediately apparent, it can be determined by simply going back to the applicable part of the reading and picking out the correct answer directly.

The last type of question may concern interpretation. After studying the information in an article, a comparable or hypothetical situation may be posed, and it will be left to you to interpret how what you have read applies to it.

It is ironic, but you may find it easier to read the questions before reading the passage presented. This is somewhat of a backward approach to reading comprehension questions, but it will alert you to what is considered important, and hence what to look for in the article, thus saving time.

Sample questions complete with answers and supporting explanations follow. The questions presented are not copies of past exams, but they do represent a good overview of what to expect on the actual exam.

SAMPLE QUESTIONS FOR READING COMPREHENSION
PASSAGE 1

All crimes, regardless of their nature, leave some degree of evidence behind. How an officer goes about gathering physical evidence can make the difference between offering evidence that is material and relevant in a trial versus that which is bound to be thrown out under cross-examination.

Preservation of the crime scene is the number one priority before and during the actual investigation. The number of investigators or specialists surveying the crime scene should be kept to an absolute minimum. Unauthorized persons should be removed from the premises until the investigation is complete. Bystanders can inadvertently step on or otherwise destroy or remove valuable evidence. In fact, some people have been known to obstruct justice willfully by destroying evidence in the hope of protecting a friend or relative. For obvious reasons, efforts should also be made to protect evidence from the elements, such as wind, sun, rain, or snow.

Not only is minimizing the potential for evidence contamination very important, but so is the way an officer proceeds with the search for and collection of evidence. The mechanics of the search itself, if conducted in a careful and orderly manner, can preclude duplication (i.e., covering the same area twice) in the investigation. This search and collection need to be carried out within a reasonable time because certain kinds of evidence are perishable (principally organic compounds such as blood and semen) and begin to deteriorate quickly. In addition to the time element, temperatures higher than 95° Fahrenheit or below freezing can also have a detrimental effect on such evidence.

In the course of the actual search itself, officers should be on the lookout for any evidence prior to actually entering the crime scene. Normally, searches are begun by scanning the floor and walls, finally proceeding to the ceiling. When marking and securing evidence, investigators should be extremely careful not to destroy any of it. Dropping a delicate article or accidently marking or scratching items are two examples of how evidence can be damaged. All evidence, once located, should be cataloged (recorded), listing a description and relative location where found in the crime scene. This compiling of records essentially provides the chain of evidence prosecutors can use at trial to secure a conviction.

Answer Questions 1 through 5 on the basis of Passage 1.

1. What would be an appropriate title for this passage?
   A. How best to secure criminal convictions through evidence handling
   B. What an officer should not do during the investigation of a crime scene
   C. The intricacies of evidence gathering
   D. Procedural guidelines and cautions for crime scene investigations.

2. What two words would be considered suitable adjectives in summarizing the content of this article?
   A. Prudent and compulsory
   B. Intelligent and inquisitive
   C. Circumspect and expeditious
   D. Attentive and compliant

3. Officer Pat Gregory was quick to respond to a warehouse burglary after receiving an anonymous tip. The burglars were not on the premises when Officer Gregory arrived. However, in their haste to flee they had left a crowbar on the warehouse floor. The warehouse door had obviously been jimmied to allow entry. Officer Gregory, in confirming that belief, picked up the crowbar and carefully placed the prying edge against the impression marks made on the door. The crowbar was placed in its original position on the warehouse floor after Officer Gregory had confirmed his suspicions. Assuming someone other than Officer Gregory was responsible for the burglary investigation, Officer Gregory's actions were
   A. Right, because the evidence, even though it had been moved, was replaced in its original position.
   B. Wrong, because he may have left an extra scratch or even traces of paint from the crowbar in the impression on the door.
   C. Right, because his confirmation will save another investigator valuable time.
   D. Wrong, because he should have wrapped the crowbar handle in either plastic or a paper towel prior to picking it up.

4. Which type of evidence given below is most prone to deterioration with time and temperature extremes?
   A. Blood stains
   B. Fired casings and bullets
   C. Hairs and fibers
   D. Dirt and soil particles

5. Which of the following is *not* considered an underlying objective for investigators in sealing off a crime scene?
   A. To prevent willful obstruction of justice by persons close to the investigation
   B. To prevent persons outside of the investigative unit from inadvertently destroying evidence
   C. To illustrate to the public that police know what they are doing
   D. To preserve the crime scene as is

PASSAGE 2

In 1969, the Supreme Court made a landmark decision in overturning a lower California Appeals Court and California Supreme Court ruling. The case in question involved Ted Chimel, who was arrested for the burglary of a local coin shop. Incidental to his arrest, authorities thoroughly searched his residence against his wishes. Officers were successful in locating evidence that implicated Mr. Chimel in the coin shop robbery. That evidence was used in the trial to convict Mr. Chimel. Both the California Appeals Court and the California Supreme Court upheld the decision. It was, however, reversed by the Supreme Court, which held that Mr. Chimel's Fourth and Fourteenth Amendment rights were violated when the search (incident to the arrest and without a warrant) went beyond that area of his person or the area within his reach from which he might have obtained a weapon. Consequently today, how and what is searched is rigidly defined. Incident to arrest, an officer is only allowed to search the person and area within proximate reach for a potential weapon. Searches can not be expanded further unless there is a warrant issued by a magistrate specifying exactly what can be searched or the arrested person gives permission or an officer has reasonable belief that another person's life may be in danger. The word *reasonable* is and has been subjected to various interpretations in the courts. The most dependable way of conducting a search without the "color of authority" potentially affecting the outcome of a trial is with a written warrant from an impartial magistrate.

Answer questions 6 through 10 on the basis of Passage 2

6. What would be an appropriate title for this passage?
   A. *Chimel vs. California* (1969)
   B. Search and seizure guidelines as established by the Supreme Court
   C. The consequences of an unreasonable search
   D. The disadvantages of not utilizing a warrant

7. The word *incident* (to arrest) as it is applied in the reading most nearly means:
   A. as a preliminary
   B. dependent on
   C. in the course of
   D. preparatory

8. (*Note:* When selecting your answer, consider only the original case decision.)
   Police Officer Tom McClintock pulled over a motorist for a minor speeding infraction. As Officer McClintock was issuing a citation, he noticed the pungent smell of marijuana. He placed the driver under arrest. A quick check of the suspect's shirt pockets revealed three marijuana joints. Nothing else was in plain view. However, upon examining the trunk, he found two kilos of cocaine. Officer McClintock acted:
   A. Properly and within the full limits of warrantless search of the vehicle.
   B. Properly by searching the suspect as well as the entire vehicle.
   C. Improperly because according to the *Chimel vs. California* decision, the "area within the suspect's immediate control" would preclude the search of the trunk without a warrant.
   D. Improperly because according to the *Chimel vs. California* decision he should have obtained permission from the suspect to search the passenger seats.

9. Which of the following factors could ultimately determine the legality of a warrantless search in the court's view?
   A. The position of the arresting officers in relation to the arrestee
   B. The degree of physical restraint placed on the arrestee
   C. The relative degree of ease or difficulty of the arrestee reaching a given area
   D. All of the above

10. According to the reading, which of the following statements is the most accurate?
   A. Mr. Chimel's Fourteenth Amendment rights were violated in the landmark case of *Chimel vs. California*.
   B. Warrants give a broad definition as to what area can be searched during criminal investigations.
   C. Warrants, in effect, remove the prospect of a court's consideration of whether "color of authority" may have in any way biased the case.
   D. The California Supreme Court overturned Mr. Chimel's conviction on the basis that his civil rights were neglected.

PASSAGE 3

Robbery, by definition, is not a crime against property; rather, it is considered a crime against a person. If someone illegally takes the property of another by means of force or the threat of force, the law prescribes that a robbery has been committed. On the other hand, if property of some value is stolen from a person directly and the aspect of force is absent in the crime, the incident is then considered larceny. Whether it is petty or grand larceny is dependent upon the value of the property stolen.

This definition by itself may seem fairly straightforward. However, several factors need to be taken into consideration when determining if, indeed, a robbery did take place or if, instead, the crime was larceny. If intimidation such as libel, extortion, or blackmail precludes the use of force and is used to obtain property from another person, this is not considered robbery. Additionally, if an individual is unaware that property is being stolen from his or her person because he or she is either inattentive or unconscious, the action constitutes larceny, not robbery.

Finally, the use of force must be preliminary in the commission of the theft for it to be considered a robbery. If force takes place after the perpetrator has committed the crime, it cannot be considered a robbery. Both the timing and circumstances of a theft can make a crucial difference in how that crime will be charged according to common law.

Answer questions 11 through 15 on the basis of Passage 3

11. Bill Smith had a few too many drinks one evening at a local tavern. Instead of attempting to drive home, he decided to go to the city park and "sleep it off" on a park bench. As Mr. Smith was sleeping, two juveniles rifled through his coat and pants pockets for his wallet. The two came away disappointed because their "take" was only $5. According to the passage, which of the statements given below is the most accurate?
   A. The theft would be considered robbery because if Mr. Smith had been awake, the juveniles were prepared to use force to obtain his wallet.
   B. The theft is purely considered petty larceny because force was absent.
   C. The theft would be considered robbery since $5 cash was taken.
   D. The theft would not be considered robbery because neither juvenile was in unlawful possession of a weapon.

12. Jack Arnold was riding the bus, as was his daily routine in commuting to work. This particular Monday morning, however, a larger than usual crowd took the bus downtown. Jack elected to stand in the aisle to provide a seat for a mother and her infant. A few stops later, there was standing room only. This was, in Tom Bessinger's mind, the perfect opportunity to pick someone's pocket. Tom was a real pro at lifting wallets and not getting caught. The stop-and-go action of the bus allowed Mr. Bessinger to "accidently" bump into his victim (in this case, Mr. Arnold) and create the minor distraction needed to pick the wallet. Consequently, it was only when Mr. Arnold went to lunch that he discovered his wallet was missing. In this case, it can be said that Tom Bessinger committed:

    A. Robbery, because his bumping into the victim constitutes force

    B. Larceny, because the victim was totally unaware of the theft

    C. Robbery, because cash and credit cards were taken from the person of another

    D. No crime was committed, because Mr. Arnold didn't report the incident to the authorities

13. Linda Minn was riding the subway to the Fourteenth Street station at 11:30 p.m. At this hour the subway was practically empty of passengers. Rob White, a heroin addict, was on the same subway train and sensed opportunity when he saw Ms. Minn's purse lying on the seat beside her. As the train began to pull into the Fourteenth Street station, Mr. White nonchalantly walked over to Ms Minn and grabbed her purse from the seat. Ms. Minn immediately began to yell for help. By the time anyone came to her assistance, Mr. White had fled the Fourteenth Street station. In this case, Mr. White could be charged with

    A. Robbery, because the victim was fully aware of theft

    B. Robbery, because Ms. Minn was in a state of panic from the incident

    C. Larceny, because Ms. Minn gave little resistance to the theft

    D. Larceny, because even though Ms. Minn may have screamed, Mr. White did not use force to acquire the purse

14. Having spent most of his life in the Bronx, Ben Harris was no stranger to violence. One evening, after visiting a corner grocery store, Mr. Harris was confronted by two juveniles who demanded his wallet. Rather than risk the potential of one of the offenders producing a weapon, Mr. Harris complied with their demands. A minute later, however, Mr. Harris decided he had had all he was going to take. He pursued the two offenders and a fistfight quickly ensued. Mr. Harris was beaten badly and required immediate medical attention. In this case, what should the two juveniles be charged with?

    A. Larceny, because the aspect of force was not a precondition to Mr. Harris handing over his wallet

    B. Robbery, because the two juveniles had an altercation with Mr. Harris in connection with the theft of the wallet

    C. Larceny, because the two offenders were juveniles

    D. Robbery, because Mr. Harris thought that one or both of the juveniles may have been armed

15. All of the following were mentioned in the reading as forms of intimidation that preclude the use of force *except*

    A. Extortion

    B. Bribery

    C. Libel

    D. Blackmail

PASSAGE 4

According to Webster's dictionary, duress is defined as

(1) compulsion by threat or force; coercion. (2) constraint or coercion of a degree sufficient to void any legal agreement entered into or any act performed under its influence. (3) forcible restraint, especially imprisonment.

In other words, duress implies that an individual is not acting of his or her free will. Specifically, under duress, someone may act wrongfully without criminal intent. However, whoever dictates the wrongful behavior of another by duress is responsible for the criminal intent.

Therefore, someone who commits a crime under a threat against his or her person, will not be held accountable for the criminal act (murder being the exception). In the courts' view of the matter, the conduct of the person actually committing the crime is justifiable under such circumstances. However, once the threat ceases to exist, any further acts contributing to the commission of a crime can no longer be justifiable. The courts further point out that the threat perceived by anyone forced into conducting criminal activity must be in the present, not the future. The prospect of the threat of force being carried out at some future time if the individual in question doesn't cooperate is not reason enough for criminal behavior to continue. Any criminal act under such circumstances is committed with intent and is therefore subject to prosecution.

Answer questions 16 through 20 on the basis of Passage 4

16. What would be an appropriate title for this passage?
    A. The complete definition of *duress* according to Webster's
    B. Duress; the perfect defense
    C. The definition and legal parameters of duress
    D. Duress; a synonym for criminal immunity

17. A person can commit most forms of criminal activity under duress without being guilty, except for:
    A. Robbery
    B. Burglary
    C. Libel
    D. Murder

18. Mary Adams, an assistant manager for a clothing retailer, was about to lock up the business for the evening when she was approached by two men. One of the men proceeded to tell Ms. Adams that they knew where she lived and, if she didn't go back into the store and empty the vault which contained the day's receipts of cash and checks, they would be at her house within the week to "finish" her and her family. Assuming that Ms. Adams complied with their demands while the two perpetrators remained outside the store, it would be considered that
    A. Ms. Adams was indeed acting under duress and would be exempt from prosecution for theft
    B. Ms. Adams would not be viewed by the courts as acting under duress
    C. Ms. Adams was acting under duress because of the threat made to finish her and her family
    D. None of the above

19. Frank "Little Joe" Lorenzo was determined to join a local gang composed of his peers. After completing various rites, Mr. Lorenzo learned that his ultimate acceptance into the organization entailed his committing arson against a residence of the leader's choosing. Mr. Lorenzo was about to back out for moral reasons when one of the gang's members pulled out a gun and handed him a Molotov cocktail. Mr. Lorenzo was told in no uncertain terms that if he didn't follow through, he was going to be shot. Mr. Lorenzo begrudgingly did commit the act and was ultimately inducted into the gang. Strangely enough, Mr. Lorenzo somewhat enjoyed burning the house. Under the circumstances, which of the following statements below would be considered true?

    A. Mr. Lorenzo would be guilty of arson because he enjoyed doing it
    B. Mr. Lorenzo would be guilty of arson because he was the one who actually threw the Molotov cocktail.
    C. Mr. Lorenzo would not be considered guilty of arson because he is morally against a crime of that nature.
    D. Mr. Lorenzo would not be considered guilty of arson because he was coerced at gunpoint.

20. Mike Johnson was armed with a shotgun when he walked into Cascade Savings and Loan. Mr. Johnson walked directly up to Phil Stevens, a customer waiting in line to make a bank transaction, and ordered him to assist in the impending robbery. Mr. Stevens was handed several sacks and told to go teller to teller and empty each till. Mr. Stevens complied under the threat of being shot. Mr. Johnson began to have second thoughts about his actions and hastily left the premises. Mr. Stevens saw Johnson retreat out of the building, but he went ahead with what he was told to do. In this case, Mr. Stevens

    A. Could be charged with robbery, because duress ceased to apply when Johnson left the building
    B. Could not be charged with robbery, because he was under duress to comply with Johnson's demands
    C. Could be charged with robbery, because regardless of the circumstances, Mr. Stevens should not have aided Mr. Johnson in the commission of a robbery
    D. Could not be charged with robbery, because Mr. Stevens was an innocent bystander randomly selected to assist in a crime

Vocabulary

The next twenty-five (25) questions will test your vocabulary. Study how the word in the question is used in the context of the sentence. In many cases, the meaning of unfamiliar terms can be discerned. If this method still leaves doubt, attempt to break the word down using the etymology tables provided earlier. Between these two methods, most words seen in entry-level police officer exams can be determined.

1. Establishing the point at which to arrest someone is an important factor in determining the *admissability* of evidence. *Admissability* most nearly means
    A. condition
    B. likelihood of being allowed
    C. necessity
    D. interpretation

2. The prospect of imminent danger to either the public or law enforcement personnel constitutes *exigent* circumstances. *Exigent* most nearly means
   A. broad and far reaching
   B. extenuating
   C. requiring immediate action
   D. unfortunate

3. A *cursory* search of the area was made prior to leaving. *Cursory* most nearly means
   A. extensive
   B. thorough
   C. superficial
   D. detailed

4. Lawfully impounded inventory should not be used as a *pretext* to search for evidence. *Pretext* most nearly means
   A. precondition
   B. means
   C. rule
   D. excuse

5. The Exclusionary Rule was adopted for the purpose of upholding the *integrity* of the courts. *Integrity* most nearly means
   A. moral character
   B. superiority
   C. fairness
   D. improbity

6. The report said that the accused was convinced that the danger of serious harm was *imminent*. *Imminent* most nearly means
   A. justifiable
   B. impending
   C. remote
   D. irrelevant

7. The landmark case would serve as a *precedent* for future court rulings. *Precedent* most nearly means
   A. source of confusion
   B. majority view
   C. visible reminder
   D. none of the above

8. The State of New York could not try Gary Willhouse for kidnapping because it did not have *jurisdiction*. *Jurisdiction* most nearly means
   A. justification
   B. authority
   C. enough power
   D. probable cause

9. The theft of professional services and public utilities is still considered theft of property, albeit *intangible* property, whether taken by deception or by failure to pay for such services. *Intangible* most nearly means
   A. insignificant
   B. invaluable
   C. not corporeal
   D. white collar

10. The evidence was ruled *immaterial* to the case at hand. *Immaterial* most nearly means
    A. not pertinent
    B. admissible
    C. substantive
    D. relevant

11. The fact that Mr. Wilson had been convicted twice for trafficking in narcotics lessened his *credibility* as a star witness. *Credibility* most nearly means
    A. trustworthiness
    B. anxiety
    C. incredulity
    D. demure

12. Violence was so common in one neighborhood that residents soon became *indifferent* to the occurrences. *Indifferent* most nearly means
    A. attentive
    B. apathetic
    C. intolerant
    D. indignant

13. Cheryl was quite *overt* in her sexual advances toward an undercover officer. *Overt* most nearly means
    A. shy
    B. blunt
    C. conspicuous
    D. slow

14. There can be fairly substantial *disparities* in what police officers earn depending on where they live and serve. *Disparities* most nearly means
    A. penalties
    B. similarities
    C. compensations
    D. differences

15. Detective Peterson was hoping his actions would not be *misconstrued* as aggressive. *Misconstrued* most nearly means
    A. misinterpreted
    B. judged
    C. criticized
    D. analyzed

16. Officer Mitchell demonstrated flagrant *incompetence* by not mirandizing the suspect at the time of the arrest. *Incompetence* most nearly means
   A. inability
   B. inhibition
   C. incongruity
   D. disregard

17. It is *imperative* that someone be told at the time of his or her arrest what specifically it is that he or she is being arrested for. *Imperative* most nearly means
   A. unimportant
   B. immaterial
   C. compulsory
   D. considerate

18. Officer Miller experienced some degree of *trepidation* every time he had to unholster his handgun in the line of duty. *Trepidation* most nearly means
   A. having power
   B. hesitation
   C. quandary
   D. trembling

19. The buildings in the downtown core were pretty *dilapidated*. *Dilapidated* most nearly means
   A. modern
   B. tall
   C. neglected
   D. new

20. The purpose of investigative detention is to resolve an *ambiguous* circumstance. *Ambiguous* most nearly means
   A. infallible
   B. uncertain
   C. argumentative
   D. interesting

21. Officers are instructed not to act *condescendingly* toward citizens in the line of duty. *Condescending* most nearly means
   A. discourteous
   B. harsh
   C. unprofessional
   D. patronizing

22. Unconscious intoxicated persons should be transported to a nearby medical facility by an ambulance instead of a patrol car to alleviate potential civil *liability*. *Liability* most nearly means
   A. responsibility
   B. exemption
   C. scrutiny
   D. considerations

23. The phone calls were intended to *intimidate* the witness. *Intimidate* most nearly means

    A. comfort   B. ostracize   C. frighten   D. relieve

24. Building containment for the two officers was nearly impossible because there were too many means of *egress* for the suspect. *Egress* most nearly means

    A. entrance
    B. exits
    C. approach
    D. attack

25. The purpose of traffic control is two-fold; to *expedite* traffic and to eliminate potential traffic conflicts. *Expedite* most nearly means

    A. deter
    B. speed the progress of
    C. prevent congestion
    D. monitor

ANSWER SHEET FOR READING COMPREHENSION SAMPLE QUESTIONS

1. Ⓐ Ⓑ Ⓒ Ⓓ
2. Ⓐ Ⓑ Ⓒ Ⓓ
3. Ⓐ Ⓑ Ⓒ Ⓓ
4. Ⓐ Ⓑ Ⓒ Ⓓ
5. Ⓐ Ⓑ Ⓒ Ⓓ
6. Ⓐ Ⓑ Ⓒ Ⓓ
7. Ⓐ Ⓑ Ⓒ Ⓓ

8. Ⓐ Ⓑ Ⓒ Ⓓ
9. Ⓐ Ⓑ Ⓒ Ⓓ
10. Ⓐ Ⓑ Ⓒ Ⓓ
11. Ⓐ Ⓑ Ⓒ Ⓓ
12. Ⓐ Ⓑ Ⓒ Ⓓ
13. Ⓐ Ⓑ Ⓒ Ⓓ
14. Ⓐ Ⓑ Ⓒ Ⓓ

15. Ⓐ Ⓑ Ⓒ Ⓓ
16. Ⓐ Ⓑ Ⓒ Ⓓ
17. Ⓐ Ⓑ Ⓒ Ⓓ
18. Ⓐ Ⓑ Ⓒ Ⓓ
19. Ⓐ Ⓑ Ⓒ Ⓓ
20. Ⓐ Ⓑ Ⓒ Ⓓ

ANSWER SHEET FOR VOCABULARY SAMPLE QUESTIONS

1. Ⓐ Ⓑ Ⓒ Ⓓ
2. Ⓐ Ⓑ Ⓒ Ⓓ
3. Ⓐ Ⓑ Ⓒ Ⓓ
4. Ⓐ Ⓑ Ⓒ Ⓓ
5. Ⓐ Ⓑ Ⓒ Ⓓ
6. Ⓐ Ⓑ Ⓒ Ⓓ
7. Ⓐ Ⓑ Ⓒ Ⓓ
8. Ⓐ Ⓑ Ⓒ Ⓓ
9. Ⓐ Ⓑ Ⓒ Ⓓ

10. Ⓐ Ⓑ Ⓒ Ⓓ
11. Ⓐ Ⓑ Ⓒ Ⓓ
12. Ⓐ Ⓑ Ⓒ Ⓓ
13. Ⓐ Ⓑ Ⓒ Ⓓ
14. Ⓐ Ⓑ Ⓒ Ⓓ
15. Ⓐ Ⓑ Ⓒ Ⓓ
16. Ⓐ Ⓑ Ⓒ Ⓓ
17. Ⓐ Ⓑ Ⓒ Ⓓ
18. Ⓐ Ⓑ Ⓒ Ⓓ

19. Ⓐ Ⓑ Ⓒ Ⓓ
20. Ⓐ Ⓑ Ⓒ Ⓓ
21. Ⓐ Ⓑ Ⓒ Ⓓ
22. Ⓐ Ⓑ Ⓒ Ⓓ
23. Ⓐ Ⓑ Ⓒ Ⓓ
24. Ⓐ Ⓑ Ⓒ Ⓓ
25. Ⓐ Ⓑ Ⓒ Ⓓ

ANSWERS TO READING COMPREHENSION AND VOCABULARY SAMPLE QUESTIONS

1. *D.* Only D best describes the scope of the article. Selections A and C are, at best, ambiguous in defining the content of the reading. Selection B was, in fact, mentioned in the passage, but it only addresses what an officer is not to do rather than providing a more complete overview of what is involved in evidence collection, as the passage does.

2. *C.* Circumspect and expeditious are the correct selections. The article points out that an officer has to look around a crime scene carefully and then be expeditious or prompt in gathering the evidence found in order to avoid potential contamination.

3. *B.* Selection B is correct because the officer may have inadvertently damaged crucial evidence or even created false leads for investigators, if, in fact, the crowbar on the floor was not the tool used to gain entry. Selection A may seem correct, but Officer Gregory, no matter how good his intentions may have been, actually moved the evidence from its original position. Selection C is not a viable concern for Officer Gregory. Selection D further exemplifies the potential for contaminating crucial evidence (i.e. misplacement of physical evidence).

4. *A.* Selection A is the correct answer because the article mentioned that organic compounds are more prone to deterioration with time and temperature extremes and cites blood as an example. Hair is considered organic in nature as well, but it does not have the same kind of enzymatic or bacterial breakdown as blood. The remaining selections are inorganic and not subject to the same kind of degradation from the elements.

5. *C.* Only C is considered as being false. The rest of the alternatives provided are, in fact, underlying objectives for authorities to rope off a given crime scene.

6. *B.* Selection A was indeed discussed, but it fails to include the entire content of the article. Selections C and D touch only on specifics and do not properly summarize the passage's underlying meaning.

7. *B.* Selection B is the correct interpretation of the word "incident" as used in the reading.

8. *C.* Statements A and B are patently false according to the *Chimel v. California* decision. Selection D is false also because the passenger seats are considered to be within the immediate reach of the suspect, and therefore Officer McClintock is indeed within his rights to search that area without a warrant.

9. *D.* Selections A, B, and C are all factors that limit areas that an arrestee may reach, albeit for a weapon or just the fact that it is within their area of control. After the *Chimel v. California* decision, courts take three factors into consideration when determining what a reasonable search without a warrant may entail.

10. *C.* Selection A is correct, but the question asks for the most accurate statement of the four given. This selection would have been more complete had it specified that his Fourth Amendment rights were violated as well. Selection B is incorrect because warrants are very specific with regard to what can be searched. They are not broad in definition. Selection D is incorrect because it was the Supreme Court of the United States, not the California Supreme Court, that reversed a lower court's decision in Chimel's case.

11. *B.* Selection A is incorrect because the intent of the juveniles, in the event the victim woke up, was never established in the passage. The reader can only speculate as to the outcome. Selection C is incorrect because the dollar value of property taken from a person is not the

determining factor in deciding whether the crime is robbery or larceny. Selection D is incorrect for two reasons, the first being that this issue wasn't mentioned in the passage, and the second that the threat of force can be accomplished without the physical presence of a weapon.

12. *B.* Selection A is incorrect because Tom Bessinger's method of operation is not considered force or the threat of force, particularly when the victim is unaware of the theft in the first place. Selection C is wrong because the reading didn't stipulate if there were cash or credit cards involved. Additionally, the taking of cash or credit cards from the person of another is, by itself, not a definition of robbery according to the passage. Selection D is incorrect because a crime did take place; it just wasn't discovered or reported immediately.

13. *D.* Neither Statement A nor statement B constitutes grounds for Mr. White to be charged with robbery. Selection C is incorrect because Ms. Moen offered no resistance to Mr. White during the theft.

14. *A.* Selection A is correct. Despite what Mr. Harris may have perceived as being a threat (as suggested in C), the fact is that the pair did not use force or the threat of force to obtain his wallet. They merely demanded he hand it over without the predication of dire consequences if he did not comply. Choice B is incorrect because the altercation took place after the theft. The altercation itself was not a precondition to the juveniles obtaining the wallet. Choice C is wrong because the age of the offenders has no bearing on whether a theft is considered a larceny or a robbery.

15. *B.* Only bribery was not mentioned in the reading.

16. *C.* Selection A was mentioned in the reading, but it fails to describe the contents of the entire passage. Selections B and D were neither mentioned nor implied in this reading.

17. *D.* Murder was pointed out in the passage as being the one exception. In a court's view, it is necessary to take one's own life before that of another.

18. *B.* Statements A and C both assume that Ms. Adams, a future defendant in a court of law, could use duress as a defense against the charge of theft. While it was true that the two men did make a threat against her to coerce her cooperation in the theft, it was done so in future terms. In other words, they would be back at a later time to execute the threat against her. The courts would view that she also had ample time to have contacted and involved the authorities to stop such a plot. She also might have been able to call the police from inside the store while the two men were waiting outside.

19. *D.* Choice A is incorrect because Mr. Lorenzo's change of feelings regarding the arson is not the issue that determines whether or not he is guilty. The fact that he was coerced under gunpoint to commit the crime is the crucial point. Choice B is true in that Mr. Lorenzo did indeed throw the Molotov cocktail, but the important point is that intent was absent because he was forced to commit the act. Choice C is incorrect for the same reason given for A.

20. *A.* Statement B is true up to the point Mr. Johnson leaves the premises. At that point, the defense of "under duress" would no longer apply. Choice C is incorrect because Mr. Stevens was under the threat of death to comply, circumstances understandable in a court of law for Mr. Stevens to participate in a robbery without demonstrating intent. However, circumstances changed at the point Mr. Johnson left the Savings and Loan. Selection D is true as far as what actually happened to Phil Stevens, but it does not necessarily preclude his liability for assisting Mr. Johnson.

Note: The answers have been provided for the vocabulary section without explanation. If further reference is needed, consult a dictionary.

1. B
2. C
3. C
4. D
5. A
6. B
7. D
8. B
9. C
10. A
11. A
12. B
13. C
14. D
15. A
16. A
17. C
18. D
19. C
20. B
21. D
22. A
23. C
24. B
25. B

Your score for each exercise would be as follows:
For the reading comprehension exercises:
    18–20 correct, EXCELLENT
    16–17 correct, GOOD
    13–15 correct, FAIR
    less than 13 correct, POOR

For the vocabulary exercises:
    23–25 correct, EXCELLENT
    21–22 correct, GOOD
    19–20 correct, FAIR
    less than 19 correct, POOR

Situational Judgment and Reasoning

OF ALL THE SECTIONS IN THIS STUDY GUIDE, this one covers the bulk of questions seen on most exams. The types of questions involving judgment and reasoning are varied, but include such topics as

- Interdepartmental protocol
- Public relations
- Appropriate use of equipment and related safety practices.
- How to best handle emergency situations
- Chart and table interpretation
- Sentence-order logistics
- Composite-sketch cross-comparisons.

All questions draw upon your ability to think and reason.

The first type of question involves general police procedure and policy. These questions do not necessitate complete familiarity with police procedures. Rather, enough information is provided within the question to answer it solely on the basis of common sense. Keep in mind that the problem in the question must be identified first. How to best solve that problem within the scope of alternatives provided, in the quickest and safest manner should be apparent.

Questions of this nature can be fairly difficult to study for. Common sense or the power of reasoning is not something that can be learned from a study guide. The best advice that can be offered is to read each question carefully and completely. Often words such as *always, except, not, least,* and *first* can entirely change the meaning of the question. Any answers that seem to be illegal or contradictory or pose a threat to the public or police personnel are probably incorrect. Options that appear self-serving or contrary to the goal of the police, to serve and protect, are probably wrong as well. Look at the example given below and determine the correct answer:

> Police officers are told that consent searches can be conducted in lieu of a warrant provided that the person who granted the search has the authority to do so. The courts also hold that permission must be knowingly, voluntarily, and intelligently given to legitimize such searches. Which of the consent searches given below would be considered the most questionable in view of these prerequisites?
>
> A. A parent giving police officers the consent to search the guest bathroom used by their teenage son.
> B. A landlord permitting police to search a common storage area shared by tenants and himself.
> C. A hysterical wife who permits police to search her husband's sports car.
> D. All of the above constitute legitimate consent searches.

If you chose C, you are correct. A parent, landlord, and wife are all parties who have joint access to or control of the property in question. However, the wife's state of mind may preclude a competent waiver of rights.

A second type of question seen on exams involves the use of tables or charts that contain specific information. On the basis of what is given, correlations or relationships may need to be extrapolated, or the figures they contain may need to be understood and recognized for their significance. Look at the sample given below.

Lieutenant Blackmore was reviewing crime reports compiled for the month of September in Sector Thirteen. Incident report details are as follows:

DATE	DAY	CRIME INVOLVED	TIME OCCURRED	STREET LOCATION
9/1	Wednesday	Burglary	1:17 a.m.	2200 block of 1st Avenue
9/2	Thursday	Burglary	10:39 p.m.	100 block of 3rd Street
9/6	Monday	Malicious Mischief	2:15 a.m.	3300 block of 16th Avenue
9/10	Friday	Larceny	3:30 p.m.	1600 block of 3rd Street
9/10	Friday	Rape	9:36 p.m.	300 block of 16th Avenue
9/15	Wednesday	Burglary	3:45 a.m.	1500 block of 1st Avenue
9/18	Saturday	Malicious Mischief	5:00 p.m.	1200 block of 3rd Avenue
9/22	Wednesday	Burglary	2:20 a.m.	3800 block of 1st Avenue
9/23	Thursday	Domestic Dispute	5:15 p.m.	2300 block of 16th Avenue
9/25	Saturday	Malicious Mischief	12:29 a.m.	1400 block of 1st Street
9/26	Sunday	Malicious Mischief	5:45 p.m.	1700 block of 3rd Avenue
9/26	Sunday	Malicious Mischief	7:50 a.m.	1900 block of 3rd Avenue
9/27	Monday	Burglary	10:20 p.m.	3300 block of 16th Avenue
9/28	Tuesday	Burglary	1:52 p.m.	500 block of 1st Street

Shift schedules are as follows

TOUR I   8:00 a.m.–4:00 p.m.

TOUR II   4:00 p.m.–midnight

TOUR III   midnight–8:00 a.m.

If Lieutenant Blackmore wanted to assign extra patrols in an effort to reduce the incidence of burglary and malicious mischief, which of the following actions would most likely achieve that goal?

A. Assign a Tour II patrol unit to 1st Avenue on Wednesdays and a Tour II patrol unit to 3rd Avenue during the weekends.

B. Assign a Tour III patrol unit to 1st Avenue on Wednesdays and a Tour II patrol unit to 3rd Avenue during the weekends.

C. Assign a Tour II patrol unit to 3rd Street on Thursdays and a Tour II patrol unit to 3rd Street on Fridays.

D. Assign a Tour I patrol unit to 1st Avenue on Wednesdays and a Tour III patrol unit to 3rd Avenue during the weekends.

If you selected B, you were correct. According to the chart, burglaries occur most frequently early Wednesday mornings on 1st Avenue during the third tour shift (1:17 a.m., 3:45 a.m., and 2:20 a.m.). The other burglaries can be considered isolated incidents that demonstrate no discernable patterns. Malicious mischief incidents, on the other hand, occur most frequently on weekend evenings on 3rd Avenue during the second tour shift (Saturday 5:00 p.m., and Sunday 5:45 p.m.). Again, the remainder of cases could be considered isolated incidents, and for the purpose of the question, they can be ignored. Trends are what are important. If appropriate correlations are made, emphasis patrols will stand a better chance of being an effective deterrent.

Two other forms of judgment and reasoning questions often seen are sentence-order logistics and composite-sketch cross-comparisons.

Sentence-order logistics simply involves four or five separate sentences which when combined properly describe an incident found in a police report. The sentences appear in a random order from which you will need to rearrange them into their proper chronological order. Look at the example given below and try to determine the correct sequence of events:

> Detective Connelly was assigned to investigate the homicide of Don Merriweather, the owner of a small downtown pawn shop. Detective Connelly's incident report contained the following five sentences:
>
> 1. Mr. Merriweather died at 6:30 p.m. at Methodist General Hospital as a result of the attack.
> 2. Mr. Merriweather resisted the assailant's demands and was consequently shot twice in the chest.
> 3. Under the threat of being shot, Mr. Merriweather was told to open the safe.
> 4. The assailant, currently unknown, forced entry through the back door.
> 5. The unknown perpetrator attempted but could not gain access to the back room vault.

The easiest strategy is to determine what took place first and last. In this case, the perpetrator had to break into the store first to set off the chain of events that occurred. The result, of course, is Mr. Merriweather's death. By looking at the choices of sentence arrangement below, the correct answer can be arrived at fairly easily through the process of elimination.

A	3	4	1	2	5
B.	2	3	4	5	1
C.	4	1	5	3	2
D.	4	5	3	2	1

If you selected the combination of Sentences 4, 5, 3, 2, 1 you were correct. Only D lists the fifth sentence as the beginning of the incident and Sentence 1 as the end. Since one of the answers must be correct, it can be confidently assumed that D is the correct answer. The other three sentences are insignificant for the most part. The key here, however, is that you must be sure of what took place in the beginning and at the end. Misinterpreting one or both of these will in all likelihood cause you to pick the wrong answer.

Unfortunately, not all questions will be as easy as this example. Some questions will have two or more answers that properly account for the beginning and end of a hypothetical incident. Those choices are the ones that deserve further scrutiny. Read the story as prescribed by each of these choices and see if they follow a logical sequence. Chances are, one of the stories will seem somewhat out of place and should therefore be eliminated from further considerations. Look at the second example provided below and try to apply the following technique.

Officer Martin was writing an incident report regarding a suicide attempt. His report contained the following five sentences.

1. Ms. Hargrove dialed 911 and explained that her boss, Mr. Abernathy, was on a fourth story ledge threatening to jump.
2. Mr. Abernathy had obvious reservations about jumping by the way he was clinging to the ledge.
3. Mr. Abernathy was arrested for attempted suicide and sent to Eastern State Hospital for psychological evaluation.
4. Mr. Abernathy told his secretary, Ms. Hargrove, she would be well taken care of after his death.
5. I persuaded Mr. Abernathy not to jump.

A.	3	4	2	1	5
B.	4	5	2	1	3
C.	4	1	2	5	3
D.	4	2	5	1	3

It should have been fairly evident that Sentence 4 took place first and Sentence 3, last. That, by itself, eliminates A. However, the three remaining choices list Sentences 4 and 3 as first and last, respectively. So, go to B, read the sentences in that order, and see if that story makes sense. In this case, Sentence 5 seems clearly out of context following the fact that Mr. Abernathy had just told his secretary she was going to be well cared for after his death. At that point, how could his secretary understand his true motives until he was actually out on the window ledge? Also, that "I" persuaded Mr. Abernathy not to jump statement is made by Officer Martin. This story seems to be disjointed, so it can be eliminated as a viable choice. Choice C seems very plausible as the correct answer, but it would be premature to come to that conclusion without giving D its due consideration. Here again, Sentence 2 following Sentence 4 seems somewhat out of order. The same holds true for Sentence 5 following Sentence. 2. The real clincher is Sentence 1 following Sentence 5. How can Mr. Abernathy be persuaded not to jump by Officer Martin when Ms. Hargrove hasn't even summoned the police yet? Therefore, D can be eliminated, and it can be assumed that C has to be the correct answer. This type of question is really not very difficult if you reason them out in this manner. Just keep a good perspective on what the story is about, and don't rush your conclusions.

The other form of judgment and reasoning questions you may encounter on the exam is composite-sketch cross-comparison. You will be given a sketch of a suspect, accompanied by sketches of four other people. You are to select the one out of the four sketches given that is actually the suspect attempting to disguise him or herself. It is important to note here that it is generally assumed that the suspect in question has not undergone any surgical procedures to change physical appearance. Working on that premise, ears, eyes, nose, mouth, cheekbone structure, chin, scars, and facial lines will not vary. However, the suspect may grow a beard or moustache, change hair styles, or wear eyeglasses or various assortments of clothing in an attempt to conceal his or her true identity.

As you compare these sketches, try to overlook these features and concentrate only on those aspects that cannot easily be changed. Usually, one or two of the composite sketches provided are quite apparent they are not sketches of the suspect. However, the remaining two sketches can have very subtle yet discernable differences that challenge a test taker's judgment skills. It can't be emphasized enough to focus on only those characteristics that cannot be changed.

One last hint here is as you work through this kind of questions, line out those sketches or choices that you have concluded cannot be the suspect. This will eliminate the potential for any confusion or backtracking and will ultimately narrow the field down to the correct choice.

When you work your way through the exercises provided in this section of the study guide, use your best judgment to discern the right answers. The correct answers, complete with explanations, are provided at the end of the exercise.

SAMPLE QUESTIONS ON SITUATIONAL JUDGMENT AND REASONING

1. Officer Pratt has just arrested an elderly woman for criminal trespass after she refused to leave the premises of a state government office. Out of respect for her age and potential for discomfort, Officer Pratt elected not to place her in handcuffs prior to transporting her to the station for booking. What would this be considered?
    - A. Good policy, because it demonstrates that police do care about the public, including those placed under arrest.
    - B. Good policy, because under the circumstances, Officer Pratt has full control of the situation.
    - C. Bad policy, because Officer Pratt is subject to a greater potential risk of being assaulted.
    - D. Bad policy, because Officer Pratt would appear too soft or lacking authority in the way he handled the incident.

2. Late one Friday evening, Officer Kent comes across a man who is unconscious in an alley. Further scrutiny reveals that the subject has an empty syringe clenched in his hand. Officer Kent attempts to wake the man but is unable to do so. Which of the actions given below would be the most appropriate for Officer Kent to undertake next?
    - A. Arrest the man for possession of illegal drug paraphernalia.
    - B. Ignore the situation and let the man wake up of his own accord.
    - C. Take the man into protective custody and transport him to a regional detoxification treatment facility.
    - D. Call for an ambulance immediately to transport the subject to a medical facility.

3. While you are patrolling a small strip plaza, you witness two individuals in the parking lot exchanging drugs for money. No sooner has the transaction taken place than both suspects become aware of your presence and take off running in opposite directions. What would be your best course of action at this point?
    - A. Give chase to the suspect who has the drugs.
    - B. Give chase to the suspect who has the money.
    - C. Fire a warning shot, and order the pair to halt.
    - D. Write down a complete physical description of both suspects, and issue a warrant for their arrest.

4. A young woman approaches you while you are on duty and explains that a street vendor has ripped her off for $25. She is very adamant that he be arrested immediately. Under the circumstances, what is the best way to handle this situation initially?
    - A. Comply with the woman's demands and place the street vendor under arrest.
    - B. Explain to the woman that there is nothing you can do because it is a civil matter and should be settled by the use of a good attorney.
    - C. Investigate the matter further by talking to the street vendor in question and then decide what action, if any, needs to be taken.
    - D. Go to the street vendor in question and demand that he return the $25 to the woman or face the possibility of arrest.

5. An off-duty police officer attending a neighborhood social function is approached by one of the neighbors and told that obscene phone calls have been a real problem recently. What is the best advice the officer could give to this person?

   A. To call the phone company and notify officials there first. Phone numbers and telephone listings can be changed.

   B. Try to outdo the caller in terms of vulgarities and obscenities.

   C. Encourage the caller to call back in the hopes of tracing the offender.

   D. Give no advice whatsoever, because he is off-duty and such a discussion would detract from the festivities.

6. During the apprehension of a robbery suspect, your partner fails in several regards to serve as an adequate backup. What is the best means to initially address such a serious error?

   A. Report your partner's inaction directly to an immediate superior.

   B. Confront the officer directly and discuss the problem.

   C. Wait until the time comes when he needs backup and in retaliation refuse to provide it.

   D. File a written request for a more competent partner.

7. An officer had just dropped off two prisoners for booking when he noticed that a $100 bill had been inadvertently left on the back seat of the patrol car. What is the most appropriate action this officer should take?

   A. Give the money to an immediate supervisor and request that it be sent to the Police Officers' Benevolence Society.

   B. Keep the money and make no mention of its existence.

   C. Ask both of the prisoners if they lost the money.

   D. Submit a formal written report on the matter and turn it in for evidence storage.

8. Police Officer Jones witnesses an altercation between two men. As he approaches closer in an attempt to stop the fight, one of the men pulls out a knife and stabs the other in the chest. The victim immediately collapses. It is quite obvious to Officer Jones that the chest wound is bleeding profusely. Under the circumstances, which of the options given below represent the best actions Officer Jones should take initially?

   A. Immediately pursue the assailant to attempt arrest.

   B. Radio for an ambulance, and then take statements from witnesses.

   C. Attempt to slow the bleeding, and summon medical assistance.

   D. File an incident report describing everything he witnessed, and issue a warrant for the arrest of the suspect.

9. While you are off duty and attending a Sunday luncheon, a woman learns you are a police officer. She then explains that a traffic citation she received earlier in the week was totally unjustified. What should you do?

   A. Tell her that tickets are never issued unless they are totally warranted.

   B. Explain that since you were not there at the time of the issuance, it would be difficult to say one way or the other.

   C. Tell her that you will investigate the matter as soon as you begin your shift.

   D. Tell her you will fix the ticket since she comes across as an honest individual.

10. While on patrol, you receive a call to investigate an indecent exposure incident at a nearby residence. Upon your arrival, you see a middle-aged man in an overcoat standing in the driveway. What is the best course of action at this point in time?
    A. Draw your weapon and shoot the individual because he is a sexual psychopath who is a threat to the public.
    B. Ascertain from the complainant if the individual standing in the drive is the person who committed indecent exposure.
    C. Immediately place the man in the overcoat under arrest.
    D. Explain to the complainant that people who commit indecent exposure are harmless and will usually leave if they are ignored.

11. During a routine patrol, Officer Matthews comes across a downed power line in the middle of the roadway. No arcing or burning is apparent. What is the appropriate way for Officer Matthews to handle such a situation?
    A. Secure the area immediately, and call the electric utility repair department.
    B. Pick up the wire, and move it to the side of the road, where it would no longer pose a hazard to traffic.
    C. Attempt to move the wire to the side of the road with a stick or other such object to avoid direct contact.
    D. File a report on the matter, and then resume patrol.

12. Which of the following crimes would be least likely to be affected by an increased police presence?
    A. Larceny
    B. Criminal trespass
    C. Murder
    D. Robbery

13. In the course of his evening patrol, Officer Ricks discovers a fire in a ground-floor hallway of a two-story apartment complex. What should be Officer Ricks' first response to the fire?
    A. Attempt to gain control of the fire by using the fire extinguisher posted in the hallway.
    B. Run through the entire building and notify all occupants that they should evacuate immediately.
    C. Contact the fire department and utilize the public address system in the patrol car to alert any occupants to the fire.
    D. Investigate the cause of the fire for the purpose of having a detailed report for fire department personnel.

14. What is the most compelling reason officers must be brief, yet accurate, in relaying information over a police radio network?
    A. To appear professional to others who may be listening.
    B. Because air time is expensive, and therefore it saves the department considerable expense.
    C. Protracted messages may be misinterpreted or misconstrued.
    D. Since many departments use the same radio network, officers should not tie up the line with long messages.

15. What is the most important reason that a police officer wears a badge?
    A. It represents an effort to maintain a professional appearance.
    B. It serves as a means of identification.
    C. It is meant to convey authority.
    D. It serves to intimidate people whom police have a run-in with.

16. While you are responding to a felony in progress, your immediate supervisor dictates instructions over the radio that you do not fully hear or comprehend. What should you do?
    A. Presume what was said was insignificant and continue your approach.
    B. Ask your superior to repeat the instructions.
    C. Place yourself in the shoes of the commanding officer and try to reason out on your own what he or she would consider important.
    D. Act on your own judgment because after completion of police academy training you have the skills to effectively discern what should be given priority.

17. Officer Fitzsimmons receives a call to investigate a silent alarm at a commercial warehouse. Which of the following actions would be considered an improper way of handling the call?
    A. Approach the building with both your lights and siren on in an attempt to minimize the potential take of a burglar.
    B. Make a cautious and indirect approach to the front of the building.
    C. Attempt to contain the building until further help arrives.
    D. If the owner shows up, do not allow him or her to enter the building until after the premises have been searched.

18. Which of the cases listed below would probably be considered the most difficult for law enforcement officials to investigate?
    A. Auto theft
    B. Malicious mischief
    C. Child abuse/neglect
    D. Securities fraud

19. Officer Clinton is assigned traffic control at a construction site where street signs have recently been changed. Officer Clinton observes a motorist commit an infraction. What should Officer Clinton do?
    A. Ignore the incident because of the recent changes.
    B. Pull over the offender and issue a warning.
    C. Pull over the offender and issue a citation.
    D. Take note of the license plate and if the same motorist commits the infraction again, then issue a citation.

20. While attending a baseball game one afternoon, you notice the placement of some kind of incendiary device connected to an electronic timer beneath the bleachers. As an off-duty police officer, what should you do?
    A. Take a closer look, and perhaps attempt to disarm the device.
    B. Tell everyone to evacuate the area because there is a bomb in the stands.
    C. Contact the field manager to have the game stopped, and evacuate the public to a safe area.
    D. Call the bomb squad, and let them handle the entire matter.

21. You are assigned traffic control at a particular intersection for a parade. An ambulance with its emergency lights and sirens going needs to cross the intersection. What should you do?
    A. Redirect the ambulance to circumvent the parade route.
    B. Temporarily stop the parade and allow the ambulance to proceed through the intersection.
    C. Call your immediate supervisor for direction or permission to stop the parade.
    D. Direct the ambulance driver to proceed to a point at least one block in front of the parade procession and then attempt the crossing.

22. During the course of interrogating a suspect, all of the approaches given below would elicit information important to the case except:
    A. Demonstrate a degree of understanding of the individual.
    B. Be a good listener.
    C. Develop a benevolent rapport with the suspect.
    D. Minimize the significance of what this individual is suspected to have done.

23. The National Advisory Commission on Criminal Justice Standards and Goals states that every police agency should immediately establish programs that encourage members of the public to take an active role in preventing crime, provide information leading to the arrest and conviction of criminal offenders, facilitate the identification and recovery of stolen property, and increase liaison with private industry in security efforts. What does the above statement imply?
    A. Citizen involvement is imperative in crime prevention.
    B. Citizens better educated about the law should take criminal matters into their own hands.
    C. Crime should be the major concern of the criminal justice system and only a secondary consideration for the community.
    D. Planning, education, and training of the citizenry in crime prevention will lessen the overall workload for the criminal justice system.

24. Officers are told not to appear at places within their patrol jurisdiction at regular intervals. What is the best reason for this policy?
    A. A police officer can more thoroughly patrol his or her beat.
    B. Staggered inspection times gives the public the impression that police officers are constantly on patrol.
    C. A regular routine inspires complacency.
    D. Established patterns of patrol make it easier for the criminal element to go about its business without the threat of getting caught.

25. Good defense posture is absolutely necessary to implement effective defensive tactics. All of the following would be considered good form except:
    A. Keeping your feet moderately spread and staggered.
    B. Keeping your legs and back straight.
    C. Bending the knees.
    D. Lowering the buttocks.

Read the following laws and classifications listed below. Answer Questions 26 through 36 on the basis of these statutes.

405—Receiving or Concealing Stolen Property in the First Degree
    A. An individual is guilty if he/she knows the property to be stolen and willfully receives or conceals said property with the intent to either deprive the rightful owner of its use or use it for his/her personal gain. Value of stolen property must be in excess of $1500.

415—Receiving or Concealing Stolen Property in the Second Degree

A. An individual is guilty if he/she knows the property to be stolen and willfully receives or conceals said property with the intent to either deprive the rightful owner of its use or use it for his/her personal gain. Value of stolen property must be in excess of $250 but not to exceed $1500; or

B. receiving or concealing a stolen firearm; or

C. receiving or concealing a stolen credit card.

420—Receiving or Concealing Stolen Property in the Third Degree

A. An individual is guilty if he/she knows the property to be stolen and willfully receives or conceals said property with the intent to either deprive the rightful owner of its use or use it for his/her personal gain. Value of stolen property must not exceed $250.

430—Larceny in the First Degree

A. An individual is guilty if he/she has the intent to permanently deprive another of property or services and either uses said property for his/her own personal gain or disposes of it for other compensation. Value of property or services, not including a motor vehicle, must be in excess of $1500; or

B. any property taken from the person of another.

435—Larceny in the Second Degree

A. An individual is guilty if he/she has the intent to permanently deprive another of property or services and either uses said property for his/her own personal gain or disposes of it for other compensation. Value of property or services, not including a motor vehicle, must be in excess of $250, but not exceed $1500; or

B. credit card theft.

440—Larceny in the Third Degree

A. An individual is guilty if he/she has the intent to permanently deprive another of property or services and either uses said property for his or her own personal gain or disposes of it for other compensation. Value of property or services, not including a motor vehicle, must not exceed $250.

450—Misappropriation of Misdelivered or Lost Property

A. An individual is guilty if he/she comes into the possession of misdelivered or lost property of another, bearing some form of identification of the rightful recipient or owner and fails to take reasonable measures in returning said property.

460—Auto Larceny

A. An individual is guilty if he/she appropriates the use of a motor vehicle without consent of the owner; or

B. accepts transportation in a vehicle known to be stolen; or

C. demonstrate the intent to permanently deprive, encumber, liquidate, pledge, or otherwise transfer any interest in said vehicle to parties other than the rightful owner.

470—Blackmail

A. An individual is guilty if he/she (public officials excluded) utilizes a threat, be it verbal or written, to acquire property not rightfully due him/her.

26. John Worthington, a county building inspector, tells Mr. Sherman that his office building is not quite in compliance with county building codes. However, for $1000, which would be far below the cost of upgrading the building to current standards, Mr. Worthington would "overlook" the infraction. According to the statutes provided, what would Mr. Worthington be guilty of?

    A. 470—A

    B. 430—B

    C. 435—A

    D. None of the above

27. Howard Bartlett, an ex-employee of a local cable TV company, hooked himself up to the local cable services without having the authorization to do so or notifying the company. Two months later, a cable repair technician discovers the illegal hookup and promptly disconnects the service. It was determined that Mr. Bartlett had not paid for two months of services, valued at $45. According to the statutes provided, Mr. Bartlett would be guilty of?

    A. 440—A

    B. 420—A

    C. 430—A

    D. Nothing, since he used to work for the company in question

28. United Parcel Service inadvertently left a package which should have been delivered to a neighbor down the block at the McCartney residence. When Mr. McCartney got home from work, he found the package behind the screen door. Mr. McCartney immediately recognized the mistake but opened the package anyway. The contents turned out to be a $250 cassette deck. Since the package was not insured and did not require a signature, Mr. McCartney chose to keep the article. Later that same evening, Mr. McCartney told his wife that he had gone to the mall and bought her the stereo equipment she had long wanted. According to the statutes, what would Mr. McCartney be guilty of?

    A. 440—A

    B. 450—A

    C. 420—A

    D. 470—A

29. (Refer to Question 28.) Which of the statutes provided would describe Mrs. McCartney's involvement?

    A. 440—A

    B. 450—A

    C. 420—A

    D. She committed no crime

30. Tom Meeker, a high school dropout, successfully hot-wired a friend's 1982 Monte Carlo and decided to take it for an afternoon joyride. At about 3:30 p.m., Tom saw Henry Weisgerber walking home from school and offered him a ride home in his "new car." According to the statutes, what is Mr. Meeker guilty of?

    A. 405—A

    B. 430—A

    C. 460—A

    D. Meeker committed no crime

31. (Refer to Question 30.) Which of the statutes provided would describe Henry Weisgerber's involvement?

    A. 405—A

    B. 460—A

    C. 460—B

    D. Weisgerber committed no crime

32. On the way home from work, Kim Mills happened across a roadside vendor selling jewelry. One particular item, a silver and turquoise bracelet, caught her interest and she inquired about the price. The vendor explained, in all sincerity, that the bracelet was worth $250. However, because it was "hot," he would part with it for $75. Ms. Mills was ecstatic about the price and promptly bought the bracelet. According to the statutes provided, what would Ms. Mills be guilty of?

    A. 420—A

    B. 415—C

    C. 415—A

    D. Ms. Mills committed no crime

33. Jerry Whitmore's daily use of cocaine was an expensive proposition. He could no longer afford to maintain his habit on the basis of what he earned at work. Due to his desperation to avoid withdrawal, he took a purse from a woman waiting at a Metro bus stop. The purse contained $375 in cash and another $200 in traveler's checks. According to the statutes provided, what is Mr. Whitmore guilty of?

    A. 415—A

    B. 430—A

    C. 430—B

    D. 435—A

34. Cassandra Carston went to a local pawn shop and bought a reasonably priced .38-caliber pistol for self-protection. Two weeks later, a detective called Ms. Carston and informed her that the pistol she had bought was stolen property. An officer was sent to her residence shortly thereafter to confiscate the weapon as evidence. Under the circumstances, what would Ms. Carston be guilty of?

    A. 450—A

    B. 430—B

    C. 415—B

    D. Ms. Carston committed no crime

35. For the lack of something to do on a Saturday afternoon, three juveniles threw bricks through the windows of a 1989 Buick Skylark. There was no damage to the body of the vehicle; however, the cost of replacing the windows was $1250. Under the statutes provided, what would the juveniles be charged with?

    A. 430—A

    B. 435—A

    C. 460—C

    D. None of the above

36. Sandra Brenston called Steven Whitlock and threatened to expose his homosexuality to close friends and the public unless he agreed to send her $1500. Under the circumstances, Ms. Brenston's actions would be considered unlawful according to which of the statutes provided below?

    A. 415—A
    B. 435—A
    C. 470—A
    D. None of the above

37. Officer Collins wrote an incident report regarding a burglary of a private residence. The following five sentences were taken out of the text of that report in no particular order:

    1. Value of property recovered: $345.
    2. Value of property reported stolen: $345.
    3. Doug Clavering is presently in the Fuller County jail in lieu of $50,000 bail.
    4. He apparently accessed the dwelling via an unlocked kitchen window.
    5. Doug Clavering was arrested and charged with Second Degree Burglary.

    Which of the following alternatives represents the correct logical order of events?

A.	4	2	1	5	3
B.	4	1	2	5	3
C.	3	5	2	1	4
D.	4	1	5	2	3

38. Officer Harper wrote an incident report regarding a forgery. The following five sentences were taken out of the text of that report in no particular order:

    1. Ms. Larson had asked Mrs. Hennessy, the store checkout clerk, if she could postdate her check by one week.
    2. Harold Craswell, the store manager, detained Ms. Larson.
    3. I placed Ms Larson under arrest for check forgery at 7:45 p.m.
    4. Cindy Larson picked out four dresses totaling $492 in value.
    5. Mrs. Hennessy said the telecheck security system determined that the check was being written on a closed account.

    Which of the following alternatives represents the correct chronological order of events?

A.	4	1	5	2	3
B.	4	2	1	5	3
C.	2	4	3	5	1
D.	1	4	5	2	3

39. Officer Conners wrote an incident report regarding a DWI (Driving While under the Influence) traffic offense. The following five sentences were taken out of the text of that report in no particular order:

    1. The owner of the vehicle, Mr. Keith Denner of 1419 9th Street, was wanted for failure to appear for an earlier charge of reckless driving.
    2. Mr. Denner assured me it was medicine prescribed to him that caused some drowsiness.
    3. Mr. Denner's blood alcohol level registered 0.19%.
    4. At 1:37 a.m., I noticed the driver of a 1990 Jeep Cherokee swerving erratically between the lines on Warren Avenue.
    5. He agreed to take the breathalizer test.

Which of the following alternatives represents the correct chronological order of events?

A.	4	1	2	3	5
B.	4	2	1	5	3
C.	4	1	2	5	3
D.	4	3	2	1	5

40. Officer Becker wrote an incident report regarding a shoplifting that had taken place in a hardware store. The following five sentences were taken out of the text of that report in no particular order.

1. He had asked the woman, Susan Daly, whether she intended to pay for the article underneath her coat.

2. I received the call to investigate a woman being held on suspicion of shoplifting at 8:30 p.m.

3. The store detective, Sid Lowry, had noticed a woman place a curling iron beneath her coat.

4. Susan Daly was placed under arrest for petty larceny.

5. She told Sid that she had a good lawyer and would definitely sue the establishment for false arrest.

Which of the following alternatives represents the correct chronological order of events?

A.	2	5	3	1	4
B.	3	1	5	2	4
C.	5	3	2	4	1
D.	3	2	1	5	4

Questions 41 through 45 involve composite-sketch cross-comparison. Look at the original sketch of the subject on the left and then try to discern which of the four other sketches to the right (labeled a, b, c, d) provided is the same individual attempting to disguise his or her appearance. Unless otherwise stated, assume the individual in question has not undergone any surgery.

41.

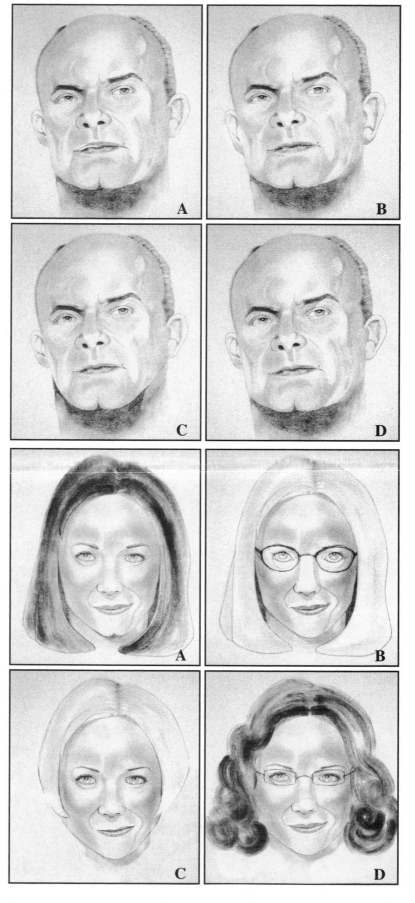

42.

43.

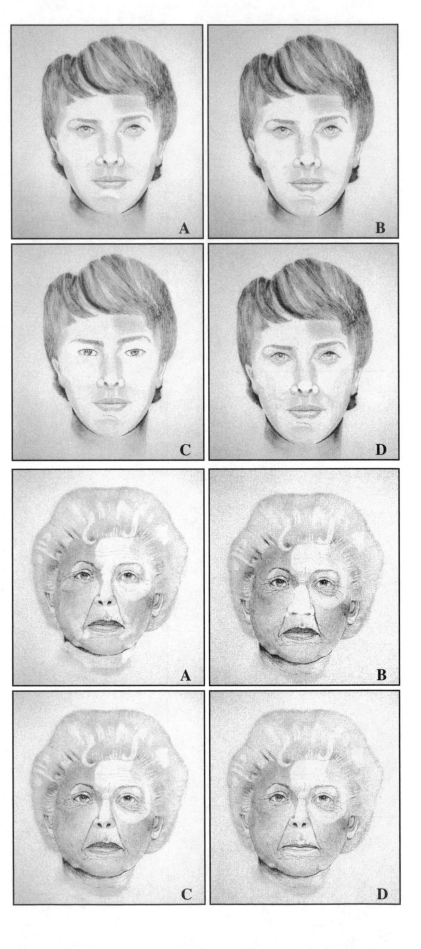

44.

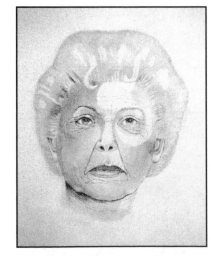

45.

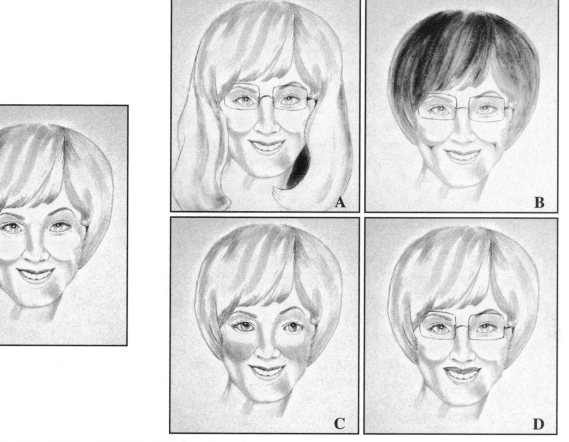

ANSWER SHEET FOR SAMPLE QUESTIONS ON SITUATIONAL JUDGMENT AND REASONING

1. Ⓐ Ⓑ Ⓒ Ⓓ	16. Ⓐ Ⓑ Ⓒ Ⓓ	31. Ⓐ Ⓑ Ⓒ Ⓓ	
2. Ⓐ Ⓑ Ⓒ Ⓓ	17. Ⓐ Ⓑ Ⓒ Ⓓ	32. Ⓐ Ⓑ Ⓒ Ⓓ	
3. Ⓐ Ⓑ Ⓒ Ⓓ	18. Ⓐ Ⓑ Ⓒ Ⓓ	33. Ⓐ Ⓑ Ⓒ Ⓓ	
4. Ⓐ Ⓑ Ⓒ Ⓓ	19. Ⓐ Ⓑ Ⓒ Ⓓ	34. Ⓐ Ⓑ Ⓒ Ⓓ	
5. Ⓐ Ⓑ Ⓒ Ⓓ	20. Ⓐ Ⓑ Ⓒ Ⓓ	35. Ⓐ Ⓑ Ⓒ Ⓓ	
6. Ⓐ Ⓑ Ⓒ Ⓓ	21. Ⓐ Ⓑ Ⓒ Ⓓ	36. Ⓐ Ⓑ Ⓒ Ⓓ	
7. Ⓐ Ⓑ Ⓒ Ⓓ	22. Ⓐ Ⓑ Ⓒ Ⓓ	37. Ⓐ Ⓑ Ⓒ Ⓓ	
8. Ⓐ Ⓑ Ⓒ Ⓓ	23. Ⓐ Ⓑ Ⓒ Ⓓ	38. Ⓐ Ⓑ Ⓒ Ⓓ	
9. Ⓐ Ⓑ Ⓒ Ⓓ	24. Ⓐ Ⓑ Ⓒ Ⓓ	39. Ⓐ Ⓑ Ⓒ Ⓓ	
10. Ⓐ Ⓑ Ⓒ Ⓓ	25. Ⓐ Ⓑ Ⓒ Ⓓ	40. Ⓐ Ⓑ Ⓒ Ⓓ	
11. Ⓐ Ⓑ Ⓒ Ⓓ	26. Ⓐ Ⓑ Ⓒ Ⓓ	41. Ⓐ Ⓑ Ⓒ Ⓓ	
12. Ⓐ Ⓑ Ⓒ Ⓓ	27. Ⓐ Ⓑ Ⓒ Ⓓ	42. Ⓐ Ⓑ Ⓒ Ⓓ	
13. Ⓐ Ⓑ Ⓒ Ⓓ	28. Ⓐ Ⓑ Ⓒ Ⓓ	43. Ⓐ Ⓑ Ⓒ Ⓓ	
14. Ⓐ Ⓑ Ⓒ Ⓓ	29. Ⓐ Ⓑ Ⓒ Ⓓ	44. Ⓐ Ⓑ Ⓒ Ⓓ	
15. Ⓐ Ⓑ Ⓒ Ⓓ	30. Ⓐ Ⓑ Ⓒ Ⓓ	45. Ⓐ Ⓑ Ⓒ Ⓓ	

ANSWERS TO SAMPLE QUESTIONS ON SITUATIONAL JUDGMENT AND REASONING

1. *C.* When suspects are handcuffed, the officer is protected from being assaulted and the suspect is deterred from escaping. This holds true for all persons arrested, including little old ladies.

2. *D.* Taking into account the fact that the man could not be awakened, and the presence of the empty syringe, which may be indicative of illicit drug use, it should be assumed by Officer Kent that a life-threatening condition prevails. Selection D is the only choice that offers immediate medical care. Detoxification centers offer programs that can be responsible for people recovering from their dependence on alcohol or drugs but are not emergency medical care facilities.

3. *A.* Since the possession of money by itself does not constitute a crime, the best approach would be to apprehend the suspect that has the illegal drugs. The other individual can be implicated at a later time. Issuing a warrant for the arrest of both suspects is all well and good, but the officer's best chance of apprehending the suspects would be to give immediate chase. Firing a warning shot is not condoned because it could put the public at risk.

4. *C.* Before an officer takes any action against parties involved in a dispute of this nature, he or she should find out the entire story from both sides. At that point, an officer can effect proper disposition of the matter.

5. *A.* This selection represents the best advice that could be given. Selections B and C would, in all likelihood, exacerbate the problem. Selection D is wrong because, regardless of the fact the officer is off duty, it is the officer's duty to serve and protect the public. Ethics do not change at the end of a shift.

6. *B.* Selection B would be the most appropriate approach to handle an incident of this nature. If the question had implied that this was a recurrent problem, then A would have been the appropriate response. Retaliation or "getting even" is an attitude unbecoming of a professional police officer. Inadequate backup can result in an officer being seriously injured or killed. Selection D is on the same order as A. It should be considered only after the officer has been addressed directly and the problem continues to persist.

7. *D.* Choice D is the best way a law-enforcement officer can protect him or herself from false claims of theft. Giving the money to a police charity or outright keeping the money would be wrong, illegal, and contrary to the ethics expected of a police officer. Choice C is incorrect because witnesses should be questioned by an investigator assigned to the case. The money could serve as important evidence which could further incriminate the prisoners for the crimes committed.

8. *C.* Since it was obvious to Officer Jones that the victim of the stabbing was bleeding severely, it is imperative that he attempt to stop or at least slow the bleeding by applying pressure to the wound. Someone can bleed to death in just minutes. A person's life takes precedence over all other matters.

9. *B.* This statement represents a truthful middle-of-the-road reply which neither further exacerbates this person's irritation over getting the ticket nor implies that you will do anything to rectify it. The other choices provided would be wrong for these very reasons.

10. *B.* Before taking any action, an officer needs to collect as much information as he or she can. Only after that has occurred, can he or she take appropriate steps to alleviate the problem. Both Selections A and C automatically assume that the man standing in the driveway is the

suspect in question. It could turn out that this individual was just a curious neighbor or an innocent bystander. Choice B would confirm or deny the identity of the man. Choice D is obviously wrong because indecent exposure is a crime and should be treated as such by law-enforcement officers.

11. *A.* All downed power lines, cables, etc., should be treated as though they are "hot." The absence of arcing or burning does not necessarily indicate that the line is de-energized. Selections B and C can both result in the officer being electrocuted. Selection D is incorrect even though a report of the incident is filed, if the officer leaves the area to continue patrol, the situation remains a potential threat to the public. The area should be secured until utility repair crews arrive and take control of the matter.

12. *C.* Murder, nine times out of ten, is a spontaneous event that lacks premeditation. The other crimes are somewhat more predictable and, as such, an increased police presence can serve as an effective preventative measure.

13. *C.* Fire department personnel are better qualified to handle such situations. After the fire department has been notified, the police officer's PA system should suffice to alert residents to the emergency. Once fire officials arrive at the scene, they have charge over future operational directives. Law-enforcement officers can further assist firefighters by handling traffic and crowd control.

14. *D.* Police radio networks are essentially party lines. When various agencies subscribe to the same transmission procedures, often officers cut one another off the air or make it difficult for an officer to even get on the air if messages are not kept to an effective minimum.

15. *B.* Selection A is true to some extent; however, the badge more importantly serves as a means to identify the police officer. Both Selections C and D are false on their own merit.

16. *B.* Problems that occur in coordinating police activities can almost always be traced to poor communication between officers. If a direction is not fully comprehended or clearly heard, it is better to have it repeated than to undertake action on your own initiative. Effective teamwork is imperative for any kind of operation to be conducted efficiently. The other choices run counter to this concept.

17. *A.* The advantage of a silent alarm is the element of surprise. This is obviously forfeited if the officer handles the call in the way described in Statement A. The remaining choices are considered correct procedure.

18. *C.* Child abuse and neglect are the greater cause of concern. Both of these crimes normally occur within the privacy of a home. Law enforcement intervention into family life can generate deep feelings of resentment and distrust. What constitutes acceptable corporal punishment for children versus that which is considered excessive, as well as abusive, force can be a relative grey area also. The other crimes are of a more tangible nature that can more easily be addressed by law enforcement personnel.

19. *B.* The best course of action would be just to issue a warning. Remember, the change of traffic signs had occurred only recently. Motorists can be complacent when commuting over the same route every day. The warning for a first-time offender would be more appropriate than a citation. This will, at least, bring the change to the motorist's attention without unnecessarily penalizing them. Selection A is wrong because if the infractions were to continue, a traffic accident or injury could result.

20. *C.* Statement C would be the most appropriate action to take because time may be of the essence. Notifying the bomb squad would be prudent, too; however, the extra time taken in waiting for their arrival would be better spent in removing the public from danger. Statement B would be incorrect because the announcement of the fact that there was a bomb on the premises might initiate a panic, and the situation would be made worse. Statement A puts both you and the public at risk if you do not have the necessary training.

21. *B.* It can be safely assumed that someone is in need of immediate medical attention. The preservation of someone's life takes precedence over all other circumstances. Selections A, C, and D complicate the matter by unnecessarily detaining the ambulance and wasting critical time.

22. *D.* By minimizing the significance of what the suspect is reported to have done, you would make it seem the police condone such actions. The suspect would then feel a little less guilty and consequently less compelled to answer questions from interrogators. Choices A, B, and C are all conducive to obtaining a better response from the suspect at the time of interrogation.

23. *A.* Only A best sums up the statement's implications. Choice B is false on its own merit. Choice C is incorrect because crime should be a primary concern for the community, not just for the criminal justice system. Selection D was neither said nor implied.

24. *D.* Letting criminals know precisely when a patrol car is scheduled for a given area basically defeats the purpose of patrolling a beat. Selection C may be true to some extent. The remaining selections are false on their own merit.

25. *B.* Choices A, C, and D all contribute to lowering the center of gravity of a police officer. Officers in this stance are more difficult to move or knock off balance. On the other hand, an officer doing what is prescribed in B would have a high center of gravity and a very narrow base of support. Consequently, a person in this stance is moved fairly easily. Balance and a low center of gravity are key to a good defense posture.

26. *D.* Selection A may initially seem the correct choice; however, blackmail is exclusive of public officials. This incident would be described as extortion, a term not given in the statutes provided.

27. *A.* Mr. Bartlett utilized two months of cable service with full intent not to pay. Since the value of the services was $45, Mr. Bartlett would be guilty of larceny in the third degree. Selection D is irrelevant.

28. *B.* Mr. McCartney intentionally misappropriated misdelivered merchandise. Consequently, Statute 450—A would be applicable for the circumstances described. This could also be qualified as a larcenous act (Statute 440—A); however, Statute 450—A is more precise in defining what had actually taken place.

29. *D.* Mrs. McCartney would not be guilty of any crime. As far as she knows, her husband had simply bought the equipment at the mall. The aspect of criminal intent is absent.

30. *C.* Statute 460—A comprehensively defines what Mr. Meeker did.

31. *D.* Mr. Weisgerber's believed that the 1982 Monte Carlo was Mr. Meeker's new car. The circumstances of how Meeker came into possession of the car was not discussed. Therefore, Mr. Weisgerber *un*knowingly accepted transportation in a stolen motor vehicle, and as such, is not subject to prosecution.

32. *A.* Ms. Mills had knowingly purchased stolen property valued at $250. Statute 420—A would be applicable to the action taken on Ms. Mills' behalf. Selection C would have been the correct answer had the bracelet had an actual value in excess of $250.

33. *C.* Statute 430—B specifically states that any property taken from the person of another qualifies as first degree larceny. Selection D is true in the respect that $575 in cash and travelers checks were stolen and therefore fits within the value limits of Statute 435—A. However, the crime is considered more serious when property is directly taken from the person of another. Consequently, what would have otherwise been considered second degree larceny is upgraded to the more serious offense of first degree larceny.

34. *D.* Selection C would have been the correct answer had Ms. Carston knowingly purchased a stolen firearm. Her only understanding of the matter was that she bought a reasonably priced firearm at a legitimate local business. If anyone deserves further investigation and perhaps prosecution under Statute 415—B, it would be the proprietor of the pawn shop.

35. *D.* Selection C would not be considered a correct answer because the juveniles' intent was to damage the vehicle, not steal it. This action would constitute malicious mischief, which was not addressed among the statutes provided.

36. *C.* Statute 470—A would be fully applicable to the case in question.

37. *A.* It was fairly evident that Sentence 4 and Sentence 3 took place first and last, respectively. Selection C is therefore eliminated on that basis alone. By looking at the second, third, and fourth numbers given in each of the remaining alternatives, Selections B and D can be eliminated. Property has to be identified and reported as stolen prior to its recovery. Both Selections B and D have this expected order reversed.

38. *A.* Selection D could have been a correct choice if Mrs. Hennessy were a regular clerk delegated to assist customers with questions. However, since she is a checkout clerk, it can be presupposed that Ms. Larson had picked out the articles of clothing first and then, at the time of being checked out, inquired about postdating her check as a means of payment. It can be safely assumed that Statements 4 and 3 are the first and last events to happen, thereby eliminating C. By scrutinizing the second and third numbers of A and B, you can safely assume that A is the correct choice. It would not make sense that, as B implies, Ms. Larson asked about postdating a check after the store manager detained her.

39. *C.* Statement 4 is obviously the beginning of Officer Conner's report. Unfortunately, all four choices given suggest that as well. However, Statement 3, being the conclusionary statement to the report, must be preceded by the fact that Mr. Denner agrees to have the breathalizer test in the first place (Statement 5). Therefore, Selections A and D can be eliminated on that basis. Selection B is incorrect because Statement 1 should precede Statement 2. It can be assumed that Officer Conners ran the plates first to learn who the owner of the vehicle was and to determine if there were any wants and warrants. Once the subject was pulled over the license and registration confirmed that Mr. Denner was the operator/driver of the vehicle. It is at this point that Mr. Denner offers the excuse made in the report.

40. *B.* The first event of this report would be Detective Lowry initially witnessing the shoplifting incident that culminated in Ms. Daly's arrest for petty larceny. Therefore, A and C can be eliminated on that basis alone. By looking at the second and third numbers in D, it can be safely surmised that Officer Becker would not receive the call to investigate a suspected shoplifter prior to Mr. Lowry's confronting the suspect in the first place. The process of elimination leaves B as being the correct answer.

41. *D.* Subject A has different lips.
Subject B has different ears.
Subject C has a narrower lower face.

42. *D.* Subject A has a cleft chin.
Subject B has different eyes and a wider nose.
Subject C has a wider face and different lips.

43. *B.* Subject A does not have a scar beneath the lower lip.
Subject C has different eyes.
Subject D has different facial lines.

44. *C.* Subject A has fewer facial lines.
Subject B has a larger nose.
Subject D has smaller lips.

45. *A.* Subject B has deep-set dimples.
Subject C has different eyes and a higher cheekbone structure.
Subject D has larger lips.

Your score for this exercise would rate as follows:
    41–45 correct, EXCELLENT
    36–40 correct, GOOD
    31–35 correct, FAIR
    Less than 31 correct, POOR

Directional Orientation

AS MENTIONED EARLIER IN THIS STUDY GUIDE, a superb memory is a real benefit to a police officer. However, when this quality is coupled with a good sense of directional orientation, the police officer is an invaluable asset to his or her department. If a police officer is familiar with the directional layout of the city or district that encompasses his or her beat, he or she can respond to emergencies in a safer and more efficient manner. On the other hand, a misdirected approach to an emergency can waste valuable time and perhaps further endanger the lives of those involved and the public in general. For these reasons, police departments are interested in determining a test applicant's directional abilities.

Most of the directional orientation questions seen on past exams have been of three types. The first variety of question asks what would be the most efficient way of getting from one point on a street map to another. If a vehicle is involved, it is assumed that no traffic violations may be committed en route unless otherwise stipulated. For example, no U-turns are permitted, and it is prohibited to travel in the wrong direction on a one-way street. The alternatives provided for these kinds of question deserve close scrutiny. Don't immediately assume that the first possible answer found is the correct choice. Very often, two possible routes will be given, one of which will be shorter and more efficient. This fact can be easily overlooked if each of the four alternatives provided is not given equal consideration and the incorrect choices eliminated accordingly. Reaching premature conclusions on any question, for that matter, is an open invitation to poor test performance.

The second type of question examines how well you can follow explicit directions. A specific route is outlined, and you need to determine what or where the final destination is. This task may seem quite easy, but it is surprising how far off in the wrong direction you can go if you misinterpret any direction given even slightly.

The third type asks the directional location of an object in relation to a person or specific landmark. This could simply come in the form of someone asking how to get to a destination, or it may concern the relative location of two different buildings. This type of question is probably the easiest to solve because you can figure out any direction by looking at the legend of the illustration given (e.g., see compass at right).

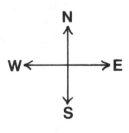

Even if the legend specifies only one direction, you can easily extrapolate any other direction as needed.

On the exam, a city or precinct grid will be given, on the basis of which questions will be asked. Be sure to read and follow the directions for each question word for word; do not assume anything. It is also important to approach these questions from the perspective of the person asking them. A northern heading from the questioner's standpoint may very well be an altogether different heading for you, depending on the way you look at the map. A right turn for the questioner could mean a left turn for you. To circumvent this confusion, simply rotate the diagram to view it from the same direction that the questioner is looking from. This will eliminate any disorientation when directions are discussed. As a final tip, you can more clearly determine correct answers by lightly sketching on the diagram provided all proposed or alternative routes in the question. This will allow for better contrast and easier discernment of the correct answer. If there are several questions relating to the same diagram, it is important to erase the previous sketching between questions. Otherwise, you will end up with a confusing array of lines, which can lead to a wrong answer.

SAMPLE QUESTIONS FOR DIRECTIONAL ORIENTATION

Answer Questions 1 through 10 on the basis of Diagram A on page 90.

1. Where is the Post Office in relation to the Second Precinct police station?
   A. South
   B. North
   C. East
   D. West

2. Assume that an officer is issuing a traffic citation to a motorist on Blaine Avenue between Ashton and Washington Boulevard. The same officer receives a call to investigate a burglary at Briarwood Apartments. Assuming that all traffic regulations are followed, which of the alternative routes provided below would be considered the best?
   A. East on Blaine Avenue half a block and then north one block on Ashton.
   B. West on Blaine Avenue half a block, north on Washington Boulevard one block, and then west on Foster Avenue one block.
   C. West on Blaine Avenue half a block, north on Washington Boulevard one block, and then east on Foster Avenue one block.
   D. East on Blaine Avenue half a block and then south one block on Ashton.

3. Officer Riley was parked directly out in front of City Hall on Dresden Avenue when she received a dispatch to investigate an assault and battery in the southwest corner of John Hopkins Park. Assuming that all traffic regulations are followed, what would be the best approach for Officer Riley to take?
   A. West on Dresden Avenue, south on Washington Boulevard for two blocks, and then one block west on Foster Avenue.
   B. West on Dresden Avenue one block and then south on Blakeview three blocks.
   C. West on Dresden Avenue, south one block on Washington, and then west one block on Chester Avenue.
   D. West on Dresden Avenue, south one block on Washington Boulevard, west one block on Chester Avenue, and then one block south on Blakeview.

4. On Dresden Avenue between Blakeview and Washington Boulevard, Officer Livingston noticed an elderly man who appeared somewhat disoriented. When she asked to see some form of identification, he explained that he must have left his wallet at home. He went on to say that he was staying with relatives, but unfortunately could not remember their address. He could, however, recall the fact that he had walked two blocks west, three blocks north and half a block east to get to his present location. According to the diagram, where would his point of origin be?
   A. The Ashton and Blaine Avenue intersection.
   B. The Foster Avenue and Washington Boulevard intersection.
   C. The Ashton and Foster Avenue intersection.
   D. The Police Department.

5. Where is First Interstate Bank in relation to the police station?
   A. Northeast
   B. North
   C. Southwest
   D. South

6. If a pedestrian were to ask a police officer standing in front of the precinct headquarters for directions to get to the fire department building, which of the following would be the best response?

   A. Go to Washington Boulevard, turn left, go three blocks, then turn left and go one block.

   B. Go to Blakeview, turn left, and go three blocks north.

   C. Go to Washington Boulevard, turn right, go three blocks; then turn left and go one block.

   D. Go to Blakeview, turn right, and go three blocks.

7. Four juveniles were seen by nearby residents trying to start a fire in a dumpster parked against the southeast corner of City Hall. The fire department was the first agency called, and at the outset of the alarm, the four suspects dispersed in different directions. The first suspect ran one and a half blocks west, two blocks south, and then one block east. The second suspect ran half a block east, two blocks south, and then one block west. The third suspect ran half a block west, three blocks south, and then one block east. The fourth suspect ran half a block west, one block south, one block east, one block south, and then finally one block east. On the basis of this information, which suspect would be nearest to the Redcliffe Apartments?

   A. Suspect 1

   B. Suspect 2

   C. Suspect 3

   D. Suspect 4

8. (Refer to Question 7.) Assume you are standing on the sidewalk that borders the northeast side of John Hopkins Park. From this point, which of the four suspects pass(es) close enough to be visually identified?

   A. Suspect 1

   B. Suspect 2

   C. Suspect 3

   D. Both Suspects 2 and 3.

9. Officer Tilder was driving south on Blakeview between Chester and Dresden Avenues when she was dispatched to a robbery in progress at the First Interstate Building. All traffic regulations aside, what would be considered the most expeditious approach?

   A. Turn right at the upcoming intersection and proceed two blocks.

   B. Turn left at the upcoming intersection and proceed two blocks.

   C. Make an immediate U-turn, turn right at the upcoming intersection and proceed two blocks.

   D. Make an immediate U-turn, turn left at the upcoming intersection and proceed two blocks.

10. According to the map, where are the Briarwood Apartments in relation to the Redcliffe Apartments?

    A. Southwest

    B. Northeast

    C. East

    D. West

DIAGRAM A

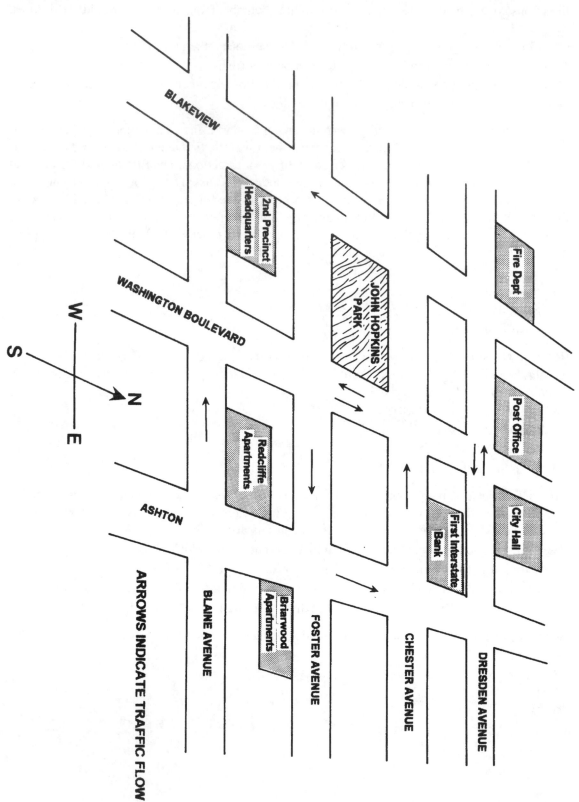

DIAGRAM B

Arrows indicate traffic flow; numbered addresses indicate single-family detached dwellings or businesses.

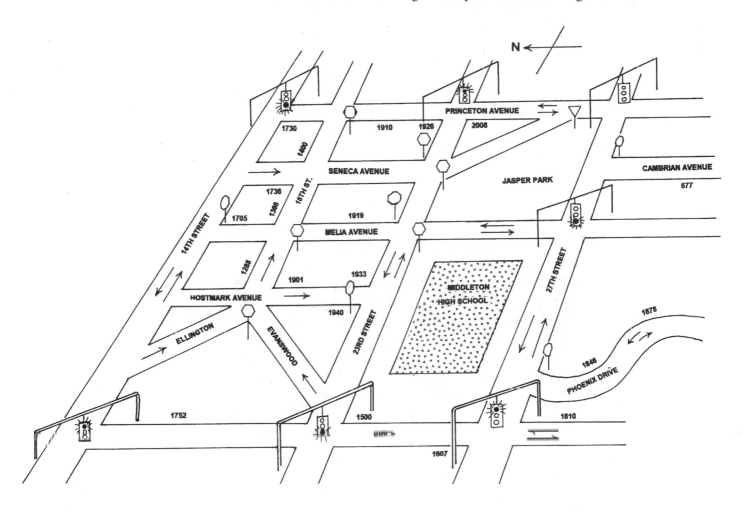

Facts to Be Aware of:

- At 0830 hours the intersection of Melia Avenue and 27th Street was closed for two hours by road repair crews.
- At 1015 hours 14th Street between Hostmark and Melia Avenues had to be closed for one hour by utility crews because of a downed power line.
- At 1145 hours the intersection of Princeton Avenue and 23rd Street had to be closed for one and a half hours to clear a two-car accident. This incident was handled by another patrol unit.
- At 1700 hours firefighters had to close the intersection of Brice and 23rd Street to fight a residential fire. The incident lasted one hour and 45 minutes; southbound traffic was permitted on Brice at 1845 hours. Traffic through the intersection was back to normal by 1930 hours.

Answer Questions 11 through 25 on the basis of Diagram B.

11. Where is Middleton High School in relation to Jasper Park?
    A. West
    B. East
    C. North
    D. South

12. Assuming that traffic regulations are followed, what is the direction of traffic flow on Evanswood Road?
    A. Southwest
    B. Southeast
    C. Northeast
    D. Northwest

13. Assuming Officer Johnson had just turned off Brice and was headed east on 14th Street, what would be the quickest route to take to get to the southeast section of Jasper Park without breaking any traffic regulations?
    A. Turn on Ellington, go east on 18th Street to Princeton Avenue, turn right, and go approximately two blocks south on Princeton Avenue.
    B. Continue on 14th Street to Seneca Avenue, turn south, and go on Seneca Avenue to Princeton Avenue.
    C. Continue on 14th Street to Seneca Avenue, turn north, and then go approximately three blocks on Seneca.
    D. Turn on Ellington, go south on Hostmark to 23rd Street, turn east on 23rd Street, go to Seneca Avenue, and then go southeast approximately one block on Seneca Avenue.

14. If Officer Sheldon were driving north on Melia Avenue between 23rd and 27th, which of the four choices given below would afford a nonstop means of getting to an apartment complex located at 1910 Princeton Avenue?
    A. Turn west on 23rd Street, go one block, turn north on Hostmark Avenue, go two blocks, turn east on 14th Street, go three blocks, and then turn right and go approximately one and a half blocks.
    B. Continue on Melia Avenue to 18th Street, turn east, go two blocks, and then turn right.
    C. Turn right at the next intersection, go two blocks, make a left turn and go approximately half a block.
    D. Turn left at the next intersection, go to the first lighted intersection and turn right, go to the next lighted intersection and turn right, go to the next lighted intersection and make another right turn, and then go approximately one and a half blocks.

15. Assuming Officer Spangler were patrolling the 1400 block of 14th Street at noon, what would be considered the quickest legal route to investigate a car-pedestrian accident at the intersection of Princeton Avenue and 27th Street?
    A. Go east on 14th Street, turn right on Princeton Avenue, and go to the accident site approximately three blocks south.
    B. Go west on 14th Street, turn left on Seneca Avenue, and go to Princeton Avenue and 27th Street.
    C. Go north on 14th Street, turn right on Princeton Avenue, and go to the accident site approximately three blocks south.
    D. Go west on 14th Street, turn north on Seneca Avenue, and go to Princeton Avenue and 27th Street.

16. If Officer Johnston were at the intersection of Hostmark Avenue and 18th Street and went three blocks east, one block north, and then two blocks west, where would he be in relation to his starting point?
    A. Northwest
    B. Southwest
    C. Northeast
    D. Southeast

17. Assume you are working central dispatch and are aware of the present locations of four patrol units. Patrol Unit 23 is parked on the 1400 block of 23rd Street; Patrol Unit 25 is parked on the 1300 block of 14th Street; Patrol Unit 27 is parked on the 600 block of Cambrian Avenue; and Patrol Unit 29 is parked on the 1900 block of Hostmark Avenue. If you were to receive an emergency call at 1025 hours regarding breaking and entering of a residence located at 1846 Phoenix Drive, which of the patrol units could respond most quickly? (Note: Speed limits for all the streets depicted on the map are the same.)
    A. Patrol Unit 23
    B. Patrol Unit 25
    C. Patrol Unit 27
    D. Patrol Unit 29

18. (Refer to Question 17.) Suppose you were to receive an emergency call at 1237 hours regarding a domestic dispute at 1910 Princeton Avenue. Which of the four patrol units described would be best able to respond to the call?
    A. Patrol Unit 23
    B. Patrol Unit 25
    C. Patrol Unit 27
    D. Patrol Unit 29

19. Based on the locations of the patrol units described in Question 17, where is Patrol Unit 27 in relation to Patrol Unit 25?
    A. North
    B. South
    C. East
    D. West

20. Assume Officer Davenport was heading west on 14th Street between Seneca Avenue and Melia Avenue when she received a call at 1915 hours to investigate a person attempting to pass a fraudulent check at a 7-11 store located at 1810 Brice. Considering her present location, which of the routes described below would be considered the most expeditious means of getting there?
    A. Continue west on 14th Street to Brice, and then turn left and go directly to the location.
    B. Turn left on Melia, right on 23rd Street, and then left on Brice.
    C. Turn left on Hostmark, right on Evanswood, right on 23rd, and then left on Briar.
    D. Turn north on Melia, west on 27th Street, and then south on Brice.

21. All of the following statements are true except:
    A. Traffic regulations aside, the shortest means of getting to the intersection of 23rd Street and Brice from the intersection of 14th Street and Melia Avenue would be to go to 18th Street on Melia Avenue, turn right, go one block, turn southwest on Evanswood, and then turn right on 23rd Street.
    B. The only one-way street that runs southeast is Ellington.
    C. The quickest means of getting to the east entrance of Middleton High School from 1730 Princeton Avenue for a noontime class would be to drive two blocks south to 23rd Street, go west on 23rd for two blocks, and then make a left on Melia Avenue and go approximately half a block.
    D. Both Choices B and C are incorrect.

22. Supposing police headquarters was located at the southeast corner of Princeton Avenue and 27th Street, and Police Officer Baker had just placed someone under arrest at 1752 Brice. According to the arrest report filed later, the time of arrest coincidentally was at 1752 hours. With that information known, which of the routes given below would be the most likely way Officer Baker transported the person arrested to the police station for further processing?
    A. South on Brice to 27th Street, and then east on 27th Street to Princeton Avenue.
    B. South on Brice to 23rd Street, east on 23rd Street to Seneca Avenue, and then southeast on Seneca Avenue to Princeton Avenue.
    C. South on Brice to 23rd Street, east on 23rd Street to Princeton Avenue, and then south on Princeton Avenue one block.
    D. None of the above.

23. According to the previous question, where in relation to police headquarters was Officer Baker at the time of the arrest?
    A. Southeast
    B. West
    C. Northwest
    D. North

24. Without regard for traffic regulations, what would be considered the quickest route to get from 1730 Princeton Avenue to 677 Cambrian Avenue to respond to a noontime drive-by shooting?
    A. Go south on Princeton Avenue to 27th Street, turn right on 27th Street, and go one block before turning left.
    B. Go west on 14th, turn left on Melia, go three blocks, turn left on 27th, and go one block before turning right.
    C. Go west on 14th, turn left on Seneca Avenue, go three blocks and merge onto Princeton Avenue, turn east on 27th Street, and go one block before turning left.
    D. Both Selections B and C would be considered viable options.

25. A high school student leaving the school premises via the east entrance (not specifically depicted on the map) would be on which road?
    A. 23rd Street
    B. Melia Avenue
    C. 27th Street
    D. Brice

DIAGRAM C

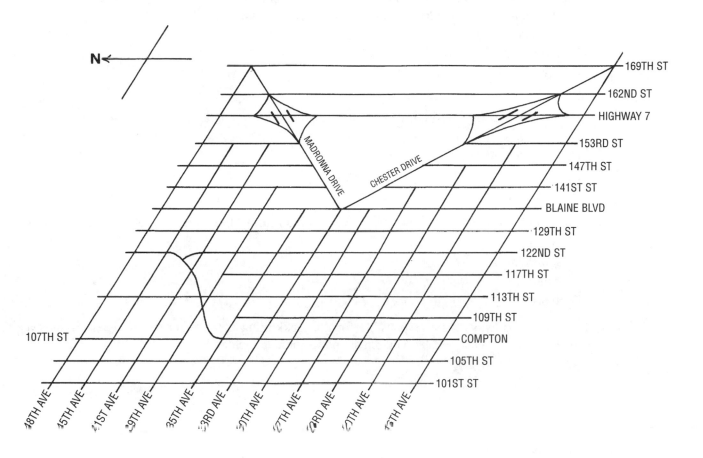

The map above represents four different law-enforcement agency jurisdictions. The State Patrol is responsible for the area bounded by 162nd Street, 48th Avenue, 153rd Street, and 16th Avenue. The County Sheriff is responsible for the area east of Blaine Boulevard excluding the portion handled by the State Patrol. The Downtown Precinct is responsible for the area bounded by Blaine Boulevard, 48th Avenue, Compton 30th Avenue, 101st Street and 16th Avenue. The 23rd Precinct is responsible for the area bounded by Compton, 48th Avenue, 101st Street, and 30th Avenue.

Answer Questions 26 through 33 on the basis of Diagram C

26. According to Diagram C, if a motorist became stranded on Chester Drive between 141st and 147th, which agency should respond to render roadside assistance?
    A. County Sheriff
    B. State Patrol
    C. 23rd Precinct
    D. Downtown Precinct

27. Technically, the southwest corner of 30th Avenue and Compton falls under whose jurisdiction?
    A. Downtown Precinct
    B. 23rd Precinct
    C. State Patrol
    D. County Sheriff

28. In which direction is a vehicle traveling on Compton from 41st Avenue to 35th Avenue headed?
    A. South
    B. Northeast
    C. Southwest
    D. North

29. Rain-slick roadways were responsible for the jackknifing of a tractor-trailer rig on Madrona Drive overpass. What agency would respond to such an incident?
    A. County Sheriff
    B. State Patrol
    C. 23rd Precinct
    D. Downtown Precinct

30. A vehicle traveling eight blocks north on Blaine Boulevard from 16th Avenue and then another four blocks west would end up in whose jurisdiction?
    A. State Patrol
    B. Downtown Precinct
    C. 23rd Precinct
    D. Unable to determine from the information given.

31. A residence on the northeast corner of 162nd Street and 16th Avenue falls in whose jurisdiction?
    A. 23rd Precinct
    B. State Patrol and/or County Sheriff
    C. State Patrol
    D. County Sheriff

32. A police officer desiring to get onto Highway 7 from the intersection of 109th Street and 20th Avenue could take which of the routes provided below?
    A. Drive eight blocks east and one block south, and then turn right.
    B. Drive five blocks north, then another five blocks east to merge directly onto Chester Drive, and continue to the Hwy 7 on ramp.
    C. Drive six blocks east and three blocks north, and then make a right turn onto Chester Drive, and continue to the Hwy 7 on ramp.
    D. Drive two blocks north and then another seven blocks east to merge directly onto Chester Drive, and continue to the Hwy 7 on ramp.

33. If a pedestrian were to walk five blocks east from Compton and 35th Avenue, then four blocks north, and then another block east, where would the intersection of Madrona Drive and Chester Drive be in relation to this person's final location?
    A. South
    B. North
    C. Northeast
    D. West

34. The following information was taken from a police report detailing what happened when a teenager lost control of his vehicle. After you have read the report, determine which of the four sketches provided below accurately depicts the incident described.

>   Blaine Williams was standing on the southeast corner of Piedmont and First Avenue when he noticed a Toyota pickup heading south on First Avenue begin to swerve erratically before entering the Piedmont intersection. The vehicle then went the wrong way on Piedmont (a one-way street), sideswiped a vehicle parked on Piedmont between First and Second Avenues, and then collided with another vehicle parked on the southeast corner of Second Avenue and Piedmont, narrowly missing two pedestrians waiting for a Metro bus.

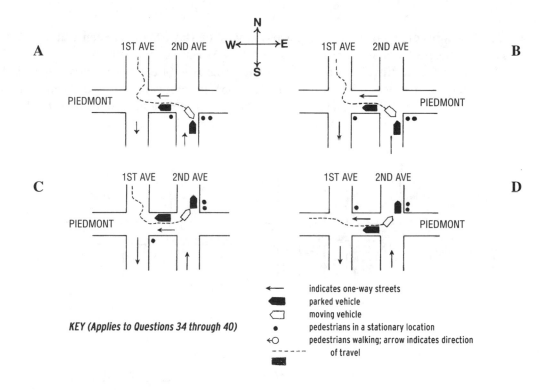

KEY (Applies to Questions 34 through 40)

←—— indicates one-way streets
parked vehicle
moving vehicle
• pedestrians in a stationary location
←O pedestrians walking; arrow indicates direction of travel
------ of travel

35. The following information is a statement from a witness that was used in compiling a police report detailing the circumstances surrounding a robbery of a small convenience store. After you have read it, determine which of the four sketches provided below accurately depicts the incident described.

>   Jacob Morris was waiting for a taxi on the southeast corner of Third Avenue and A Street when he heard two shots from the store directly across Third Avenue. Moments later, he witnessed a middle age man accompanied by a male juvenile run kitty corner from the store and then proceed two blocks north before turning east and disappearing from view.

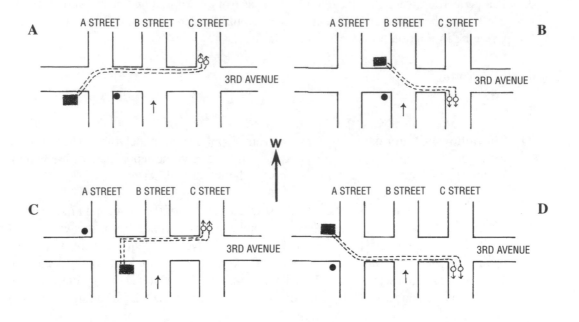

36. Joyce Robins claimed to have been walking west on Bay Street between 12th and 15th when she saw the suspect's vehicle, heading east on Bay Street, swerve in front of an oncoming car and drive over the northwest curb of 15th Avenue and Bay Street before crossing 15th Avenue and crashing into the second building north from the northeast corner of 15th Avenue and Bay Street. If Officer Hildbrandt wanted to document the witness's statement in his report, which of the four sketches provided below would accurately represent what she says happened?

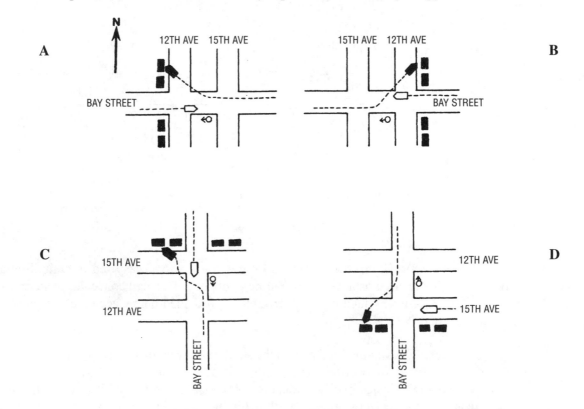

37. Bob Meinke claimed that he had been walking west on 20th Street and was halfway across the Aster Street crosswalk when a late-model Ford pickup traveling south on Aster Street failed to stop for the red light. It narrowly missed hitting Bob before swerving southwest and rear-ending a vehicle parked on the south side of 20th Street. If these statements were to be incorporated into a police report, which of the four sketches below would serve as an accurate representation?

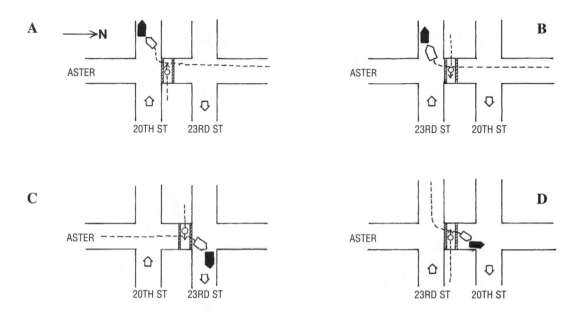

38. Teresa Billings was jogging south on Venetta and was about to cross 7th Street when she noticed that the driver of a Honda Prelude failed to stop for a stop sign on Hayward at the 7th Street intersection. Consequently, as the vehicle continued south on Hayward, it broadsided another vehicle, which had the right of way and was heading west on 7th Street. This story was corroborated by another witness standing at the southwest corner of 7th Street and Venetta. Which of the following sketches accurately depicts the circumstances just described?

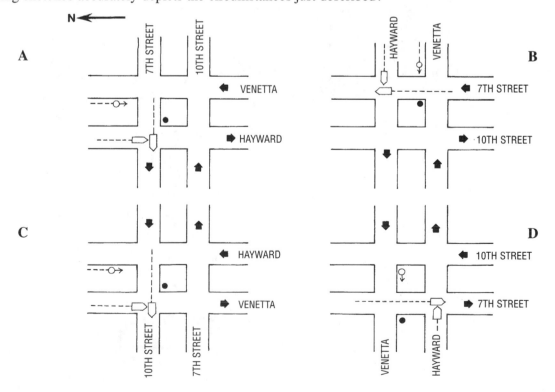

39. (Refer to Question 38.) After you have determined the correct map that depicts the incident described, where in relation to the jogger is the second witness?

    A. North

    B. East

    C. South

    D. West

40. In Question 38, in which direction was the vehicle that committed the traffic infraction headed?

    A. North

    B. East

    C. South

    D. West

ANSWER SHEET TO DIRECTIONAL ORIENTATION QUESTIONS

1. Ⓐ Ⓑ Ⓒ Ⓓ
2. Ⓐ Ⓑ Ⓒ Ⓓ
3. Ⓐ Ⓑ Ⓒ Ⓓ
4. Ⓐ Ⓑ Ⓒ Ⓓ
5. Ⓐ Ⓑ Ⓒ Ⓓ
6. Ⓐ Ⓑ Ⓒ Ⓓ
7. Ⓐ Ⓑ Ⓒ Ⓓ
8. Ⓐ Ⓑ Ⓒ Ⓓ
9. Ⓐ Ⓑ Ⓒ Ⓓ
10. Ⓐ Ⓑ Ⓒ Ⓓ
11. Ⓐ Ⓑ Ⓒ Ⓓ
12. Ⓐ Ⓑ Ⓒ Ⓓ
13. Ⓐ Ⓑ Ⓒ Ⓓ
14. Ⓐ Ⓑ Ⓒ Ⓓ

15. Ⓐ Ⓑ Ⓒ Ⓓ
16. Ⓐ Ⓑ Ⓒ Ⓓ
17. Ⓐ Ⓑ Ⓒ Ⓓ
18. Ⓐ Ⓑ Ⓒ Ⓓ
19. Ⓐ Ⓑ Ⓒ Ⓓ
20. Ⓐ Ⓑ Ⓒ Ⓓ
21. Ⓐ Ⓑ Ⓒ Ⓓ
22. Ⓐ Ⓑ Ⓒ Ⓓ
23. Ⓐ Ⓑ Ⓒ Ⓓ
24. Ⓐ Ⓑ Ⓒ Ⓓ
25. Ⓐ Ⓑ Ⓒ Ⓓ
26. Ⓐ Ⓑ Ⓒ Ⓓ
27. Ⓐ Ⓑ Ⓒ Ⓓ
28. Ⓐ Ⓑ Ⓒ Ⓓ

29. Ⓐ Ⓑ Ⓒ Ⓓ
30. Ⓐ Ⓑ Ⓒ Ⓓ
31. Ⓐ Ⓑ Ⓒ Ⓓ
32. Ⓐ Ⓑ Ⓒ Ⓓ
33. Ⓐ Ⓑ Ⓒ Ⓓ
34. Ⓐ Ⓑ Ⓒ Ⓓ
35. Ⓐ Ⓑ Ⓒ Ⓓ
36. Ⓐ Ⓑ Ⓒ Ⓓ
37. Ⓐ Ⓑ Ⓒ Ⓓ
38. Ⓐ Ⓑ Ⓒ Ⓓ
39. Ⓐ Ⓑ Ⓒ Ⓓ
40. Ⓐ Ⓑ Ⓒ Ⓓ

ANSWERS TO DIRECTIONAL ORIENTATION QUESTIONS

1. *B.* North

2. *C.* Both A and D are incorrect because these approaches run counter to the traffic flow. Selection B is incorrect because going west on Foster Avenue would place the officer in the vicinity of John Hopkins Park.

3. *D.* Selection A is wrong because it runs against the traffic flow. Selection B is incorrect because Officer Riley would pass her intended destination by one block. She would be closer to precinct headquarters than the southwestern corner of John Hopkins Park. Selection C would place Officer Riley at the northwest corner of John Hopkins Park.

4. *A.* This kind of question requires backtracking, in this case half a block west, three blocks south, and then two blocks east. This would place this elderly man's approximate point of origin at the Ashton and Blaine Avenue intersection.

5. *A.* Northeast

6. *D.* The question is a little tricky. Since it was a pedestrian inquiring for directions, attention need not be paid to one-way streets. Therefore, the most direct route would be simply to walk three blocks north on Blakeview, and the fire station should be seen on the northwest corner of Dresden Avenue and Blakeview. Only D suits the description. Selections B and C would actually place the pedestrian outside the boundaries of this precinct. Selection A is a possible route to get to the fire station; however, D is shorter.

7. *C.* The escape routes taken by the four suspects are highlighted in the diagram below. Suspect 3 is seen to be the closest to the Redcliffe Apartments.

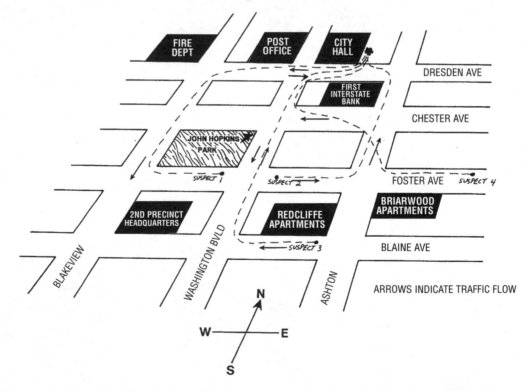

8. *D.* The star in John Hopkins Park marks the vantage point described in the question. If you were looking northeast, both Suspects 2 and 3 would pass close enough that fairly good physical descriptions could be obtained. Selections B and C are correct; however, D would be considered the best overall choice.

9. *B.* Selections A and D are incorrect because Officer Tilden would actually be heading away from the robbery and ultimately end up at a point beyond the map area provided. Selection C is incorrect because Officer Tilden would end up on Dresden Avenue at Ashton. The First Interstate Bank fronts Chester Avenue and Ashton. If the question had wanted a secondary or indirect approach, this option would have been considered appropriate.

10. *B.* Northeast. Selection A would have been correct had the question reversed its point of reference.

11. *A.* West. This question can be answered by simply filling in the compass points not provided in the legend. This methodology will alleviate any potential confusion on this question as well as other questions pertaining to the same legend.

12. *C.* Northeast. Selection A is incorrect because it runs counter to one-way traffic flow.

13. *B.* Both A and D are possible routes to get to the destination described; however, note the numerous intersections posted with stop signs. Officer Johnson would lose valuable time by stopping at each intersection. While the actual distance involved in B is comparable to the other routes detailed, it offers Officer Johnson a nonstop means of getting to the southeast part of Jasper Park. Selection C is incorrect because if Officer Johnson were to go north on Seneca Avenue for three blocks, he would be headed in a direction opposite to that intended.

14. *D.* Selection A is incorrect because driving north on Hostmark Avenue runs counter to the one-way-street designation. (*Note:* Even though the question does not address traffic regulations, it should be assumed that traffic laws must be obeyed *unless* otherwise specified.) Selection B is wrong because of the stop sign present at the Princeton and 18th Avenue intersection. Selection C is wrong as well, because the stop sign at Seneca and the stoplight on Princeton Avenue would require Officer Sheldon to stop twice. Only D affords a nonstop route for Officer Sheldon to get to the apartment complex on Princeton Avenue.

15. *B.* Selection A is incorrect because the intersection of Princeton Avenue and 23rd Street is closed from 1145 hours to 1315 hours (11:45 a.m. to 1:15 p.m., respectively) because of a two-car accident.

   (*Note:* It should be mentioned here that many exams seen recently vacillate between the use of military time and regular (civilian) time. Many police departments utilize military time in filling out various reports. Therefore, you should be aware of both uses. Military time is basically figured on a twenty-four hour clock; 0100 hours represents 1:00 a.m., 0200 hours represents 2:00 a.m., 1200 hours represents noon, 1600 hours represents 4:00 p.m., 2200 hours represents 10:00 p.m., and so on. Minutes are figured the same as for civilian time. For instance, 0830 hours represents 8:30 a.m., 0945 hours represents 9:45 a.m., 1515 hours represents 3:15 p.m., etc. Be aware of both forms of time because invariably you will be expected to understand the differences.)

   Selection C is incorrect because you cannot go north on 14th Street. Fourteenth Street is a two-way street that runs east and west. Selection D is wrong as well, because you cannot go north on Seneca Avenue. Seneca Avenue is a one-way street that runs south from 14th Street.

16. *C.* If Officer Johnston were to follow these directions, he would end up at the intersection of 14th Street and Melia Avenue, which is northeast of his point of origin.

17. *D.* Selection C may seem the correct choice initially. However, remember that the intersection of Melia Avenue and 27th Street is closed between the hours of 8:30 and 10:30 a.m. for road repair. Therefore, since Brice is the only route available to get to Phoenix Drive, D would be considered the best.

18. *B.* Here again another choice (i.e., A) may seem the most expeditious means of responding to the call. However, remember that the intersection of Princeton Avenue and 23rd Street is closed between 11:45 a.m. and 1:15 p.m. because of a two-car accident. Patrol Unit 23 would have to drive west to Melia and then east on 18th Street in order to reach the point referred to in the question. Patrol Unit 25 would be considered the closest.

19. *B.* South

20. *A.* Even though the fire department had to close the intersection of 23rd Street and Brice earlier, southbound traffic on Brice was allowed after 1845 hours. Choice A was then made possible, since the call came in at 1915 hours. Choice B, however, is not possible because westbound traffic on 23rd Street was not permitted through the Brice intersection until 1930 hours. Choice C is incorrect for the same reasons as B in addition to the fact that Officer Davenport would be going the wrong way on Evanswood, which is a one-way street. Choice D is wrong because Officer Davenport cannot travel north on Melia from 14th Street. Had this alternative called for him to drive south instead, D might have been considered the correct answer.

21. *D.* Selection B is wrong because the tail end of Seneca Avenue runs southeast as well. Selection C is wrong, too, because the intersection of Princeton Avenue and 23rd Street is closed between 11:45 a.m. and 1:15 p.m. due to a traffic accident.

22. *D.* None of the selections are correct because each route takes the officer through the intersection of 23rd Street and Brice, which is closed between the hours of 5:00 and 6:45 p.m. The arrest occurred at 1752 hours (i.e., 5:52 p.m.).

23. *C.* Northwest.

24. *B.* The question does stipulate that traffic regulations need not be followed; however, that would not eliminate the two-car accident that obstructs the intersection of Princeton Avenue and 23rd Street during the noon hour. Choice C is incorrect because turning east on 27th Street would place the officer outside the boundaries of the map provided.

25. *B.* Melia Avenue.

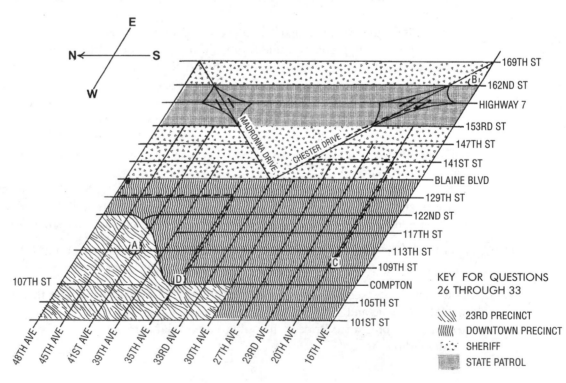

26. *A.* County Sheriff.

27. *A.* Downtown Precinct.

28. *C.* Southwest.

29. *B.* State Patrol.

30. *C.* 23rd Precinct (See Point A on the map).

31. *D.* Only the County Sheriff, not the State Patrol (see Point B on the map). 162nd Street serves as the boundary between the area served by the State Patrol and that handled by the sheriff. The area east of 162nd Street, which includes the residence in question, falls within the sheriff's jurisdiction.

32. *C.* Selection A is incorrect because going one block south of 20th Avenue on 153rd Street would result in driving away from the Chester Drive overpass. Selection B is incorrect because these directions place the officer at the intersection of 35th Avenue and Blaine Boulevard, which does not merge directly with Chester Drive. Selection D is incorrect for similar reasons. Two blocks north would place the officer on 27th Avenue, which does not merge into Chester Avenue. Rather, it terminates at 141st Street. (See route shown in map from Point C).

33. *A.* South. (See route shown on map from Point D).

34. *B.* Selection A is incorrect because it fails to correctly identify the positioning of Blaine Williams. It places the witness at the southwest corner of 2nd Avenue and Piedmont. Selection C is incorrect because it places the accident at the northeast corner of 2nd Avenue and Piedmont. Selection D is wrong for the same reasons as C, as well as the fact that the vehicle in question did not enter Piedmont from 1st Avenue and that the witness location is misplaced as well.

35. *D.* Selection A has Mr. Morris positioned at the northeast corner of 3rd Avenue and A Street. Selection B improperly depicts the location of both the witness and the store on B Street. Selection C places the witness on the southwest corner of 3rd Avenue and A Street and improperly defines the escape route taken by the pair.

36. *C.* (*Note:* Frequently, examiners provide questions that intentionally mix up points of reference. Don't let this confuse you. Analyze each map individually and determine the correct answer through the process of elimination. One other suggestion would be to establish compass points in each of the four sketches. This will tend to alleviate any directional errors.)

Selection A is wrong for a number of reasons. The suspect's car is headed west, not east, on Bay Street; fails to swerve in front of the car heading east on Bay Street; crosses the northeast curb of 12th Avenue and Bay Street, not the northwest curb of 15th Avenue and Bay Street; and crashes into a building on 12th Avenue, not 15th Avenue.

Selection B is incorrect because it shows the witness walking east, not west, on Bay Street; the suspect's vehicle was headed west, not east, on Bay Street, before crashing into a building on 12th Avenue instead of 15th Avenue.

Selection D is incorrect because the suspect's vehicle crosses the southwest curb of 15th Avenue and Bay Street, not the northeast corner; the vehicle is not shown to swerve in front of an oncoming vehicle; and the suspect's vehicle is shown crashing into a building south of the southeast corner of Bay Street and 15th Avenue, not two buildings north of the northeast corner of 15th Avenue and Bay Street.

37. *A.* Selection B is incorrect because it shows Mr. Meinke walking west on 23rd Street, not 20th Street, and the accident occurs on 23rd Street instead of 20th Street. Selection C is wrong for basically the same reasons as B, in addition to the fact that Mr. Meinke is walking due east, not west. Selection D is incorrect because here again the accident happens on 20th Street, not Aster. Additionally, Mr. Meinke is walking east, not west, across Aster on 23rd Street instead of 20th Street. (*Note:* This answer should have been fairly obvious because only Sketch A demonstrated an accident occurring on 20th Street.)

38. *B.* Selection A is incorrect because the second witness who corroborates the story of the person jogging is positioned at the southeast corner of 7th Street and Hayward instead of the southwest corner of 7th Street and Venetta. Selection C is incorrect for too many reasons to mention. Selection D is incorrect because the jogger's position and the second witness's position are just the opposite of where they should be.

39. *C.* South.

40. *C.* South.

Your score for this exercise would rate as follows:
    37–40 correct, EXCELLENT
    33–36 correct, GOOD
    29–32 correct, FAIR
    less than 29 correct, POOR

Report Writing, Grammar, and Spelling

THE ABILITY OF A POLICE OFFICER to write authoritative investigative reports is important for several reasons. Probably among the most significant is that such reports serve as official, permanent records, which detail circumstances surrounding law-enforcement activity. Additionally, these same recorded facts may be used as potential leads by people outside of the initiating department (e.g., FBI, DEA, GPS, etc.) to further an investigation. The reports can also be forwarded to the criminal justice system to be used in determining what form of disciplinary action should be taken or to make a penalty assessment.

Police reports are also important at the administrative level. Data can be extrapolated and statistical correlations made regarding problem traffic areas, high crime districts, recurrent criminal trends, and the like. Departmental manpower can then be put to more effective use by focusing attention on such areas. Reports can also play a key role in promotion and budget recommendations. The ramifications of good report writing are considerable.

During the exam, you will not be expected to write an actual police report. However, the test questions will follow one of two different formats. One form involves reading a narrative. A blank report form of some kind is furnished in conjunction with the reading. You will then be required to find information within the reading pertinent to various sections of the report.

The second format is essentially the opposite of the first. You are provided with a report that has already been filled out. From it, you will need to extract information appropriate to the question asked. This exercise is not difficult, but a little care should be used in determining the who, what, when, where, why, and how factors of any particular incident. The reason for such caution is that there may be several facts in a crime scene that could go in one part of a report.

For example, there may be several *who*s contained in one report. For instance, who is the complainant (i.e., the victim or reportee of the purported crime)? who is the perpetrator? who is the witness, if there is one? who responded to the incident; who filed the report? It can be easy to misconstrue information inserted into a police report if close attention is not paid to the question at hand. The best advice here is to read either the narrative or prepared report through once to familiarize yourself with what has taken place. Then, read each question carefully and go back to the reading and discern what information is being requested. Once you have worked through the exercises provided in this study guide, you should be prepared for comparable questions on the actual exam.

The second part of this chapter involves basic grammar and spelling, two very important aspects of good report writing. Written police reports are essentially the official records of incidents. If the information contained in the report is vague, grammatically incorrect, or grossly misspelled, not only does it detract from the competence and professionalism of the officer in question, but it also reflects poorly on the department as a whole. Well-written reports communicate better and serve to expedite, not hinder, the complaint-issuing process.

It is not the intention of this book to provide instruction in basic grammar. If you feel that this may be one of your weaker areas, there are volumes of material available at your local library dedicated to this subject. Rather, test questions comparable to those seen on past exams are given with answers and explanations.

This chapter also reviews a few basic spelling rules that can lend substantial assistance to those who struggle in this area. Additionally, an extensive list of words that have been seen on past exams, as well as those studied at various training academies, has been compiled and included in this section. This does not guarantee that words other than those compiled will not be seen on your exam; however, it will offer a fairly comprehensive study of the word base you will most likely encounter on the actual exam.

Read the narrative provided on the next page and then use the blank report form provided on page 109 to answer Questions 1 through 10. (*Note:* Answer sheets for this exercise and others throughout this section are placed at the end of this chapter.)

On Monday, November 7, 1992, Officer Brad Tomkins, Badge Number 136, was assigned to patrol the east side of Precinct 13 from 0700 hours to 1530 hours. Officer Tomkins received a dispatch from 911 at 0815 hours to investigate a possible car theft at 2215 Winfield Street. CENCOM had received a call five minutes earlier from a Mr. Saravich claiming that someone had broken into his next-door neighbor's garage overnight and stolen the family's 1991 Honda Accord while the family was away on vacation. Officer Tomkins' response time was just under five minutes. Upon arrival, Mr. Saravich, a 45-year-old black male who resides at 2217 Winfield Street, told the officer that it was he who had placed the call. He further explained that he was watching the house for Mr. and Mrs. Turnley while they were vacationing in Hawaii. At 8:05 a.m. (0805 hours), he noticed that the garage door had been left open and the neighbor's car was missing. Knowing that he was the only person who had been left a key to the residence, he called the police. Officer Tomkins was told that the Turnleys were staying at the Lahina Hotel, Suite 265, in Maui and could be reached by calling (919) 562-5251. Their home phone number is 565-1212. Mr. Saravich also mentioned that if he needed to be reached his home phone number was 753-2125. During the weekday afternoons, he works as a part-time claims adjuster for Safeco, Inc., and could be reached at 832-5621. Officer Tomkins walked around to the rear of the house and noticed distinctive pry marks on the jamb of the garage door. The door leading from the garage to the interior of the home did not appear to have been tampered with. All other windows and doors of the home seemed secure. Mr. Saravich could not ascertain whether anything else of value had been stolen from the garage. That determination would have to be made when the Turnleys returned home from their trip. Coincidentally, Mr. Saravich had been the agent that sold the Turnleys their comprehensive auto insurance policy (Allstate carried their homeowners insurance). He was able to offer Officer Tomkins a complete description of the missing vehicle. The vehicle was a white, four-door, 1991 Honda Accord registered to Howard and Mary Turnley, Washington State license number DAL-542, VIN number P34GL55421Z1476CD, and it carried a blue book (fair market) value of approximately $12,000. With that, Officer Tomkins completed his investigation at 0845 hours and submitted copies of the report to Sergeant Hunt. The report was classified under Auto Theft and assigned case number 66-54201.

① File #

GENERAL REPORT   (All entries must be typed or printed)

② Case #

③ Incident ④ Arrest ⑤ Vehicle ⑥ Property	⑦ Precinct of Report	⑧ Report Name/Offense/Charge	⑨ Type

⑩ Date Occurred	⑪ Time	⑫ Date Discovered	⑬ Time	⑭ Date Reported	⑮ Time	⑯ ☐ In Person ☐ Written ☐ By Phone ☐ Radioed In	⑰ Day of Week

⑳ Residence	⑲ Business	⑱ Auto	㉑ Will victim prosecute? Yes / No	㉒ Occupants at home at the time of offense? Yes / No	㉓ Is property insured? Yes / No

㉔ Entry Point?	㉕ Entry Method?	㉖ Was Force Used? Yes / No	㉗ Name: Insurance Co./Agent

VICTIM

㉘ Name: (Business) Last First Middle	㉞ Race	㉟ Sex	㊱ Age
㉙ Address: Street City State Zip	㉛ Home Phone		㊲ Date of Birth
㉚ Occupation ㉝ Place of Employment Street City State Zip	㉜ Business Phone		

㊳ Victim ㊴ Witness ㊵ Suspect ㊶ Arrested	㊷ Name: Last First Middle (Maiden)	Race	Sex	㊾ Age
	㊸ Address: Street City State Zip	㊹ Home Phone		Date of Birth

Business Name Street City State ZIP ㊺ Business Phone (Reportee) ㊻ Occupation (Reportee)

Physical Ident.	Outstanding Mark/Scar	㊼ Height	㊽ Weight	㊾ Build	㊿ Complexion	51 Hair	How Worn	52 Eyes	53 Glasses ☐ Yes ☐ No

Description of Clothing

54 Reportee 55 Witness 56 Suspect 57 Arrested	58 Name: Last First Middle (Maiden)	Race	Sex	Age
	59 Address: Street City State Zip	60 Home Phone		Date of Birth

Physical Ident.	Outstanding Mark/Scar	61 Height	62 Weight	63 Build	64 Complexion	65 Hair	How Worn	66 Eyes	67 Glasses ☐ Yes ☐ No

68 Description of Clothing

VEHICLES

69 Stolen 70 Recovered	73 License No.	74 State	75 Year	76 Type	Loc. Stolen Loc. Recov.	A
71 Wanted / Suspect	77 Vehicle Identification Number (VIN)				Loc. Stolen Rec. Outside	B
Victim / Impnd. - Hold	78 Year	79 Make	80 Model		Stolen Out Loc. Recov.	C
Impound / 72 Inv/Cond	81 Body Style	82 Color	Tow Truck Oper. No.			

Imp. Hold: Requested By Tow Truck Business Name

Tow From:

PROPERTY

83 Stolen	What is it?	Serial Number
84 Lost	Brand Name/Make	Model/Caliber
Found	Action	Barrel Length
Damgd.		
85 $ Theft	86 Type & Wheel Size	87 Frame Color
$ Damage	88 Fender Color	89 Seat Color
90 Total $	Unique Features	

TIME

91 Dispatched	92 Arrived	93 In Service	94 Signature of Reporting Officer/Person	95 Badge/Identification Number	96 Approved By

Evidence Seized Yes ☐ No ☐	DIST	Board	Detective Div.	Patrol Div.	Court	Prosecutor City Atty.	TOTAL
		Traffic	Armed Forces Pol.	Coroner	JUV	Other	

1. Which of the times provided below would be the correct entry for Box 13?
   A. 0815   B. 0845   C. 0805   D. 0820

2. Which of the times provided below would be the correct entry for Box 15?
   A. 0815   B. 0845   C. 0805   D. 0810

3. The number 66-54201 should be entered in which box?
   A. 1   B. 2   C. 77   D. 95

4. Which of the following addresses would be entered in Box 29?
   A. 2215 Winfield Street
   B. 2217 Winfield Street
   C. 2251 Winfield Avenue
   D. Lahina Hotel, Suite 265, Maui, Hawaii

5. Assuming that Box 54 is checked, which of the following numbers would be appropriate for Box 60?
   A. 832-5621
   B. 562-5251
   C. 753-2125
   D. 565-1212

6. What date should be entered in Box 14?
   A. 10-7-92
   B. 11-2-92
   C. 11-7-92
   D. 11-2-91

7. In which box would the number P34GL55421Z4176CD appropriately be inserted?
   A. Box 73
   B. Box 77
   C. Box 80
   D. None of the above

8. Box numbers 91 and 92 should be reported as?
   A. 0805 hours and 0810 hours, respectively.
   B. 0815 hours and 0820 hours, respectively.
   C. 0810 hours and 0845 hours, respectively.
   D. 0805 hours and 0845 hours, respectively.

9. The number 136 would be correctly entered in which box?
   A. Box 2
   B. Box 76
   C. Box 85
   D. Box 95

10. Which name would be correctly entered in Box 96?
    A. Turnley
    B. Saravich
    C. Hunt
    D. Tompkins

Look over the completed NOI (Notice of Infraction)/court docket provided below. Answer Questions 11 through 20 on the basis of the information provided in this report.

UNIFORM COURT DOCKET

☑ TRAFFIC INFRACTION   ☐ CRIMINAL TRAFFIC

☐ NON-TRAFFIC INFRACTION   ☐ CRIMINAL NON-TRAFFIC

☐ CITY/TOWN OF _CLEARWATER_   PLAINTIFF VS. NAMED DEFENDANT

IN THE ☐ DISTRICT ☑ MUNICIPAL COURT OF _PORTLAND_

STATE OF OREGON COUNTY OF _THURSTON_

THE UNDERSIGNED CERTIFIES AND SAYS THAT IN THE STATE OF _OREGON_

DRIVER'S LICENSE NO.	STATE	EXPIRES	SOCIAL SECURITY NUMBER
HALL TS344PC	CO	94	653-02-5552

NAME LAST	FIRST	INITIAL	☐ INTERPRETER NEEDED
HALL	TALON	S	

ADDRESS _5742 EVERGREEN BLVD_   ☐ IF NEW ADDRESS PASSENGER

CITY	STATE	ZIP CODE	EMPLOYER
DENVER	CO	67521	OCCIDENTAL INC.

SEX	RACE	DATE OF BIRTH	HEIGHT	WEIGHT	EYES	HAIR	RESIDENTIAL PHONE NO.
M	W	06-18-52	602	200	HAZ	BRO	(602)535-6752

VIOLATION DATE ON OR ABOUT

MONTH	DAY	YEAR	TIME 24 HOUR
09	15	92	1:30PM

AT LOCATION	M.P.	CITY/COUNTY OF
I-5	92	THURSTON

DID OPERATE THE FOLLOWING VEHICLE/MOTOR VEHICLE ON A PUBLIC HIGHWAY AND

VEHICLE LICENSE NO.	STATE	EXPIRES	VEH. YR.	MAKE	MODEL	STYLE	COLOR
ADK 573	CO	93	89	GMC	4DR	SUBURBAN	BRN/BLK

TRAILER #1 LICENSE NO.   STATE   EXPIRES   TR. YR.   TRAILER #2 LICENSE NO. STATE   EXPIRES   TR. YR.

OWNER/COMPANY IF OTHER THAN DRIVER	ADDRESS	CITY	STATE	ZIP CODE
OCCIDENTAL INC	1270 1RST AVE	DENVER	CO	67521

ACCIDENT NO. PD I F	BAC READING	COMMERCIAL VEHICLE ☑ YES ☐ NO	HAZARD PLACARD ☐ YES ☐ NO	EXEMPT VEHICLE ☐ FARM ☐ R.V.	☐ FIRE ☐ OTHER

DID THEN AND THERE COMMIT EACH OF THE FOLLOWING OFFENSES/INFRACTIONS

1. VIOLATION/STATUTE CODE	DESCRIPTION	VEHICLE SPEED	IN A	ZONE	☐ RADAR ☐ PACE ☐ AIRCRAFT
54.67.375	SPEEDING	72		60	

2. VIOLATION/STATUTE CODE   DESCRIPTION

PENALTY/BAIL U.S. FUNDS $ 40.00

APPEARANCE DATE	MO.	DY.	YR.	TIME	A.M. P.M.	BOOKING DATE	DATE NOTICE ISSUED 09-15-92

WITHOUT ADMITTING HAVING COMMITTED EACH OF THE ABOVE INFRACTIONS/OFFENSES, I PROMISE TO RESPOND AS DIRECTED ON THIS NOTICE.

I CERTIFY (OR DECLARE) UNDER PENALTY OF PERJURY UNDER THE LAWS OF THE STATE OF OREGON THAT I HAVE RESONABLE GROUNDS/PROBABLE CAUSE TO BELIEVE AND DO BELIEVE THE ABOVE NAMED PERSON COMMITTED THE ABOVE INFRACTION(S) AND/OR OFFENSE(S) CONTRARY TO LAW.

OFFICER	NUMBER
FRANK TALMADGE	154

X _Talon Hall_ DEFENDANT'S SIGNATURE   DATE 09-15-92   PLACE CLEARWATER, OR.

ABSTRACT OF JUDGEMENT	INFRACTION			COMPLAINT/CITATION				PENALTY		
	INF	RESPONSE	DISPOSITION	CRG	PLEA	CNG	FINDING	FINE	SUSPENDED	SUB-TOTAL
	1	C NC	C NC D P	1	G NG		G NG D BF	$	$	$
	2	C NC	C NC D P	2	G NG		G NG D BF	$	$	$
								$	$	$

FINDING/ JUDGEMENT DATE	TO SERVE	WITH	DAYS SUSPENDED	CREDIT FOR TIME SERVED	OTHER COSTS $
ABSTRACT MAILED TO OLYMPIA	RECOMMENDED NONEXTENSION OF SUSPENSION		LICENSE SURRENDER DATE		TOTAL COSTS $

11. According to the court docket, what was Mr. Hall cited for?
    A. Criminal traffic infraction
    B. Criminal nontraffic infraction
    C. Traffic infraction
    D. Nontraffic infraction

12. In which state was the defendant's license issued?
    A. Oregon
    B. Colorado
    C. Washington
    D. Iowa

13. What is the defendant's hair color?
    A. Blond
    B. Black
    C. Brown
    D. Red

14. When and where was the notice of infraction issued?
    A. 09-15-92/Thurston County
    B. 06-18-52/Denver, Colorado
    C. 09-15-92/Clearwater County
    D. 11-15-92/Portland, Oregon

15. The vehicle driven by the defendant is considered to be a
    A. Commercial vehicle
    B. Recreational vehicle
    C. Farm vehicle
    D. It was not indicated on the NOI

16. Mr. Hall committed what kind of offense, specifically?
    A. Improper passing
    B. Failure to comply with restrictive signs
    C. Improper lane usage
    D. Speeding

17. Officer Frank Talmadge determined that the defendant was committing the infraction specified in the NOI through which means?
    A. Aircraft
    B. Radar
    C. Pace
    D. Was not indicated on the citation.

18. When is the license of the vehicle in question due to expire?
    A. 1989
    B. 1994
    C. 1992
    D. 1993

19. As indicated on the citation, what is the defendant's DOB?
    A. 05-17-75
    B. 09-15-92
    C. 06-18-52
    D. 08-18-52

20. According to the information recorded in this court docket, all of the following statements are true except?
    A. The vehicle driven by Mr. Hall is owned by a corporation.
    B. Mr. Hall was driving 12 MPH in excess of the posted speed limit.
    C. The vehicle in question is a two-tone General Motors Suburban.
    D. The defendant's home address is 1270 First Avenue, Denver, CO 67521.

SAMPLE QUESTIONS FOR GRAMMAR

Questions 21 through 40 are specifically designed to test your knowledge of proper English usage and grammar. This section is meant only as a basic review of what is traditionally taught in high school. If you feel unsure about some of the rules, it is strongly advised that you study supplemental material which addresses this subject. A quick refresher course in writing can always be beneficial, regardless of the potential exam implications.

Each question will provide four complete sentences. You will have to determine which sentence, if any, is grammatically correct. The answers to these questions, complete with explanations detailing why the incorrect sentence structures are wrong, are provided toward the back of this section.

21. A. The Policeman's Ball (an event established three years ago) has become a widely publicized festivity.
    B. These kinds of preparatory study guides are instructive.
    C. The grand jury has agreed on the verdict.
    D. All of the above sentences are grammatically correct.

22. A. Detective Hanley is at his best in filing detailed field interview reports.
    B. Officer Briggs was upset at me.
    C. Rookie police officer Dan Clemms only made one error on his first street assignment.
    D. None of the above sentences are grammatically correct.

23. A. Sergeant Hill has arrested a woman identified by the victim's mother as the person she saw leaving the scene of the crime.
    B. The gang of juveniles fleed in several directions at the sight of Officer Jenkins.
    C. After completing the accident report, the rest of the day was easy.
    D. None of the above sentences are grammatically correct.

24. A. A gun was found lose in her purse.
    B. The mayor effected many changes in police personnel.
    C. The Thomas-Gains Community Service award was presented to both my partner and myself.
    D. All of the above sentences are grammatically correct.

25. A. Its about time they implemented that policy.
    B. The suspect was told to lay his gun down on the ground.
    C. Everyone shaked my hand at the conference.
    D. All of the above sentences are grammatically correct.

26. A. Officer Bartelli's response was quick and emphatic.
    B. Steve Jones's nightstick was missing.
    C. In general, it's relatively quiet out there.
    D. All of the above sentences are grammatically correct.

27. A. To Lieutenant James, Patrolman Heath was borderline irresponsible.
    B. Each officer is bringing their own lunch.
    C. In summary: the prosecutor has proven a clear case of negligent homicide.
    D. None of the above sentences are grammatically correct.

28. A. The M.O. is very unique, but I cannot recall whom it is.
    B. This is the portable TV set that was knocked over during the argument.
    C. Detective Connely remarked "that he felt fatigued."
    D. None of the above sentences are grammatically correct.

29. A. Richard and Sue said that their planning on a backpacking trip in October.
    B. "Your checkbook balance is wrong" she said, "add your deposit slips again."
    C. I have a partner who served three consecutive tours in Vietnam.
    D. All of the above sentences are grammatically correct.

30. A. To work effectively, a police officer should keep his firearm cleaned and oiled.
    B. Bill was real livid.
    C. There isn't an unbroken window in the abandoned warehouse.
    D. All of the above sentences are grammatically correct.

31. A. Judith Merriweather chairwoman of Crime Stoppers Blockwatch has announced the merger.
    B. We shall always remember him as a compassionate police officer, said the minister.
    C. Where has John Carrington been at?
    D. None of the above sentences are grammatically correct.

32. A. The nature of police work both gave me excitement and satisfaction.
    B. The patrolman did not say whether he had completed the preliminary assessments.
    C. The applicant has had three years of undergraduate study at ohio state university.
    D. None of the above sentences are grammatically correct.

33. A. Steve and I attended the safety seminar sponsored by Kelso, Inc.
    B. Captain Felder has an leather recliner and an oak file cabinet he would like to sell.
    C. Carroll would like to join us to.
    D. All of the above sentences are grammatically correct.

34. A. The store manager payed little attention to the threat made by the suspect.
    B. How can you expect everyone to do his duty when you place them under intense scrutiny?
    C. Whom did you call?
    D. All of the above sentences are grammatically correct.

35. A. There is not no easy way of solving the problem of teenage drug abuse.
    B. Your official hiring date (once the background check proves satisfactory) will be the first Tuesday of next month.
    C. The new department policy was poorly planned, it lacked both insight and reality.
    D. None of the above sentences are grammatically correct.

36. A. Margarets new car has turned out to be a lemon.
    B. Talking, not arguing, is the best way to handle domestic disputes.
    C. That sort of trite remarks will ruin your career.
    D. All of the above sentences are grammatically correct.

37. A. Frank had a holier than thou attitude after tipping off authorities about an illegal gambling operation.
     B. A good police officer has courage, strength, and is patient.
     C. None of the administrators speaks well of Captain Martin.
     D. None of the above sentences are grammatically correct.

38. A. People seldom attend help sessions nevertheless they are proven to be extremely helpful for most.
     B. It almost seems impossible to meet the deadline established.
     C. Please fill out your job application form carefully, concisely, and truthfully.
     D. None of the above sentences are grammatically correct.

39. A. Before I worked for the department, I had never used a handgun.
     B. Officer Miller crouched besides the victim.
     C. Your going to the demonstration whether you like it or not.
     D. All of the above sentences are grammatically correct.

40. A. The Bill of Rights guarantees individual freedoms.
     B. The reason for Dave's absence was because he felt sick.
     C. Nobody else decisions are more respected than Sergeant Collin's.
     D. All of the above sentences are grammatically correct.

SPELLING

Spelling questions can make up five to ten percent of the police officer exam. Consequently, this area warrants a degree of review even by those who have fairly good spelling skills. A basic list of guidelines that can be of assistance when the proper spelling of a word is in doubt is provided. Pay particular attention to any exceptions pointed out in these guidelines. Test questions often center around such exceptions. As mentioned earlier, a list of words that have been seen on past exams has been compiled for your study. There is a good chance that most of the spelling questions that may be seen on your actual exam will be included in this list.

Once you have studied these spelling rules and the list, move on to the sample spelling test questions that follow. Do not use a dictionary for reference because you will not be allowed to use one during the actual exam. The answers to these sample questions are provided at the back of this chapter.

SPELLING GUIDELINES

1. If you add a suffix that begins with a vowel to a word that ends in the letter *e* (silent), you should drop the final *e*. For instance, the word DINE and the suffix -ING are combined to form the word DINING. Other examples would be COMING, LOVING, CONTINUOUS, DEPLORABLE, etc.

    However, if the word in question ends in soft GE or CE, the letter *e* may be kept before either -ABLE or -OUS. For instance, the word MANAGE plus ABLE is spelled MANAGE-ABLE. Other examples would include TRACEABLE, ENFORCEABLE, ADVANTAGEOUS, COURAGEOUS, etc.

    One other exception is to keep the letter *e* in the present participle of the words SINGLE, DYE, and EYE: SINGEING, DYEING, and EYEING.

2. If you add a suffix that begins with a consonant, (i.e., *-ment, -ly*) the spelling will not normally change. For instance, the words MOVEMENT, LONELY, CARELESSNESS, EXTREMELY, etc. illustrate this rule. Exceptions are JUDGMENT, ARGUMENT, ACKNOWLEDGMENT, and TRULY.

3. If a suffix is added to words that end in *y*, the *y* must be changed to *i* unless the suffix itself begins with *i*. For instance, HAPPY and -NESS are combined to spell HAPPINESS. Other examples include BUSINESS, MERCILESS, and DEFIANT. However, words such as STUDY or CARRY which end in *y* do not change with the addition of a suffix (STUDYING and CARRYING).

4. The use of the suffix -SEDE, -CEDE, or -CEED is quite simple. SUPERSEDE is the only word spelled with -SEDE. SUCCEED, PROCEED, and EXCEED are the only words that incorporate -CEED as a suffix. All other comparable words are spelled with the -CEDE ending: RECEDE, INTERCEDE, PRECEDE, etc.

5. In most cases, prefixes can be added to words without affecting the spelling of the word in question. For example, MIS- added to SPELL produces MISSPELL. Other examples would include MALCONTENT, UNNECESSARY, INACCURATE, and IRREVERENT.

6. Use *i* before *e* except after *c* or when it sounds like the same for letter *a*. For instance, the words BELIEVE, CHIEF, YIELD, GRIEF, etc. demonstrate the proper spellings in the absence of *c*. RECEIVE, PERCEIVE, and DECEIT are a few examples that reverse the order of *i* and *e*. Examples of words in which *ei* sounds like *a* are NEIGHBOR, THEIR, WEIGHT, etc. They follow the same rules of spelling that apply to words having the letters *e* and *i* following *c*. Other words that seem to be an exception to these rules are NEITHER, SEIZE, FORFEIT, EITHER, LEISURE, WEIRD, COUNTERFEIT, and FOREIGN.

7. If you intend to change the form of a single-syllable action word that ends in a consonant preceded by a vowel, you must double the final consonant. For instance, PLAN, SAD, and SIT change to PLANNING, SADDEN, and SITTING.

   The final consonant must be doubled to change the form of a two-syllable word that ends in a consonant preceded by a vowel and which is accented on the second syllable. For instance, the words REFER, REMIT, and OCCUR can have their respective spellings changed to REFERRING, REMITTANCE, and OCCURRING. However, if you are using a two- or three-syllable word and the addition of a suffix results in the change of accent from the final syllable to a preceding one, you should not double the final consonant. For instance, the words TRAVEL, REFER, and CANCEL would be spelled TRAVELING, REFERENCE, and CANCELING according to this rule.

8. Adjectives which end with the letter *l* may be changed to a corresponding adverb by simply adding -*ly* to the word. For instance, LEGAL, ACCIDENTAL, and UNUSUAL may be changed to LEGALLY, ACCIDENTALLY, and UNUSUALLY.

   If you desire to combine suffixes and prefixes that end in -*ll*, usually one -*l* is dropped from the word. For instance, the words ALL-TOGETHER, ALL-READY, and MIND-FULL would appropriately be combined to spell ALTOGETHER, ALREADY, and MINDFUL.

9. If the intent is to change a singular to a plural, this can usually be accomplished by simply adding -*s* to the word: for instance, CHIPS, RULES, TIMES, etc. If the word in question ends in *s* or an *s*-like sound (i.e., *sh*, *ch*, *ss*, *x*, and *z*) then a plural may be formed by adding -*es*: for instance, CRUSHES, ANNEXES, DISHES, etc. Be aware, however, that some words require irregular changes to become plural. For instance, ALUMNUS to ALUMNI, THIEF to THIEVES, WOMAN to WOMEN, and CRISIS to CRISES, just to name a few.

10. If you are unsure of whether a word's ending is properly spelled -ISE or -IZE, you can be relatively assured that the latter choice is correct more often than it is wrong. American usage seems to prefer -IZE in most instances. ADVISE, DESPISE, SURPRISE, and SUPERVISE are just a few of the -ISE exceptions. ORGANIZE, UTILIZE, CENTRALIZE, and AUTHORIZE are typical words that incorporate -IZE.

There are, of course, other, minor rules to spelling that have not been discussed here. However, this list of guidelines encompasses most of what will concern you on the actual exam. Keep this list in mind as you work through the sample questions provided.

SAMPLE QUESTIONS FOR SPELLING

41. Prior to the Miranda case, police officers felt that it was _UNNECESSERY_ to explain to a defendant his or her rights at the time of the arrest. How should the word underlined in this sentence be spelled?
    A. UNECESSARY
    B. UNNECCESSARY
    C. UNNECESSARY
    D. No change is required because the word in question is spelled correctly.

42. Most people probably _EXSEDE_ the speed limit by five to ten miles per hour. How should the word underlined in this sentence be spelled?
    A. EXCEED
    B. EXCEDE
    C. EXSEED
    D. No change is required because the word in question is spelled correctly.

43. Kids learning to drive seem to have difficulty with the aspects of _PARALLEL_ parking. How should the underlined word be spelled?
    A. PARRALEL
    B. PARALELL
    C. PEARALLEL
    D. No change is required because the word in question is spelled correctly.

44. Sex offenders need to be _SUPERVICED_ closely. How should the underlined word be spelled?
    A. SUPERVIZED
    B. SUPERVISED
    C. SUPERVIZZED
    D. No change is required because the word in question is spelled correctly.

45. The witness claims to _RECKINIZE_ two of the three people we have in custody. How should the underlined word be spelled?
    A. RECOGNISE
    B. RECOGNIZE
    C. REKOGNIZE
    D. No change is required because the word in question is spelled correctly.

46. Howard wants the reports on his desk no later than _WENSDAY_. How should the underlined word be spelled?
    A. WENDSDAY
    B. WEDSDAY
    C. WEDNESDAY
    D. No change is required because the word in question is spelled correctly.

47. It was very difficult to tell the difference between the *COUNTERFIET* and the real thing. How should the underlined word in the sentence be spelled?

    A. COUNTORFEIT

    B. COUNTERFIT

    C. COUNTERFEIT

    D. No change is required because the word in question is spelled correctly.

48. The defense attorney hoped that his client would receive a lenient *JUDGEMENT* since it was a first-time offense. How should the underlined word in the sentence be spelled?

    A. JUDGMENT

    B. JUGMENT

    C. JUDGMENTE

    D. No change is required because the word in question is spelled correctly.

49. The whole incident proved to be *EMBARRASSING*. How should the underlined word in the sentence be spelled?

    A. EMBARASSING

    B. EMBARRASING

    C. EMBERRASSING

    D. No change is required because the word in question is spelled correctly.

50. Only recently have repeat offenders *RECEEVED* harsher sentences. How should the underlined word in the sentence be spelled?

    A. RECEIVED

    B. RECIEVED

    C. RECCIVED

    D. No change is required because the word in question is spelled correctly.

51. Considering the circumstances, her actions seemed *JUSTAFIABLE*. How should the underlined word in the sentence be spelled?

    A. JUSTIFYABLE

    B. JUSTEFIABLE

    C. JUSTIFIABLE

    D. No change is required because the word in question is spelled correctly.

52. *OCASIONALLY*, you will be required to put in overtime. How should the underlined word in the sentence be spelled?

    A. OCASSIONALLY

    B. OCCASIONALLY

    C. OCCASIONALY

    D. No change is required because the word in question is spelled correctly.

53. After chasing the suspect for several blocks, Officer Miller had to stop to catch his *BREATHE*. How should the underlined word in the sentence be spelled?

    A. BREATH

    B. BREETH

    C. BRETHE

    D. No change is required because the word in question is spelled correctly.

54. Most defendants in a court of law have the assistance of *COUNSUL*. How should the underlined word in the sentence be spelled?

    A. COUNCIL

    B. COUNSELL

    C. COUNSEL

    D. No change is required because the word in question is spelled correctly.

55. She had a lot of *MISCELLANEOUS* items in her purse. How should the underlined word in the sentence be spelled?

    A. MISSCELLANEOUS

    B. MISCELANEOUS

    C. MISCELLANIOUS

    D. No change is required because the word in question is spelled correctly.

56. Mayor Blackmore has received a lot of *CORRESPONDENCE* on the issue. How should the underlined word in the sentence be spelled?

    A. CORRASPONDENCE

    B. CORRESPONDENTS

    C. CORESPONDANCE

    D. No change is required because the word in question is spelled correctly.

57. Madison is a large *MUNICPALITY*. How should the underlined word in the sentence be spelled?

    A. MUNICSIPALITY

    B. MUNICIPALITY

    C. MUNECAPALITY

    D. No change is required because the word in question is spelled correctly.

58. Her testimony seemed *CONTREDICTORY* to statements she made earlier. How should the underlined word in the sentence be spelled?

    A. CONTRADICTORY

    B. CONTRADICTERY

    C. CONTRADICTARY

    D. No change is required because the word in question is spelled correctly.

59. Officer Blaine *PERSONALY* took responsibility for the incident. How should the underlined word in the sentence be spelled?

    A. PERSONELLY

    B. PERSONOLY

    C. PERSONALLY

    D. No change is required because the word in question is spelled correctly.

60. The severity of the accident made it difficult to determine the *IDENTAFICATION* of the victims involved. How should the underlined word in the sentence be spelled?

    A. IDENTIFICATION

    B. IDENTIFACATION

    C. IDINTIFICATION

    D. No change is required because the word in question is spelled correctly.

ANSWER SHEET FOR SAMPLE REPORT WRITING/INTERPRETATION QUESTIONS

1. Ⓐ Ⓑ Ⓒ Ⓓ
2. Ⓐ Ⓑ Ⓒ Ⓓ
3. Ⓐ Ⓑ Ⓒ Ⓓ
4. Ⓐ Ⓑ Ⓒ Ⓓ
5. Ⓐ Ⓑ Ⓒ Ⓓ
6. Ⓐ Ⓑ Ⓒ Ⓓ
7. Ⓐ Ⓑ Ⓒ Ⓓ

8. Ⓐ Ⓑ Ⓒ Ⓓ
9. Ⓐ Ⓑ Ⓒ Ⓓ
10. Ⓐ Ⓑ Ⓒ Ⓓ
11. Ⓐ Ⓑ Ⓒ Ⓓ
12. Ⓐ Ⓑ Ⓒ Ⓓ
13. Ⓐ Ⓑ Ⓒ Ⓓ
14. Ⓐ Ⓑ Ⓒ Ⓓ

15. Ⓐ Ⓑ Ⓒ Ⓓ
16. Ⓐ Ⓑ Ⓒ Ⓓ
17. Ⓐ Ⓑ Ⓒ Ⓓ
18. Ⓐ Ⓑ Ⓒ Ⓓ
19. Ⓐ Ⓑ Ⓒ Ⓓ
20. Ⓐ Ⓑ Ⓒ Ⓓ

ANSWER SHEET FOR SAMPLE GRAMMAR QUESTIONS

21. Ⓐ Ⓑ Ⓒ Ⓓ
22. Ⓐ Ⓑ Ⓒ Ⓓ
23. Ⓐ Ⓑ Ⓒ Ⓓ
24. Ⓐ Ⓑ Ⓒ Ⓓ
25. Ⓐ Ⓑ Ⓒ Ⓓ
26. Ⓐ Ⓑ Ⓒ Ⓓ
27. Ⓐ Ⓑ Ⓒ Ⓓ

28. Ⓐ Ⓑ Ⓒ Ⓓ
29. Ⓐ Ⓑ Ⓒ Ⓓ
30. Ⓐ Ⓑ Ⓒ Ⓓ
31. Ⓐ Ⓑ Ⓒ Ⓓ
32. Ⓐ Ⓑ Ⓒ Ⓓ
33. Ⓐ Ⓑ Ⓒ Ⓓ
34. Ⓐ Ⓑ Ⓒ Ⓓ

35. Ⓐ Ⓑ Ⓒ Ⓓ
36. Ⓐ Ⓑ Ⓒ Ⓓ
37. Ⓐ Ⓑ Ⓒ Ⓓ
38. Ⓐ Ⓑ Ⓒ Ⓓ
39. Ⓐ Ⓑ Ⓒ Ⓓ
40. Ⓐ Ⓑ Ⓒ Ⓓ

ANSWER SHEET FOR SAMPLE SPELLING QUESTIONS

41. Ⓐ Ⓑ Ⓒ Ⓓ
42. Ⓐ Ⓑ Ⓒ Ⓓ
43. Ⓐ Ⓑ Ⓒ Ⓓ
44. Ⓐ Ⓑ Ⓒ Ⓓ
45. Ⓐ Ⓑ Ⓒ Ⓓ
46. Ⓐ Ⓑ Ⓒ Ⓓ
47. Ⓐ Ⓑ Ⓒ Ⓓ

48. Ⓐ Ⓑ Ⓒ Ⓓ
49. Ⓐ Ⓑ Ⓒ Ⓓ
50. Ⓐ Ⓑ Ⓒ Ⓓ
51. Ⓐ Ⓑ Ⓒ Ⓓ
52. Ⓐ Ⓑ Ⓒ Ⓓ
53. Ⓐ Ⓑ Ⓒ Ⓓ
54. Ⓐ Ⓑ Ⓒ Ⓓ

55. Ⓐ Ⓑ Ⓒ Ⓓ
56. Ⓐ Ⓑ Ⓒ Ⓓ
57. Ⓐ Ⓑ Ⓒ Ⓓ
58. Ⓐ Ⓑ Ⓒ Ⓓ
59. Ⓐ Ⓑ Ⓒ Ⓓ
60. Ⓐ Ⓑ Ⓒ Ⓓ

For your convenience, a reference list of words seen on various police officer exams has been provided below. It should be noted that this list of words does not preclude the possibility of seeing other words or variations of the same word on the actual exam. However, this reference list should account for a majority of spelling questions most likely encountered on the test.

abandoned	assistance	chief	credibility
abduction	assistants	circle	criminal
accelerator	associate	circumstance	criteria
accessories	assortment	citizen	cruising
accident	athletics	coarse	curfew
accomplice	attorney	cocaine	current
accountability	attraction	coerce	custody
acquaintance	attribute	coherent	cylinder
acquitted	authorization	collaborate	damage
across	automatic	collar	deceased
adjacent	available	collision	decent
administrative	backward	colonel	decision
admissible	bail	coming	defendant
admission	bale	commercial	delinquent
admonition	bandage	commission	demeanor
adultery	barricade	committed	depression
affidavit	beginning	communication	descent
affirmation	behavior	community	description
aggravated	beige	complainant	detention
alcohol	believe	comply	diesel
allege	belligerent	concealed	different
always	bicycle	conscience	disappear
ammunition	boulevard	conscious	disappointed
analysis	brake	consent	discipline
anonymous	break	conspiracy	dispatched
answer	breathalyzer	construction	disperse
apparent	bruise	continue	disposition
appeal	building	contraband	disseminate
application	bulletin	conviction	dissent
appraise	bureau	cooperate	district
apprehend	burglary	coroner	disturbance
approximately	business	corporation	duress
argument	cache	corps	during
arraignment	calendar	corpse	eight
arrangement	campaign	correctional	elementary
arrest	captain	corrective	embarrass
arson	carnal	corroborate	embezzlement
arterial	carrying	cough	emergency
artery	cartridge	council	emphasize
article	cashier	counsel	employee
artificial	casualty	counterfeit	enforcement
asked	ceiling	coupon	epileptic
asphyxiated	cemetery	court	equipment
assault	chauffeur	courteous	erratic

evidence	identified	larceny	nervous
examination	illegal	latent	neurotic
exceed	illiterate	legal	niece
except	imitation	leisure	ninety
excite	immediately	length	noisy
exercise	impact	liability	noticeable
exhaust	impaired	liable	notify
experience	implementation	liaison	obligation
explanation	impossible	libel	obnoxious
explosion	impression	liberty	obscene
expression	incest	license	observed
extension	incident	lieutenant	obsolete
extortion	incorrigible	liquor	obstacle
familiar	incriminate	loiter	occasion
felony	indecent	loose	occupant
feminine	indicate	lose	occur
financial	indict	loss	occurred
forcibly	indigent	malicious	odor
foreign	individual	manual	offender
forfeit	informant	marijuana	official
forgery	inherent	marital	operator
fornication	inherit	medal	opinion
forth	initial	medical	opportunity
forty	injured	menace	opposite
fourteen	inquiry	metal	ordinance
fourth	inscribed	metropolitan	oxygen
fracture	instead	microfiche	painful
fraudulent	insufficient	microphone	parallel
frequent	insurance	mileage	parole
friend	intelligent	minor	participate
fugitive	intercourse	minute	passed
furniture	interest	miranda	passenger
gambling	interrogate	miscellaneous	past
garbage	intersection	mischief	patience
gauge	intervention	misdemeanor	patients
genuine	interview	misspelled	peace
government	intimidation	mitigate	pedestrian
grease	intoxicating	molest	penalty
grievance	investigation	motorcycle	perform
guardian	it's	municipal	perjury
handkerchief	its	muscle	permanent
hazard	jealous	mustache	permit
headache	jewelry	naive	persecute
hemorrhage	judgment	narcotics	persistent
heroin	juvenile	nausea	personal
homicide	khaki	necessary	personnel
horizontal	knife	negative	perspiration
hostage	knowledge	neglect	physical
hurrying	label	negotiable	physician
hydrant	laboratory	neighbor	piece

planning	receipt	sieve	telephone
pneumatic	receive	signature	temperature
polygamy	reckless	silhouette	temporary
polygraph	recognize	similar	terrorism
positive	recommendation	simultaneous	testimony
possession	recurrence	sincc	theater
potential	reference	sincerity	their
pregnancy	refuse	siphon	there
prejudice	registration	skeleton	they're
prejudiced	regrettable	skeptical	thieves
preliminary	reimburse	skidded	thorough
premises	relevant	sleight	thought
prescription	religious	slight	threw
preservation	remember	sobriety	throat
previous	renewal	socialize	through
principal	representation	sodomy	tissue
principle	reputation	sophisticated	to
probably	resistance	specimen	together
probationary	respiration	spontaneous	tongue
procedure	responsible	sprain	too
proceeded	restitution	statement	tourniquet
process	revoked	stationary	toxicology
profane	revolver	stationery	traffic
professional	rhythmic	statute	transferred
prohibitive	robbery	sterilize	translucent
promiscuous	routine	stomach	trespassing
proposition	sacrifice	strangulate	truancy
prosecute	sanitary	strictly	Tuesday
prostitution	satisfactory	striped	two
proximity	Saturday	stripped	typewriter
psychology	scene	subject	ultimatum
pulse	schedule	submitting	unconscious
pungent	scheme	subpoena	unnecessary
punitive	secretary	substantiate	urgent
pursuit	seen	subtle	using
putrefy	segregate	succeed	utility
pyrotechnic	seize	successful	vacuum
quality	semiautomatic	suffocate	vagrancy
quantity	sense	suicidal	valuable
questionnaire	sentence	summons	vehicle
quiet	sequester	superintendent	velocity
quite	sergeant	supervisor	verify
racial	serial	surveillance	version
radical	several	susceptible	vertical
raid	severely	suspect	vicinity
rally	sexual	suspicion	vicious
ramification	sheriff	symptom	victim
rationalization	shining	tamper	visible
raucous	shone	tattoo	volume
realize	shown	technician	voluntary

waist	weigh	witness	you're
warehouse	welfare	women	young
warrant	whether	wounded	your
waste	whiskey	wrapper	
weather	whole	wreck	
Wednesday	whore	yield	

ANSWERS TO SAMPLE REPORT WRITING QUESTIONS

1. *C.* 0805 hours. The narrative stated directly that Mr. Saravich had noticed that the garage door had been left open and his neighbor's vehicle was missing at exactly 0805 hours.

2. *D.* 0810 hours. Choice A may seem like the correct answer; however, 0815 is the time Officer Tomkins was dispatched to the Winfield Avenue residence. The narrative goes on to say that CENCOM had received the call from Mr. Saravich five minutes earlier.

3. *B.* 66-54201 is the case number assigned to the report. A file number was not provided.

4. *A.* Subtle changes in street addresses such as "Avenue" instead of "Street" or transposing the numerical portion of an address render an answer incorrect. Selection D is where the victims (in this case, the Turnley family) are currently staying. However, the home address where the actual incident took place is appropriate for Box 29.

5. *C.* Since it was Mr. Saravich who reported the incident to the police, his home phone number would be placed in Box 60. Selection A is Mr. Saravich's business number.

6. *C.* November 7, 1992

7. *D.* Selection B is incorrect because the number 14 in the VIN is transposed to 41.

8. *B.* Officer Tomkins was dispatched to the Turnley residence at exactly 0815 hours. The reading further stated that it took Officer Tomkins approximately five minutes to get there.

9. *D.* 136 is Officer Brad Tomkin's badge number.

10. *C.* Sergeant Hunt.

11. *C.* Traffic infraction.

12. *B.* Colorado (CO).

13. *C.* Brown.

14. *A.* 09-15-92/Thurston County.

15. *A.* Commercial vehicle.

16. *D.* Speeding.

17. *B.* Radar.

18. *D.* 1993. Selection B would have been the correct answer had the question asked when Mr. Hall's driver's license was due to expire.

19. *C.* 06-18-52.

20. *D.* The defendant's home address was listed as 5742 Evergreen Boulevard, Denver, CO 67521.

ANSWERS TO SAMPLE GRAMMAR QUESTIONS

21. *D.* A. Parentheses can be used to enclose explanations within a sentence.

    B. The word *these* is plural and correctly modifies the plural noun, *study guides*.

    C. *Grand jury* is considered a collective noun and therefore requires the singular word *has*.

22. *A.* The sentence correctly uses the present tense to illustrate a point.

    B. The word *at* exemplifies the incorrect use of a preposition. The word *with* would be considered appropriate.

    C. "Only made" exemplifies the incorrect placement of an adverb. It should be turned around to read "made only."

23. *A.* This sentence correctly uses a subordinate clause in stating what had happened.

    B. The word *fleed* does not exist; the appropriate word should be *fled*.

    C. The sentence contains an inappropriate dangling modifier that fails to identify who filled out the accident report. One way to write this sentence better would be this: After he completed the accident report, he found the rest of the day easy.

24. *B.* *Affect* means "influence"; here *effect* ("cause," "bring about") is needed.

    A. The word "lose" is considered a verb that means the opposite of win. The proper adjective to use in this case is "loose," which means unrestrained.

    C. *Myself* is a reflexive pronoun that should not be substituted for *I* or *me*.

25. *B.* *Lay* is the correct transitive verb to be used in this statement.

    A. *Its* is a contraction of "it is." An apostrophe is needed between the letters *t* and *s*. *Its* is a possessive pronoun.

    C. *Shaked* is not recognized as a word. *Shook* is the appropriate word needed in this sentence.

26. *D.* A. The apostrophe is correctly used to indicate possession.

    B. With a singular noun that ends in *s*, in this case *Jones*, it would be correct to indicate possession either by adding an apostrophe after *s* in *Jones* (*Jones'*) or by adding an apostrophe and *s* (*Jones's*). However, it would have been incorrect to write *Joneses*.

    C. The comma is appropriately used to set apart the introductory phrase, and the apostrophe is used correctly to indicate the contraction.

27. *A.* The comma is appropriately used in the sentence after the introductory phrase. Without it, the sentence seems confused and may be misunderstood.

    B. There must be agreement between the pronoun and what it stands for. *His* or *hers* would be considered correct instead of *their*.

    C. The colon is used correctly; however, the first word of a complete statement that follows a colon should be capitalized.

28. *B.* *That* is the appropriate pronoun since it refers to an object, in this case a TV set.

    A. *Who* and *whom* can refer only to people. Since a method of operation instead of people is being described, the word *whose* which is a possessive of *who* would be considered the correct choice, referring to the person with that M.O.

    C. Quotation marks should not be used to set off indirect quotations. The absence of quotation marks would be acceptable.

29. *C.* The adjective clause is appropriately introduced by the pronoun *who*.

    A. *Their* is a possessive of *they*. Instead, the contraction *they're* is needed.

    B. A common splice should not be used in divided quotations. A period after *said* and capitalizing *add* would be one correct revision.

123

30. *C.* The singular verb agrees with the singular noun.
A. This statement sounds ridiculous, not to mention that a modifier must modify something. A more appropriate statement would read, "The police officer should keep his firearm cleaned and oiled to make it work effectively."
B. Adverbs modify adjectives, verbs, and other adverbs. Therefore, it should read, "Bill is very livid."

31. *D.* A. Commas were not used to set off words in parenthetical opposition. Commas should be placed at "Merriweather, chairwoman" and "Blockwatch, has."
B. Quotation marks should always be used to enclose a quotation. They should be placed prior to the word "We" and after the word "officer."
C. "Where has John Carrington been?" This would be a more appropriate way of asking the question. *At* is unnecessary and ungrammatical.

32. *B.* *Whether* is properly used as a conjunction in this statement.
A. A correlative conjunction was not appropriately placed next to the words it connects. A better way to restructure this sentence would be this: The nature of police work gave me both excitement and satisfaction.
C. Ohio State University is considered to be a proper name and should therefore be capitalized.

33. *A.* *I* (instead of *me*) is the correct choice of first-person pronoun as subject of *attended*.
B. *A* instead of *an* should be used before "leather recliner."
C. *To* is a preposition that expresses motion or direction toward something. Instead, the adverb *too* should be used to indicate "in addition."

34. *C.* *Whom* is the proper pronoun to use instead of *who*.
A. *Paid* is the correct substitute.
B. *His* is considered singular, and therefore *them* should be replaced by *him*.

35. *B.* Commas would have worked as well; however, parentheses are suitable to set off parenthetical expressions.
A. *Not* should be left out of the sentence. *Not* and *no* combined in a statement can render an expression ineffective.
C. A colon should be used instead of the comma when there is restatement of the idea.

36. *B.* Commas are effectively used to set off contrasted phrases.
A. There is need for an apostrophe to demonstrate possession (*Margaret's*).
C. Plural adjectives must be used to modify plural nouns. Therefore, *that* should be replaced with *those*.

37. *D.* A. *Holier than thou* is intended to be a single compound unit and therefore requires hyphenation (*holier-than-thou*).
B. Ideas within a sentence must be parallel or presented in the same form. The correct way of expressing the same idea is this: A good police officer has courage, strength, and patience.
C. *Speaks* fails to agree with the plural subject, administrators. *Speak* would be correct.

38. *C.* The descriptive words in the statement are in complete agreement with one another.
A. Any time there are two complete thoughts within a sentence that uses the connecting word *nevertheless*, it should be preceded with a semi-colon and followed by a comma.
B. An adverb should be placed close to the word it modifies. *Seems* and *almost* should be reversed.

39. *A.* Punctuation and tense are correctly used in this statement.
    B. *Besides* is an advert that means "in addition to." On the other hand, *beside* is a preposition that means "by the side of."
    Your is a possessive of *you*. *You're*, which is a contraction of *you are*, is what is needed in this statement.

40. *A.* "Bill of Rights" is appropriately capitalized.
    B. *Because* makes poor use of a conjunction. *That* would be more appropriate.
    C. *Else* must illustrate possession by adding an apostrophe and *s* (*else's*).

ANSWERS TO SAMPLE SPELLING QUESTIONS

41. *C.* UNNECESSARY

42. *A.* EXCEED

43. *D.* PARALLEL

44. *B.* SUPERVISED

45. *B.* RECOGNIZE

46. *C.* WEDNESDAY

47. *C.* COUNTERFEIT

48. *A.* JUDGMENT

49. *D.* EMBARRASSING

50. *A.* RECEIVED
    (*Note:* Sometimes the very word that you are trying to determine the correct spelling for may exist elsewhere in the test. In this case, *received* was used in the previous question. While this may be atypical of the actual exam, be mindful of the fact that this method may serve as a cross-check of your work.)

51. *C.* JUSTIFIABLE

52. *B.* OCCASIONALLY

53. *A.* BREATH is the proper spelling of the noun that refers to respiration. *Breathe* is the proper spelling of the verb that refers to inhaling and exhaling. (*Note:* You may be given spelling questions that may require not only correct spelling but vocabulary discernment as well. This question is a prime example of what could be involved. First, determine which word is applicable to the context of the sentence, and then select the correct spelling.)

54. *C.* COUNSEL
    Selection A is the correct spelling for a conference group or assembly.

55. *D.* MISCELLANEOUS

56. *D.* CORRESPONDENCE
    Selection B is the proper spelling of the noun that refers to writers.

57. *B.* MUNICIPALITY

58. *A.* CONTRADICTORY

59. *C.* PERSONALLY

60. *A.* IDENTIFICATION

Your score for the exercises would rate as follows:

     54–60 correct, EXCELLENT

     47–53 correct, GOOD

     40–46 correct, FAIR

     less than 40 correct, POOR

Mathematics

AS A POLICE OFFICER, you will need to have good mathematical ability to determine everything from property values to blood alcohol levels. Mathematics is important beyond your career, as well. The implications in your personal life can be as far reaching as calculating depreciation values on real estate for tax purposes to simply balancing your checkbook.

Mathematics treats exact relations existing between quantities in such a way that other quantities can be deduced from them. In other words, you may know a basic quantity, but to derive further use from that quantity, it is necessary to apply known relationships (that is, formulas).

For example, let's say you wanted to know how many revolutions a tire would have to make to roll a distance of exactly 20 feet. Outside of physically rolling the tire itself and using a tape measure, it would be impossible to solve such a problem without mathematics. However, by applying math, we can exploit known relationships to derive the answer.

If we know that the diameter of the tire is 40 inches, we can easily determine the tire's perimeter or circumference. In geometric terms, the tire is a circle and the known formula for determining the circumference of a circle is to multiply the diameter by π (which is 3.1416). The symbol π is referred to in mathematics as *pi*. Therefore, our tire's circumference is 40 x 3.1416 = 125.66 inches.

Since we now know that the circumference of the tire is 125.66 inches, we can learn how many revolutions a tire with this circumference would need to go exactly 20 feet. However, we cannot simply divide 125.66 inches into 20 feet because we are dealing with two entirely different units of measure, inches and feet.

Therefore, we need to convert feet into inches. We know that there are 12 inches in one foot, so 20 feet x 12 inches = 240 inches. Now we can divide 125.66 inches into 240 inches to find the answer we need. In this case, the tire would have to make 1.91 revolutions to roll exactly 20 feet. You can see by this example how known relationships can help find an unknown.

This chapter is designed with the purpose of reviewing only those aspects of math that have been predominantly seen on past exams. If you find any areas of weakness after completing the exercises, it would be in your best interest to get additional reference material from your library.

The subjects reviewed in this section include fractions, decimals, ratios, proportions, and geometry. Each of these areas is discussed briefly, and some examples demonstrate its application. At the end of this section, there are practice exercises for you to complete. Answers and explanations are provided separately so you can check your performance.

MATHEMATICAL PRINCIPLES

A. FRACTIONS

Fractions are essentially parts of a whole. If you have $^1/_2$ of something, this means you have 1 of 2 equal parts. If you have $^7/_8$ of something, this means you have 7 of the 8 equal parts available.

The 1 of $^1/_2$ is the *numerator*, which tells the number of parts used. The 2 is the *denominator*, which tells how many parts the whole has been divided into. As a general rule, if the numerator is less than the denominator, the fraction is called *proper*. On the other hand, if the numerator is greater than or equal to the denominator, the fraction is called *improper*. See the examples below:

$^1/_3$ is a proper fraction
$^2/_3$ is a proper fraction
$^3/_3$ is an improper fraction (Note: this fraction has a value of 1).
$^7/_3$ is an improper fraction.

A mixed number is simply a whole number plus a fractional part. For example, $2^1/_3$ is a mixed number. If there is a need to change a mixed number into an improper fraction, simply multiply the whole number by the denominator of the fraction and add the resulting product to the numerator. For example:

$$2^1/_3 = (2 \times 3) + 1 \text{ divided by } 3 = {}^7/_3, \text{ an improper fraction}$$

If it is necessary to change an improper fraction into a mixed number, simply divide the numerator by the denominator. The quotient is the whole number; the remainder is left over the denominator and the remaining fraction reduced to its lowest terms. For example:

$$\frac{15}{10} = 1\frac{5}{10} = 1^1/_2$$

The fraction $^{15}/_{10}$ is improper, and 15 divided by 10 is 1 with 5 left over, so $1^1/_2$ is the resulting mixed number reduced.

When we need to add, subtract, divide, or multiply fractions, certain rules need to be understood and followed. One basic rule is that multiplication or division should be done prior to addition or subtraction.

To start, when you add or subtract fractional numbers, you must always use a common denominator. For example:

$$^1/_4 + {}^2/_4 = {}^3/_4$$
$$^3/_6 - {}^1/_6 = {}^2/_6$$

Notice that the solution's denominator remains the same, while the variable is the numerator (that is, $^1/_4 + {}^2/_4$ does not equal $^3/_8$, nor does $^3/_6 - {}^1/_6 = {}^2/_0$ or 0).

The same thing applies to mixed numbers as well.

$$2^1/_4 + 1^3/_4 = 3^4/_4.$$

$^4/_4$ is an improper fraction that can be reduced to 1. Therefore,

$$2^1/_4 + 1^3/_4 = 4$$

But what happens when you have to add or subtract two fractions that have different denominators? Look at two such examples below:

$$^3/_7 + {}^1/_2 = X$$
$$^5/_8 - {}^1/_3 = X$$

Before anything can be figured out, it is essential that we find the least common denominator (LCD) for each problem. Looking at the former example ($^3/_7 + {}^1/_2 = X$), we need to find the LCD for 7 and 2.

In this case, it happens to be 14 (that is, 7 and 2 each divide evenly into 14, and 14 is the smallest number for which that is true). Now that we are working the problem in units of fourteenths, it is easy to figure the values of the numerators involved. For example:

$$^3/_7 = ^x/_{14}$$

To find X, you need to divide 7 into 14 and multiply the resulting quotient by the numerator:

$$14 \div 7 = 2, \ 2 \ x \ 3 = 6; \text{ therefore, } ^3/_7 = ^6/_{14}$$

Work in a similar manner for all fractions.

$$^1/_2 = ^x/_{14}, \ 14 \div 2 = 7, \ 7 \ x \ 1 = 7, \text{ therefore } ^1/_2 = ^7/_{14}$$

Now that we have a common denominator, we can add or subtract numbers as we please. In this case,

$$^6/_{14} + ^7/_{14} = ^{13}/_{14}$$

This is a proper fraction that cannot be reduced any further.

Try your hand at the second example, $^5/_8 - ^1/_3 = X$. If you followed the format below to arrive at the answer of $^7/_{24}$, you were correct.

$$^5/_8 = ^x/_{24}, \ 24 \div 8 = 3, \ 3 \ x \ 5 = 15; \text{ therefore } ^5/_8 = ^{15}/_{24}$$

$$^1/_3 = ^x/_{24}, \ 24 \div 3 = 8, \ 8 \ x \ 1 = 8, \text{ therefore, } ^1/_3 = ^8/_{24}$$

$$^{15}/_{24} - ^8/_{24} = ^7/_{24}$$

This is a proper fraction that cannot be reduced further.

To add or subtract mixed numbers with different fractions, the same rule applies. The only difference is that whole numbers can be treated as fractions themselves if they need to be borrowed from. For example,

$$5^2/_8 - 3^3/_4 = X$$

First we need to convert the fractions separately. The LCD for both fractions is 8. Therefore, we calculate that $^3/_4 = ^6/_8$.

Since $^2/_8 - ^6/_8$ would leave us with a negative number, we need to borrow from the whole number (that is, 5). Therefore, we can look at $5^2/_8$ as $4^{10}/_8$. Thus, the problem now reads $4^{10}/_8 - 3^6/_8 = X$.

As the problem now reads, we can subtract the whole numbers (4 and 3) separately, thus $4 - 3 = 1$. The fractions $^{10}/_8$ and $^6/_8$ can be subtracted separately as well; thus $^{10}/_8 - ^6/_8 = ^4/_8$ or $^1/_2$.

Now, put the whole number answer and the fractional answer together and we arrive at the total solution, $X = 1^1/_2$.

To multiply fractions or mixed numbers it is not necessary to determine an LCD. Rather, the product of the numerators is divided by the product of the denominators. Several examples are shown below:

$$^6/_7 \ x \ ^5/_8 = \frac{6 \ x \ 5 = 30}{7 \ x \ 8 = 56} = ^{30}/_{56}$$

which is equivalent to (or "reduces to") $^{15}/_{28}$

$$4 \times 7^{1}/_{3} = {}^{4}/_{1} \times {}^{22}/_{3} = \frac{4 \times 22 = 88}{1 \times 3 = 3} = 29^{1}/_{3}$$

When you need to divide fractions or mixed numbers, convert the divisor to its reciprocal (reverse numerator and denominator) and then multiply. For example:

$$^{7}/_{8} \div {}^{1}/_{2} = X$$

$(^{2}/_{1}$ is the reciprocal of $^{1}/_{2})$. Thus,

$$^{7}/_{8} \times {}^{2}/_{1} = {}^{14}/_{8}, \text{ or } 1^{3}/_{4} \text{ reduced.}$$

Another example involving mixed numbers is

$$6^{5}/_{8} \div 3^{1}/_{3} = X$$

This equals $^{53}/_{8} \times {}^{3}/_{10}$ (reciprocal of $3^{1}/_{3}$) $= {}^{159}/_{80}$, or $1^{79}/_{80}$, reduced

B. DECIMALS

Decimals are basically another means to represent fractional numbers. The difference is that in decimals all fractions are expressed in factors of 10. The placement of the decimal point determines if it is a measure concerning tenths, hundredths, thousandths, ten thousandths, etc., and directly influences the size of the whole numbers involved. Look at the illustration below that depicts the same number with different decimal placements and examine the consequent change in value:

- 4,459.1340 = Four thousand, four hundred fifty-nine and one hundred thirty-four thousandths.
- 44,591.340 = Forty-four thousand, five hundred ninety-one and thirty-four hundredths.
- 445,913.40 = Four hundred forty-five thousand, nine hundred thirteen and four tenths.
- 4,459,134.0 = Four million, four hundred fifty-nine thousand, one hundred thirty-four.

When conducting addition or subtraction of decimals, the place values (that is, decimal points) of decimals must be in vertical alignment. Just as mixed numbers require a common denominator so decimals require this alignment. In this respect, the common denominator is that tenths are under tenths, hundredths are under hundredths, etc. Thus, you are adding or subtracting comparable units. For example:

$$\begin{array}{r} 6.5432 \\ +\ 73.43 \\ \hline 79.9732 \end{array} \quad \text{or} \quad \begin{array}{r} 50.432 \\ -\ 12.07 \\ \hline 38.362 \end{array}$$

When multiplying decimals, it is necessary to treat them as whole numbers. Once you have determined the product, the decimal point is moved to the left the same number of places as there are numbers after the decimal point in both the decimals being multiplied. For example:

$$\begin{array}{r} 5.678 \\ \times\ \ .02 \\ \hline 11345 \\ 0000 \\ \hline 0.11356 \end{array}$$

In this case, there are 5 numbers to the right of the decimal (678 and 02); therefore, 11356 should have the decimal placed in front of the first 1. The final number is 0.11356.

Dividing decimals is as simple as multiplication. When utilizing long division, simply move both place values to the right so that the divisor becomes a whole number. The decimal point then needs to be placed in the quotient above the place it has been moved to in the number being divided. At that point, each of the numbers can be treated as whole numbers and ordinary long division can be used. For example:

$$7.62 \div 3.11 = X$$
$$3.11 \overline{)\ 7.62} = X$$

We need to move the decimal point over two places to render the divisor a whole number. Note the placement of the decimal in the quotient.

$$311. \overline{)\ 762.} = X$$

Then,

$$
\begin{array}{r}
2.450 \\
311 \overline{)\ 762.} \\
622 \\
\hline
1400 \\
1244 \\
\hline
1560 \\
1555 \\
\hline
5
\end{array}
$$

and $X = 2.450$

With this rule in mind, it is very easy to convert fractions to decimals. Use the example below, and observe the placement value.

The fraction $^{16}/_{23}$ is proper. But, when using long division to determine a decimal, we would divide 23 into 16.

$$
\begin{array}{r}
.6956 \\
23 \overline{)\ 16.0} \\
138 \\
\hline
220 \\
207 \\
\hline
130 \\
115 \\
\hline
150 \\
138 \\
\hline
12
\end{array}
$$

or 0.696, rounded off.

C. PERCENTAGES

The term percentage by itself means "divided by one hundred." For example, 15% means 15 ÷ 100. A percentage shows what portion of 100 a given number constitutes. For example, if someone had 100 plants and gave away 20 to a friend, that would mean he or she gave away $^{20}/_{100}$ or 0.20 of the stock. To determine the percentage of plants given away, we would simply multiply 0.20 by 100, giving us 20%. Let's look at another problem and determine the percentages involved:

> If a fire truck had 300 feet of $1^1/_2$ inch hose and three firefighters took 100 feet, 75 feet, and 125 feet respectively to attend to a fire, what percentage did each firefighter carry?

> Since we already know the total length of hose involved, it is a simple matter to solve for percentages.

Firefighter A	Firefighter B	Firefighter C
$\dfrac{100 \text{ feet}}{300 \text{ feet}} \times 100$	$\dfrac{75 \text{ feet}}{300 \text{ feet}} \times 100$	$\dfrac{125 \text{ feet}}{300 \text{ feet}} \times 100$
$= 33\%$	$= 25\%$	$= 42\%$

When you add these percentages together, you get 100% of hose used.

D. RATIOS AND PROPORTIONS

A ratio is simply two items compared by division. For instance, it is known that there are 3500 residents for every 1 patrolman in the city of Birmingham. If this were to be properly expressed as a ratio, it would be 3500:1 or 3500/1. As a rule, if a ratio is expressed as a fraction, it should be reduced. One other rule to remember is that a ratio should not be expressed as a mixed number.

A proportion, on the other hand, is an equation that shows that two ratios are equal. One of the more common types of questions seen on past exams concern speed and distance proportions. For example, if a car can travel 5 miles in 6 minutes, how far can it travel in 30 minutes, assuming the same speed is maintained? This kind of problem would first be set up as two separate ratios and then placed in a proportion to determine the unknown.

RATIO 1 $\quad \dfrac{5 \text{ miles}}{6 \text{ minutes}} \quad$ RATIO 2 $\quad \dfrac{X \text{ miles}}{30 \text{ minutes}}$

In proportional form we then have; $\quad \dfrac{5 \text{ miles}}{6 \text{ minutes}} = \dfrac{X \text{ miles}}{30 \text{ minutes}}$

Once the proportion is established, you can cross multiply the proportion figures and obtain this: $6X = 5 \times 30$.

To solve for X, one of two basic algebraic laws needs to be applied. The addition law for equations states that the same value can be added or subtracted from both sides of an equation without altering the solution. The second basic law is the multiplication law for equations. This states that both sides of an equation can be multiplied or divided by the same number without changing the final solution.

These two laws are used to solve equations that have only one variable. In the case of $6X = 5 \times 30$, we will implement the multiplication/division law to determine X. If we divide both sides of the equation by 6, we can then figure how many miles the car would travel in 30 minutes.

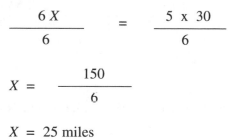

$$\frac{6X}{6} = \frac{5 \times 30}{6}$$

$$X = \frac{150}{6}$$

$$X = 25 \text{ miles}$$

When working with direct proportions like this, you have to be careful not to confuse them with inverse proportions. An example would be two gears with differing numbers of teeth that run at a given number of revolutions per minute (rpm).

Let's say one gear has 30 teeth and runs at 60 rpm, while the other gear has 20 teeth and runs at X rpm. Find X.

We could set it up as a direct proportion:

$$\frac{30 \text{ teeth}}{20 \text{ teeth}} = \frac{60 \text{ rpm}}{X \text{ rpm}}$$

$$\frac{30X}{30} = \frac{60 \times 20}{30}$$

$$X = \frac{1200}{30}$$

$$X = 40 \text{ rpm}$$

Since we recall from mechanical principles that a gear with fewer teeth turns faster than a gear with more teeth, we know that the ratios demonstrated by this proportion are *incorrect*. Rather, it should be inversely proportional. Therefore, it is important when coming across a question of this nature to utilize the reciprocal of one of the ratios in the equation to set up the proportion. For example:

$$\frac{20 \text{ teeth}}{30 \text{ teeth}} = \frac{60 \text{ rpm}}{X \text{ rpm}}$$

or

$$\frac{30 \text{ teeth}}{20 \text{ teeth}} = \frac{X \text{ rpm}}{60 \text{ rpm}}$$

Both of these are correct proportions.

$$\frac{20X}{20} = \frac{30 \times 60}{20}$$

$$X = \frac{1800}{20}$$

$$X = 90 \text{ rpm}$$

$X = 90$ rpm is the correct answer, given the fact this gear has the smaller number of teeth.

E. GEOMETRY

(*Note:* Even though geometric problems are rarely seen on police officer exams, the review of very basic rules is warranted. If, by chance, you run across such questions on your exam, you will then be that much better prepared.)

Any object that requires space has dimensions which can be measured in length, width, and height. If all three of these measurements are used to quantify the size of a given object, it can be said that it is three-dimensional, or solid. If only two measurements, such as length and width, can be determined, it is considered to be two-dimensional, or a plane. A line is essentially a one-dimensional figure because it has no height or width, only length.

Two-dimensional objects frequently seen in geometry are:

1. *Rectangle:* a plane formed from two pairs of parallel lines that are perpendicular to one another. Its area can be determined by multiplying length by width. For example: A rectangle measuring 9 feet by 6 feet has an area of 54 square feet.

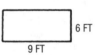

2. *Square:* a rectangle with sides of equal length. The area of a square is found in the same way as for a rectangle.

3. *Triangle:* a closed plane shape that has three sides. Its area can be determined by multiplying $\frac{1}{2}$ times the base times the height. For example: A triangle with a 10-foot base and 5-foot height has an area of 25 square feet ($\frac{1}{2}$ x 10 x 5). (A right triangle has one angle that is 90 degrees; that is, two sides are perpendicular).

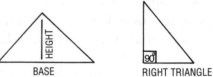

4. *Circle:* a closed plane curve whose circumference is equidistant from the center. A line from the center of the circle to its circumference is a radius. The diameter of a circle is the radius times two. The area of a circle is equal to πR^2 ($\pi = 3.1416$). For example: A circle with a radius of 10 feet has an area of π x $10^2 = 314.16$ square feet. If, on the other hand, we wanted to determine the circumference, we would multiply π by the diameter or $\pi 2R$. In this case, the circumference = 3.1416 x 10 x 2, or 62.83 feet.

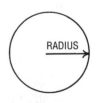

The space occupied by a three-dimensional object is called its *volume.* If we want to know the volume of a rectangular solid, we take the area of a rectangle times its height. For example: This rectangular solid has an area of 50 square feet (that is, 10 feet x 5 feet). When we multiply 50 square feet x 3 feet, we can determine its volume, which in this case is 150 cubic feet.

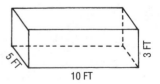

A square solid, is a cube. Since all sides are equal in length, we can simply cube the length (L^3) to determine its volume.

For example, let's say one side measures 2 feet in length. The volume of this cube would equal 2 x 2 x 2, or 8 cubic feet.

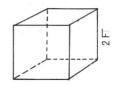

The volume for a sphere is found by using the equation

$$V = \frac{4}{3} \pi R^3.$$

For example, if the radius of a ball is 3 inches, what would its volume be?

$$(\frac{4}{3}) \times (3.1416) \times (3)^3 = \frac{4}{3} \times 3.1416 \times 27 = 113.09 \text{ cubic inches}$$

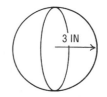

The volume of a cylinder is found by using the equation

$$V = \pi R^2 \text{ (Height)}.$$

For example, if a tin can has a radius of 4 inches and a depth of 8 inches, what is its volume?

$$(3.1416) \times (4)^2 \times (8) = 3.1416 \times 16 \times 8 = 402.12 \text{ cubic inches}$$

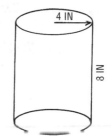

One other aspect of geometry that may be seen on police officer exams concerns right triangles. The Pythagorean theorem states that the square of the side opposite the right angle equals the sum of the squares of the other sides, or $A^2 + B^2 = C^2$. For example,

If side $A = 5$ feet and side $B = 10$ feet.
$5^2 + 10^2 = C^2$
$25 + 100 = C^2$
$125 = C^2$

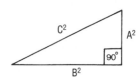

Therefore, C is equal to the square root of 125, or 11.2.

Next you will find some sample questions on mathematical principles so you can test your skills in this area. Solutions to the problems are given at the end of the exercise to verify your work.

SAMPLE QUESTIONS FOR MATHEMATICS

1. $17\frac{3}{4} - 8\frac{1}{4} = X$. Which of the following equals X?
   A. $9\frac{2}{4}$ B. $9\frac{1}{8}$ C. $9\frac{1}{2}$ D. 9

2. $9 - \frac{3}{8} = X$. Which of the following equals X?
   A. $8\frac{3}{8}$ B. $8\frac{5}{8}$ C. 9   D. $7\frac{3}{8}$

3. $9\frac{1}{4} + 18\frac{2}{4} + 20\frac{1}{4} = X$. Which of the following equals X?
   A. $48\frac{1}{4}$ B. $48\frac{1}{2}$ C. $43\frac{1}{4}$ D. 48

4. $6^{1}/_{3} - 4^{5}/_{6} = X$. Which of the following equals X?
   A. $1^{1}/_{4}$ B. $1^{1}/_{2}$ C. $1^{3}/_{4}$ D. $1^{3}/_{6}$

5. $4^{2}/_{3} + 1^{1}/_{6} - 2^{1}/_{8} = X$. Which of the following equals X?
   A. $3^{17}/_{24}$ B. $3^{1}/_{4}$ C. $3^{3}/_{16}$ D. $3^{5}/_{18}$

6. $12^{3}/_{8}$ x $2^{5}/_{7} = X$. Which of the following equals X?
   A. $32^{33}/_{25}$ B. $32^{17}/_{18}$ C. $33^{33}/_{56}$ D. $34^{1}/_{3}$

7. 7 x $^{1}/_{2}$ x $^{3}/_{7} = X$. Which of the following equals X?
   A. $1^{3}/_{7}$ B. $1^{1}/_{4}$ C. $1^{3}/_{4}$ D. $1^{1}/_{2}$

8. $8^{3}/_{4} \div 2^{1}/_{2} = X$. Which of the following equals X?
   A. $1^{7}/_{8}$ B. $3^{1}/_{8}$ C. $3^{1}/_{2}$ D. $4^{1}/_{10}$

9. If the number $5^{2}/_{3}$ were changed from a mixed number to a decimal, which of the following is correct, assuming it is rounded off to hundredths?
   A. 5.67 B. 5.66 C. 5.6 D. 5.7

10. 6.71 x $0.88 = X$. Which of the following equals X?
    A. 5.0948 B. 5.887 C. 5.91 D. 5.9048

11. $132.069 - 130.69 = X$. Which of the following equals X?
    A. 0.379 B. 1.379 C. 1.739 D. 1.793

12. $8.53 + 17.671 = X$. Which of the following equals X?
    A. 16.524 B. 23.102 C. 26.201 D. 25.012

13. $15.75 \div 4.12 = X$. Which of the following equals X?
    A. 3.823 B. 3.283 C. 3.023 D. 3.803

14. $6.75 + 8.372$ x $3.14 = X$. Which of the following equals X?
    A. 47.48 B. 33.04 C. 37.48 D. 34.03

15. 9 x $5.2 \div 18.76 = X$. Which of the following equals X?
    A. 0.40 B. 15.75 C. 28.06 D. 2.49

16. $17 - 14.87 \div 2.5 + 3.61 = X$. Which of the following equals X?
    A. 4.46 B. 0.35 C. 14.66 D. 4.64

17. If 23.6 were changed into a percentage of its relationship to the number 1, which of the following would be correct?
    A. 23.6% B. 0.236% C. 236% D. 2360%

18. The fraction $^{3}/_{7}$ represents what percentage?
    A. 41.85% B. 42.85% C. 48.25% D. 43.35%

19. If someone were to withdraw $237.00 from a savings account that totaled $3,000.00, what percent of the money is left in the account?
    A. 92.1% B. 83.7% C. 94.1% D. 89.7%

20. The number 13 is 75% of what number?
    A. 15.49 B. 16.35 C. 16.99 D. 17.33

21. If a screw has a pitch that requires it to be turned 30 times to advance it two inches, what ratio correctly reflects the relationship?
    A. 2:30 B. 30:2 C. 2:15 D. 15:1

22. According to the directions on a bottle of liquid fertilizer, it is supposed to be mixed in water at the rate of 3 tablespoons per gallon before applying to a garden. How many tablespoons of fertilizer would be required for 20 gallons of water?

  A. 20   B. 40   C. 60   D. 80

23. $$\frac{5}{8} = \frac{X}{32}$$ Which of the following equals X?

  A. 10   B. 20   C. 25   D. 30

24. $$\frac{3/5}{1/2} = \frac{X}{15}$$ Which of the following equals X?

  A. 18   B. 16.5   C. 19.2   D. 16

25. What is the area of a rectangle if it is 6 feet long by 4 feet wide?
  A. 10 square feet
  B. 64 square feet
  C. 24 cubic feet
  D. 24 square feet

26. If a township is a square section of territory and one side is known to be 6 miles in length, how many square miles would the township occupy?
  A. 16 square miles
  B. 18 square miles
  C. 36 square miles
  D. 42 square miles

27. What is the circumference of a gear that has a $5^7/_8$ inch diameter?
  A. 18.05 inches   B. 16.57 inches   C. 19.45 inches   D. 18.46 inches

28. If a triangle had a base of 8 feet and a height of 3.5 feet, what would its area be?
  A. 12 square feet
  B. 14 square feet
  C. 16 square feet
  D. 20 square feet

29. If a rectangular object is 20 feet long by 15 feet wide and has a height of 4 inches, what would be its approximate volume be?
  A. 1200 cubic feet
  B. 1200 square feet
  C. 100 cubic feet
  D. 100 square feet

30. If one side of a cube measures 36 inches, what is its volume?
  A. 46,000 cubic inches
  B. 46,656 square inches
  C. 46,656 cubic yards
  D. 1 cubic yard

31. If a fully inflated basketball has a diameter of 12 inches, how much volume would it occupy?
    A. 904.78 cubic inches
    B. 673.54 cubic inches
    C. 509.78 cubic inches
    D. 475 cubic inches

32. If a can has a height of 16 inches and a volume of 1256.64 cubic inches, what is its diameter?
    A. 10 inches   B. 11 inches   C. 12 inches   D. 12.5 inches

33. The Pythagorean theorem concerns what kind of geometric shape?
    A. Equilateral triangle
    B. Scalene triangle
    C. Right triangle
    D. Acute triangle

34. If the length of side *A* of a right triangle is 8 feet and the length of side *C* (the hypotenuse) is 12.8 feet, what is the length of side *B*?
    A. 8 feet   B. 10 feet
    C. 12 feet   D. 12.3 feet

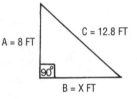

35. What is the area of the figure below?
    A. 44 square centimeters
    B. 46 square centimeters
    C. 48 square centimeters
    D. 50 square centimeters

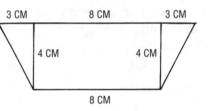

36. If a basement's floorplan has the dimensions shown below, how many square feet would it cover?
    A. 1000
    B. 995
    C. 988
    D. 984

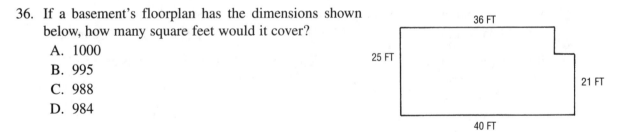

37. What is the length of a diagonal line inside a square that measures 81 square feet?
    A. 9.82 feet   B. 10.38 feet   C. 12.73 feet   D. 14.71 feet

38. If 34 inches represents 34% of the diameter of a particular circle, what is the area of the circle?
    A. 4,891 square inches
    B. 5,432 square inches
    C. 6,971 square inches
    D. 7,854 square inches

39. If you were told that a specific tire could roll 200 yards in 27.28 revolutions, what is the radius of the tire?

    A. 42 inches   B. 84 inches   C. 37.5 inches   D. 75 inches

40. What is the volume of the figure shown below? (Hint: Look at this diagram as half of a cylinder on top of a rectangular solid).

    A. 376.7 cubic centimeters

    B. 348.2 cubic centimeters

    C. 336.7 cubic centimeters

    D. 329.8 cubic centimeters

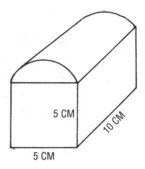

5 CM   10 CM   5 CM

ANSWER SHEET FOR SAMPLE MATHEMATICS

1. Ⓐ Ⓑ Ⓒ Ⓓ	15. Ⓐ Ⓑ Ⓒ Ⓓ	29. Ⓐ Ⓑ Ⓒ Ⓓ	
2. Ⓐ Ⓑ Ⓒ Ⓓ	16. Ⓐ Ⓑ Ⓒ Ⓓ	30. Ⓐ Ⓑ Ⓒ Ⓓ	
3. Ⓐ Ⓑ Ⓒ Ⓓ	17. Ⓐ Ⓑ Ⓒ Ⓓ	31. Ⓐ Ⓑ Ⓒ Ⓓ	
4. Ⓐ Ⓑ Ⓒ Ⓓ	18. Ⓐ Ⓑ Ⓒ Ⓓ	32. Ⓐ Ⓑ Ⓒ Ⓓ	
5. Ⓐ Ⓑ Ⓒ Ⓓ	19. Ⓐ Ⓑ Ⓒ Ⓓ	33. Ⓐ Ⓑ Ⓒ Ⓓ	
6. Ⓐ Ⓑ Ⓒ Ⓓ	20. Ⓐ Ⓑ Ⓒ Ⓓ	34. Ⓐ Ⓑ Ⓒ Ⓓ	
7. Ⓐ Ⓑ Ⓒ Ⓓ	21. Ⓐ Ⓑ Ⓒ Ⓓ	35. Ⓐ Ⓑ Ⓒ Ⓓ	
8. Ⓐ Ⓑ Ⓒ Ⓓ	22. Ⓐ Ⓑ Ⓒ Ⓓ	36. Ⓐ Ⓑ Ⓒ Ⓓ	
9. Ⓐ Ⓑ Ⓒ Ⓓ	23. Ⓐ Ⓑ Ⓒ Ⓓ	37. Ⓐ Ⓑ Ⓒ Ⓓ	
10. Ⓐ Ⓑ Ⓒ Ⓓ	24. Ⓐ Ⓑ Ⓒ Ⓓ	38. Ⓐ Ⓑ Ⓒ Ⓓ	
11. Ⓐ Ⓑ Ⓒ Ⓓ	25. Ⓐ Ⓑ Ⓒ Ⓓ	39. Ⓐ Ⓑ Ⓒ Ⓓ	
12. Ⓐ Ⓑ Ⓒ Ⓓ	26. Ⓐ Ⓑ Ⓒ Ⓓ	40. Ⓐ Ⓑ Ⓒ Ⓓ	
13. Ⓐ Ⓑ Ⓒ Ⓓ	27. Ⓐ Ⓑ Ⓒ Ⓓ		
14. Ⓐ Ⓑ Ⓒ Ⓓ	28. Ⓐ Ⓑ Ⓒ Ⓓ		

ANSWERS TO MATHEMATICS SAMPLE QUESTIONS

1. *C.* $3/4 - 1/4 = 2/4$ and should be reduced to $1/2$.
$17 - 8 = 9$; therefore, $X = 9^{1}/_{2}$

2. *B.* $9 - 3/8 = X$; $9 = 8^{8}/_{8}$; then, $8/8 - 3/8 = 5/8$;
therefore, $X = 8^{5}/_{8}$

3. *D.* $9^{1}/_{4} + 18^{2}/_{4} + 20^{1}/_{4} = X$;
$1/4 + 2/4 + 1/4 = 1$; $9 + 18 + 20 = 47$; therefore,
$X = 47 + 1 = 48$

4. *B.* $6^{1}/_{3} - 4^{5}/_{6} = X$; $1/3 = 2/6$, therefore,
$5^{8}/_{6} - 4^{5}/_{6} = X$; $5 - 4 = 1$ and $8/6 - 5/6 = 3/6$
$3/6$ is reduced to $1/2$; therefore, $X = 1^{1}/_{2}$. Choice D is the correct answer also, but it is not in reduced form.

5. *A.* $2/3$, $1/6$, $1/8$ have the LCD of 24; therefore,
$2/3 = 16/24$, $1/6 = 4/24$, $1/8 - 3/24$

$$\frac{16}{24} + \frac{4}{24} = \frac{20}{24} \qquad \frac{20}{24} - \frac{3}{24} = \frac{17}{24}$$

$(4 + 1) = 5$; $(5 - 2) = 3$; therefore $X = 3^{17}/_{24}$.

6. *C.* $12^{3}/_{8} = 99/8$; $2^{5}/_{7} = 19/7$
$99/8 \times 19/7 = 1881/56 = 33^{33}/_{56}$

7. *D.*

$$\frac{7}{1} \times \frac{1}{2} = \frac{7}{2} \qquad \frac{7}{2} \times \frac{3}{7} = \frac{21}{14}$$

$21/14 = 1^{7}/_{14}$; when this is reduced, $X = 1^{1}/_{2}$

8. *C.* $8^{3}/_{4} = 35/4$, $2^{1}/_{2} = 5/2$
$35/4 \div 5/2 = 35/4 \times 2/5 = 70/20$
$70/20 = 3^{10}/_{20}$, or $3^{1}/_{2}$ when reduced; $X = 3^{1}/_{2}$

9. *A.*   The whole number 5 remains unchanged; however, $2/3$ is the same as saying 2 divided by 3. Therefore, when rounded off to hundredths, the fraction is 0.67. Thus, the decimal should be 5.67. Choice B is correct, except that it has not been rounded off as requested. Choices C and D are not correct because both are rounded off to tenths, not hundredths.

10. *D.* $6.71 \times .88 = X$. $X = 5.9048$

11. *B.*
$$\begin{array}{r} 132.069 \\ -\ 130.690 \\ \hline 1.379 \end{array}$$

therefore, $X = 1.379$

12. *C.*
$$\begin{array}{r} 17.671 \\ +\ 8.53 \\ \hline 26.201 \end{array}$$

therefore, $X = 26.201$

13. *A.* 15.75 divided by 4.12 should be looked at as 1575 divided by 412; then the decimals are reinserted. The answer is 3.8223, or 3.823 rounded off to thousandths.

14. *B.* You should remember that multiplications and divisions are always carried out before additions or subtractions. Another similar rule states that when several multiplications and divisions occur together, you should do them in the order they are given. In this case, we first multiply 8.372 by 3.14, giving us 26.29. Now, add 26.29 to 6.75. Therefore, $X = 33.04$.

15. *D.* Multiply 9 x 5.2, then divide the result by 18.76.

16. *C.* Remembering the rules discussed in answer 14, division must be done first; 14.87 divided by 2.5 should be looked at as 148.7 divided by 25, or 5.95. Thus,

$$17 - 5.95 + 3.61 = X$$

$$\begin{array}{r} 17.00 \\ -\ 5.95 \\ \hline 11.05 \end{array} \qquad \begin{array}{r} 11.05 \\ +\ 3.61 \\ \hline 14.66 \end{array}$$

$$X = 14.66$$

17. *D.* 23.6 multiplied by 100 = 2360%.

18. *B.* 3.0 divided by 7 = 0.4285; then 0.4285 x 100 = 42.85%.

19. *A.*
$$\begin{array}{r} 3000.00 \\ -\ 237.00 \\ \hline 2763.00 \end{array}$$

then, 2763.0 divided by 3000 = 0.921. Finally, 0.921 x 100 = 92.1%.

20. *D.* This kind of percentage problem needs to be worked as a proportion. We would get the following:

$$\frac{75}{100} = \frac{13}{X} \; ; 75X = 1300$$

$$X = \frac{1300}{75} = 17.33$$

21. *D.* Since the ratio is $^{30}/_2$, as with fractions, it should be reduced as low as possible, preferably to 1. In this case, 30:2 can be reduced to 15:1.

22. *C.* The ratio is 3:1 in this problem. Therefore,

$$\frac{3 \text{ Tbsp}}{1 \text{ gal}} = \frac{X \text{ Tbsp}}{20 \text{ gal}}$$

$X = 3 \text{ x } 20$, which is 60.

23. *B.*

$$\frac{5}{8} = \frac{X}{32}$$

$$8X = 160,$$

$$X = \frac{160}{8} = 20.$$

24. *A.*

$$\frac{^3/_5}{^1/_2} = \frac{X}{15} \; ; \; ^1/_2 X = 9; \text{ thus } ^1/_2 X \text{ x } 2 = 9 \text{ x } 2$$

Therefore, $X = 18$

25. *D.* A rectangular area as determined by the following equation

$A = \text{length x width.}$
Therefore, 6 feet x 4 feet = 24 sq feet.

26. *C.* Since the area of a square is equal to the length of one side squared, we simply square 6 miles (that is, 6^2) giving us 36. Therefore, a township occupies 36 square miles.

27. *D.* The first step in this problem is to change the fraction $^7/_8$ into a decimal since π is in decimal form. Thus, we divide 7 by 8 giving us .875. The gear's diameter is 5.875 in decimal form. The equation, Circumference = Diameter x π (3.1416). Therefore,

5.875 diameter x 3.1416 = 18.4569 inches or 18.46 inches rounded to hundredths.

28. *B.* Since the area of a triangle is equal to $^1/_2$ x base x height, we can plug in the numbers accordingly, giving us the following:

$$(^1/_2)(8)(3.5) = 14 \text{ square feet}$$
The area is 14 square feet.

29. *C.* The volume of a rectangle is found by using the formula A = Length x Width x Height. Before we use this equation, all units must be the same (that is, inches or feet). In this case, it is easier to convert the height to feet.

$$\frac{4 \text{ inches}}{12 \text{ inches/feet}} = .3333 \text{ feet}$$

Area = 20 feet x 15 feet x .33 feet
Area = 99.90 cubic feet, or approximately 100 cubic feet.

30. *D.* The easiest way to solve this problem is to recognize that 36 inches = 1 yard. Since 36^3 is a sizable number to to multiply, we will use the simpler alternative of 1^3. Therefore, $1^3 = 1$ cubic yard. This is a common unit of measure in the construction field when ordering specific volumes of dirt, rock, concrete, etc. Choice B would be correct if the number were in cubic inches. Square inches determine only the area of a two-dimensional shape.

31. *A.* A basketball fully inflated can be thought of as a sphere. To determine its volume, we need to use the equation

$^4/_3$ x π (3.1416) x R^3
The diameter is given as being 12 inches, therefore its radius is equal to $^1/_2$ the diameter (that is, 6 inches).

$$\frac{4}{3} \quad \text{x} \quad \frac{3.1416}{1} = \frac{12.5664}{3} = 4.1888$$

$6^3 = 6$ x 6 x 6 = 216 cubic inches
4.1888 x 216 = 904.78 cubic inches, rounded to hundredths

32. *A.* Since the geometric shape in the question is a cylinder, we need to examine the equation Volume = $\pi R^2 H$. If we plug our known values into this equation, it would read

$$1256.64 = \pi (3.1416)(X)^2 (16 \text{ inches}).$$

$$\frac{1256.642}{3.1416 \text{ x } 16} = X^2$$

$$25 = X^2; \text{ therefore, } X = 5$$

Remember, 5 inches represents only the radius; the diameter would equal 5 x 2 = 10 inches.

33. *C.* Right triangle.

34. *B.* Implementing the Pythagorean theorem, $A^2 + B^2 = C^2$, we can determine X with simple algebra to solve for one variable.

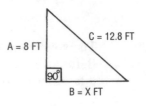

$A^2 = 8^2 = 64$
$C^2 = 12.8^2 = 163.84$
$64 + X^2 = 163.84$
$X^2 = 163.84 - 64$
$X = \sqrt{99.84}$
Therefore, $X = 10$ feet.

35. *A.* In geometric terms this is considered to be a trapezoid, which is a quadrilateral with two sides parallel and the other two sides not parallel. To figure the area, we can see it as one rectangle (*A*) and two triangles (*B*) and (*C*).

The rectangular area is equal to Length x Width, therefore,

8 x 4 = 32 square centimeters (cm)

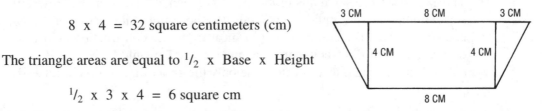

The triangle areas are equal to $\frac{1}{2}$ x Base x Height

$\frac{1}{2}$ x 3 x 4 = 6 square cm

Since triangles *B* and *C* have the same dimension, we just multiply 6 x 2 = 12 to determine their total area combined. Therefore, *A* + *B* + *C* = total area of trapezoid.

32 square cm + 12 square cm = 44 square cm

36. *D.* With the dimensions given, we can assume it has a rectangular shape. The easiest way to approach this question is to figure the total area of the basement as a rectangle and subtract the area missing in the corner.

40 feet x 25 feet = 1,000 square feet;
Side *A* = 25 feet – 21 feet or 4 feet
Side *B* = 40 feet – 36 feet or 4 feet

The area of the missing corner is 4 feet x 4 feet or 16 square feet. Therefore, this basement's total area is

1000 square feet – 16 square feet = 984 square feet.

37. C. The area of a square is the length of one side squared. If the square given is 81 square feet in area, then the square root of 81 will give us the length of the square's side which, in this case, is equal to 9. Since we are dealing with right angles in the square, we can apply the Pythagorean theorem to determine the length of the diagonal. Therefore,

$$9^2 + 9^2 = X^2$$

$$81 + 81 = X^2$$

$$162 = X^2; \quad X = 12.73 \text{ feet}$$

38. D. First, we need to figure the diameter. If we know that 34 inches is 34% that is, .34, of the diameter, we can set up a proportion to solve it. Our proportion would be:

$$\frac{34 \text{ inches}}{.34} = \frac{X}{1.00}$$

$$\frac{.34X}{.34} = \frac{34}{.34}$$

therefore, $X = 3,400$ divided by 34.

Since the diameter is 100 inches, the following formula can be applied to determine the area of the circle in question.

$A = \pi R^2$. The radius is equal to $\frac{1}{2}$ the diameter or in this case, $100 \times .50 = 50$ inches.

Therefore,

$$A = 3.1416 \times 50^2 \text{ inches}$$
$$A = 3.1416 \times 2,500 \text{ square inches}$$
$$A = 7,854 \text{ square inches}$$

39. A. First, if we divide 27.28 revolutions into 200 yards, we can determine how many yards (or inches) this tire could travel after one revolution. We arrive at 7.33 yards. Then, since the diameter of this tire is referred to in inches, not yards, we simply multiply 7.33 yards x 36 inches/yard to give us 263.88 inches. In other words, for every 1 revolution this tire makes it can travel 263.88 inches. This number is the tire's circumference. If we know the tire's circumference, using the equation

Diameter x 3.1416 = Circumference

we can easily figure the tire's diameter.

$$X \text{ x } 3.1416 = 263.88 \text{ inches}$$

$$\frac{X \text{ x } 3.1416}{3.1416} = \frac{263.88 \text{ inches}}{3.1416}$$

$$X = 83.99 \text{ or } 84 \text{ inches in diameter.}$$

Since the question wanted the radius of the tire, we can simply divide the diameter by 2, giving us an answer of 42 inches.

40. *B.* The volume of the rectangular solid is equal to its Length x Width x Height.

10 cm x 5 cm x 5 cm = 250 cubic centimeters.

The volume of a cylinder is equal to π x radius squared x height. Since the width of the rectangular solid can be considered the diameter of the cylinder, the radius is $^1/_2$ the diameter or in this case, 5 cm divided by 2 equals the radius of 2.5 cm. The length of the rectangular solid can be considered the height of the cylinder. Therefore,

3.1416 x 2.5^2 cm x 10 cm = volume of cylinder
3.1416 x 6.25 cm x 10 cm = 196.35 cubic cm.

However, there is only half of a cylinder on top of the rectangular solid, so the cylinder represents only 98.2 cubic cm volume in the illustration shown. Now, add both volumes you have determined to give the total volume of this geometric shape.

250 cubic cm + 98.2 cubic cm = 348.2 cubic cm.

Practice Examination I

THE TIME ALLOWED for the entire examination is $2^1/_2$ hours. Directions: Each question has four answers, lettered A, B, C, and D. Choose the best answer and then, on the answer sheet provided on page 185 (which you can remove from the book), find the corresponding question number and darken the circle corresponding to the answer you have selected.

Questions 1–20 are based on four sketches and associated personal data below. Study the material for 12 minutes. Do not exceed the time allowed; if you do, you will forfeit the true sense of how an exam is actually conducted. When your time is up, turn to the questions provided without making further reference to the composites just studied.

SUSPECT 1

NAME: Evan Scott Ballantine

ALIAS: Chester Scott, Hank Ballestros

DOB: July 23, 1954

HEIGHT: 6'3"

WEIGHT: 225 pounds

HAIR: Blond

EYES: Brown

RACE: White

SEX: Male

SCARS OR
MARKS: Quarter-size birthmark on left forearm

SOCIAL
SECURITY
NUMBER: 720-22-5941 and 312-52-7751
Wanted for second degree murder and first degree sexual assault

CRIMINAL
RECORD: Second degree assault and battery. Consider armed and dangerous.

CASE
NUMBER: 55-1101

SUSPECT 2

NAME: Roger Thorsen

ALIAS: None

DOB: October 13, 1975

HEIGHT: 5'11"

WEIGHT: 177 pounds

HAIR: Black

EYES: Hazel

RACE: Black

SEX: Male

SCARS OR
MARKS: None known

SOCIAL
SECURITY
NUMBER: 872-00-5593

Wanted for first degree arson and grand theft

CRIMINAL
RECORD: Second degree manslaughter

AWWS (Automated Want and Warrant System) number: 512-05

SUSPECT 3

NAME:	Jane Robinson
ALIAS:	None
DOB:	November 17, 1963
HEIGHT:	5'7"
WEIGHT:	135 pounds
HAIR:	Black (greying)
EYES:	Green
RACE:	White
SEX:	Female
SCARS OR MARKS:	Several pronounced pockmarks on the forehead (presumed to be smallpox-related)
SOCIAL SECURITY NUMBER:	750-32-4711
	Wanted for first degree extortion and bribery
CRIMINAL RECORD:	No priors
NCIC FILE NUMBER:	40-751

SUSPECT 4

NAME: Kathy Fitz

ALIAS: Elaine Roberts

DOB: February 13, 1969

HEIGHT: 5'10"

WEIGHT: 140 pounds

HAIR: Red

EYES: Blue

RACE: White

SEX: Female

SCARS OR
MARKS: Two-inch-long scar on left side of neck directly beneath the ear

SOCIAL
SECURITY
NUMBER: 205-11-7350

Wanted for first degree kidnapping and second degree assault

CRIMINAL
RECORD: Second degree malicious mischief

CLETS FILE
NUMBER: 51-59

Answer Questions 1 through 20 on the basis of the composites just studied. *DO NOT REFER TO THE COMPOSITES.*

1. What was Roger Thorsen specifically wanted for?
    A. First degree extortion and grand theft
    B. Grand theft and first degree arson
    C. First degree kidnapping and first degree assault
    D. First degree murder and second degree sexual assault

2. Which of the four suspects utilizes multiple aliases?
    A. Roger Thorsen
    B. Kathy Fitz
    C. Jane Robinson
    D. Evan Ballantine

3. In trying to further elude the authorities, which of the four suspects given utilizes multiple Social Security numbers?
    A. Suspect 1   B. Suspect 2   C. Suspect 3   D. Suspect 4

4. What was on Kathy Fitz's record for prior convictions?
    A. First degree extortion
    B. First degree assault and battery
    C. Second degree malicious mischief
    D. Second degree manslaughter

5. Which of the four suspect files was assigned an AWWS case number?
    A. Elaine Robinson
    B. Roger Thorsen
    C. Jane Robinson
    D. Kathy Fitz

6. All of the suspects were Caucasian with the exception of
    A. Suspect 1
    B. Suspect 2
    C. Suspect 3
    D. All suspects were Caucasian, according to the files provided

7. What did Jane Robinson's file indicate that her height and weight were, respectively?
    A. 5'10" and 135 pounds
    B. 5'11" and 140 pounds
    C. 5'7" and 135 pounds
    D. 5'10" and 140 pounds

8. Which suspect was described as having smallpox scars on the forehead?
    A. Suspect 1   B. Suspect 2   C. Suspect 3   D. Suspect 4

9. Which of the dates given below represent Elaine Roberts' date of birth?
    A. 2-13-69
    B. 7-13-75
    C. 11-17-63
    D. 10-23-54

10. Which of the four suspects did not utilize an alias in the commission of his or her crimes?
    A. Suspect 1
    B. Suspect 2
    C. Suspects 2 and 4
    D. Suspects 2 and 3

11. Whose Social Security number is 872-55-0093?
    A. Elaine Roberts
    B. Roger Thorsen
    C. Jane Robinson
    D. None of the above

12. Which of the suspects has blond hair and brown eyes?
    A. Roger Thorsen
    B. Evan Ballantine
    C. Kathy Fitz
    D. None of the above

13. The picture to the right is a composite sketch of whom?
    A. Hank Ballestros
    B. Evan Ballentine
    C. Chester Scott
    D. Roger Thorsen

14. According to the criminal files provided, which suspect was considered to be armed and dangerous?
    A. Suspect 1
    B. Suspect 2
    C. Suspect 3
    D. Suspect 4

15. According to CLETS file number 51-59, which of the following Social Security Numbers applies to the suspect in question?
    A. 211-05-7305
    B. 205-11-7350
    C. 251-05-7305
    D. 205-73-0511

16. According to NCIC file number 40-751, what crime or crimes was the suspect in question wanted for?
    A. Grand theft and first degree arson
    B. First degree assault
    C. Bribery and first degree extortion
    D. Second degree sexual assault and first degree murder

17. Which suspect was described as having a birthmark the size of a quarter on the right forearm?
    A. Suspect 1
    B. Suspect 3
    C. Suspect 4
    D. None of the above

18. Which choice below inaccurately describes Suspect 1?

    A. Sex: Male

    B. Eyes: Hazel

    C. DOB: 7-23-54

    D. Weight: 225 pounds

19. Which of the numbers provided below correctly identifies the case number of Suspect 1?

    A. 512-05

    B. 11-5501

    C. 55-1101

    D. 59-51

20. All of the following Social Security numbers are identified as belonging to one of the four suspects described with the exception of

    A. 800-72-5953

    B. 750-32-4711

    C. 720-22-5941

    D. 312-52-7751

21. Police personnel in most jurisdictions are percieved by the general public as being spread to thin to fulfill all the responsibilities that come with serving the community.

    The above statement, in terms of English usage,

    A. Is structurally incorrect

    B. Contains one or more misspellings

    C. Lacks necessary punctuation and/or capitalization

    D. Is correct in all aspects

22. One of the areas that has been affected by budgetary constraint is job training.

    The above statement, in terms of English usage,

    A. Is structurally incorrect

    B. Contains one or more misspellings

    C. Lacks necessary punctuation and or capitalization

    D. Is correct in all aspects

23. Drug Awareness and Resistance Education programs are designed for juveniles contemplating the use of drugs and their parents.

    The above statement, in terms of English usage,

    A. Is structurally incorrect

    B. Contains one or more misspelling

    C. Lack necessary punctuation and/or capitalization

    D. Is correct in all aspects

24. Undercover investigators must exercise a great deal of caution in planning and affecting communication with supervisory personnel.

    The above statement, in terms of English usage,

    A. Is structurally incorrect

    B. Contains one or more misspellings

    C. Lacks necessary punctuation and/or capitalization

    D. Is correct in all aspects

25. It is recommended that, when at all possible, apparent suicides should be handled with the same degree of attention given a homicide.

    The above statement, in terms of English usage,

    A. Is structurally incorrect

    B. Contains one or more misspellings

    C. Lacks necessary punctuation and/or capitalization

    D. Is correct in all aspects

26. Police Officer Harris eluded to the hazards of joining a gang when he referred to a list of juveniles who have been killed in gang-related incidents.

    The above statement, in terms of English usage,

    A. Is structurally correct

    B. Contains one or more misspellings

    C. Lacks necessary punctuation and/or capitalization

    D. Is correct in all aspects

27. Involuntary commitment is possible through a mental health professional when the suspect refuses appropriate treatment, is a danger to him- or herself or others and can be detained for 14 to 60 days.

    The above statement, in terms of English usage,

    A. Is structurally incorrect

    B. Contains one or more misspellings

    C. Lacks necessary punctuation and/or capitalization

    D. Is correct in all aspects

28. The evidentiary value of labratory tests on fibers varies greatly depending on the quantity of fibers collected and the uniqueness of the characteristics found during the examination.

    The above statement, in terms of English usage,

    A. Is structurally incorrect

    B. Contains one or more misspellings

    C. Lacks necessary punctuation and/or capitalization

    D. Is correct in all aspects

29. It is not uncommon in many jurisdictions for felony cases to be referred by the district attorneys office to a city attorneys office for the purpose of reducing the charges to a misdemeanor.

    The above statement, in terms of English usage,

    A. Is structurally incorrect

    B. Contains one or more misspellings

    C. Lacks necessary punctuation and/or capitalization

    D. Is correct in all aspects

30. Larceny is defined as the felonious taking and carrying away of someone else's personal property, without they're consent, with the intention of permanently depriving that person of its use or possession.

    The above statement, in terms of English usage,

    A. Is structurally incorrect

    B. Contains one or more misspellings

    C. Lacks necessary punctuation and/or capitalization

    D. Is correct in all aspects

31. Many states explicitly prohibit the placement of some or all types of juveniles in adult institutions.
    The above statement, in terms of English usage,
    A. Is structurally incorrect
    B. Contains one or more misspellings
    C. Lacks necessary punctuation and/or capitalization
    D. Is correct in all aspects

32. A legal obligation against the state is an obligation that would form the basis of a judgement against the state in a court of competant jurisdiction should the legislature permit the state to be sued.
    The above statement, in terms of English usage,
    A. Is structurally incorrect
    B. Contains one or more misspellings
    C. Lacks necessary punctuation and/or capitalization
    D. Is correct in all aspects

Answer Questions 33 through 35 on the basis of the reading provided below:

Black's Law Dictionary defines assault as "any willful attempt or threat to inflict injury upon the person of another, when coupled with an apparent present ability to do so, and any intentional display of force such as would give the victim reason to fear or expect immediate bodily harm." According to one state's criminal statutes, the crime of assault is further subclassified depending on the severity of the offense committed. First degree assault involves the use of a firearm or deadly weapon or any other means which is likely to result in the victim being severely harmed or killed. This form of assault is considered a Class A felony.

Second degree assault involves intentional assault that consequently inflicts substantial bodily harm to the victim or assault of another for reason of committing a felony or with the intent to cause bodily harm, inadvertently passes a pathogen on to the victim. This form of assault is considered a Class B felony.

Third degree assault involves the assault of any law enforcement officer or public employee while performing their assigned duties, or any criminal negligence that results in bodily harm to the victim, or the willful intent to assault another to avoid lawful apprehension or detention. This form of assault is considered a Class C felony.

Fourth degree assault involves any kind of assault except for those already described. This form of assault is simply considered a gross misdemeanor.

It should be noted that if there are multiple assaults of varying degrees committed, the defendant shall be charged with the most severe offense.

33. Paul goes to his estranged wife's apartment knowing that her boyfriend, John, is visiting. When John opens the front door to let Paul in, Paul immediately starts a physical altercation that results in a small facial laceration and two broken ribs to John. Accordingly, if John has intentions to prosecute, Paul may be charged with which of the following:
    A. Class A felony
    B. Class B felony
    C. Class C felony
    D. Gross misdemeanor

34. As Officer Beaumont was attempting to place Margaret Williams into the back of his patrol car for transport and subsequent booking into the county jail for suspected prostitution, Ms. Williams stomped on his right foot with her high-heeled shoe. Officer Beaumont sustained injuries to his right toe resulting in light duty assignment for three weeks. Ms. Williams should be charged with which of the following crimes, according to the reading:
    A. First degree assault
    B. Second degree assault
    C. Third degree assault
    D. No crime, because she was already being charged with prostitution

35. Tom Briggs, a reputed cocaine addict, was confronted by Bill Evans, a store manager, and accused of shoplifting two cameras. Mr. Briggs, feeling cornered, produced a syringe that he claimed was contaminated with the AIDS virus. He indicated he would without reservation stick Mr. Evans with it if Mr. Evans failed to get out of the way. The police, who had been summoned earlier, arrived and quickly subdued the suspect. Toxicology reports later confirmed that the syringe was, in fact, clean. Outside of shoplifting, Mr. Briggs should be additionally charged with which crime according to the reading? (*Note:* Disregard aspect of robbery).
    A. First degree assault
    B. Second degree assault
    C. Third degree assault
    D. Mr. Briggs can't be charged with anything besides shoplifting, because lab results on the syringe turned out to be negative for the AIDS virus.

Answer Questions 36 through 38 on the basis of the reading provided below:

> Homicide is defined in *Black's Law Dictionary* as "the act of a human being taking the life of another human being either through felonious, excusable, or justifiable means."
>
> First degree murder involves causing the death of another; with premeditated intent or, through indifference to life, causing circumstances which create a grave risk and actually result in the death of another; or causing the death of another, whether the victim or a third party, in the commission or attempt to commit rape, robbery, arson, burglary, or kidnapping, or in flight therefrom. First degree murder is considered a Class A felony.
>
> Second degree murder involves intentionally causing the death of another without premeditation, or during the commission or attempt to commit offenses not specifically mentioned under first degree murder or flight therefrom. Second degree murder is considered a Class A felony.
>
> First degree manslaughter involves a person recklessly causing the death of another, or the intentional and unlawful killing of a fetus by causing injury to the mother. First degree manslaughter is considered a Class B felony.
>
> Second degree manslaughter involves criminal negligence that results in the death of another. Second degree manslaughter is considered a Class C felony.
>
> Homicide by abuse involves causing the death of either a child under the age of 15 or a dependent adult suffering from severe developmental disabilities through a pattern of extreme indifference to life. Homicide by abuse is considered a Class A felony.

36. Elaine Stevens and Joyce Patterson had gotten into a heated argument over the use of some food stamps. When Ms. Patterson realized that Mrs. Stevens had neither the means nor the desire to reimburse her for the alleged loss, she pushed Mrs. Stevens to the floor and kicked her in the stomach. Consequently, Mrs. Stevens, who was in her third trimester of pregnancy, suffered

severe abdominal pain. After she summoned help on the telephone, firefighter paramedics transported her to County General Emergency. Despite the efforts of the hospital personnel, she miscarried two hours later. According to the reading, under the circumstances, Ms. Patterson should be charged with which of the following crimes?

A. Class A felony

B. First degree murder

C. Homicide by abuse

D. Class B felony

37. Ricky Matthews was driving his 1991 Ford Taurus west on Interstate 80 when he made an improper lane change that forced another vehicle off the road. The driver of that vehicle, Tracy Cummings, was killed instantly when her car collided with an oak tree. Mr. Matthews' blood alcohol level registered far above what was legally tolerated by the state. In this instance, according the reading, Mr. Matthews should be charged with which offense?

A. Class A felony

B. Class C felony

C. First degree manslaughter

D. He should not be charged with anything besides driving while under the influence (DWI).

38. Mr. and Mrs. Bradford's marriage had been on shaky ground for several months. One evening during dinner, an argument ensued concerning the family's finances. It was all that Mrs. Bradford could take, and she spontaneously grabbed a knife lying on a kitchen counter and stabbed Mr. Bradford several times in the neck and back. Mr. Bradford died three hours later in the critical care unit at Mercy Hospital. According to the reading, which offense should Mrs. Bradford be charged with?

A. Murder in the first degree

B. Manslaughter in the first degree

C. Murder in the second degree

D. Manslaughter in the second degree

Answer Questions 39 through 42 on the basis of the reading provided below:

Extortion is defined as the obtaining of property or services from another by wrongful use of actual or threatened force, violence, or fear.

First degree extortion involves the direct or indirect threat to cause future bodily injury or physical damage to the property of another or to subject the person threatened to restraint or confinement. First degree extortion is a Class B felony punishable by up to 10 years in prison.

Second degree extortion involves the direct or indirect threat to expose a secret, whether true or not, that instills contempt or hatred toward another; to withhold crucial testimony or disseminate false testimony that affects another person's legal defense or claim; to perpetuate a strike or boycott to obtain property unrelated to the event itself; or to act in a way harmful to another person's safety, health, business, or personal relationships. Second degree extortion is a Class C felony punishable by up to 7 years in prison.

Bribery is defined as the offering, giving, receiving, or soliciting of anything of value to influence action as an official or in the discharge of legal or public duty. Any person whose official conduct is connected with the administration of government is subject to this legal provision. Bribery is a Class A felony punishable by up to 15 years in prison.

39. Ann Compton threatened a neighbor who was currently standing trial for first degree theft that she would make a materially false statement against her defense in court if she did not receive $500. Under these circumstances and according to the preceding narrative, which of the following could Ms. Compton be charged with:
    A. Class A felony
    B. Perjury
    C. Class C felony
    D. The narrative is not applicable to this situation

40. Harold Russell, a recently furloughed convict, telephones one of the witnesses who had testified against him in court ten years earlier. He explains that the streets are unsafe these days, and that the witness or his wife may have an unfortunate "accident" if they are not careful. At this point, Mr. Russell hangs up. Accordingly, Mr. Russell could be prosecuted under which of the following statutes if the witness in question was the Mayor?
    A. Bribery
    B. First degree extortion
    C. Second degree extortion
    D. None of the above

41. Barb Waterhouse threatened to expose a local congressman's extramarital affair if he failed to enact legislation that would render harsher sentences for repeat sex offenders. If the congressman made local authorities aware of the threat, Ms. Waterhouse could be prosecuted under which of the following statutes?
    A. Bribery
    B. First degree extortion
    C. Second degree extortion
    D. None of the above

42. Dan Evans, a person twice convicted for the collection of unlawful debt, calls Charlie McKay and explains in no uncertain terms that if he does not pay the $1800 owed as interest from an earlier gambling activity, Mr. Evans and some "friends" would break both of Charlie's legs later in the week. On the presumption that Mr. Evans is arrested and prosecuted for the offense, how much prison time could Mr. Evans potentially face?
    A. 7 years
    B. 10 years
    C. 15 years
    D. None of the above

Below are hypothetical codes established by a statue law committee to address various infractions. Each code has three parts: a title, a chapter, and a section, in that order. Review each of these before proceeding with Questions 43 through 53.

RCX 38.12.012 concerns the operation of a nonhighway vehicle under the influence of a controlled substance or alcohol.

RCX 38.47.071 concerns certificates of registration and ownership.

RCX 38.49.008 concerns the operation of nonhighway vehicles.

RCX 38.32.047 concerns the operation of a motor vehicle with a revoked or suspended license.

RCX 38.23.047 concerns driving with a revoked or suspended license.

RCX 38.32.074 concerns driving without a valid driver's license.

RCX 38.23.074 concerns unauthorized persons allowed to drive a motor vehicle.

RCX 43.67.132 concerns the striking of an unattended car or other property.

RCX 43.76.312 concerns the injury or death of a person as a result of striking an unattended vehicle or property.

RCX 43.74.132 concerns driving while under the influence of drugs or alcohol.

RCX 43.10.509 concerns assisting another to start a vehicle equipped with an ignition interlock device.

RCX 43.21.075 concerns failure to stop and give identification to an officer.

RCX 43.12.057 concerns obedience to directions given by firefighters, flaggers, or police officers.

RCX 43.21.057 concerns refusal to give information or cooperation to a police officer.

RCX 48.12.018 concerns reckless driving.

RCX 48.12.081 concerns the attempt to elude pursuing police vehicles.

RCX 48.21.018 concerns homicide by a motor vehicle.

RCX 48.21.075 concerns persons under the influence of a controlled substance or alcohol.

RCX 48.10.509 concerns a nonappearance in court after signing a written promise to show up.

RCX 48.01.72 concerns racing vehicles on a public street or highway.

RCX 48.15.017 concerns vehicular assault.

RCX 48.51.071 concerns leaving children in an unattended vehicle while the engine is running.

43. Officer Pettibone was driving behind a 1985 Thunderbird when he noticed that its right rear tail light was out. Before attempting to stop the vehicle, he made a routine check of the vehicle's license number. According to dispatch, the vehicle in question had a license that had been revoked three months earlier. Officer Pettibone immediately turned on his emergency lights and attempted to pull the suspect over. However, the suspect went through two stoplights and struck an unattended parked vehicle before Officer Pettibone could effect an arrest. A breathalyzer test administered to the driver at the scene registered above the legal limit of 0.1%. On the basis of this situation, which of the alternatives provided below would most comprehensively address the infractions committed by the driver?

    A. RCX 38.32.047, RCX 38.12.012, RCX 43.67.132, RCX 48.12.018, RCX 48.12.081, and RCX 43.21.075

    B. RCX 48.12.081, RCX 48.12.018, RCX 43.74.132, RCX 43.21.075, RCX 43.67.132, and RCX 38.32.047

    C. RCX 48.12.081, RCX 43.74.132, RCX 48.12.018, RCX 43.67.132, RCX 38.32.047

    D. RCX 48.21.075, RCX 38.32.047, RCX 43.67.132, RCX 43.21.075, RCX 48.12.081, and RCX 48.12.018

44. In a fit of jealousy, Mark Kilpatrick attempted to run over his ex-girlfriend with his Honda Civic before crashing into a light standard. Fortunately, the victim suffered only minor bruises to her left leg and a small laceration to her right elbow. The suspect was also believed to have been on amphetamines at the time of the incident. Pursuant to arrest, Mr. Kilpatrick could be comprehensively charged with which of the following?

    A. RCX 43.67.132, RCX 48.21.018, RCX 43.74.132, and RCX 48.12.018
    B. RCX 48.12.018, RCX 43.74.132, RCX 43.76.312, and RCX 48.15.017
    C. RCX 48.15.017, RCX 43.67.132, RCX 48.12.018, and RCX 43.74.132
    D. RCX 48.12.018, RCX 48.21.075, RCX 48.15.017, and RCX 43.67.132

45. Chris Marshall double-parked in front of a convenience store so she could run in for a quick cup of coffee. The car's engine was left running so Mrs. Marshall's two kids, ages 1 and 3, would not get cold. The children were strapped in rear seat restraints. When Officer Daniels saw Mrs. Marshall return to the vehicle, he ran the plate number through dispatch and then pulled her over one and a half blocks later. The car's plates were valid; however her driver's license had expired two months earlier. When Officer Daniels asked whether the home address on her expired license was still current, Mrs. Marshall refused to answer. She felt that her ex-husband would somehow become involved. Under the circumstances, which of the alternatives provided below would comprehensively cover the infractions committed by Mrs. Marshall?

    A. RCX 38.32.074, RCX 48.15.017, and RCX 43.21.057
    B. RCX 48.51.071, RCX 43.21.057, and RCX 38.23.047
    C. RCX 43.21.075, RCX 38.32.074, and RCX 48.51.071
    D. RCX 43.21.057, RCX 38.32.074, and RCX 48.51.071

46. A mechanic who was caught bypassing ignition interlock systems for people willing to pay $250 would be appropriately charged and prosecuted under which code?

    A. Title 10, Chapter 509, Section 43
    B. Title 43, Chapter 1, Section 509
    C. Title 431, Chapter 05, Section 9
    D. Title 43, Chapter 10, Section 509

47. Bill Heston, a local farmer, was driving his tractor south on State Highway 60 to get to one of his alfalfa fields. State Trooper Don Weiss had seen the traffic back up, and when he got to the front of the line, he immediately pulled Mr. Heston over to the shoulder of the road. In attempting to comply with Officer Weiss, Mr. Heston inadvertently ran over a milepost before coming to a complete stop. Mr. Heston was put through a field sobriety test. The results neither confirmed nor denied that Mr. Heston was intoxicated. However, a breathalyzer reading indicated that Mr. Heston's blood alcohol level was below the legal limit. Under the circumstances, which of the alternatives provided below would comprehensively account for the infractions committed by Mr. Heston?

    A. RCX 38.12.012 and RCX 43.67.132
    B. RCX 38.49.008 and RCX 43.67.132
    C. RCX 43.21.075, RCX 43.67.132, and RCX 38.49.008
    D. RCX 43.67.132, RCX 38.32.074, and RCX 38.49.008

48. Tom and Richard McCann were racing their convertibles down Second Avenue when Tom lost control of his vehicle. It jumped a curb, struck and killed two pedestrians waiting to cross in the crosswalk. When officers arrived at the scene, they learned that Tom's driver's license had been suspended thirty days earlier for reckless driving. Drugs or alcohol were not believed to have been factors contributing to the accident. Under the circumstances, Richard McCann should be charged with which of the following?

   A. RCX 38.32.047, RCX 48.12.018, and RCX 48.01.72

   B. RCX 38.23.047, RCX 48.01.72, RCX 48.12.018, and RCX 48.15.017

   C. RCX 48.01.72, RCX 48.12.018, RCX 38.23.047, and RCX 43.74.132

   D. None of the above alternatives are completely correct

49. On the basis of the previous question, Tom McCann should be charged with which of the following?

   A. RCX 48.12.018, RCX 48.01.72, and RCX 38.23.047

   B. RCX 48.01.72, RCX 48.12.018, and RCX 38.23.047

   C. RCX 38.23.047, RCX 48.01.72, and RCX 48.12.018

   D. None of the above alternatives are completely correct

50. Joe Evans was in a hurry to meet a friend at the Four Corners Tavern. Unfortunately, the shortest route there went through a temporary detour due to a residential fire. Because he was late, Mr. Evans had no intention of driving any further than he had to. Against the direction of a volunteer firefighter, Mr. Evans drove through the congestion of emergency vehicles and over two charged hoses without the benefit of ramps. Motorcycle Patrolman Carl Best witnessed the infraction and promptly pulled Mr. Evans over. When Officer Best called dispatch to run Mr. Evans' license to determine if there were any wants or warrants, he discovered that Mr. Evans did, in fact, have a warrant out for his arrest. Apparently, Mr. Evans had not shown up for an earlier hearing in municipal court to explain mitigating circumstances involved in an unrelated incident. Officer Best asked Mr. Evans several questions pertaining to the incident at hand; however, no reply was offered. Pursuant to the defendant's arrest, he could be comprehensively charged with which of the following alternatives?

   A. RCX 48.10.509, RCX 43.21.057, and RCX 43.12.057

   B. RCX 43.12.057, RCX 43.12.075, and RCX 48.10.509

   C. RCX 43.21.057, RCX 38.47.071, RCX 43.12.057, and RCX 48.10.509

   D. RCX 38.23.074, RCX 48.10.509, RCX 43.21.057, and RCX 43.12.057

51. Mrs. Hartford had just purchased a new Audi A4. After she left the dealership with the new vehicle, Mrs. Hartford was pulled over by a state patrolman conducting a random license and vehicle inspection test. Her license checked out fine; however, she could not produce an owner's registration. Mrs. Hartford did not have any outstanding wants or warrants. Under the circumstances, Mrs. Hartford was given a written warning instead of a notice of infraction. Had it been an NOI rather than a warning, Mrs. Hartford could have been charged with which of the following?

   A. RCX 38.32.007

   B. RCX 38.23.509

   C. RCX 38.47.071

   D. RCX 38.02.071

52. Kate Jennings was accompanied by her older sister, Kathy (ages 15 and 18, respectively) when Kate drove to the local grocery store. On the way back home, Kate encountered a small patch of black ice that caused her to lose control of the vehicle and sideswipe an unattended parked vehicle. A neighbor witnessed the incident and immediately called 911. A police officer was quick to respond. Kate did not have a learner's permit. Under the circumstances, Kathy should be charged with which of the following?
    A. RCX 38.23.074
    B. RCX 38.32.074
    C. RCX 38.23.047
    D. RCX 38.47.071

53. On the basis of the previous question, Kate should be charged with which of the following?
    A. RCX 38.23.074
    B. RCX 38.32.074
    C. RCX 38.23.047
    D. RCX 38.47.071

54. Sergeant Bernstein's report was seemingly *redundant* in a couple of areas. *Redundant* most nearly means
    A. Incomprehensible
    B. Repetitious
    C. Concise
    D. Easy to understand

55. Cliff's *facetiousness* with the law officer landed him a jail term. *Facetiousness* most nearly means
    A. Serious nature
    B. Blitheness
    C. Wisecracking
    D. Stubborn attitude

56. Jurors were not permitted to *divulge* any information to a third party while sequestered. *Divulge* most nearly means
    A. Conceal
    B. Distort
    C. Expose
    D. Disclose

57. The minor infraction was enough to warrant permanent *expulsion*. *Expulsion* most nearly means
    A. Displacement
    B. Replacement
    C. Disgrace
    D. Subjugation

58. Many people are of the belief that the rights and privileges guaranteed by the Constitution are the main factor preventing total *anarchy* in this nation. *Anarchy* most nearly means
    A. Compatibility
    B. Conformity
    C. Disorder
    D. Harmony

59. Jerry had nothing but *contempt* for the legal system once Judge Skyler refused to dismiss his speeding ticket. *Contempt* most nearly means
    A. Disdain
    B. Praise
    C. Respect
    D. High regard

60. The suspect freely made her confession without *coercion* in the hope of gaining a lighter sentence. *Coercion* most nearly means
    A. Reservations
    B. Assistance
    C. Stipulation
    D. Intimidation

61. It was an *alleged* accident that Ms. Phelps overdosed on sleeping pills. *Alleged* most nearly means
    A. Guaranteed
    B. Credible
    C. Indisputable
    D. Purported

62. The defense attorney repeated the witness's statement *verbatim*. *Verbatim* most nearly means
    A. Imprecisely
    B. Word for word
    C. Perfunctory
    D. Eloquently

63. Vice Detective Sid Morrissey is a *proficient* interrogator. *Proficient* most nearly means
    A. Incompetent
    B. Prodigious
    C. Expert
    D. Amateur

64. Mr. Austin was a little *ambiguous* concerning his whereabouts at the time of the murder. *Ambiguous* most nearly means
    A. Vague
    B. Explicit
    C. Recalcitrant
    D. Too relaxed

65. The victim was *asphyxiated* in her sleep. *Asphyxiated* most nearly means
    A. Uncomfortable
    B. Distressed
    C. Suffocated
    D. Restless

Answer Questions 66 through 68 on the basis of this flow chart.

STATE AND FEDERAL COURT SYSTEMS

66. Which court may review a decision made by a state supreme court?
    A. Intermediate appellate court
    B. Federal Supreme Court
    C. U.S. district court
    D. None of the above

67. All of the following lower courts with limited jurisdictions have only one avenue of appeal except:
    A. Juvenile court
    B. Small claims court
    C. Traffic court
    D. Municipal court

68. According to the flow chart, all of the following statements are true except
    A. Only one court has three potential avenues of appealing a decision.
    B. Decisions arrived at in U.S. Claims Court can be appealed directly to the federal circuit court of appeals.
    C. Decisions heard in the federal Supreme Court can originate from only three different venues.
    D. All of the above are correct.

69. Second degree arson constitutes knowingly and maliciously causing a fire which damages any structure or property adjoining it, a motor vehicle, or any other tangible property. First degree reckless burning constitutes inadvertently damaging the property of another through reckless burning. On the basis of these definitions, what one word could be used, for the purpose of prosecution, to establish discernable differences between the two?

    A. Justification

    B. Intent

    C. Procedure

    D. None of the above

70. When someone's neighbor ends up being convicted of a heinous crime, people are initially surprised that such a thing could happen. However, after the fact, people are quick to point out that the felon had expressionless eyes, never smiled, or possessed some other physical characteristic that did not seem normal. On the basis of this observation, the truth of the matter is that

    A. Potential criminals are recognizable and as such should be supervised closely.

    B. People who never smile are particularly prone to violence.

    C. Certain physical traits provide insight into and enable one to predict someone's future actions.

    D. There really is no such thing as a standardized criminal appearance.

71. A preliminary hearing is a proceeding in which a magistrate decides whether a crime has been committed or if there is probable cause to believe the defendant committed the act. If it is decided that neither of these can be determined, it is within the magistrate's authority to have the charges dropped and the defendant released. However, if enough evidence is presented to substantiate one or both of these considerations, the defendant can be ordered held for further trial proceedings.

    In the case of John Matthews, Police Sergeant Perry Miller witnessed the defendant sit on a park bench that was located reasonably close to a drug cache that had been purposefully left for a drug buy arranged earlier. Mr. Matthews made no attempt to possess the drugs. However, he did seem fidgety, having probably recognized the situation for what it really was. He promptly left the area. According to this reading, pursuant to his arrest and appearance in a preliminary hearing, the defendant should be

    A. Released for a lack of any evidence implicating him in narcotics trafficking

    B. Held because he was fidgety at the time, indicating a guilty conscience

    C. Held because he promptly left the scene for reasons apparent to the officers involved

    D. Released simply because he seems too nervous to be the kind that deals in drugs

72. If a police department wanted to project a more positive image to the public, which of the following would be the most effective means to accomplish this goal?

    A. Treat persons suspected of committing felonies with a little less force and more dignity

    B. Demonstrate equal enforcement of the criminal code as established by the state with respect to all persons charged

    C. Address select community groups and meetings and explain the department's intentions

    D. Police officers should be professional, courteous, and helpful when conducting routine traffic enforcement.

73. During a routine traffic stop, the placement of a police vehicle is important to the safety of the officer. All of the following procedures would be considered correct in this respect, except

    A. Pull approximately 10–15 feet behind the violator's vehicle

    B. Park offset approximately half the vehicle width to the right

    C. Park the police vehicle with the front end angled to the left

    D. All of these will afford some degree of protection for the officer

74. Most witnesses to crimes are ineffective observers. Unlike a police officer, they lack the developed skill to remember in detail the people who break the law or the events involved. Which of the statements provided below would accurately summarize the contents of this passage?

    A. Police officers have recall abilities that are over and above those of the public they serve.

    B. As a general rule, witnesses to crime have lower mental capabilities.

    C. Violations of the law are not always recognized by people. Consequently, details of a crime are usually sketchy.

    D. Most people are not truly cognizant of their surroundings.

75. If it is known that over 80% of the people are right-handed, it can be reasonably assumed that an officer's safest approach to a suspect wielding a gun in a nighttime situation would be

    A. Stay low and go to the suspect's right

    B. Stay low and go to the left

    C. Stay low and go to the right

    D. Approach the suspect in a direct line

76. If an officer arrives at a crime scene where the suspect has already fled, he or she should check the condition of any victims at the scene. If medical assistance is required, the officer should stay with the victim(s) and administer first aid until paramedics arrive. Additionally, the crime scene should be protected for the express purpose of gathering evidence. Officers should interview the victim(s) and take statements from any potential witnesses regarding the incident. All evidence should be collected and cited accordingly on the initial incident report.

    Officer Myers arrived at a scene where a woman had been forcibly raped and stabbed to death. As Officer Myers began to fill out an incident report, a curious bystander found a knife discarded in a hedgerow in close proximity to the body. The man handed the knife to the officer. At this point, Officer Myers took the man's name and address for future reference and then asked him to leave the immediate area. According to the narrative, Officer Myers' actions would be considered

    A. Proper because he stayed with the victim during the time he filled out the incident report

    B. Improper because the crime scene was left unprotected prior to the completion of gathering evidence

    C. Proper because he had obtained information necessary to locate the bystander involved for future questioning

    D. Improper because he did not seek out potential witnesses to the incident

77. Sergeant Jeff Love received a dispatch to investigate an aggravated assault. When he arrived at the scene, two male juveniles, wearing jackets bearing gang insignia, were kneeling beside someone who had sustained severe bruises and lacerations to his face. Officer Love was told by one of the two bystanders that they had been attacked unprovoked by two members of a rival gang. The attackers had then ducked into a vacant warehouse across the street. After getting a full description of the suspects, Officer Love called and waited for backup before conducting a thorough search of the area where the attackers were last seen. According to the information in Question 76, Officer Love's actions would be considered

    A. Proper because he had gotten all the information necessary to complete an incident report

    B. Improper because he wasted valuable time in collecting witness statements instead of immediately giving chase to the suspects involved

    C. Proper because he waited at the scene for backup to arrive

    D. Improper because the victim of the assault did not received immediate medical attention from him

78. Often it is said that law enforcement officers are their own worst enemies. Minor oversights and complacency in procedures and situations can often result in violence to officers. Those who have been spared or survived a particular incident are amazed at their own negligence in times of stress. What would it be reasonable to deduce from this?
   A. Law enforcement officers should guard themselves against complacency at all times.
   B. Law enforcement officers should avoid stressful situations altogether.
   C. Compared to veteran officers, rookie law enforcement officers are probably at more of a risk of making such mistakes.
   D. The element of danger involved in an arrest can be completely eliminated by following certain basic operational safeguards.

Answer Questions 79 through 81 on the basis of the statistics compiled below from a hypothetical municipality.

Type of crime	Number of cases	Average number of manhours assigned per case	Estimated total economic impact (loss in dollars)
Aggravated assault	117	1.5	NA
Arson	14	4.0	720,000
Auto theft	62	2.75	1,100,000
Burglary	312	3.75	925,000
Embezzlement	32	2.5	700,000
Fraud	79	1.5	1,250,000
Gambling	43	1.0	NA
Larceny	1320	3.5	3,750,000
Murder	42	17	NA
Narcotics	981	1.0	NA
Forcible rape	52	10.5	NA
Robbery	674	4	2,600,000
Shoplifting	520	1.5	1,300,000
Vandalism	720	0.5	125,000

79. Assuming that crime against property includes arson, burglary, vandalism, larceny, robbery, embezzlement, auto theft, and shoplifting, what percentage of the total annual caseload would these crimes constitute?
   A. 71%
   B. 74%
   C. 76%
   D. none of these

80. The Commission on Law Enforcement and Administration of Justice set a goal of reducing the homicide rate by at least 15% within the next two years. Approximately how much would this trim the number of deaths per year indicated in this study?
   A. 7   B. 4   C. 3   D. 2

81. The crime that requires the second-highest number of man-hours per case constitutes what percentage of the total crimes committed?
   A. 1%   B. 2%   C. 3%   D. 4%

Answer Question 82 on the basis of the chart below.

CRIME INDEX OFFENSE, PERCENT DISTRIBUTION

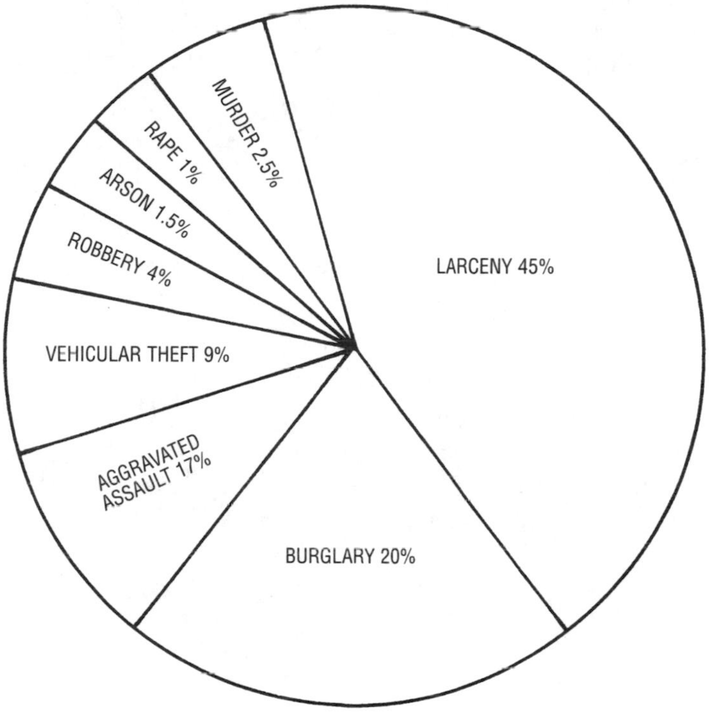

82. If there were a total of 10,000 offenses reported and the percent distribution of the crimes was as indicated in the chart, how many actual aggravated assault cases would there be?
    A. 2000
    B. 1850
    C. 1700
    D. None of these

83. If it is reported that one robbery is committed every 45 seconds, one burglary every 10 seconds, and one aggravated assault every 27 seconds, how many of each crime would be committed per hour?
    A. 90, 200, 270, respectively
    B. 80, 360, 133, respectively
    C. 75, 400, 230, respectively
    D. None of the above

84. If the Sheriff's Department responded to 245 traffic accidents for the month and the other 8% of its calls were attributed to stranded motorists, how many calls did the Sheriff's Department receive altogether?
    A. 248   B. 253   C. 266   D. 275

85. If a police applicant scored 80%, 82%, 90%, and 87% on her first four exams, what kind of grade would be required on the fifth exam to acquire an overall average of 87%?
    A. 87%   B. 89%   C. 96%   D. 98%

86. The sketch provided below is a floor plan of the room where a suicide occurred. Point A is the point where the victim in question had fallen after shooting herself. Point B marks the bullet's exit. With the information provided, how far (in feet) did the bullet travel from Point A before striking the corner of the wall?

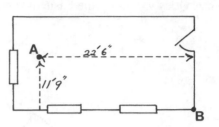

   A. 21.75

   B. 24.70

   C. 25.38

   D. 26.25

87. Using a compass point method in making a crime scene sketch, Detective O'Hara determined that both victims of the double homicide (Points B and C) were at 90 degrees to one another, with the doorway (Point A) serving as the reference point. If the distances to Points B and C from Point A were 15'6" and 17'3", respectively, what would the distance between the two bodies be?

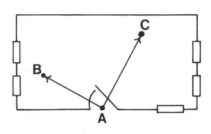

   A. 23.19

   B. 21.74

   C. 19.23

   D. 16.52

88. A Superior Court judge recently told a board of commissioners that for the year, domestic filings increased 32% and juvenile filings increased 41%. Assuming the Superior Court's annual caseload for both kinds of filings was 231 and 163 respectively, what had been the respective number of filings in the previous year?

   A. 192 and 123, respectively

   B. 175 and 116, respectively

   C. 182 and 119, respectively

   D. 205 and 131, respectively

89. Sergeant Bob Wyse utilized a wheel search pattern in his investigation of a case involving a homicide. In searching for fiber, thread, and hair samples that could potentially help the case, Sergeant Wyse meticulously covered an area that extended 15 feet in all directions from the victim. How many square feet of area did this search pattern account for?

   A. 706.86 square feet

   B. 1237.41 square feet

   C. 2103.5 square feet

   D. 2827.44 square feet

Study the uniform crime report provided below to answer Questions 90 through 93.

| Criminal Offense | Males | | | | Females | | | |
| | Total | | Under 18 | | Total | | Under 18 | |
	1985	1990	1985	1990	1985	1990	1985	1990
Murder & nonnegligent manslaughter	13,141	15,906	1,015	1,293	6,750	6,953	1,501	1,709
Robbery	49,192	46,702	2,950	2,893	23,471	23,405	2,090	2,740
Forcible rape	16,531	19,603	983	1,107	1,006	1,180	105	145
Burglary	67,985	82,996	13,580	14,012	9,706	11,340	936	1,050
Arson	9,512	10,759	235	257	123	137	13	29
Motor vehicle theft	72,503	73,415	12,509	12,703	24,600	24,807	1,326	1,349
Larceny	426,719	503,971	29,601	35,803	290,439	312,482	18,901	18,996
Aggravated assault	232,500	256,319	18,900	23,752	137,506	145,990	15,403	18,901

90. In the five-year period indicated in the survey, which criminal offense committed by male juveniles experienced the greatest percentage increase?
    A. Murder and nonnegligent manslaughter
    B. Forcible rape
    C. Larceny
    D. Aggravated assault

91. According to the most recent statistics, how many more times is a man likely to commit murder or nonnegligent manslaughter than a woman?
    A. 3:1   B. 2.67:1   C. 2.29:1   D. 2.2:1

92. Motor vehicle theft accounts for what percentage of the total crimes committed by female juveniles?
    A. 1%   B. 3%   C. 5%   D. 7%

93. Which category of offenders demonstrates the largest percentage decrease in robbery?
    A. Adult males
    B. Juvenile males
    C. Adult females
    D. Juvenile females

94. Police Officer Dave Cuen was sent to investigate the death of an infant belonging to a professional couple living in an upscale neighborhood. Sudden Infant Death Syndrome (SIDS) was suspected as the cause of death. Officer Cuen needed to ask several questions of the parents regarding the care and health of the baby prior to its death. Below are various questions posed by the officer in order to complete his report. Considering the sensitivity of the issue, which of the questions tended to illustrate a judgmental bias?
    A. "When you realized the child was unresponsive, what did you do?"
    B. "Did you notice anything different about the infant?"
    C. "When did you last check the infant?"
    D. "Are you positive the baby was not sick?"

95. Each of the sentences below have been taken out of an incident report supplement detailing the circumstances surrounding a burglary. The sentences are not arranged in any particular order. Select the alternative that represents the facts as they would appear chronologically in the report.

 1. While conducting routine patrol in the 2700 block of Maple Avenue, I received a dispatch at 2052 hours to investigate a burglary in progress at 3625 Hannibal Street.

 2. The two suspects did not stop when ordered to.

 3. I lost the suspects in the alley between the 3900 block of Hannibal Street and the 3900 block of McGregor Way.

 4. The two-story home was completely dark.

 5. While waiting for backup, I heard the distant noise of glass breaking toward the rear of the home.

   A. 5, 3, 2, 4, 1
   B. 1, 5, 2, 3, 4
   C. 1, 4, 5, 2, 3
   D. 1, 4, 5, 3, 2

96. The following sentences are notes taken from an officer's activity log detailing a notice of infraction given to a motorcyclist earlier in the week. The sentences are not arranged in any particular order. Select the alternative that represents the facts as they would appear chronologically in the official activity log.

 1. At 1117 hours, I observed a motorcyclist going 15 mph over the acceptable speed limit for a designated school area.

 2. He was very adamant that he had not been speeding through the school area and seemed hesitant in offering his license as requested.

 3. I was assigned to patrol the Hale Elementary School area between the hours of 1100 and 1245 Monday through Wednesday.

 4. I gave him a citation for exceeding the speed limit in front of a school and a written warning for the expired license.

 5. His driver's license had been expired for almost a month.

   A. 1, 3, 2, 4, 5
   B. 3, 1, 5, 2, 4
   C. 3, 1, 2, 4, 5
   D. 3, 1, 2, 5, 4

97. Police Officer Hank Johnson had filed a missing person report earlier in the week. Each of the sentences provided below has been taken directly out of that report. The sentences are not arranged in any particular order. Select the alternative that represents the facts as they would appear chronologically in the report.

 1. The party was hosted by the McNeil family, who live at 290 NW Brookdale Boulevard.

 2. A vehicle of that general description had been reported stolen the same evening.

 3. At 0800 hours, Mrs. Beth Hallestad called to report that her 13-year-old daughter, Tracy, and her best friend had not returned home from a party held the previous night.

 4. Mrs. Hallestad provided a complete physical description.

 5. Mr. McNeil recalled seeing the two leave in a late model Toyota pickup at approximately 11:15 p.m.

   A. 4, 3, 1, 5, 2
   B. 1, 3, 4, 5, 2
   C. 3, 4, 5, 2, 1
   D. 3, 4, 1, 5, 2

98. The following sentences are notes taken from an officer's activity log detailing an attempted suicide. The sentences are not arranged in any particular order. Select the alternative that represents the facts as they would appear chronologically in the officer's activity log.

　1. Mr. Crawford was placed in protective custody at 1950 hours.

　2. I attempted to talk Mr. Crawford out of what he was attempting to do.

　3. I was walking my beat when a passerby by the name of Ms. Dora Sanders pointed out someone threatening to jump from a third-story window.

　4. I radioed for immediate backup to cordon off the area as well as the Fire Department for their assistance.

　5. The person identified himself and explained the motive for his actions.

    A.   3, 4, 5, 2, 1

    B.   3, 5, 4, 2, 1

    C.   3, 2, 5, 4, 1

    D.   3, 2, 4, 5, 1

Answer Questions 99 through 101 on the basis of the passage below.

The number located at the top of a driver's license consists of the first five letters of the last name, the first letter of the first name, and the first letter of the middle name. The birth year when subtracted from 100 produces the first two numerical digits. A check digit inserted by the computer produces the third numerical digit. A code for the month of birth and a code for the day of birth are inserted toward the end. Month and day codes are represented below:

MONTHS	DAYS		
JANUARY - A	01 - A	13 - M	25 - Y
FEBRUARY - B	02 - B	14 - N	26 - Z
MARCH - D	03 - C	15 - O	27 - 1
APRIL - F	04 - D	16 - P	28 - 2
MAY - G	05 - E	17 - Q	29 - 3
JUNE - H	06 - F	18 - R	30 - 4
JULY - J	07 - G	19 - S	31 - 5
AUGUST - L	08 - H	20 - T	
SEPTEMBER - O	09 - I	21 - U	
OCTOBER - P	10 - J	22 - V	
NOVEMBER - R	11 - K	23 - W	
DECEMBER - T	12 - L	24 - X	

99. According to the formula prescribed, John Doe Smith, born 10-26-56, would be issued which of the following driver's license numbers?

    A. JDSMITH44ZP9

    B. SMITHJD449PZ

    C. DJSMITH449PZ

    D. SMITHJD44PZ

100. According to the formula prescribed, Jason Lowell Halvorson, born June 16, 1975, would be issued which of the following driver's license numbers?

    A. HALVOJL251HP

    B. HALVEJL523PH

    C. HALVOLJ25H1P

    D. HAVOJL521HP

101. According to the formula prescribed, Vicki Jean Bartenolli, born August 30, 1963, would be issued which of the following driver's license numbers?

    A. VJBARTE378L4

    B. JVBART837L4

    C. BARTEJV371L4

    D. BARTEVJ378L4

Answer Questions 102 through 105 on the basis of the passage below:

The month expiration tab on a passenger vehicle or a truck displays the month in which the vehicle's registration expires. A color-code scheme has been implemented to identify the part of the year that registrations needs to be renewed.

    Yellow: January, February, and March
    Green: April, May, and June
    Red: July, August, and September
    Black: October, November, and December

Anything other than a passenger vehicle or a truck follow the scheme presented below:

    Red: January, February, and March
    Yellow: April, May, and June
    Black: July, August, and September
    Green: October, November, and December

The year expiration tab displays the year in which the vehicle registration expires. This identification needs to be present only on the rear plate. All tab numbers are recorded on the vehicle registration form. Government vehicles are exempt from registration fees and expiration tabs, and are identified accordingly. Corporations that own fleet vehicles are exempt as well; a vehicle that falls into that category is issued a permanent fleet registration tab that is renewed in October of each year.

102. The color code for identifying month expiration tabs on recreational vehicles (e.g., snowmobiles) is regulated by what type of system?

    A. Monthly

    B. Quarterly

    C. Semi-annual

    D. Yearly

103. Fleet vehicles owned by corporations are on what type of registration renewal system?

    A. Monthly

    B. Quarterly

    C. Annual

    D. Exempt

104. If Joe Collier owned a new 1993 Buick LeSabre whose vehicle registration was due to expire in September of the year following its purchase, which of the following descriptions would be considered true?

    A. The month expiration tab would be black, and the year expiration tab would indicate 93

    B. The month expiration tab would be black, and the year expiration tab would indicate 94

    C. The month expiration tab would be red, and the year expiration tab would indicate 93

    D. The month expiration tab would be red, and the year expiration tab would indicate 94

105. Shawn Turner drove a 1980 Ford Fairlane to and from various state departments to conduct official business. If the vehicle was purchased in July by the government agency he worked for, what would be the correct color code and year tab for the eight-year-old vehicle?

  A. Red and 88, respectively, placed on both the front and back license plates
  B. Black and 88, respectively, placed on both the front and back license plates
  C. Red and 88, respectively, placed on the rear plate only.
  D. None of the above

Answer Questions 106 through 112 on the basis of the map provided below.

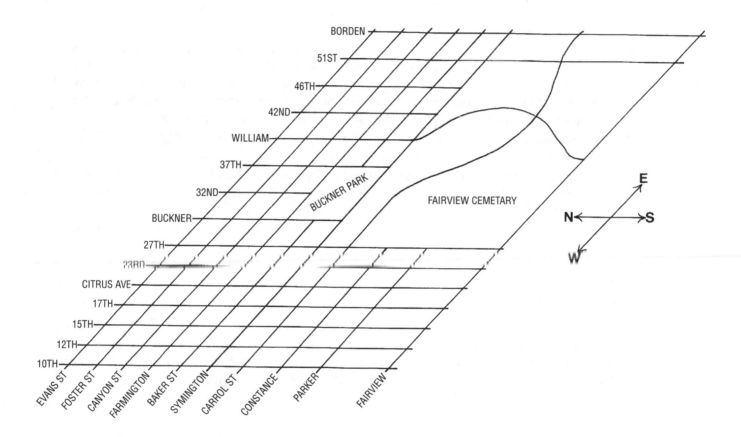

106. If Officer Preston was conducting traffic enforcement at 17th and Parker and was radioed to investigate a burglary in progress at a residence located on Canyon Street between 32nd Avenue and 37th Avenue, what general direction must he head?

    A. North

    B. Northeast

    C. Southeast

    D. South

107. Buckner Park adjoins which corner of the Fairview Cemetery?

    A. Northeast

    B. South

    C. Northwest

    D. Southeast

108. Assume that Evans, Canyon, Baker, Carrol, and Parker are one-way streets that direct traffic flow west; all odd-numbered avenues are one-way streets that direct traffic flow south; all other streets not accounted for can be considered two-way streets. Which of the alternatives provided below would be considered legal means for an officer working traffic enforcement at the intersection of 17th and Parker to respond to a felony in progress at 37th and Evans?

    A. Go from Parker on 17th Avenue to Evans and then turn right on Evans and continue six blocks

    B. Go one block south on 17th Avenue, turn left, go one block and make another left turn, go eight blocks, turn right and go five blocks before turning left and driving one more block north

    C. Go one block south on 17th Avenue, one block east on Fairview, eight blocks north on Citrus Avenue, four blocks east on Foster, one block north on 32nd Avenue, and then one block east on Evans Street.

    D. Go three blocks west, seven blocks north, ten blocks east, one block north, and then one block west.

109. Look at the previous question again. Assume the streets not named in the question are one-way roads that direct traffic flow west; all other streets are to be considered two-way, and even-numbered avenues are one-way roads that direct traffic flow south. Which of the alternatives provided below would be considered a legal means for an officer currently parked at the intersection of 10th Avenue and Constance to get to 46th Avenue and Foster Street in order to investigate a vehicular assault?

    A. Go one block north, turn right and continue to William Avenue, turn left, go to Canyon Street, turn right, go to 46th Avenue, turn left, and drive one more block.

    B. Go two blocks east, turn left and go to Evans Street, turn right, and continue to 46th Avenue before turning right again and driving one more block south.

    C. Go one block south and turn left, go two blocks east and turn left again, go eight blocks and then turn right, go ten blocks east before turning right again, and drive one more block due south.

    D. Go one block south and turn left, go two blocks east and turn left again, go eight blocks before turning right, go nine blocks east before turning right again, and drive one more block due south.

110. If Patrol Officer Marsha White, who is currently positioned at 15th Avenue and Baker Street, is dispatched to investigate a homicide that has occurred in the far northeast corner of the Fairview Cemetery, which of the routes provided below would afford her the quickest means to respond? (Assume all streets are two-way and have identical speed limits.)
    A. Go one block south, turn left, and go approximately eleven blocks east; the scene should be in view on the right side.
    B. Go approximately ten blocks east before turning south and driving one more block.
    C. Go two blocks south, turn left, and go to 51st Avenue before turning north and driving approximately one more block. The scene should be in view on the left.
    D. Go one block south, turn right, and go approximately eleven blocks west. The scene should be in view on the left.

111. Field Training Officer Ralph Sexton was accompanying a new police recruit on his first patrol assignment. The 23rd Precinct station house was located at the southeast corner of Citrus Avenue and Canyon Street. On the presumption that they had started from there and drove two blocks east, one block south, and four blocks east, then turned right and followed that road to its end, then turned west and continued to the first intersection encountered, and then turned right and west one block before turning left and stopping at a point one block further on, what direction is their new location in relation to headquarters?
    A. Northwest
    B. Southeast
    C. West
    D. South

112. Assume that the precinct station house is located at the same place as in the previous question. The entire length of 46th Avenue is closed for a repaving project; the intersection of Borden Avenue and Farmington Street is closed between 1:15 p.m. and 3:20 p.m. for a natural gas line repair, and a load of debris dumped unlawfully on Carrol Street between Williams Avenue and 27th Avenue obstructs both lanes of traffic between 2:45 p.m. and 3:15 p.m. Under these circumstances, if Officer Bob Marshall was dispatched from the precinct station at 1450 hours to investigate a two-car accident that had occurred at 51st Avenue and Canyon Street, which of the routes given below would serve as a viable means of response? (Assume that all streets are two-way).
    A. Drive directly east nine blocks.
    B. Go three blocks south, nine blocks east, and then three blocks north.
    C. Go seven blocks south, turn left, and four intersections later turn left again, and then continue to Canyon Street.
    D. Go four blocks south, turn left, and five intersections later turn left again and continue to Canyon Street before making a left turn and driving one more block west.

113. Detective Brad Jones was sent to investigate a homicide in a low income housing project. Four witnesses each claimed to have gotten a relatively good view of the suspect as he fled the crime scene. Mrs. Dorothy Williams claimed that the suspect was a Caucasian male of light complexion with reddish-blonde hair and blue eyes, standing approximately 5'11", weighing 175 pounds. Mrs. William French described the suspect as being a Latin male of light complexion, approximately 6 feet tall, 180 pounds, with light brown hair and green eyes. Mr. William Becket described the suspect as being a Caucasian male, approximately 5'11" tall, weighing 190 pounds, with sandy blonde hair and hazel eyes. Mr. Howard Werner described the same person as a Caucasian male with medium complexion, standing approximately 5'6" tall, weighing 175 pounds, with brown hair and blue eyes. Judging from these descriptions, which witness probably offered the most accurate description of the suspect in question?

A. Mr. Becket

B. Mrs. Williams

C. Mr. Werner

D. Mrs. French

114. Some states issue driver's licenses that incorporate a lenticular security feature on the part of the license that includes the operator's signature and birthdate. This feature is simply a series of raised bumps on the card's laminate. What is the most probable reason for doing this?

A. It serves as identification for blind persons.

B. It hinders potential alterations.

C. It can still provide the information even after years of wear.

D. It helps to prevent a driver's license from inadvertently being lost.

115. Commercial security for store proprietors is important in reducing the incidence of theft. Which of the tactics given below would probably have the least effect on reducing the potential for robbery?

A. Place checkout stands in highly visible locations.

B. Keep minimum cash in the till.

C. Make bank deposits at irregular intervals.

D. Install good lighting and mirrors.

116. Fingerprints are important in evidence collection. Latent prints are described as the indistinct impressions left by the perspiration or oily secretions that are exuded from the fingers onto those objects that are touched directly. Which of the following conditions would have a detrimental effect on the quality of a latent print?

A. Hot and humid weather

B. Warm and dry weather

C. Cold and dry weather

D. Weather has no bearing on the quality of latent prints.

The blank booking form on the next page is to be used as a reference for Questions 117 through 125. You may refer back to this form to answer the questions.

① DATE OF REPORT	② BOOKING NO.	③ PRECINCT NO.	④ BADGE NO. OF ARRESTING OFFICER	⑤ TYPE F - FELONY M - MISDEMEANOR O - OTHER	⑥ EVIDENCE BOOKED ☐ YES ☐ NO

⑦ COMPLAINT FILED (CHARGES & COUNTS)

⑧ INVESTIGATING OFFICER'S NAME & ADDRESS:	⑨ ARRAIGNMENT DATE	⑩ TIME	⑪ COURT

㉕ ARRESTEE'S NAME:	㉗ SSN	⑫ ARREST DISPOSITION:

㉖ ARRESTEE'S ADDRESS:	⑬ D.A. FELONY REFERRAL:
	⑭ 72-HOUR RELEASE:

㉘ SEX	㊲ SCARS, PECULIARITIES:	⑮ FELONY WARRANT SERVED:
㉙ AGE/DOB	㊳ EMPLOYER'S NAME & ADDRESS:	⑯ MISDEMEANOR WARRANT SERVED:
㉚ RACE		⑰ FELONY COMPLAINT FILED:
㉛ HAIR	㊴ IN CASE OF EMERGENCY CALL: NAME: ADDRESS:	
㉜ EYES	RELATION: PHONE NO.:	⑲ OTHER:
㉝ HEIGHT	㊵ ARRESTEE'S VEHICLE: YR: MAKE: MODEL: COLOR:	⑳ PRIOR ARREST DISPOSITION:
㉞ WEIGHT	㊶ PRESENT LOCATION OR IMPOUNDMENT:	㉑ NAME OF PROBATION OFFICER:
㉟ MEDICAL PROBLEMS:		㉒ PRECINCT NO., IF AVAILABLE:
		㉓ TIME SERVED FOR OFFENSE:
㊱ ALIAS (AKAs):		㉔ PLACE WHERE TIME SERVED:

⑱ MISDEMEANOR COMPLAINT FILED:

SEE APPLICABLE CODES BELOW

CODE	㊷ NAME	ADDRESS	HOME PHONE:	BUSINESS PHONE:

SEX:
O—MALE
Y—FEMALE

RACE:
1—CAUCASIAN
2—HISPANIC
3—AFRICAN AMERICAN
4—ASIAN
5—NATIVE AMERICAN

DATE OF BIRTH:
NUMERIC CODE SHOULD EXPRESS
MONTH-DAY-YEAR

EYES:
BROWN—BRO
BLUE—BE

GREEN—GE
HAZEL—HZ
GREY—GR
BLACK—B

HAIR:
BROWN—B
GREY—GE
BLACK—BA
BLONDE—DN
RED—R
BALD—NA

HEIGHT:
WEIGHT:
3 DIGIT NUMERIC CODE SHOULD
EXPRESS WEIGHT

SCARS/PECULIARITIES:
A—DEFORMITY
B—AMPUTATION
C—SCARS
D—TATTOO

LOCATION OF MARK:
1—FINGER
2—HAND
3—ARM
4—FOOT
5—LEG
6—CHEST
7—NECK
8—FACE

VEHICLE DESCRIPTION:
2 DOOR—2
4 DOOR—4
TRAILER—T
TRUCK—TK
VAN—N
STATION WAGON—W
CONVERTIBLE—K

CODES:
S—SPOUSE
A—BROTHER
D—SISTER
G—PARENT OR GUARDIAN
J—OTHER RELATIVE
M—FRIEND
O—ACCOMPLICE

ANY TIME ENTRIES IN THIS REPORT SHOULD BE EXPRESSED IN MILITARY FORM.

A hypothetical arrest composite is presented below. Go over the information carefully before answering questions 117 through 125.

On September 17, 1992, Michael J. Connors was arrested at his home at 2025 Parker Boulevard, Auburn, Washington, for the manufacture of and intent to deliver a controlled substance and unlawful possession of a firearm by a felon, both of which are considered Class B felonies. Another person on the premises, Timothy Russell, who claimed to be a friend of the arrestee, was also arrested, for conspiracy to distribute a controlled substance. He was booked in the Auburn County jail (see arrest report #15-503).

Officer John Halden, Badge Number 363, was the arresting officer. Officer Halden currently resides on Creston Drive in Auburn, Washington. One hundred twenty grams of what is suspected to be cocaine and a .38-caliber pistol with the serial number 51105350 were placed in the evidence storage locker at Precinct 14 for future court exhibition. The arraignment of the suspect has been set for September 20, 1992, at 1:00 p.m. in Breston County District Court. Records indicate that the suspect has been convicted twice for assault and once for distribution of a controlled substance. He has served three years and two months in Humbolt Correctional and was paroled in October 1990, according to Officer Thurston Whitby, who was his probation officer at the time. Michael J. Connors has been known to have used the alias Mark E. Preston while engaging in drug-trade activity. Mr. Connors is a 37-year-old white male, 6', 195 pounds, with brown hair and hazel eyes. He is known to be a diabetic requiring insulin. One physical mark worth noting is a black eagle tattoo on his right forearm. Mr. Connors currently works for Hawthorne, Inc., located at 679 E. Marston Place, Auburn, Washington. His Social Security number is 508-27-4110, and another card found in his possession indicates that his stepmother, Andrea Stevens, who lives at 2042 Barrangton Avenue, Waverly, Iowa, should be contacted in case of an emergency. Her phone number is (319) 563-2751. Mr. Connors' two-tone white-on-blue 1990 Ford four-door station wagon was impounded by Hand K Towing, at 4357 H Street, Auburn, Washington. Below are the names and addresses of people Mr. Connors asked to be notified pending his trial.

1. (Stepfather) George C. Nichols, 1459 E. Parkhurst, Federal Way, WA, home phone (206) 951-4321, business phone (206) 573-4444.
2. (Cousin) Arthur B. Gladstone, 160-D Magnuson Way Apartments, Colville, IA, home phone (515) 723-5678.
3. (Neighbor) Tina Weatherby, 2037 Parker Boulevard, Auburn, WA, home phone (206) 951-5541, business phone (206) 591-8741.
4. (Friend) Timothy Russell, 906 Forrest Drive, Auburn, WA, home phone (206) 933-5441.

117. According to the narrative, what information should be placed in Box 2 with regard to Mr. Connors' arrest?
    A. 15-503
    B. 511-05-5350
    C. 363
    D. None of the above

118. What information concerning Mr. Connors should be placed in Box 30 of this report?
    A. White
    B. Asian
    C. Black
    D. None of the above

119. What information concerning Mr. Connors should be placed in Box 33 of this report?
    A. 6'
    B. Brown
    C. 600
    D. 195 pounds

120. With regard to Mr. Connors' arrest, whose name should be inserted in Box 21?
    A. John Halden
    B. Thurston Whitley
    C. Arthur Gladstone
    D. Timothy Russell

121. The name Mark E. Preston would be appropriately inserted into what box on a booking report prepared for Mr. Connors?
    A. Box 36
    B. Box 39
    C. Box 42
    D. None of the above

122. What information would be placed in Box 10 with regard to Mr. Connors' arraignment?
    A. 9-17-92
    B. 9-20-92
    C. 1:00 p.m.
    D. None of the above

123. All of the following are true with respect to the booking report prepared on Mr. Connors except
    A. 0, 1, 9-20-92, and B would be inserted in Boxes 28, 30, 29, and 31
    B. YES, Breston County District Court, 195 pounds, and HZ would respectively be inserted in Boxes 6, 11, 34, and 32
    C. F, 363, Conspiracy to distribute a controlled substance, and 508-27-4110 would be inserted in Boxes 5, 4, 7, and 27 respectively
    D. Both A and C

124. All of the following are true with respect to the booking report prepared on Mr. Connors' except
    A. HZ, black colored eagle tattooed on right forearm, 90-FORD-4-W-White/blue, and Humbolt Correctional would be inserted in Boxes 32, 37, 40, and 24, respectively
    B. Andrea Stevens would be inserted in Box 39
    C. Diabetic, N/A, Hand K Towing-679 E. Marston Place, Auburn, WA, and the name George Nichols would be inserted in Boxes 35, 22, 41, and 42, respectively
    D. All of the above are incorrect

125. What would be the appropriate report code used by the authorities to indicate Mr. Timothy Russell's relation to Mr. Connors?
    A. G
    B. M
    C. A
    D. None of the above

ANSWER SHEET TO PRACTICE EXAM I

1. (A) (B) (C) (D)
2. (A) (B) (C) (D)
3. (A) (B) (C) (D)
4. (A) (B) (C) (D)
5. (A) (B) (C) (D)
6. (A) (B) (C) (D)
7. (A) (B) (C) (D)
8. (A) (B) (C) (D)
9. (A) (B) (C) (D)
10. (A) (B) (C) (D)
11. (A) (B) (C) (D)
12. (A) (B) (C) (D)
13. (A) (B) (C) (D)
14. (A) (B) (C) (D)
15. (A) (B) (C) (D)
16. (A) (B) (C) (D)
17. (A) (B) (C) (D)
18. (A) (B) (C) (D)
19. (A) (B) (C) (D)
20. (A) (B) (C) (D)
21. (A) (B) (C) (D)
22. (A) (B) (C) (D)
23. (A) (B) (C) (D)
24. (A) (B) (C) (D)
25. (A) (B) (C) (D)
26. (A) (B) (C) (D)
27. (A) (B) (C) (D)
28. (A) (B) (C) (D)
29. (A) (B) (C) (D)
30. (A) (B) (C) (D)
31. (A) (B) (C) (D)

32. (A) (B) (C) (D)
33. (A) (B) (C) (D)
34. (A) (B) (C) (D)
35. (A) (B) (C) (D)
36. (A) (B) (C) (D)
37. (A) (B) (C) (D)
38. (A) (B) (C) (D)
39. (A) (B) (C) (D)
40. (A) (B) (C) (D)
41. (A) (B) (C) (D)
42. (A) (B) (C) (D)
43. (A) (B) (C) (D)
44. (A) (B) (C) (D)
45. (A) (B) (C) (D)
46. (A) (B) (C) (D)
47. (A) (B) (C) (D)
48. (A) (B) (C) (D)
49. (A) (B) (C) (D)
50. (A) (B) (C) (D)
51. (A) (B) (C) (D)
52. (A) (B) (C) (D)
53. (A) (B) (C) (D)
54. (A) (B) (C) (D)
55. (A) (B) (C) (D)
56. (A) (B) (C) (D)
57. (A) (B) (C) (D)
58. (A) (B) (C) (D)
59. (A) (B) (C) (D)
60. (A) (B) (C) (D)
61. (A) (B) (C) (D)
62. (A) (B) (C) (D)

63. (A) (B) (C) (D)
64. (A) (B) (C) (D)
65. (A) (B) (C) (D)
66. (A) (B) (C) (D)
67. (A) (B) (C) (D)
68. (A) (B) (C) (D)
69. (A) (B) (C) (D)
70. (A) (B) (C) (D)
71. (A) (B) (C) (D)
72. (A) (B) (C) (D)
73. (A) (B) (C) (D)
74. (A) (B) (C) (D)
75. (A) (B) (C) (D)
76. (A) (B) (C) (D)
77. (A) (B) (C) (D)
78. (A) (B) (C) (D)
79. (A) (B) (C) (D)
80. (A) (B) (C) (D)
81. (A) (B) (C) (D)
82. (A) (B) (C) (D)
83. (A) (B) (C) (D)
84. (A) (B) (C) (D)
85. (A) (B) (C) (D)
86. (A) (B) (C) (D)
87. (A) (B) (C) (D)
88. (A) (B) (C) (D)
89. (A) (B) (C) (D)
90. (A) (B) (C) (D)
91. (A) (B) (C) (D)
92. (A) (B) (C) (D)
93. (A) (B) (C) (D)

94. Ⓐ Ⓑ Ⓒ Ⓓ
95. Ⓐ Ⓑ Ⓒ Ⓓ
96. Ⓐ Ⓑ Ⓒ Ⓓ
97. Ⓐ Ⓑ Ⓒ Ⓓ
98. Ⓐ Ⓑ Ⓒ Ⓓ
99. Ⓐ Ⓑ Ⓒ Ⓓ
100. Ⓐ Ⓑ Ⓒ Ⓓ
101. Ⓐ Ⓑ Ⓒ Ⓓ
102. Ⓐ Ⓑ Ⓒ Ⓓ
103. Ⓐ Ⓑ Ⓒ Ⓓ
104. Ⓐ Ⓑ Ⓒ Ⓓ

105. Ⓐ Ⓑ Ⓒ Ⓓ
106. Ⓐ Ⓑ Ⓒ Ⓓ
107. Ⓐ Ⓑ Ⓒ Ⓓ
108. Ⓐ Ⓑ Ⓒ Ⓓ
109. Ⓐ Ⓑ Ⓒ Ⓓ
110. Ⓐ Ⓑ Ⓒ Ⓓ
111. Ⓐ Ⓑ Ⓒ Ⓓ
112. Ⓐ Ⓑ Ⓒ Ⓓ
113. Ⓐ Ⓑ Ⓒ Ⓓ
114. Ⓐ Ⓑ Ⓒ Ⓓ
115. Ⓐ Ⓑ Ⓒ Ⓓ

116. Ⓐ Ⓑ Ⓒ Ⓓ
117. Ⓐ Ⓑ Ⓒ Ⓓ
118. Ⓐ Ⓑ Ⓒ Ⓓ
119. Ⓐ Ⓑ Ⓒ Ⓓ
120. Ⓐ Ⓑ Ⓒ Ⓓ
121. Ⓐ Ⓑ Ⓒ Ⓓ
122. Ⓐ Ⓑ Ⓒ Ⓓ
123. Ⓐ Ⓑ Ⓒ Ⓓ
124. Ⓐ Ⓑ Ⓒ Ⓓ
125. Ⓐ Ⓑ Ⓒ Ⓓ

ANSWERS TO PRACTICE EXAM I

Refer to the composite sketches and files for any clarification on Questions 1 through 20.

1. *B.* Grand theft and first degree arson

2. *D.* Evan Ballantine

3. *A.* Suspect 1

4. *C.* Second degree malicious mischief

5. *B.* Roger Thorsen

6. *B.* Suspect 2

7. *C.* 5'7" and 135 pounds

8. *C.* Suspect 3

9. *A.* 2-13-69

10. *D.* Suspects 2 and 3

11. *D.* None of the above

12. *B.* Evan Ballantine

13. *D.* Roger Thorsen

14. *A.* Suspect 1

15. *B.* 205-11-7350

16. *C.* Bribery and first degree extortion

17. *D.* None of the above

18. *B.* Eyes: Hazel

19. *C.* 55-1101

20. *A.* 800-72-5953

21. *B.* The word *to* that follows the word *spread* should be spelled *too*, which is an adverb that indicates "in addition." *Percieved* is misspelled as well. It should be *perceived*. Remember the basic rule: *i* before *e* except after *c*.

22. *A.* Since *areas* is plural, it needs to be followed by *have been* instead of *has been*.

23. *A.* This statement is confusing due to a misplaced modifier. The statement would be better structured by placing *for* prior to *their parents*.

24. *B.* Affect is a verb that means "to act upon." *Effect* is a noun that means "something produced by an agency or cause."

25. *D.* This statement is grammatically correct in every way.

26. *B.* Elude means "to escape or avoid." *Allude* means "to refer to indirectly."

27. *C.* A comma should have been placed after *others*.

28. *B.* Labratory should be spelled *laboratory*.

29. *C.* Apostrophes need to be placed before *s* in *attorneys* to indicate possession (*attorney's*).

30. *A.* *They're* is an improperly used contraction meaning "they are." *Their* is also wrong since it is plural where singular is needed. Replacing *they're* with *his or her* would render the statement gramatically correct.

31. *D.* This statement is grammatically correct in every way.

32. *B.* The words *judgement* and *competant* are both misspelled. The correct spellings are *judgment* and *competent*.

33. *B.* The injuries sustained by the victim are not severe enough to constitute first degree assault. Second degree assault better defines these circumstances.

34. *B.* Even though third degree assault specifically mentions the involvement of a law enforcement authority, police officers are also people. Since Officer Beaumont's injury was substantial, the offense committed by Ms. Williams should be upgraded to the more serious charge of second degree assault.

35. *A.* The fact that the syringe tested negative for the virus is irrelevant. AIDS is a life-threatening illness, and Mr. Briggs used that threat against Mr. Evans in an attempt to escape. Therefore, Mr. Briggs should be charged with first degree assault as well as shoplifting.

36. *D.* Specifically, Ms. Patterson should be charged with first degree manslaughter, a Class B felony.

37. *C.* Mr. Matthews' actions would be considered reckless, especially with alcohol involved. Ms. Cummings' death should be treated as first degree manslaughter. Selection D is incorrect because no act committed by anyone in a state of intoxication is deemed less criminal as a result of his or her condition.

38. *C.* The key word in this story is *spontaneous*. Mrs. Bradford lacked premeditation in killing her husband. Consequently, it would be considered second degree murder instead of first degree murder.

39. *C.* Ms. Compton has committed second degree extortion, a Class C felony.

40. *D.* Even though Mr. Russell had implied the threat of physical harm to either the witness or his wife, it cannot be classified as either bribery or extortion because he did not ask to receive anything in the way of property or services. This is more along the lines of malicious harassment, which was not discussed in the narrative.

41. *A.* Since Ms. Waterhouse stood to gain a favor from a public servant because of the threat, she could be prosecuted for bribery.

42. *B.* Under the circumstances, Mr. Evans can be prosecuted for first degree extortion, which carries a maximum sentence of ten years in prison.

43. *B.* Selection A should include RCX 43.74.132 instead of RCX 38.12.012 because the Thunderbird can operate on a public highway. Selection C fails to account for failure to stop, which is RCX 43.21.075. Selection D lists the code RCX 48.21.075 that applies only to people in general; in this case, however, it is the driver who is intoxicated. Therefore, RCX 43.74.132 would be applicable.

44. *C.* Selection A should include RCX 48.14.017 instead of RCX 48.21.018 because the victim sustained only minor injuries. Selection B incorrectly substitutes RCX 43.76.312 for RCX 43.67.132. It was the actual vehicular assault (RCX 48.15.017) that caused the victim to suffer injuries. Selection D incorrectly substitutes RCX 48.21.075 for RCX 43.74.132. The driver was under the influence of an illegal substance.

45. *D.* Selection A is incorrect because RCX 48.15.017 (vehicular assault) did not occur. Instead, RCX 48.51.071 (leaving children unattended in a running vehicle) needs to be accounted for. These two codes can be easily mistaken if numbers are transposed. Selection B indicates Ms. Marshall as driving with a revoked or suspended license (RCX 38.23.047). The truth of the matter is that she was driving with an expired driver's license, which is covered by RCX 38.32.074. Selection C wrongly implies that Ms. Marshall did not stop for Officer Daniels to answer any questions (RCX 43.21.075). In fact, she did stop her vehicle but refused to answer Officer Daniels' question. Code RCX 43.21.057 would be applicable. Here again, care must be exercised not to accidentally transpose numbers, as that will result in two entirely different codes.

46. *D.* Decimals are used to separate the three components of a code. Selection D is the appropriate breakdown of the code in question.

47. *B.* Selection A is wrong for the reason that Mr. Heston was not intoxicated at the time of the incident. RCX 38.49.009 would better define this situation. Selection C is wrong because Mr. Heston did pull over immediately for Officer Wiess. RCX 43.21.075 would be an inappropriate citation. Selection D is wrong because we can assume Mr. Heston did have a valid driver's license since the reading did not mention otherwise. Therefore, RCX1 38.32.074 would not apply.

48. *A.* Selection B is wrong because Richard McCann did not commit vehicular assault (RCX 48.15.017). Selection C is wrong because RCX 43.74.132 (driving under the influence) would not apply.

    (*Note 1:* RCX 38.32.047 and RCX 38.23.047 mean basically the same thing. Either one would be considered correct.)

    (*Note 2:* Racing is considered to be reckless driving even if an accident does not result.)

49. *D.* All three selections (A, B, and C) correctly apply; however, they all fail to address RCX 48.21.018, vehicular homicide. Notice that A, B, and C are the same; only their order has been changed.

50. *A.* Selection B is incorrect in citing RCX 43.12.075 (failure to stop and provide identification to a police officer). Instead, RCX 43.21.057 should be applied, since the defendant refused to answer Officer Best's questions. Selection C is incorrect in citing RCX 38.47.071 because the certificate of ownership and registration were of no consequence. Selection D is wrong because RCX 38.23.074 (unauthorized persons driving a motor vehicle) was not an issue.

    (*Note:* Reckless driving could probably be thrown in as well; however, since it was not offered in any of the choices presented, this prospect must be overlooked.)

51. *C.* Only C (certificate of registration) is correct. The other choices were not included in the list of codes provided.

52. *A.* Kathy can be charged with allowing an unauthorized person to drive a motor vehicle (i.e., RCX 38.23.074). It can be assumed that she had a valid driver's license, but that really was not the issue since she was not driving the vehicle. Therefore, B cannot be considered. Selections C and D are inapplicable as well.

53. *B.* Since Kate was doing the driving, B would be the appropriate charge. The remainder of the selections are inapplicable.

54. *B.* Repetitious

55. *C.* Wisecracking

56. *D.* Disclose

57. *A.* Displacement

58. *C.* Disorder

59. *A.* Disdain

60. *D.* Intimidation

61. *D.* Purported

62. *B.* Word for word

63. *C.* Expert

64. *A.* Vague

65. *C.* Suffocated

66. *B.* According to the flow chart presented, only the U.S. Supreme Court can review a state supreme court decision.

67. *A.* Juvenile Court can appeal either directly to a trial court or to an intermediate appellate court.

68. *D.* Selection A refers to bankruptcy court. Selection C refers to the U.S. court of appeals, the federal circuit court of appeals, and the state supreme court.

69. *B.* Intent presupposes knowledge, which in a court of law must be proven by either direct or inferred evidence.

70. *D.* The observation described in the question dismisses the correlation of physical characteristics and criminal activity. Selection D properly summarizes this fact.

71. *A.* The reading is specific as to why a person is held or released after a preliminary hearing. Since there has been no presentation of direct evidence against the defendant, he should be released.

72. *D.* More often than not, citizens come into contact with the police over a traffic incident. The other selections given in this questions may or may not promote the desired effect. However, the manner in which a police officer handles a traffic incident leaves a lasting impression on those involved.

73. *B.* In most cases, violators pull off onto the shoulder of the road. You can see by the illustration that the implementation of Selection B would not provide a safety corridor for the officer.

　　Parking offset to the left would protect the officer from any oncoming traffic. Selection C accomplishes the same. Selection A offers the patrolman a good field of observation of both the driver and vehicle. This would not be the case if the officer were to pull up any closer to the violator in question.

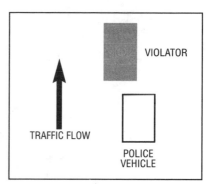

74. *D.* Selection C may be partially true, but D best encompasses what was meant by the passage. Most people see but do not actually observe or consciously register the actions and movements of people or objects, events, and surrounding circumstances.

75. *C.* Both A and B are basically one and the same and can be eliminated on those grounds. Selection C would be considered correct since most people will shoot high and to the right. Responding in this manner will lessen the possibility of being shot. Selection D is wrong because it would render the officer an easy target for the suspect.

76. *B.* By allowing bystanders in the immediate area of the crime, Officer Myers may have allowed evidence to become contaminated. The remaining choices fail to follow procedure as stated in the question.

77. *D.* Selections A and B are false on their own merit. Selection C may seem to be the correct choice; however, Officer Love should be waiting with the victim to lend medical assistance. "Severe facial lacerations" implies severe bleeding. Waiting for backup in order to give pursuit is a secondary consideration.

78. *A.* Officer laxity, rather than a lack of knowledge of proper procedure, is the prime reason for unpredicted violence to occur. Complacency must be avoided at all times. Selection B is not practical in the line of duty for a police officer. Selection C cannot be deduced from this reading. Selection D may seem correct; however, it is virtually impossible to eliminate all aspects of danger associated with an incident regardless of how closely procedures are followed. Some incidents are impossible to predict.

79. *B.* To determine what the percentage of the total annual caseload is crimes against property, the individual caseloads for each applicable crime must first be added together: (14 + 312 + 720 + 1320 + 674 + 32 + 62+ 520 = 3,654 cases involving crimes against property). This figure is then divided by the total number of all criminal cases handled for the year and then multiplied by 100 to express the number found as a percentage. Therefore,

$$\frac{3654 \text{ crimes against property cases}}{4968 \text{ total criminal cases handled}} \times 100 = 73.55$$

or approximately 74%.

80. *B.* Since the goal is to trim the homicide rate by 15% over a two-year period, this translates into a 7.5% annual reduction (i.e., 15% divided by 2 years = 7.5%). Therefore, since there were 42 murders for the year, 42 x .075 = 3.15, we can safely say the commission hopes for approximately four fewer murders per year. It is important to note that we should not round off to 3.0 because the .15 does represent a tangible amount that must be accounted for.

81. *A.* Forcible rape would constitute the second-highest number of man-hours used per case. Therefore, divide the number of forcible rape cases by the total annual caseload of all crimes and multiply the resulting number by 100 to express it as a percentage.

$$\frac{52 \text{ cases of forcible rape}}{4968 \text{ total cases handled for the year}} \times 100 = 1\%$$

82. *C.* Since 10,000 total offenses were reported, and according to the Crime Index aggravated assault accounts for 17% of the total cases, you should simply multiply 0.17 by 10,000 to get the answer, 1700.

83. *B.* First, it is necessary to figure how many seconds there are in one hour. Since there are 60 seconds per minute and 60 minutes per hour, there are 3600 seconds per hour. Then, just divide the time factor given for each crime into 3600 to arrive at the answer. Therefore:

3600 divided by 45 = 80 robberies
3600 divided by 10 = 360 burglaries
3600 divided by 27 = 133 aggravated assaults

84. *C.* Since it is known that 245 responses represents 92% of the total calls (i.e., 100%–8% = 92%), we can set up the following proportion to determine how many calls were received for the month altogether:

$$\frac{92}{100} = \frac{245}{X} \; ; \; 92X = 24,500 \; ; \; X = 266 \text{ calls}$$

85. *C.* When determining the average of test scores for an applicant, it is necessary to add all test scores together and divide by the number of tests taken. Therefore, if we know what the four previous test scores were, and the desired overall average, we can find the percent required for the last exam:

$$\frac{80\% + 82\% + 90\% + 87\% + X}{5} = 87\%$$

$$\frac{3.39 + X\%}{5} = 0.87$$

3.39 + X% = 4.35
X% = .96, X = 96%

86. *C.* Look at the two lengths provided and the bullet's trajectory as a right triangle. If we employ the Pythagorean Theorem, A^2 and B^2 can be represented as $(11'9")^2$ and $(22'6")^2$, respectively. Since we should convert to one unit of measure (we will use feet instead of inches to keep the calculations simple) the figures would then be $(11.75)^2$ and $(22.5)^2$. The bullet's trajectory is the unknown, which is represented by C^2. Therefore, $(11.75)^2 + (22.5)^2 = C^2$, and

$$138.1 + 506.25 = C^2$$
$$644.35 = C^2$$
$$25.38 = C$$

87. *A.* Here is another problem that can be looked upon as a right triangle. 15'6" and 17'3" can represent A^2 and B^2, respectively. When converting to equivalent units (i.e., feet), it would be $(15.5)^2$ and $(17.25)^2$. The distance between Points B and C can be represented as C^2. Therefore, according to the Pythagorean Theorem $(15.5)^2 + (17.25)^2 = C^2$, and

$$240.25 + 297.56 = C^2$$
$$537.81 = C^2$$
$$23.19 = C$$

88. *B.* If domestic filings were up 32% for the year, 132% = 231, and 100% = 100/132 x 231 = 175 cases. If the gain in juvenile filings was up 41% for the year, 141% = 163 and 100% = 100/141 x 163 = 115.6, or 116 cases.

89. *A.* Since we are being asked to determine the area of a circular search pattern, we simply use the geometric formula $(3.1416)R^2$. 15 feet is the radius of the area in question. Therefore, $(3.1416)(15 \text{ feet})^2 = X$ area in square feet, and

$$(3.1416)(225) = X$$
$$X = 706.86 \text{ square feet.}$$

90. *A.* Murder/homicide 1293 - 1015 = 278 additional cases

$$\frac{278 \text{ additional cases}}{1015 \text{ reference case load}} \text{ x } 100 = 27.39\% \text{ increase}$$

Forcible rape 1107–983 = 124 additional cases

$$\frac{124 \text{ additional cases}}{983 \text{ reference case load}} \text{ x } 100 = 12.6\% \text{ increase}$$

Larceny 35803 - 29601 = 6202 additional cases

$$\frac{6202 \text{ additional cases}}{29,601 \text{ reference case load}} \text{ x } 100 = 20.95\% \text{ increase}$$

Aggravated assault $23752-18900 = 4852$ extra cases

$$\frac{4852 \text{ additional cases}}{18,900 \text{ reference case load}} \times 100 = 25.67\% \text{ increase}$$

91. *C.* From the most recent figures (1990), men committed 15,906 homicides, while women committed 6953, which when divided (i.e., 15,906 divided by 6953) reflects a 2.29:1 relationship.

92. *B.* 3%. There were 44,919 crimes committed by female juveniles in 1990. 1349 of those cases constituted motor vehicle theft. To determine the annual caseload percentage for this crime, we simply divide 1349 by 44,919 and then multiply the quotient by 100. The answer is 3%.

93. *A.* Adult male. $49,192-46,702 = 2,490$

$$\frac{2490}{49,192} \times 100 = 5\% \text{ decrease in robbery cases for adult males}$$

$2,950 - 2893 = 57$

$$\frac{57}{2950} \times 100 = 2\% \text{ decrease in robbery cases for juvenile males}$$

$23,471 - 23,405 = 66$

$$\frac{66}{23,471} \times 100 = 0.3\% \text{ decrease in robbery cases for adult females}$$

$2740-2090 = 650$

$$\frac{650}{2090} \times 100 = 31\% \text{ increase in robbery for juvenile females}$$

94. *D.* Selections A, B, and C are very objective questions that should not elicit guilty feelings from either parent nor will it indicate that the police suspect the parent of any wrongdoing. Selection D however, conveys both of these biases.

95. *C.* Sentence 1 is obviously first in the report and Sentence 3 must be last, and only C accounts for this particular order. All other selections can be eliminated without further regard.

96. *B.* It can be reasonably assumed that a description of the assignment would first be mentioned in the activity log as a point of reference and the end result of this activity was that the motorcyclist received the citation. These facts would preclude A and C. Between B and D, it would have to be decided which came first, Sentence 2 or Sentence 5. Obviously, Sentence 2 would have to happen before the officer could determine that the license had expired. Therefore, B is the correct choice.

97. *D.* Sentence 3 is obviously the event that initiated the filing of the missing persons report. This fact alone precludes A and B. Between C and D, it will have to be determined whether Sentence 5 occurred before Sentence 1 or *vice versa*. Since Officer Johnson must learn where the party was before he can interview Mr. McNeil, the host, D would therefore be selected as the correct choice.

98. *A.* In this question, the knowledge that Sentence 3 and Sentence 1 happened first and last does not help in narrowing the options. However, it should be evident that the officer involved would notify headquarters of the situation and request backup to gain better control of the situation and crowd. This leaves only A as correct.

99. *B.* SMITH: First 5 letters of last name

J: First letter of first name

D: First letter of middle name

100–56 = 44: Birth year calculation

9: Check digit (could be any single number)

P: Month of birth

Z: Day of birth

100. *A.* HALVO: First 5 letters of last name

J: First letter of first name

L: First letter of middle name

100–75 = 25: Birth year calculation

1: Check digit (any single number)

H: Month of birth

P: Day of birth

101. *D.* BARTE: First 5 letters of last name

V: First letter of first name

J: First letter of middle name

100–63 = 37: Birth year calculation

8: Check digit (could be any single digit)

L: Month of birth

4: Day of birth

102. *B.* Quarterly, because there are four colors that identify the months of the year.

103. *C.* Since the reading mentioned that fleet vehicles have to renew registration only once a year, in October, it can be categorized as an annual system.

104. *D.* Since a Buick LeSabre is a passenger vehicle, red would correctly represent the month in question. The expiration tab year would correctly be identified as 1994. Selection C would have been correct had the vehicle been anything other than a passenger vehicle or truck (except a government-exempt or fleet-exempt vehicle).

105. *D.* Mr. Turner is driving a government vehicle, which is exempt from tab and registration fees.

106. *B.* Northeast

107. *C.* Northwest

108. *D.* Selection A is incorrect because the officer would be driving the wrong direction on a one-way street at two points: north on 17th Avenue and east on Evans Street. Selection B is incorrect, because after the route takes the officer in question north on Citrus Avenue and then east on Foster, which is fine up to that point, driving north on 37th Avenue runs against the traffic flow. Selection C is correct up to the point the officer turned east on Evans Street. Evans is a one-way street that directs traffic west.

109. *C.* Selection A is incorrect because the officer will be going against traffic flow on both 10th Avenue and 46th Avenue. Selection B is incorrect because the officer cannot legally go east on Constance. Selection D would place the officer at 42nd Avenue and Foster, not 46th Avenue and Foster as specified in the question.

110. *A.* Selection B is incorrect because Baker Street dead ends at Buckner Park. Selection C is a potential route that could be taken to get to the crime scenes however, it takes the officer a little out of the way in comparison with A. Selection D would place Officer White at a destination not included in the map provided.

111. *D.* Following the directions given would place both officers at 23rd Avenue and Parker Street, directly south of Precinct headquarters.

112. *C.* Selection A is not possible because 46th Avenue cannot be crossed due to road repairs. Selection B is incorrect for the same reason. Selection D is not possible because Carrol Street is closed at that hour and the intersection of Borden Avenue and Farmington is closed as well.

113. *B.* This can seem like a confusing question; however, information common among witnesses is justifiable reason to believe that what is told to investigators is accurate. The general consensus is that the suspect is a Caucasian male who is 511" and weighs between 175 and 180 pounds; he has light-colored hair and blue eyes. The witness who comes closest to describing the suspect in this manner is Mrs. Williams. Each detail she gave is verified by one or more other witnesses.

114. *B.* When a driver's license is lenticulated, it renders it difficult, if not impossible, to alter any information without the alterations being obvious. The other selections are either ridiculous or simply not true.

115. *B.* Both A and D enhance visibility, which tends to discourage robbery. Selection C avoids establishing patterns that criminals can take advantage of. Selection B however, will do nothing in itself to discourage robbery. On the other hand, if this fact is advertised or made known, it may alleviate the incentive to commit the crime.

116. *C.* Selection C will tend to close skin pores, thereby leaving a minimal amount of residue on anything touched. During warmer weather, people tend to perspire more, and consequently more readily identifiable prints will be left on most surfaces.

117. *D.* A booking report number had not been specifically given in the reading. Selection A represents an arrest report number for Mr. Russell.

118. *D.* Reference Code Number 1 should be used, according to the report. Selection A is a correct description; however, it is procedurally wrong to state the fact this way since applicable booking codes have been provided.

119. *C.* The report specifically mentions that height must be expressed as a three digit number expressing both feet and inches. Therefore, C is the correct choice.

120. *B.* Thurston Whitley was Mr. Connors' probation officer. Selection A is the arresting officer involved.

121. *A.* This name is an alias used by Mr. Connors. Box 36 would be the correct place for this information.

122. *D.* Selection C is correct with respect to the appointed time; however, the booking report makes specific reference to the fact that all time entries must be expressed in military form. Therefore, 1300 hours would be the correct information to insert in Box 10.

123. *D.* Selection A is incorrect in placing 9-20-92 in Box 29. This would reflect Mr. Connors' arraignment date, not his date of birth. Mr. Connors' age was given to be 37. Selection C is incorrect in the charges filed against Mr. Connors. Instead this lists what was filed against Mr. Russell. Both manufacture of and intent to deliver a controlled substance, plus unlawful possession of a firearm by a felon, should be placed in Box 7.

124. D. Even though the description is correct, Selection A is incorrect because it does not use the code D-3 to establish the location of the scar or peculiarity. Selection B is incomplete. Andrea Stevens' relation to Mr. Connors, home address and home phone number should be completed since the information is available. Selection C incorrectly states Hand K's impoundment yard as being located at 679 E. Marston Place; this is the address where Mr. Connors is employed. The correct insertion made into Box 41 is Hand K Towing, 4357 H Street, Auburn, WA.

125. D. Mr. Connors made reference to Mr. Russell as a friend. Mr. Russell was, in fact, arrested for conspiracy to distribute a controlled substance at the same time Mr. Connors was arrested. Therefore, from the authorities' perspective, Mr. Timothy Russell would be considered an accomplice. The code O was not offered as an option for the question.

TEST RATINGS ARE AS FOLLOWS:
    120–125 correct, EXCELLENT
    113–119 correct, VERY GOOD
    106–112 correct, GOOD
    100–105 correct, FAIR
    99 or fewer correct, UNSATISFACTORY

Go back to each question you missed and determine if the question was just misinterpreted for one reason or another, or if your response reflects a weakness in subject matter. If it is a matter of misinterpretation, try reading the question more slowly while paying particular attention to key words such as *not, least, except,* or *without.* If, on the other hand, you determine a weakness in a certain area, do not despair. That is what this study guide is for: to identify any area of weakness before you take the actual exam. Reread the material on the area of concern in this study guide. If you still feel a need for supplemental material, your local library is an excellent source.

Practice Examination II

THE TIME ALLOWED for the entire examination is $2^1/_2$ hours.

Directions: Each question has four answers, lettered A, B, C, and D. Choose the best answer and then, on the answer sheet provided on page 233 (which you can remove from the book), find the corresponding question number and darken with a soft pencil the circle corresponding to the answer you have selected.

Questions 1–8 are based on the sketch provided below. Study it for 3 minutes; do not exceed the time allowed. If you do, you will forfeit the true sense of how an exam is actually conducted. When your time is up, turn to the questions provided without making further reference to the picture just studied.

Answer Questions 1 through 8 on the basis of the sketch just studied. *DO NOT REFER TO THE PICTURE.*

1. What is the numerical address of the apartment complex nearest to the person walking on the sidewalk?
   A. 75751
   B. 75715
   C. 75709
   D. 75705

2. The street depicted in the sketch is a
   A. Two lane, one-way street
   B. Single lane, one-way street
   C. Two-way street
   D. There were no indications in the sketch to make such distinctions

3. How many people were seen in the sketch?
   A. 2
   B. 3
   C. 4
   D. 5

4. A window-mounted portable air conditioning unit was shown in the sketch as belonging to an apartment tenant. What floor of the apartment complex did this tenant reside on?
   A. Second
   B. Third
   C. Fourth
   D. Fifth

5. Judging by one of the vehicles parked in front of the apartment building, what kind of activity was apparently taking place?
   A. Someone was moving.
   B. A family was preparing to go on a picnic.
   C. Property theft was being committed.
   D. Someone was rendering roadside assistance to a stalled vehicle.

6. What kind of object is seen on the luggage rack of the vehicle referred to in the previous question?
   A. Rocking chair
   B. TV set
   C. Camping paraphernalia
   D. Chair

7. What was the only license number discernable among the parked cars shown in the sketch?
   A. LMX 430
   B. BEL 678
   C. XLM 403
   D. KNT 471

8. All of the following statements are true with respect to the vehicle being driven in the sketch except
    A. The license plate number is BLE 768.
    B. It is a four-door passenger vehicle carrying two passengers and the driver.
    C. The front portion of the vehicle is not discernable in the sketch.
    D. It was headed in the right direction on a one-way street.

Study the narrative below for 5 minutes. Do not exceed the time allowed; if you do, you will forfeit the true sense of how an exam is actually conducted. When your time is up, turn to the questions provided without making further reference to this reading.

A JUDICIAL SUMMARY OF A CRIMINAL CASE IN SUPERIOR COURT

Basically, each municipality has its own police department, which responds to calls within its jurisdiction. Unincorporated areas are usually served by some other agency or multijurisdictional law-enforcement task force. Criminal cases begin when the police are called to respond to an incident. Typically, an officer travels to the crime scene and fills out an incident report that describes the circumstances involved and lists the names and addresses of prospective witnesses. This incident report is then filed with the department and subsequently forwarded to the appropriate detective division responsible for investigating that type of crime. Detectives formalize the process by taking written statements from any witnesses, obtaining evidence, and writing a report detailing the known facts of the case. This information is then given to the prosecuting attorney. A filing unit clerk logs the case in and assigns a case number to it. At this point, a senior deputy prosecuting attorney will either approve the filing of formal charges or move to dismiss. If the senior deputy feels that sufficient evidence exists to prosecute the crime successfully, he or she pursues the case. Court clerks type the formal documentation required for the senior deputy's final approval. After approval, the documentation is given to a legal desk clerk who assigns a superior court case number as a permanent record. After it has been signed by an appropriate magistrate, the compiled paperwork is then processed by the Information and Records Department.

A defendant must be identified before charges are formally filed. Custody is not at issue here. The defendant may have already been arrested and placed in custody for the crime, or he or she may remain at large; identification is the important issue.

Once the person in question is arrested and subsequently taken to jail, he or she has the right to appear before a judge within twenty-four hours to seek a release. If a judge is reasonably assured that the defendant will honor a promise to return for the hearing, he or she is released without bail or, in other words, on personal recognizance. If, on the other hand, a defendant has a dangerous criminal history, he or she may be asked to post significant bail. In either case, the presiding magistrate must render a decision concerning the defendant's disposition by 2:00 p.m.

The Administrative Recognizance Release Program (ARRP) is a fairly recent innovation that attempts to streamline this process. If a suspect is determined to be nonviolent and has demonstrated past reliability, he or she may be released on personal recognizance prior to the hearing. If the bond set by the magistrate cannot be met by the defendant, he or she has the right to petition the court for a reduction of bail.

Once charges have been formally filed, the defendant is summoned to appear for arraignment. The arraignment is basically a formal hearing of the charges levied against the defendant. At the arraignment, it is explained that an attorney is needed (if one has not already been retained) and if the defendant cannot afford one, a court-appointed defense attorney is made available at state expense.

Within two weeks of this hearing, the defendant has to appear for another hearing called an *omnibus*. It is at this point that a plea is entered and a trial date is formally set. During the course of this hearing, both the defense attorney and the prosecuting attorney must exchange information pertinent to the case. In legal parlance, this is referred to as "discovery"; it allows all parties concerned equal access to information for formal case preparation.

A defendant who wishes to plead guilty in exchange for a lesser charge or dismissal of certain counts (plea bargaining) must do so prior to or during the omnibus hearing. If the judge accepts the plea, the defendant waives the right to trial and is convicted of the lesser charges set by the prosecution. If plea bargaining is not utilized and the defendant pleads not guilty and is in custody, a trial date must be set within sixty days of arraignment. If the defendant has been released pending trial, the trial date must be established within ninety days. These time limits preserve the defendant's right to a speedy trial. While waiting for the trial, the deputy prosecutor assigned to the case issues subpoenas for any witnesses. These subpoenas state specifically when and where witnesses must appear.

Pretrial hearings may also be required to determine whether certain incriminating evidence, offered voluntarily by the defendant after being duly informed of his or her constitutional rights, can be used by the prosecution. Court Rule 3.5 establishes that a hearing ("3.5 hearing") must be held to determine the admissibility of such evidence.

Another form of pretrial hearing occurs when a defendant attempts to prove that the evidence against him or her was seized illegally and is thus inadmissible in court. If the constitutional rights of the defendant were violated, the suppression hearing rules in favor of the defendant.

Prior to the actual trial date, either the defense or the prosecution may ask to have the trial delayed (or "continued") for various reasons. If either party wishes to avoid a deferment, a presiding judge determines if it is warranted. If there are sufficient grounds to justify it, everyone who has been subpoenaed is informed of the new place and time of the trial. Otherwise, the case is heard as scheduled.

The court may have to hear several cases in a day; however, criminal cases usually take precedence over civil cases and are assigned accordingly. Once the trial actually begins, the defendant must choose whether to have a jury hear the case or to waive that right. If the defendant prefers the jury trial, the attorneys conduct jury selection, referred to as *"voir dire."* Prospective jurors are interviewed by both counsels and accepted or eliminated depending on the attitudes they exhibit toward the defendant. At the close of jury selection, the trial begins. Attorneys make opening statements and call witnesses to testify under oath about what they know of the defendant and their connection to the crime involved. Witnesses are allowed to be cross-examined by opposing counsel.

When this phase of the trial has ended, the defendant may elect to take the stand to further defend him or herself. The state has the right to call rebuttal witnesses at the completion of such testimony. The jury is then instructed by the judge and both attorneys about what the law requires and what their duty involves. Final statements are rendered first by the prosecutor, then by the defense before deliberations begin.

A unanimous decision by jurors is required to convict the defendant. A jury that fails to agree is referred to as a "hung jury." Depending on state discretion, the case will either be dismissed or retried at a later date. Hung juries are usually the consequence of insufficient evidence. The state must prove its charge beyond a reasonable doubt to effect a conviction. If a conviction is handed down in Superior Court, a judge issues a sentence approximately four to six weeks later. State sentencing guidelines normally dictate that the punishment be appropriate for the crime. This can come either in the form of serving time in a state prison or as probation.

Answer Questions 9 through 23 on the basis of the narrative just studied. *DO NOT REFER TO THE READING.*

9. Which of the following correctly identifies the title of the passage?
   A. A Summary of Criminal Case Proceedings in Superior Court
   B. A Judicial Review of Criminal Cases in Superior Court
   C. A Judicial Summary of A Criminal Case in Superior Court
   D. A Judicial Review of Civil Cases in District Court

10. What kind of crimes were specifically addressed within the context of the reading?
    A. Felonies
    B. Misdemeanors
    C. Traffic citations
    D. None of the above

11. According to the reading, what is another term for jury selection?
    A. *Voir dire*
    B. Preliminary hearing
    C. Omnibus
    D. Probationary discretion

12. The acronym ARRP was explained in the narrative as meaning?
    A. Assessment for Responsible Release Program
    B. Administrative Recognizance Release Program
    C. Accountability Recognizance Release Program
    D. None of the above

13. According to the reading, plca bargaining arrangements must be made prior to or during which event in the judicial process?
    A. Pretrial hearing
    B. Preliminary hearing
    C. Omnibus hearing
    D. 3.5 hearing

14. If a defendant is currently in jail and defense counsel enters a not guilty plea at arraignment, how long does the court technically have to set a trial date?
    A. 24 hours
    B. $3^1/_2$ days
    C. 60 days
    D. 90 days

15. According to the reading, how long does a magistrate have to sentence a person convicted in Superior Court?
    A. 60 days
    B. 90 days
    C. 4 to 6 weeks
    D. None of the above

16. What was the legal term given that describes the exchange of information pertinent to the case between defense and prosecution attorneys?

    A. Discovery

    B. *Voir dire*

    C. Omnibus

    D. Plea bargaining

17. What was mentioned within the narrative to be of primary importance prior to charges being formally filed?

    A. Investigators furnish complete details of the crime involved

    B. Defendant identification

    C. An appropriate magistrate signature

    D. The assignment of a court case number for information and records

18. How many jurors must reach a guilty verdict before a person can be convicted in Superior Court?

    A. A simple majority

    B. A two-thirds majority

    C. A three-quarters majority

    D. It must be a unanimous decision

19. If a defendant was well aware of his or her constitutional rights and offered authorities a confession (incriminating evidence) and then later decided that the confession should not be used, which of the following hearings determines admissibility of such evidence in Superior Court?

    A. Omnibus hearing

    B. Plea-bargaining hearing

    C. 3.5 hearing

    D. Arraignment hearing

20. According to the narrative, what is another term for released without bail?

    A. Personal recognizance

    B. Probation

    C. *Voir dire*

    D. Court rule 3.5

21. All of the following statements from the reading are true except

    A. The state must prove its charges beyond a reasonable doubt before a person can be convicted in Superior Court.

    B. Magistrate precedence normally dictates the punishment appropriate for the crime.

    C. Another term for a delayed trial is "continued."

    D. Final statements for a trial are rendered first by the prosecuting attorney.

22. After the filing unit clerk logs in the case and assigns a case number to it, who was mentioned as having discretion at this point to either file formal charges against the defendant or drop the case?

    A. Superior Court magistrate

    B. Information and records department

    C. Senior deputy prosecuting attorney

    D. Superior Court clerk

23. What kind of hearing was said to be held in the event that there is some question about the legality of evidence seizure and possible infringement of a defendant's constitutional rights?
    A. Omnibus hearing
    B. Preliminary hearing
    C. Deferment hearing
    D. Suppression hearing

Answer Questions 24 through 26 on the basis of the reading given below:

Sergeant Bloomingthal was told by a joint steering committee of community blockwatch leaders that a rash of crime had recently been affecting participating neighborhoods. Specifically, Meadowlark Estates, on Humbolt Avenue and 7th Street, had seen an increase in vehicular prowling. Farmington Community Club, located on Elmhurst Boulevard and Crescent, had experienced an increase in residential burglaries. Carver Center Apartments, on Bridgeview Lane and Center Road, had seen a higher incidence of malicious mischief, and the Port Herrington Center for the Disabled, at Wilmont and Chester Boulevard, had seen a rise in petty larceny. The participants at the meeting also claimed that vehicular prowling and larceny seemed to occur more often on weekends between 8:30 p.m. and 1:30 a.m. and again between 12:30 and 6:30 p.m. Malicious mischief and residential burglary seemed to occur more often on weekdays between 6:30 and 10:30 p.m. and between 8:00 and 11:30 p.m.

24. If Sergeant Bloomingthal is in charge of patrol assignments, which of the following actions would most likely reduce the incidence of residential burglary?
    A. Assign additional patrols to Crescent Street and Elmhurst Boulevard Monday through Friday between 6:30 and 10:30 p.m.
    B. Assign additional patrols to Elmhurst and Wilmont Monday through Friday between 8:00 and 11:30 p.m.
    C. Assign additional patrols to Elmhurst and Crescent on Saturday and Sunday between 8:30 p.m. and 1:30 a.m.
    D. Assign additional patrols to Crescent and Elmhurst Boulevard Monday through Friday between 8:00 p.m. and 11:30 p.m.

25. Assuming Sergeant Bloomingthal wanted to reduce the incidence of malicious mischief in the area of concern, it would probably prove most effective to
    A. Assign additional patrols to Wilmont and Chester Monday through Friday between 6:30 and 10:30 p.m.
    B. Assign additional patrols to Bridgeview Lane and Center Road Saturday and Sunday between 12:30 and 6:30 p.m.
    C. Assign additional patrols to Center Road and Bridgeview Lane Monday through Friday between 6:30 and 10:30 p.m.
    D. Assign additional patrols to 7th Street and Humbolt Avenue Saturday and Sunday between 8:30 p.m. and 1:30 a.m.

26. All of the following statements are true except
    A. Additional patrols on Chester Boulevard and Wilmont on Saturday and Sunday between 12:30 and 6:30 p.m. would most likely reduce the incidence of petty larceny.
    B. Additional patrols on 7th Street and Humbolt Avenue on Saturday and Sunday between 8:30 p.m. and 1:30 a.m. would most likely reduce the incidence of malicious mischief.
    C. Additional patrols in Meadowlake Estates on Saturday and Sunday between 8:30 p.m. and 1:30 a.m. would most likely reduce the incidence of vehicular prowling.
    D. The incidence of residential burglary and malicious mischief would most likely remain unchanged by assigning extra patrols to work during the weekends.

27. Officer John McDonald has been deployed to conduct a secondary search of a five-block area for someone who had attempted to rape a woman at knifepoint. An alert neighbor heard the screams for help and managed to scare off the perpetrator before any harm came to the victim. Without any physical description leads, which of the following observations made by the officer would warrant sufficient suspicion to stop a subject and conduct a field interview?
    A. A man jogging in tandem with his leashed dog
    B. A male juvenile breathing heavily from pedaling a bicycle
    C. A male delivery person wearing shoes that are somewhat muddy
    D. A man dressed in a business suit with ruffled hair

28. The use of emergency lights and a siren in responding to a call is principally a matter of common sense. Which of the factors given below would be the least important consideration in the decision to implement the use of sirens and lights?
    A. Type of crime being responded to
    B. Road conditions in inclement weather
    C. Proximity to the scene of the crime
    D. Amount of traffic congestion encountered

29. Why are silent alarms considered more dangerous for a police officer to handle than audible alarms?
    A. Suspects can hear approaching sirens and prepare to resist or, worse, to directly assault the officer involved.
    B. It is almost impossible to sneak up on a suspect in complete silence so the element of surprise is unequivocally relinquished.
    C. Suspects are more prone to violence when surprised by an officer.
    D. Officers respond with the idea that complete surprise is in their corner and consequently may fail to exercise the degree of caution that would otherwise be used.

30. You respond to the scene of a burglary that has just occurred inside an office/warehouse. Considering the short response time involved, you and your partner have strong reason to believe the suspect(s) is/are still inside. Procedure dictates that additional assistance be called for a thorough building search. While you wait for backup, what would be the best way for you and your partner to conduct surveillance of the building's exterior?
    A. One officer should guard the entrance to the building while the other covers a rear exit.
    B. One officer should go inside the building while the other remains in the patrol vehicle to monitor communications.
    C. One officer should go to the left rear flank of the building while the other covers the right rear flank.
    D. One officer should go to one corner of the building while the other positions him or herself diagonally opposite.

31. Officer Bill Mason was transporting a prisoner to the station house for processing when he observed the vehicle ahead of him being driven in a flagrantly negligent manner. As the only law enforcement officer in the area, what should Officer Mason do?

    A. Allow the incident to pass since his primary duty is to transport the person he already has in custody to the station house

    B. Pull the violator over and issue an oral warning before continuing on

    C. Pull the violator over and issue a citation for the infraction before continuing on

    D. Pull the violator over and effect a custodial arrest, and then have backup transport the individual to the station for booking

32. Many state legislatures have changed laws in an effort to decriminalize minor traffic offenses while making no change for the more serious offenses. All of the following support this action except

    A. Such changes may reduce the traffic warrant backlog by offering alternative penalties.

    B. Court-issued civil penalties and potential jail time are viewed by law enforcement officials as being a comparable deterrent.

    C. The time spent in court by police officers will be significantly reduced as a result of changing the hearing procedures.

    D. Both A and C would be considered the exceptions.

33. Canine patrol units can serve as an effective way to arrest a suspect who is attempting to flee the scene of a crime. Success in utilizing such a tool depends largely on the degree to which officers can contain the suspect and prevent the crime scene from becoming contaminated with scent other than that of the suspect. Taking these two points into consideration, in which of the following circumstances would it be considered appropriate to use a patrol dog?

    A. A local high school football game that necessitates crowd control

    B. A man who takes a couple of hostages at gunpoint and then barricades himself and the hostages in an office storeroom

    C. A juvenile, suspected of burglarizing a residence, who is still believed by authorities to be within a 5- to 6-block radius

    D. A situation that involves the exchange of gunfire at a vacant warehouse between a person suspected of robbery and the authorities

34. When police departments rely on a witness to identify a file photo of a suspected person, often eight to ten photos of other people similar in appearance to the person in question will be presented as a photo montage to the witness. What is the single most important reason for doing this?

    A. It establishes credibility on the witness's part if the suspect is pointed out.

    B. It helps to suggest what kind of criminal profile is being sought by the department.

    C. It alleviates a witness's fear of mistaken identity.

    D. It insures witness privacy.

35. When detectives intend to interrogate a criminal suspect, they normally take the suspect to a relatively small room that contains only a desk and a few chairs. The room is unremarkable; nothing adorns the walls, there is a conspicuous absence of windows and phones, and only the suspect and the person(s) conducting the interrogation are allowed in the room. What is the most compelling reason for interrogating a suspect in this manner?

    A. It warns the suspect of the conditions to expect once convicted.

    B. It makes the suspect feel intimidated or insignificant.

    C. It avoids distractions and helps to gain control or authority over the suspect.

    D. It allows an interrogator to use whatever force is necessary to get a confession, without interference.

36. Fingerprints can serve as crucial evidence in an investigation. Which of the surfaces given below would yield the most definitive, high-quality print?
    A. Glass
    B. Paper
    C. Unfinished wood
    D. Brick

Answer Questions 37 through 39 on the basis of the passage given below:

Evidence is essentially a means of proof or the establishment of facts in a trial. Evidence may be manifested in trial in one of several forms. According to *Black's Law Dictionary*:

Direct evidence is a form of testimony from a witness who actually saw, heard, or touched the subject of interrogation.

Opinion evidence is a form of testimony from a witness describing what he or she thinks, believes, or infers in regard to facts in dispute, as distinguished from his or her personal knowledge of the facts themselves.

Circumstantial evidence is a form of testimony not based on actual personal knowledge or observation of the facts in controversy, but of other facts from which deductions are drawn showing indirectly the facts sought to be proved.

Real evidence are objects or items furnished for view or inspection, as distinguished from a description furnished by a witness.

37. During a murder trial, a firearms identification expert testified that the ballistics of the .44-caliber revolver recovered from the defendant at the time of arrest matched the bullet recovered from the victim's body. Additionally, the medical examiner testified that this same bullet was the cause of the victim's death. What form of evidence would both of these testimonies be considered?
    A. Direct evidence
    B. Opinion evidence
    C. Circumstantial evidence
    D. Real evidence

38. The .44-caliber bullet recovered from the body of the victim described in the previous question would be considered what form of evidence?
    A. Direct evidence
    B. Opinion evidence
    C. Circumstantial evidence
    D. Real evidence

39. A second witness testified that she did not hear any gun shots per se but she did corroborate with the first witness that the defendant was seen running down Main Street from the murder scene shortly after 10 p.m. According to the reading, this form of testimony would best be considered as:
    A. Direct evidence
    B. Opinion evidence
    C. Circumstantial evidence
    D. Real evidence

40. While Officer Sloan was conducting patrol on his assigned beat, directions issued by a superior officer over the portable radio unit were jumbled by electronic interference. If Officer Sloan did not fully understand the message, what should his response appropriately be?
    A. Spare himself the embarrassment of having the message repeated, continue with his original duty, and ask about it later.
    B. Try to interpret what parts were understood and act on that information as best as possible.
    C. Contact someone else on the force and inquire what was meant.
    D. Request to have the message repeated because of the interference.

41. Officer Beth Hopkins is searching for a shoplifting suspect among a crowd of people shopping in a mall. The store manager gave Officer Hopkins the following physical description:

    Female, approximately 30 years old, brown hair and green eyes, 6'2", 145 pounds, wearing a white jacket and denim jeans, and smoking a cigarette. Which part of this description would best aid Officer Hopkins in spotting and subsequently apprehending the suspect in question?
    A. The suspect's age
    B. The clothing worn by the suspect
    C. The height and weight of the suspect
    D. The fact that the suspect may be a chain smoker

42. Officer Bradshaw (a one-officer primary unit) pulled over a suspect van wanted in connection with a felony. Which of the following actions would be considered most appropriate in clearing the suspect vehicle?
    A. Walk up to the driver door and request identification from the driver
    B. Move along the passenger side of the vehicle in a crouched position, take a quick peek through the window to assess the number of occupants present, and then command everyone to get out of the vehicle
    C. After the driver removes himself from the vehicle, conduct a pat-down search and arrest of the suspect to the rear of the vehicle
    D. Call for backup and wait for assistance before attempting to clear the suspect vehicle

43. When Officer Daryl Sutton was within a block of where someone had reported seeing a vehicular prowler canvassing the neighborhood around 10 p.m., he shut off the patrol vehicle's headlights and stopped short of the location by using the emergency brake. When the police car was at a complete stop, the engine was then turned off. This means of approach in responding to a nighttime prowler call would be considered
    A. Proper, because every effort was made by the officer to minimize the possibility of alerting the suspect to his presence
    B. Improper, because a parking brake can be noisy and is not usually used as a means of stopping a police vehicle
    C. Proper, because he is better able to see any people or suspicious vehicles leaving the immediate vicinity
    D. Improper, because driving any distance without headlights during the evening invites a potential accident

44. Which of the following alternatives would be considered the most effective way for police to suppress criminal activity in general?

    A. Educate the public as a whole and seek citizen cooperation

    B. Conduct patrol tours in a systematically unsystematic manner

    C. Have police officers become fully aware of their jurisdictional boundaries and alternate routes (i.e., shortcuts) which can significantly reduce response time

    D. Aggressively patrol neighborhoods that are known to be problem areas

45. While walking his beat, Officer Dunkin observes a small group of youths inside the lobby of a public transit building that should have been locked for the evening. Without seeing any evidence of breaking and entering, he orders the youths to leave and radios dispatch to alert the proper authorities to secure the building. All but one of the youths comply with the officer's demands. At this point, he places the noncompliant individual under arrest for first degree criminal trespass—a gross misdemeanor. On the way to the parked patrol vehicle, the arrestee calls on his friends for assistance. If the arrestee's cohorts approach the officer in a manner that seems threatening, what would his best reaction to the situation be?

    A. Call for backup and wait out the incident

    B. Pull out his revolver and threaten to shoot the first person who moves any closer

    C. Release the prisoner

    D. Tell them they are making the biggest mistake of their lives

46. You are working traffic enforcement at a busy intersection, and you witness two people emerge armed from a credit union adjacent to your post. They run toward a vehicle being driven by an accomplice to effect escape. What would be your best reaction to this situation?

    A. Draw your weapon and order the suspects to freeze

    B. Run into the credit union to assess what had been taken

    C. Get a physical description of the suspects and their vehicle, then notify dispatch

    D. Attempt to maneuver in front of the vehicle and confront the suspects directly

47. Every police department has a bulletin board in the squadroom or elsewhere in the station house that posts information about wanted criminals, problems, law changes, crime analysis reports, etc. What is the most likely reason for a posted bulletin, supervisory order, or policy change to be rescinded?

    A. The posting date is old.

    B. It conflicts with a notice issued later.

    C. It is not readily accepted by most rank and file officers.

    D. It undermines the effectiveness of the department as a whole and is therefore ignored by most officers.

48. Officer Nichols is following a late-model Chevrolet pickup that has a broken taillight. Both vehicles are in the middle lane of Interstate 12, which is crowded with commuters attempting to get home. Which of the following would be considered the most appropriate action for Officer Nichols to take?

    A. Tap his brakes to indicate to the vehicle behind him that he intended to slow to a stop, and then issue the driver of the pickup a ticket for the infraction

    B. Activate his emergency lights and siren and attempt to pull the driver of the truck over to the shoulder of the road, where it would be relatively safe to issue a notice of infraction

    C. Follow the vehicle regardless of how far it may go, until it takes an exit ramp off the highway, and then pull the driver over to the side of the road and issue a ticket.

    D. Allow the vehicle to pass without issuing a ticket

49. When a building is being methodically searched for a suspect, what is the most probable reason all officers enter and exit the building at the same location?
    A. This method lessens the degree of scent contamination for a given area and enhances success for K-9 apprehension.
    B. It precludes those areas from serving as potential escape routes.
    C. It prevents officers leaving the building from being mistaken for suspects.
    D. An officer can always count on his flank being protected.

50. The homogeneity of a society will affect an officer's *perception* of his or her role. *Perception* most nearly means
    A. Understanding
    B. Hinderance
    C. Illusion
    D. Veracity

51. The multijurisdictional task force represents the salutary *culmination* of many local people's efforts and the cooperation of various federal law-enforcement agencies. *Culmination* most nearly means
    A. Iniquity
    B. Fulfillment
    C. Imagination
    D. Conclusion

52. State legislatures would receive greater *deference* in gender discrimination laws than those under Supreme Court doctrine. "Deference" most nearly means
    A. Compliance
    B. Share
    C. Honor
    D. Publicity

53. There were some *controversial* topics in the governor's State of the State address. *Controversial* most nearly means
    A. Arguable
    B. Prejudicial
    C. Unbelievable
    D. Boring

54. Mr. Miller was subject to arrest for *advocating* civil disobedience. *Advocating* most nearly means
    A. Supporting
    B. Conducting
    C. Abhorring
    D. Repressing

55. The defendant was *jubilant* over the verdict. *Jubilant* most nearly means
    A. Dejected
    B. Elated
    C. Exonerated
    D. Indifferent

56. In order to protect the *integrity* of this department, a high standard of ethical conduct is expected of all officers. *Integrity* most nearly means
    A. Name
    B. Uprightness
    C. Cohesiveness
    D. Suitability

57. Every police officer should *endeavor* to identify the needs of the community within his or her jurisdiction. *Endeavor* most nearly means
    A. Persevere
    B. Strive
    C. Refuse
    D. Reconcile

58. His actions were considered *flagrant* violations of departmental rules and regulations. *Flagrant* most nearly means
    A. Glaring
    B. Minor
    C. Inadvertent
    D. Significant

59. Burglary and larceny are considered to be the most *pervasive* of all the major crimes. *Pervasive* most nearly means
    A. Costly
    B. Violent
    C. Elusive
    D. Widespread

60. In general, attorneys seem to have a more *pessimistic* view of government leadership than others. *Pessimistic* most nearly means
    A. Gloomy
    B. Positive
    C. Reserved
    D. Enlightened

61. The suspect was *petulant* when asked about his past drug and alcohol abuse. *Petulant* most nearly means
    A. Cooperative
    B. Querulous
    C. Apathetic
    D. Offended

62. Assault and battery is commonplace among the *indigent*. *Indigent* most nearly means
    A. Affluent
    B. Neglected
    C. Destitute
    D. Wealthy

63. The evidence submitted in the hearing was ruled *irrelevant* to the case. *Irrelevant* most nearly means
    A. Pertinent
    B. Immaterial
    C. Important
    D. Applicable

Answer Questions 64 through 66 on the basis of the narrative provided below:

There are specific guidelines that law enforcement officers follow when making an arrest at a suspect's home. Officers should identify themselves as law-enforcement officers, state the express purpose of their visit, and wait a reasonable time for a response or an incontrovertible refusal to allow entry. This is referred to as the "knock and announce" rule. If the officer has a warrant and is refused entry by the suspect, the officer retains the right to break and enter to effect an arrest. Most state courts will not issue no-knock warrants. However, there are certain exceptions to the "knock and announce" rule. If the officer suspects that evidence crucial to the case may be destroyed while the police are waiting and complying with these standards, he or she may bypass the knock and announce rule. If the rule creates the risk of imminent escape for the suspect or risk to the public, there again is valid reason to circumvent such procedural guidelines. Three important court cases established precedent with regard to this procedure. *Payton v. New York* (1980) established that an arrest warrant must be in an officer's possession prior to entering a person's premises when permission to enter is denied and exigent circumstances (i.e., exceptions to the rules) do not exist. *Steagold v. U.S.* (1981) dictated that if the suspect is in a home other than his own, both an arrest warrant and a search warrant would be required to effect an arrest. *Watson v. U.S.* (1976) was definitive as to what constitutes a private area and what constitutes a public domain. Any place or space which is basically open to the public at large is considered to be an area that does not require a warrant to effect an arrest. The difference established in this court case is that a doorway to a person's home is considered to be a private area, thus falling under the guidelines prescribed. However, a person's porch is considered to be a public domain.

64. From both a legal and a practical perspective, the implementation of the knock and announce policy in conducting an arrest does all of the following except
    A. Reduce the possibility of violence
    B. Serve as a prelude to using any means necessary to effect an arrest
    C. Avert property damage
    D. Protect the suspect's/occupant's constitutional right to privacy

65. Officer Jake Talbott and his partner go to the home of Barry Livermore to execute an arrest warrant. After they spend a few moments waiting on the porch for the suspect to answer his door, a passing neighbor mentions that Barry was next door visiting a close friend. Officer Talbott then goes to the home next door, and after being refused admission, he enters forcibly and promptly places Mr. Livermore under arrest. According to the reading, Officer Talbott's actions were
    A. Legal, because the warrant was served after correctly following knock and announce guidelines
    B. Illegal, because the owner of the home was reluctant to permit the officer to enter
    C. Legal, because Mr. Livermore was outside his home and the situation thus did not require full compliance with knock and announce policy.
    D. Illegal, because a search warrant was not obtained in addition to the arrest warrant prior to arresting Mr. Livermore at his neighbor's house

66. Officer Blake Anderson went to a suspect's home prior to seeking an arrest warrant signed by a magistrate and by good fortune saw the suspect standing in the driveway. Officer Anderson identified himself prior to placing the suspect under arrest. Under the circumstances, according to the reading, Officer Anderson's actions were
    A. Illegal, because he failed to have an arrest warrant for the suspect in his possession
    B. Legal, because the driveway would be considered a public area and therefore would not require Officer Anderson to have a warrant to effect an arrest
    C. Illegal, because Officer Anderson did not specifically ask for permission to come onto the property
    D. Legal, because Officer Anderson did identify himself

Answer Questions 67 through 69 on the basis of the reading below:

If a police officer witnesses a traffic infraction or elects to issue a citation during the investigation of a traffic accident, the violator can do one of two things. He or she may accept the citation with the promise to respond, or he or she may refuse to sign the citation. If the violator refuses to sign, the officer may charge him or her with failure to sign and effect an arrest for a misdemeanor. If the violator elects the former, he or she will have 10 days to respond, provided the officer filed the infraction notice with the court within 48 hours from the time of issuance. Otherwise, the court dismisses the citation without prejudice. Provided the officer is in compliance with this dictate, a violator may respond by either requesting a hearing to contest the infraction, paying the appropriate penalties as assessed by state law, or requesting a hearing to explain any mitigating circumstances. A violator who does not respond may be faced with nonrenewal of his or her driver's license until all penalties are paid in full; or, worse, the prosecutor may institute a criminal complaint for failure to respond that can result in incarceration.

If a police officer recognizes that an infraction has been committed, but through either indecisiveness or the fact that the violator in question was not present at the time of the officer's arrival, he may file a written citation with the court at a later point. The officer must explain in the citation the reasonable grounds why he or she believes that an infraction was committed. If the infraction notice is filed with a court within 48 hours, and the court elects to send the citation via the U.S. Mail, the violator in question has 14 days to respond. If, on the other hand, the court elects to have the violator served directly, then he or she has only 8 days to respond. The forms of response which may be used by the violator at this point are the same as described earlier.

If the officer witnesses a standing, stopping, or parking violation, he or she may issue a citation and display it conspicuously on the vehicle. If the officer involved files the citation with the court within the time specified earlier, the violator in question will have 9 days to respond in the same manner as noted previously.

67. Officer Davis observes a vehicle double parked in front of a loading zone. Officer Davis issues a citation for the infraction and leaves a copy under the windshield wiper on the driver's side. She files the notice of infraction with the court 3 days later. Under these circumstances, how many days does the violator in question have to respond?
    A. 10
    B. 9
    C. 8
    D. None of the above

68. Officer Stone witnesses a driver go through a stop sign in an apparent attempt to merge into traffic when the opportunity availed itself. Officer Stone pulls the driver over and issues a citation for failure to stop. The driver is adamant that a tree partially obstructed his view of the sign and consequently refuses to sign the issuance. At this point, which of the following is considered to be true?

    A. The violator has the right to request a mitigating circumstance hearing
    B. The violator may contest the infraction in municipal court
    C. The driver may be charged with a misdemeanor and subsequently arrested
    D. The violator in question has 10 days to determine the means to address the charge

69. Mr. Harold Phelps receives a notice in the mail that regards a traffic infraction he had incurred earlier in the week. Assuming that the officer involved was in compliance with court standards for issuance and that the postmark on the envelope was March 10, 1992, which of the dates provided below represents the day by which Mr. Phelps has to respond to the notice or face possible prosecution for failure to respond?

    A. March 18, 1992
    B. March 19, 1992
    C. March 20, 1992
    D. March 24, 1992

Answer Questions 70 through 73 on the basis of the reading below:

> Malicious mischief is defined in *Black's Law Dictionary* as "the willful destruction of personal property from actual ill will or resentment toward its owner or possessor." This crime was formerly considered trespass by common law, but most states have made penalties for this kind of crime more severe. The spectrum of malicious mischief is sketched out below:
>
> First degree malicious mischief involves knowingly and maliciously damaging property that belongs to another where the sum of the damages exceeds $1700, or willfully interrupting a public service by damaging or tampering with a utility, a public conveyance, communications equipment, or an emergency vehicle. First degree malicious mischief is a Class B felony.
>
> Second degree malicious mischief involves knowingly and maliciously damaging property that belongs to another where the sum of the damages exceeds $300 but does not exceed $1700, or willfully creating a substantial risk of interrupting a public service by damaging or tampering with a utility, a public conveyance, communications equipment, or an emergency vehicle, or willfully causing the injury or death of any livestock owned by another. Second degree malicious mischief is a Class C felony.
>
> Third degree malicious mischief involves knowingly and maliciously damaging property that belongs to another where the sum of the damages is beneath the limits imposed by the first two statutes. Third degree malicious mischief is a gross misdemeanor if the sum of damages caused exceeds $75. Otherwise, the crime is deemed a misdemeanor.

70. For the lack of something better to do, Billy White decided to key-scratch the front right fender of a Cutlass Supreme parked in front of a small convenience store. Two people across the street witnessed the event that led to Billy's arrest. A claims adjuster from the vehicle owner's insurance firm estimated the damage would cost approximately $850 to fix. According to the reading and under the circumstances given, what should Billy White be charged with?

    A. Class B felony
    B. Class C felony
    C. Gross misdemeanor
    D. Misdemeanor

71. Robert Blakemore was considered a genius by most computer experts. For the challenge of it, Mr. Blakemore had gained unauthorized access to county courthouse records. He planted a tailor-made virus in the county's computer system that would methodically eliminate certain information from the electronic data base. Assuming that Mr. Blakemore had left some sort of trail that resulted in his arrest, which of the crimes described in this reading would apply to this case?

    A. First degree computer trespass

    B. Second degree computer trespass

    C. Class C felony

    D. Class B felony

72. Vicki Thurston wanted revenge against a classmate who embarrassed her in front of her friends at school. Vicki knew where this person lived. After school, she went to a local hardware store and bought a can of black spray paint. That same evening, Vicki went to this person's house and spray painted graffiti on the exterior of the garage. Police had little difficulty in determining the motive and who was responsible for the incident. The initial damage estimate from the homeowner's insurance carrier was approximately $300. According to the guidelines established in the reading, Ms Thurston could be prosecuted for what crime?

    A. First degree malicious mischief

    B. Second degree malicious mischief

    C. Third degree malicious mischief

    D. Class B felony

73. A woman charged with a crime who relies on the defense that her husband coerced her to commit it more often than not will have a conviction handed down rather than charges reduced or dropped. According to this statement, it can be presumed that

    A. Women are less trustworthy than men.

    B. Duress is no longer recognized by the law as being valid as a defense.

    C. Society realizes that the modern-day wife is in more control of her actions than those in the past.

    D. None of the above.

Answer Questions 74 and 75 on the basis of the procedure given below:

    Handling the mentally disturbed has always been a delicate matter for police officers. Below is a list of guidelines that many departments use in handling such calls:

    1. Make every attempt to obtain the person's voluntary cooperation.

    2. People in such a state may voluntarily commit themselves to an institution if they are 18 years of age and fully cognizant of what it means. Persons under the age of 18 can be committed by a parent or guardian.

    3. If there is reasonable cause to believe that the person in question is an imminent threat to him or herself, others, or property, a police officer can take the individual into protective custody. At this point, the person must be transferred to a mental health clinic for professional evaluation or held for professional evaluation and treatment for a period not to exceed 48 hours. Anything beyond this time requires a court order.

    4. If someone in this state is subject to lawful arrest for committing a crime, he or she should be taken into protective custody and held for evaluation under the same guidelines as explained under item 3. However, if the person arrested exhibits pronounced symptoms of mental illness, he or she should be seen by a doctor prior to or during the booking process. If the person is determined to be mentally ill, all custody officers should be duly informed.

74. Officer John White was dispatched to investigate a complaint of a person making a public nuisance of himself in front of a shopping mall entrance. When Officer White arrived, he observed a middle-aged man waving his arms and hands in an erratic manner at customers entering and leaving the mall. Officer White recognized the man as a past mental patient from the local VA hospital who had had several earlier run-ins with the police. In all previous encounters, however, he had not been considered dangerous and was not arrested. When pressed by the mall manager to do something about the problem, Officer White took the man into protective custody. According to the guidelines established in the reading, Officer White's actions would be considered

   A. Proper, because the suspect's action were threatening to mall customers
   B. Improper, because there were insufficient grounds to take the man into protective custody
   C. Proper, because the suspect was over 18 years of age and had previously been placed in a mental institution
   D. Improper, because a mental health professional should have been notified first

75. Officer Walt Markham was radioed to investigate an individual defacing public property. When Officer Markham arrived, he confronted the suspect by initially inquiring for some form of identification. He noticed a Medic Alert bracelet on the suspect's right wrist. This fact, coupled with signs of slurred and abnormal speech, peculiar mannerisms, and a mild degree of confusion, led the officer to believe the individual in question might be suffering from some form of mental illness. Officer Markham took the suspect into protective custody and booked him for second degree malicious mischief. The suspect was placed in a holding facility for three days until a mental health professional could conduct an evaluation. According to the reading, how was the suspect in question treated?

   A. Improperly, for the sole reason that the suspect was detained for too long without the issuance of a court order for further detention
   B. Properly, because all guidelines according to the reading were followed
   C. Improperly, because the suspect exhibited outward signs of mental illness and as a consequence should have been taken directly to a doctor or at least had a doctor present at the time of booking
   D. Both A and C are correct

76. Facts pertinent to a burglary investigation are given below. On the assumption that you have to complete an incident report regarding the matter, select from the four lettered statements that follow the one which most concisely describes what happened.

   - Victim's name is Ms. Sarah Oppenheimer
   - Victim's address is 1507 W. Chestnut Avenue
   - Nature of crime: Burglary
   - Approximate time of occurrence: 11:30 p.m. to 7:00 a.m.
   - Associated property damage: Back-door window pane broken

   A. Sometime between 11:30 p.m. and 7:00 a.m., the residence at 1507 W. Chestnut Avenue, owned by Ms. Sarah Oppenheimer, was burglarized
   B. Ms. Sarah Oppenheimer's residence was burglarized between 11:30 p.m. and 7:00 a.m. It is located at 1507 W. Chestnut Avenue and sustained damage to the back door
   C. Between 11:30 p.m. and 7:00 a.m., the residence of Ms. Sarah Oppenheimer, located at 1507 W. Chestnut Avenue, was burglarized after access had been gained by breaking a back-door window pane
   D. After gaining entry through a back-door window pane, Ms. Sarah Oppenheimer's house, located at 1507 W. Chestnut Avenue was burglarized between 11:30 p.m. and 7:00 a.m.

77. Facts pertinent to a traffic accident investigation are given below. On the assumption that you have to complete an incident report regarding the matter, select from the four lettered statements that follow the one which most concisely describes what happened.

   - Victim's name is Mrs. Jerome Wilson
   - Victim's vehicle: 1985 Monte Carlo
   - Accident occurred at 5:30 p.m. on the Charleston Overpass
   - Nature of crime: Hit and run
   - Associated property damage: Sideswiped left rear quarter panel
   - Description of suspect vehicle: light-colored, two door sedan; license-plate number unknown

   A. At 5:30 p.m., Mrs. Jerome Wilson was driving her 1985 Monte Carlo across the Charleston Overpass when she was sideswiped by another vehicle, which did not stop. The suspect vehicle was described by Mrs. Wilson as a light-colored, two-door sedan, license-plate number unknown. Mrs. Wilson's 1985 Monte Carlo sustained damage to the left rear quarter panel.

   B. At 5:30 p.m., Mrs. Jerome Wilson was crossing the Charleston Overpass when she was sideswiped in the left rear quarter panel by the driver of a light-colored two-door sedan that failed to stop. The license-plate number of the suspect vehicle is unknown.

   C. A 1985 Monte Carlo driven by Mrs. Jerome Wilson was sideswiped on the Charleston Overpass at 5:30 p.m. Damage to the victim's vehicle was confined to the left rear quarter panel. The suspect vehicle was a two-door sedan, license-plate number unknown, which did not stop.

   D. A light-colored, two-door sedan, license-plate number unknown, sideswiped Mrs. Jerome Wilson at 5:30 p.m. on the Charleston Overpass. The suspect vehicle did not stop. Vehicle damage was restricted to the left rear quarter panel.

78. Suppose you were at the scene of a winter traffic accident, and for the record, you had to state how cold it was in Fahrenheit degrees. If you knew it was 25° Celsius and the conversion formula

$$F = 9/5 \ (C°) + 32$$

   was handy, which of the following would be the correct entry for the incident report?
   A. 102.6°
   B. 77°
   C. 67.3°
   D. 59.4°

79. Suppose a ballistics expert made the claim that a .220 Swift's bullet would travel $1^1/_3$ yards in the same time it takes a .22-caliber bullet to travel 16 inches. How could this data be best expressed in terms of a ratio?
   A. 1.33:16
   B. 1.33:1.5
   C. 3:1
   D. 1:3

80. If a gun barrel had a bore (interior diameter) of 7 millimeters and the barrel wall's thickness is 1.725 millimeters, what is the exterior diameter of the gun barrel in question?
   A. 8.725 millimeters
   B. 9.65 millimeters
   C. 10.1 millimeters
   D. 10.45 millimeters

Answer Questions 81 through 83 on the basis of the chart given below

	Reported cases involving domestic violence	Reported fatalities resulting from domestic violence	Reported domestic violence cases that involved a firearm
1991			
17th Precinct	137	14	14
23rd Precinct	252	25	32
9th Precinct	16	1	1
1992			
17th Precinct	149	7	18
23rd Precinct	213	12	47
9th Precinct	27	2	3

81. The 23rd Precinct is shown to have had fewer reports of domestic violence in 1992 than in 1991. This reflects what percentage decrease?
    A. 13.2%
    B. 15.5%
    C. 16.7%
    D. 18.3%

82. Which precinct experienced the largest percentage increase in domestic disputes that involved a firearm from 1991 to 1992?
    A. 9th
    D. 23rd
    C. 17th
    D. Information in the survey is insufficient to make this determination

83. If the 17th Precinct experienced a 450% increase in fatalities stemming from domestic violence from 1993 to 1991, how many fatalities were there in 1993?
    A. 57
    B. 58
    C. 63
    D. 77

84. A rectangular area of 47.5 feet by 13.2 feet were roped off for a murder investigation. How many square feet does it encompass?
    A. 627
    B. 593
    C. 572.5
    D. 402

NORMAN HALL'S POLICE EXAM PREPARATION BOOK

85. Suppose a mechanic who worked for the police department had to winterize all of the patrol vehicles' coolant systems. All vehicles in question had 14-quart cooling-system capacities and currently contain a 45% antifreeze solution. If guidelines specify that a 75% solution of antifreeze is required for adequate protection against colder weather, how many quarts of the original solution would have to be drained out of each vehicle and replaced with pure antifreeze to comply with the guidelines?

A. 5.23

B. 7.64

C. 8.91

D. 9

86. If a new police cruiser can be driven 115 miles in town on 5 gallons of gas, how many miles could it be driven under the same conditions with a full tank of gas? (Consider the vehicle to have a 30-gallon capacity for the purpose of the question.)

A. 720

B. 690

C. 675

D. 650

87. Suppose a county correctional facility has enough emergency provisions on hand to sustain 240 prisoners (its capacity) for 14 days. If the current inmate populations were at 140% of the prison's capacity, how long would the same provisions last?

A. 23.5 days

B. 19.6 days

C. 15.3 days

D. 10 days

88. Suppose an investigator needed to protect a crime scene in a park against rain or other natural contaminants that could hinder an investigation. If the area of concern was circular, with a radius of 6.5 feet, how wide a square tarp would be required to sufficiently cover the area described?

A. 6.5 feet

B. 13 feet

C. 14.5 feet

D. 16 feet

89. Assume Officer Bill McPherson and Officer Terry Henderson are next-door neighbors and coincidentally work in the same department. If Officer McPherson can commute to work in 45 minutes doing an average speed of 30 mph, how fast could Officer Henderson get to work driving at an average speed of 35 mph, assuming the same route is taken and all other factors remain constant?

A. 52.5 minutes

B. 42.13 minutes

C. 38.57 minutes

D. 36.79 minutes

90. A person who desires to be a firefighter for example may set fire to a structure and endeavor to achieve a spectacular rescue in order to gain notoriety.

    The above statement, in terms of English usage,

    A. Is structurally incorrect
    B. Contains one or more misspellings
    C. Lacks necessary punctuation and/or capitalization
    D. Is grammatically correct

91. The appropriate examination and correct evaluation of real evidence is a responsibility of the technician or expert, whom by reason of his training and experience is qualified in the specialty involved

    The above statement, in terms of English usage,

    A. Is structurally incorrect
    B. Contains one or more misspellings
    C. Lacks necessary punctuation and/or capitalization
    D. Is grammatically correct

92. The importance of the proceedure becomes apparent when consideration is given to the fact that the police officer may be called to the witness stand several months after an investigation has been completed.

    The above statement, in terms of English usage,

    A. Is structurally incorrect
    B. Contains one or more misspellings
    C. Lacks necessary punctuation and/or capitalization
    D. Is grammatically correct

93. The FBI, in the uniform crime reports, predicts that the total number of robberies in the United States will increase in 2003.

    The above statement, in terms of English usage,

    A. Is structurally incorrect
    B. Contains one or more misspelling
    C. Lacks necessary punctuation and/or capitalization
    D. Is grammatically correct

94. Because Pete Mitchell was too young he was immediately disqualified from further consideration for employment.

    The above statement, in terms of English usage,

    A. Is structurally incorrect
    B. Contains one or more misspellings
    C. Lack necessary punctuation and/or capitalization
    D. Is grammatically correct

95. An incident report should be typewritten if possible; if not, it should be neatly and legibly written by pen in black or blue ink. Erasures and whiteout should be avoided; there should be no more than two to a page, and they should be neatly made and present no difficulty in reading and no possibility of misinterpretation.

    The above statement, in terms of English usage,

    A. Is structurally incorrect
    B. Contains one or more misspellings
    C. Lacks necessary punctuation and/or capitalization
    D. Is grammatically correct

96. Forgery is commited by an individual who, with intent to defraud, knowingly makes or utters a false writing that apparently imposes a legal liability on another or affects his legal right or liability to his prejudice.

   The above statement, in terms of English usage,

   A. Is structurally incorrect

   B. Contains one or more misspellings

   C. Lacks necessary punctuation and/or capitalization

   D. Is grammatically correct

97. When police officers take their lunch hour with Lieutenant Branstad, you usually end up talking about procedural policies.

   The above statement, in terms of English usage,

   A. Is structurally incorrect

   B. Contains one or more misspellings

   C. Lacks necessary punctuation and/or capitalization

   D. Is grammatically correct

98. To judges and juries, few kinds of evidence are as persuasive as fingerprints; however, investigating officers often miss fingerprints that might help insure convictions.

   The above statement, in terms of English usage,

   A. Is structurally incorrect

   B. Contains one or more misspellings

   C. Lacks necessary punctuation and/or capitalization

   D. Is grammatically correct

99. Containing a glove pouch, handcuff case, mace holder, and pen holder, a police officer wears a belt that stores much more than a gun.

   The above statement, in terms of English usage,

   A. Is structurally incorrect

   B. Contains one or more misspellings

   C. Lacks necessary punctuation and/or capitalization

   D. Is grammatically correct

Answer Questions 100 through 106 on the basis of the preliminary investigation report on the next page. You may refer back to this report to answer the questions.

① PRELIMINARY INVESTIGATION OF (CRIME): BURGLARY
② FILE #: 54-322-1
③ PCT OF REPORT: 12TH
④ DATE OF REPORT: 3-11-92

PREMISES

⑤ CRIME OCCURED IN OR ON- (RES) VAC LOT, BUSI, ST
⑥ IF RESIDENCE, ILLUSTRATE TYPE. APT, CONDO, (SINGLE FAMILY,) DUPLEX, HOTEL, MOTEL

VICTIM
⑦ LAST, FIRST, AND MIDDLE NAME: FOSTER, DENNIS EUGENE
⑩ SEX: 1
⑪ RACE: 2
⑫ DOB: 7-5-75
⑬ AGE: 18
⑧ HOME ADDRESS (H) / BUSINESS ADDRESS (B): 14071 NW 174TH ST. DENVER, CO 67504
⑨ HOME PHONE (H) / BUSINESS PHONE (B) (INCLUDE AREA CODE): (618) 575-2134
⑭ OCCUPATION: SALES ASSA / MARKET MANAGER

⑮ LOCATION OF OCCURRENCE: 14071 NW 174TH ST. DENVER, CO. 61510
⑯ DATE AND TIME OF OCCURRENCE: 3-10-92 BETWEEN 1800HRS AND 2315HRS
⑰ TYPE OF PROPERTY TAKEN: STEREO, CASH, AND FIREARMS
⑱ POINT OF ENTRY (BACK DOOR, SKYLIGHT, WINDOW, ETC.): BACKDOOR
⑲ METHOD OF ENTRY (BROKEN WINDOW, PRIED LOCK, ETC.): CHOPPED DOOR PANEL
⑳ SUSPECTED TOOL OR INSTRUMENT USED (CROWBAR, KEYS, ETC.): AXE

SUSPECTS

	㉑ RACE	㉒ SEX	㉓ HEIGHT	㉔ WEIGHT	㉕ BUILD	㉖ COMPLEX.	㉗ HAIR	㉘ EYES	㉙ AGE	㉚ NAME AND ADDRESS IF KNOWN
1	1	600	170	M	3	4	8	20	8	

㉛ DESCRIPTION OF CLOTHING: RED BALL CAP BLACK JACKET BLUE JEANS AND WHITE TENNIS SHOES
㉜ OUTSTANDING MARKS OR SCARS: 8
㉝ WEAPON USED OR SEEN: 8

	㉞ RACE	㉟ SEX	㊱ HEIGHT	㊲ WEIGHT	㊳ BUILD	㊴ COMPLEX.	㊵ HAIR	㊶ EYES	㊷ AGE	㊸ NAME AND ADDRESS IF KNOWN
2	5	1	505	130	M	5	3	8	18	8

㊹ DESCRIPTION OF CLOTHING: BRONZE JACKET WITH WHITE TRIM, DARK PANTS, AND DARK SHOES
㊺ OUTSTANDING MARKS OR SCARS: A-5 (DARK PURPLE) 1-5100
㊻ WEAPON USED OR SEEN: 3

VEHICLE

㊼ SUSPECTS / VICTIM	㊽ YEAR	㊾ MAKE	㊿ MODEL	⑤① COLOR	⑤② LICENSE # IF KNOWN	⑤③ STATE	⑤④ OTHER EXTERIOR FEATURES
SUSPECTS ✓	1995	GMC	BLAZER	BLACK	8	NJ	HALOGEN LIGHT BAR (4-LIGHTS) ON TOP

⑤⑤ OTHER FEATURES UNIQUE TO VEHICLE: RED PRIMER ON RIGHT FENDER

⑤⑥ SUSPECTS / VICTIM	⑤⑦ YEAR	⑤⑧ MAKE	⑤⑨ MODEL	⑥⓪ COLOR	⑥① LICENSE # IF KNOWN	⑥② STATE	⑥③ OTHER EXTERIOR FEATURES

CODES
A - PERSON REPORTING INCIDENT   B - WITNESS   C - RELATIVE   D - PERSON DISCOVERING INCIDENT

B
⑥④ NAME: MS. ANTONIA EVANSDALE
HOME ADDRESS (H) / BUSINESS ADDRESS (B): (H) ⑥⑤ 1297 HAWTHORNE CT. DENVER 67501
PHONE NUMBER (INCLUDE AREA CODE): (H) ⑥⑥ (618) 572-2147
OCCUPATION: WAITRESS - BESSINGERS
(B) 13571 IRST AVE, DENVER, CO
⑥⑦ (618) 735-2156

A
⑥⑨ NAME: GEORGE PETERSON
HOME ADDRESS (H) / BUSINESS ADDRESS (B): (H) ⑦⓪ 14074 NW 174TH ST. DENVER CO. 67504
PHONE NUMBER (INCLUDE AREA CODE): (H) ⑦① (618) 575-1530
⑦② OCCUPATION: RETIRED MILITARY
(B) ⑦③

⑦④ NAME:
HOME ADDRESS (H) / BUSINESS ADDRESS (B): (H) ⑦⑤
PHONE NUMBER (INCLUDE AREA CODE): (H) ⑦⑥
⑦⑦ OCCUPATION:
(B) (B) ⑦⑧

ITEMS TAKEN - CODES / PROPERTY SUMMARY

⑦⑨ QUANTITY		⑧⓪ VISIBLE DESCRIPTION	⑧① BRAND	⑧② MODEL # IF KNOWN	⑧③ GENERAL DESCRIPTION	⑧④ VALUE
3	1	LEATHER WALLET	WILSON		BROWN TRIFOLD - CONTAINER	20.00
4	1	RIFLE	WEATHERBY	MARK XII	.22 CAL. $150.00 CASH	150.00 / 700.00
4	1	PISTOL	RUGER		.22 CAL	225.00
6	2	PORTABLE TV SETS	SONY	TRINITRON	13"	85.00
6	1	TUNER	CARVER	SA-50	GOLD COLORED W/ CHERRY WOOD CABINETRY	260.00
6	1	PREAMP	CARVER	SA-117	SILVER COLORED W/ CHERRY WOOD CABINETRY	375.00
6	1	AMPLIFIER	CARVER	SA-03	" " "	375.00
6	2	SPEAKERS	DALQUIST	117-BT	CHERRY WOOD CABINETRY / BLACK CLOTH	480.00

(USE BACK OF REPORT IF EXTRA SPACE REQUIRED)

OFFICE

⑧⑤ INVESTIGATING OFFICER: CHARLES DIRKSON
⑧⑥ BADGE / ID #: 534
⑧⑦ APPROVED BY: SGT. J. MORRIS
⑧⑧ EVIDENCE SIEZED: YES / NO ✓
⑧⑨ DETECTIVE DIV
⑨⓪ JUV
⑨① PROSECUTOR CITY ATTY
⑨② CLEARED BY ARREST: YES / NO ✓
⑨③ PERSON REPORTING (SIGNATURE): George Peterson

SEX:
1—MALE
2—FEMALE

RACE:
1—WHITE
2—WHITE/HISPANIC
3—BLACK
4—BLACK/HISPANIC
5—ASIAN
6—NATIVE AMERICAN

(Height and Weight must be expressed as a three digit number)
(Use the number 8 to indicate unknown)

COMPLEXION:
1—PALE
2—DARK
3—MEDIUM
4—RUDDY
5—LIGHT BROWN

HAIR:
1—BLOND
2—RED
3—BLACK
4—BROWN
5—GREY
6—WHITE

EYE COLOR:
1—HAZEL
2—BROWN

3—GREEN
4—BLACK
5—BLUE
6—GREY

OUTSTANDING MARKS/SCARS:
(Location preceeds identification)
1—LEG
2—TORSO
3—ARM
4—HAND
5—NECK
6—FACE
A—BIRTHMARK
B—TATTOO
C—SCAR

PROPERTY SUMMARY CODES:
1—CLOTHING
2—JEWELRY
3—CURRENCY
4—FIREARMS
5—HOUSEHOLD APPLIANCE
6—ELECTRONICS (other than #5)
7—MISCELLANEOUS

WEAPONS:
1—PISTOL
2—RIFLE
3—KNIFE
4—SHOTGUN
5—BLUNT INSTRUMENT
6—EXPLOSIVE

100. According to the report, who is the complainant?
    A. Mr. Dennis Foster
    B. Ms. Antonia Evansdale
    C. Mr. George Peterson
    D. It was not specifically mentioned in the report

101. What was the date on which this incident happened?
    A. July 5, 1975
    B. February 10, 1972
    C. March 11, 1992
    D. March 10, 1992

102. To whom does the phone number (618) 572-2147 belong?
    A. The victim
    B. The witness
    C. The victim's spouse
    D. The person reporting the incident

103. The property summary statement should specify the total value of all merchandise taken. Which of the numbers given below would be an accurate assessment?
    A. $2,680.00
    B. $2,080.00
    C. $1,180.00
    D. None of the above

104. Who was the person assigned to investigate the burglary?
    A. Sergeant Morris
    B. Officer Dirkson
    C. Officer Foster
    D. Officer Evansdale

105. All of the following statements are true regarding this report except
    A. One of the suspects was described by Mr. Foster as being an Asian male, approximately 18 years of age, 5'5", medium build, light brown complexion, with black hair.
    B. The witness involved worked as a cocktail waitress at Bessingers and can be reached at work by calling (618) 735-2156.
    C. The victim of the crime works as a sales associate at Parker Lumber; a business phone number was not provided.
    D. One of the suspects involved was described by a witness as being a Caucasian male approximately 20 years of age, 6', medium build, medium complexion, with brown hair. He was also described as wearing white tennis shoes, a black jacket, blue jeans, and a red ball cap.

106. All of the following facts concerning this burglary incident are true except
    A. The single most expensive item taken from the victim was a firearm.
    B. The incident occurred sometime in the span of 4 hours and 15 minutes.
    C. The home phone numbers for the witness and person responsible for reporting the incident are (618) 735-2156 and (618) 575-1530, respectively.
    D. Police Officer Charles Dirkson (Badge #534) was in charge of the investigation. The subsequent report filed on the burglary was approved by Sergeant J. Morris.

107. Officers Rick Gaston and Harvey Duper pull over a car for a minor traffic infraction. The driver of the vehicle shoots Officer Duper in the shoulder and drives away. Which of the following immediate actions by Officer Gaston would be appropriate?

    A. Give immediate chase to the suspect vehicle

    B. Exchange gunfire so long as the suspect has not driven further than one block away

    C. Attend to his partner's injuries and radio for immediate medical assistance, then relay a description of the suspect and vehicle, including the direction in which it was last seen heading

    D. Drive his partner to the closest emergency facility for medical assistance

108. Officer Leslie Black decided to have lunch in one of the restaurants on her beat. After she finished eating, the restaurant owner refused to accept any money for the meal, explaining he wished to show his appreciation for her presence in the neighborhood. Under the circumstances, what should Officer Black do?

    A. Offer her humblest appreciation and make certain witnesses are not present

    B. Insist that she be allowed to pay for the meal or threaten to arrest the restaurant owner on bribery charges

    C. Leave enough money to cover the meal and then notify her supervisor regarding the matter

    D. Patronize the establishment more often to show her appreciation

109. Officer Pete Bradley was off duty and attended a neighborhood party. When he went to the men's room, he noticed four juveniles smoking marijuana in an adjoining bedroom. What would be Officer Bradley's best approach in handling this matter?

    A. Leave the premises immediately and offer no justification for doing so

    B. Investigate the matter further, and if his suspicions are confirmed, place the juvenile offenders under arrest

    C. Call for backup and wait on the premises for other police to show up

    D. Tell the host his suspicions, and then leave the party

110. Police Officers Kelly Martin and Jane Newton are responding to a burglary in progress. Eight blocks from their destination, they come across a severe traffic accident involving serious injury to one of the drivers involved. What would be the best response Officer Martin could make to the situation?

    A. Radio for a secondary unit to respond to the initial call, summon emergency medical assistance, and then stay at the scene to administer aid until additional help arrives

    B. Radio dispatch about the accident and continue to respond to the burglary in progress

    C. Leave Officer Newton at the scene of the accident and continue to respond to the burglary in progress

    D. Assume someone has already been notified about the accident and continue to the original destination

111. Officer Milton Hastings is currently investigating a minor traffic accident. A young woman runs up to him and claims that a stranger is in the basement of her home. What would be the best way for Officer Hastings to handle this situation?

    A. Continue with the accident investigation and assume since the young woman could not offer any proof, the story was probably fabricated

    B. Drop the accident investigation and immediately go to the young woman's home

    C. Continue with the accident investigation after radioing for another unit to respond

    D. Tell the young woman that he will go to her residence immediately after completing the reports necessary for the accident at hand

112. Dwayne Harper is working dispatch on Sunday. An elderly woman calls in to complain about a fellow officer's use of vulgar language. What is the best thing for Mr. Harper to do at this point?
    A. Explain to her that the administrative staff do not work weekends so that she should call back first thing Monday morning
    B. Take all the information provided and give the report to a supervisor first thing Monday morning
    C. Tell the complainant that he will have the offending party contact her Monday morning to resolve the issue
    D. Prepare an official reprimand for the officer involved

113. Officer Vance Hoptkins was having lunch in a small diner in another district. A young woman, remembering that Officer Hoptkins eats there fairly regularly, approached him to complain about a next-door neighbor's stereo being so loud that neither she or her baby could get any rest. Since she lived just around the block, what should Officer Hoptkins do?
    A. Explain to the woman that he was on his lunch hour and, since stereo noise is basically a public nuisance (minor nuisance), he would investigate it as soon as he finished eating
    B. Tell her to call emergency 911 and request a district car to investigate
    C. Immediately look into the matter and then resume having lunch once the problem has been rectified
    D. Radio dispatch directly to have a district car investigate the matter

114. Officer Brice Miller is working DWI patrol in the Westminster district when he pulls over a suspected drunk driver. Upon requesting identification, he learns that the driver is an off-duty police officer from a neighboring district. What would be the best way for Officer Miller to handle this situation?
    A. Put the off-duty officer through the same kind of field sobriety test given to others; if suspicions are confirmed by the test results, book the officer for DWI as he would anyone else
    B. Take his keys away and escort him home
    C. Tell the driver to go directly home and not make a report of the matter
    D. Contact his supervisor and request instructions on what action should be taken

115. Officer Frank Milligan was in pursuit of someone who had just committed a felony. Vehicle speeds were in excess of 85 miles per hour when the suspect veered off a frontage road and headed for a residential area, maintaining a high speed. At this point, Officer Milligan's best action would be which of the following?
    A. Slow down to a reasonable speed and radio dispatch where the vehicle was last seen heading
    B. Break off pursuit and attempt to locate the suspect again in another area
    C. Attempt to stop the suspect vehicle with whatever means necessary because of the risk posed to the public
    D. This is reason enough for the officer to utilize his firearm.

116. Officer Mary Coffman is preparing a preliminary investigation report for larceny. The complainant furnished the following information concerning a valuable ring that was stolen. Which of the descriptions given would probably be the most helpful in identifying and recovering the item?
    A. The ring was appraised at a value of $27,000.
    B. It was a gold ring with 13 inlaid diamonds.
    C. The ring was sized for a smaller man's ring finger.
    D. The ring had the shape of a horse's head.

117. Rumor has it that the officer assigned to be your partner has a reliability problem when serving as backup. What would be your best way to handle such a situation?

   A. Ask your supervisor for another partner

   B. Seek a legal injunction to prevent the assignment

   C. Confront the officer directly and tell him or her that you have reservations about the transfer

   D. Try to get to know the officer in question first hand

118. Officer Jim Dailey responds to a call regarding a middle-aged woman threatening to jump off the Manchester Narrows bridge. Upon arrival, he sees the woman standing precariously on a guard rail facing the water. Under the circumstances, what is the best way for Officer Dailey to handle this situation?

   A. Approach the woman slowly and then, once within arm's reach, quickly attempt to subdue her

   B. Assure the woman that if she really intended to jump, she would have done so already

   C. Ask the woman if she fully realizes the pain and embarrassment this will cause her family and friends

   D. Make the woman aware of his presence and simply be a good listener

Answer Questions 119 through 124 on the basis of the map and narrative below:

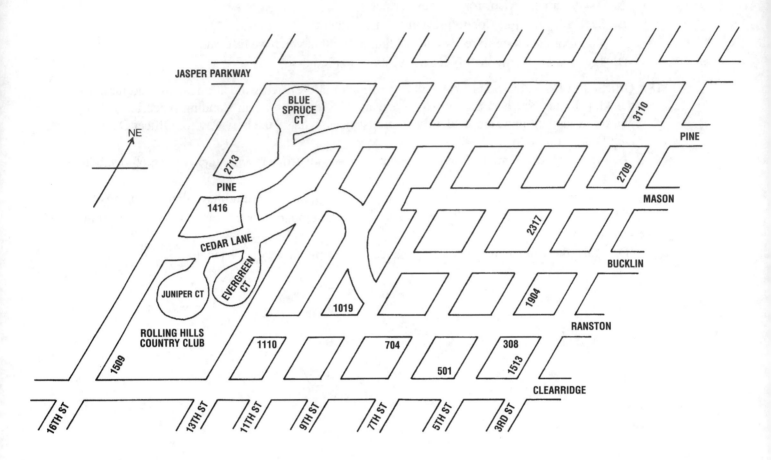

Facts to consider regarding this map:

- Pine and Ranston Avenues are one-way, heading west; all other roads are to be considered two-way streets.
- Numbers represent single family residences.

At 10:17 a.m., a two-car traffic accident involving a fatality occurs at the intersection of Jasper Parkway and 9th Street. Police close this intersection for four hours and 15 minutes to complete their investigation.

Thirteenth Street between Cedar Lane and Ranston Avenue is closed by the city's Street Department so necessary road repair can be conducted between 9:05 and 11:15 a.m.

Sector A is bounded by Cedar Lane, 9th Street, Jasper Parkway, and 16th Street.

Sector B is bounded by Bucklin, 5th Street, Ranston Avenue, 3rd Street, and 9th Street.

Sector C is bounded by 9th Street, Clearridge Boulevard, 3rd Street, Ranston Avenue, 5th Street, and Bucklin.

Sector D is bounded by 9th Street, Cedar Lane, 16th Street, and Clearridge Boulevard.

119. If a police officer were located at a residence on the 1100 block of Clearridge Boulevard, what direction would he or she have to travel to get to Third Street?

  A. Southeast

  B. East

  C. Southwest

  D. North

120. If precinct headquarters is located on the corner of 9th Street and Mason Avenue, where is the intersection of Jasper Parkway and 3rd Street in relation to the Police Department?

  A. Northeast

  B. Northwest

  C. East

  D. West

121. If a patrol vehicle were located at Blue Spruce Court and dispatched to investigate a vehicular prowler in the 500 block of Ranston Avenue, which of the routes given below would serve as the most direct and legal means of getting there?

  A. Turn left on Pine and right on 13th Street to Ranston Avenue, and then turn left on Ranston Avenue and go approximately four blocks.

  B. Turn right on Pine, left on 16th Street to Cedar Lane, left on Cedar Lane to 9th Street, left on 9th Street to Bucklin, right on Bucklin to 5th Street, and right on 5th Street and go one block before turning right.

  C. Turn right on Pine, left on 16th Street to Clearridge Boulevard, left on Clearridge to 7th Street, and then left on 7th Street and go one block.

  D. Turn left on Pine, and then turn right on 5th Street and go three blocks before turning right again.

122. Look at the previous question again. Despite the patrol vehicle's point of origin, his response to the call described effectively places the officer in which sector, according to the boundaries described in the map?

  A. Sector A

  B. Sector B

  C. Sector C

  D. Sector D

123. Suppose Police Officer Vince Howard had just completed a larceny investigation at 2713 16th Street and was dispatched at 1415 hours to assist in directing backed-up traffic at the intersection of Jasper Parkway and 3rd Street. Which of the routes provided below would serve as the best legal means of getting to the prescribed destination?

  A. Go northeast to the first intersection encountered, turn right, and then go approximately six blocks southeast.

  B. Go southeast to the first intersection encountered, turn right, and then go approximately six blocks northeast.

  C. Go southwest to the second intersection encountered, turn left, follow the road to its end, turn left, and go to Jasper Parkway before making a right turn and continuing another three blocks.

  D. Go southwest to the second intersection encountered, turn left and follow that road to its end, turn left, and turn right at the first possible intersection; then go three blocks before turning left and going another three blocks.

124. All of the following statements are true except:
    A. An officer at 704 Ranston Avenue could respond most quickly to a domestic dispute on Juniper Court by taking a right turn at the first intersection encountered and then taking the first available left turn and staying on that road until Juniper Court.
    B. An officer having breakfast at the Rolling Hills Country Club Restaurant, located on Clearridge Boulevard between 13th Street and 16th Street, could most directly go southeast on Clearridge Boulevard and take the first available left to get to a traffic accident on Pine and 13th Street reported to have occurred at 1045 hours.
    C. Sector C is basically southwest of Sector B.
    D. An officer choosing to walk his beat leaves precinct headquarters (the location was described in an earlier question) and goes two blocks northeast, three blocks southeast, four blocks southwest, two blocks northwest, and then two blocks northeast; this would place the officer exactly one block southeast of his point of origin.

125. An effective means for detectives to observe someone walking along a street without their being noticed involves using three-officer foot surveillance with vehicular backup. The latter aspect is useful primarily if the suspect enters a bus, cab, or other vehicle. Assume a suspect is walking south on the west side of a street toward an intersection. If the procedure of three-officer foot surveillance is being followed to the letter, two officers will have already taken up positions directly to the rear of the suspect, while the third officer walks parallel to the suspect's path, but on the east side of the street. The vehicle involved should remain at least half a block behind and try to avoid double parking, which would draw unnecessary attention. If the person being followed turns right at the intersection, the first officer directly behind the suspect should continue straight, crossing the intersection, and then turn west to walk parallel to the subject's course but on the opposite side of the street he or she is now on. The second officer following directly behind the suspect should continue doing so. The third officer, who originally parallelled the subject's path, should not continue straight at the intersection. Instead, he or she should head west across the street and take up a position directly behind the second officer. The same rotational procedure should be used if the suspect decides to make another turn. The vehicular back-up, on the other hand, should not attempt to stay directly with the suspect in the event of a turn. It should continue through the intersection and take up another tail position as dictated by the three officers on foot.

    Which of the diagrams provided on the next page accurately portrays the surveillance technique described in this narrative?

A

B

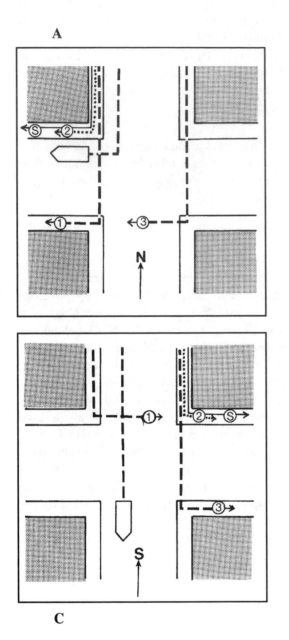

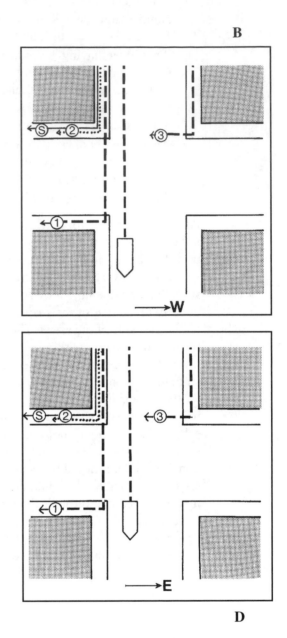

C

D

Arrows indicate direction of travel
S—Suspect
1—First officer
2—Second officer
3—Third officer
⬭ —Vehicle

ANSWER SHEET TO PRACTICE EXAM II

1. (A) (B) (C) (D)   32. (A) (B) (C) (D)   63. (A) (B) (C) (D)
2. (A) (B) (C) (D)   33. (A) (B) (C) (D)   64. (A) (B) (C) (D)
3. (A) (B) (C) (D)   34. (A) (B) (C) (D)   65. (A) (B) (C) (D)
4. (A) (B) (C) (D)   35. (A) (B) (C) (D)   66. (A) (B) (C) (D)
5. (A) (B) (C) (D)   36. (A) (B) (C) (D)   67. (A) (B) (C) (D)
6. (A) (B) (C) (D)   37. (A) (B) (C) (D)   68. (A) (B) (C) (D)
7. (A) (B) (C) (D)   38. (A) (B) (C) (D)   69. (A) (B) (C) (D)
8. (A) (B) (C) (D)   39. (A) (B) (C) (D)   70. (A) (B) (C) (D)
9. (A) (B) (C) (D)   40. (A) (B) (C) (D)   71. (A) (B) (C) (D)
10. (A) (B) (C) (D)   41. (A) (B) (C) (D)   72. (A) (B) (C) (D)
11. (A) (B) (C) (D)   42. (A) (B) (C) (D)   73. (A) (B) (C) (D)
12. (A) (B) (C) (D)   43. (A) (B) (C) (D)   74. (A) (B) (C) (D)
13. (A) (B) (C) (D)   44. (A) (B) (C) (D)   75. (A) (B) (C) (D)
14. (A) (B) (C) (D)   45. (A) (B) (C) (D)   76. (A) (B) (C) (D)
15. (A) (B) (C) (D)   46. (A) (B) (C) (D)   77. (A) (B) (C) (D)
16. (A) (B) (C) (D)   47. (A) (B) (C) (D)   78. (A) (B) (C) (D)
17. (A) (B) (C) (D)   48. (A) (B) (C) (D)   79. (A) (B) (C) (D)
18. (A) (B) (C) (D)   49. (A) (B) (C) (D)   80. (A) (B) (C) (D)
19. (A) (B) (C) (D)   50. (A) (B) (C) (D)   81. (A) (B) (C) (D)
20. (A) (B) (C) (D)   51. (A) (B) (C) (D)   82. (A) (B) (C) (D)
21. (A) (B) (C) (D)   52. (A) (B) (C) (D)   83. (A) (B) (C) (D)
22. (A) (B) (C) (D)   53. (A) (B) (C) (D)   84. (A) (B) (C) (D)
23. (A) (B) (C) (D)   54. (A) (B) (C) (D)   85. (A) (B) (C) (D)
24. (A) (B) (C) (D)   55. (A) (B) (C) (D)   86. (A) (B) (C) (D)
25. (A) (B) (C) (D)   56. (A) (B) (C) (D)   87. (A) (B) (C) (D)
26. (A) (B) (C) (D)   57. (A) (B) (C) (D)   88. (A) (B) (C) (D)
27. (A) (B) (C) (D)   58. (A) (B) (C) (D)   89. (A) (B) (C) (D)
28. (A) (B) (C) (D)   59. (A) (B) (C) (D)   90. (A) (B) (C) (D)
29. (A) (B) (C) (D)   60. (A) (B) (C) (D)   91. (A) (B) (C) (D)
30. (A) (B) (C) (D)   61. (A) (B) (C) (D)   92. (A) (B) (C) (D)
31. (A) (B) (C) (D)   62. (A) (B) (C) (D)   93. (A) (B) (C) (D)

94. (A) (B) (C) (D)
95. (A) (B) (C) (D)
96. (A) (B) (C) (D)
97. (A) (B) (C) (D)
98. (A) (B) (C) (D)
99. (A) (B) (C) (D)
100. (A) (B) (C) (D)
101. (A) (B) (C) (D)
102. (A) (B) (C) (D)
103. (A) (B) (C) (D)
104. (A) (B) (C) (D)

105. (A) (B) (C) (D)
106. (A) (B) (C) (D)
107. (A) (B) (C) (D)
108. (A) (B) (C) (D)
109. (A) (B) (C) (D)
110. (A) (B) (C) (D)
111. (A) (B) (C) (D)
112. (A) (B) (C) (D)
113. (A) (B) (C) (D)
114. (A) (B) (C) (D)
115. (A) (B) (C) (D)

116. (A) (B) (C) (D)
117. (A) (B) (C) (D)
118. (A) (B) (C) (D)
119. (A) (B) (C) (D)
120. (A) (B) (C) (D)
121. (A) (B) (C) (D)
122. (A) (B) (C) (D)
123. (A) (B) (C) (D)
124. (A) (B) (C) (D)
125. (A) (B) (C) (D)

ANSWERS TO PRACTICE EXAMINATION II

Refer to the sketch for any clarification of Questions 1 through 8.

1. *B.* 75715

2. *C.* Two-way street. The solid double yellow lines should have made this fact obvious.

3. *C.* 4. One pedestrian and three in the passing car.

4. *A.* Second floor

5. *A.* The furniture on top of the station wagon should be clue enough that someone was in the process of moving.

6. *D.* Chair

7. *A.* LMX 430

8. *D.* The selection is false, for the reason given in Question 2.

9. *C.* Judicial Summary of a Criminal Case in Superior Court

10. *D.* The reading discusses how serious criminal charges—namely, felonies—are handled in Superior Court. However, there were no direct references within the narrative.

11. *A.* *Voir dire*

12. *B.* Administrative Recognizance Release Program (ARRP)

13. *C.* Plea bargaining agreements must be heard prior to or during an omnibus hearing.

14. *C.* According to the reading, a person currently in custody must be given a trial date within 60 days of arraignment to be assured the right to a speedy trial.

15. *C.* Four to six weeks was the time given in which a judge has to sentence a convicted person.

16. *A.* Discovery

17. *B.* The reading emphasized that a defendant, whether in custody or not, must be identified prior to charges being formally filed.

18. *D.* Jurors must be unanimous; otherwise, the jury is considered hung and the charges are either dismissed or retried later.

19. *C.* Court Rule 3.5 establishes the admissibility of such evidence.

20. *A.* Personal recognizance means the same thing as release without bail.

21. *B.* State sentencing guidelines, not the judge, were mentioned near the end of the narrative as being the determining factor.

22. *C.* It was pointed out that C is the person responsible.

23. *D.* A pretrial suppression hearing would determine evidence admissibility in this case.

24. *D.* Selection D would effectively concentrate patrol efforts in the area and at the time of day most needed. In all likelihood, there would be a corresponding decrease in residential burglaries at the Farmington Community Club.

25. *C.* Selection C would effectively concentrate patrol efforts in the area and at the time of day most needed. In all likelihood, there would be a corresponding decrease in malicious mischief at the Carver Center Apartments.

26. *B.* Selections B and C are essentially describing the same neighborhood and inherent crime problem. The only difference is that B incorrectly identifies the problem plaguing Meadowlark Estates. Vehicular prowling, not malicious mischief, is the concern there.

27. *C.* Realistically, anyone in the immediate vicinity of the crime should be questioned about seeing anything or anyone unusual in the area. However, for the purpose of this question, C should warrant the most attention. The shoes might have been muddied in the attempt to flee the area through someone's yard. Most delivery people maintain an impeccable appearance.

28. *B.* Selections A, C, and D are valid points of consideration, whereas wet road surfaces or icy conditions are not reasons in themselves to take such action.

29. *D.* Unfortunately, officers do sometimes respond to silent alarms with the thought that the suspect is completely unaware that the authorities have been notified. This can lead to a potentially fatal error if appropriate caution is not exercised on the officer's behalf. Selection A is not true because common sense dictates not using the siren in responding to a silent alarm. Selection B may be true to a limited extent in close-quarter approaches, but for the most part, officers have the advantage of surprise. Selection C is untrue because if the officer catches the suspect off balance from the start, he should have control of the situation.

30. *D.* The most effective means of surveillance or visual containment is offered by the approach described in D. This method allows officers the best vantage points to monitor the entire building's exterior, not just two or three sides, as would be the case in A and C. Selection B would simply be foolhardy prior to the arrival of backup.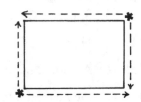

31. *D.* While negligent driving was neither defined nor implied in the reading as being a serious offense, it can be reasonably assumed that it can pose a danger to other lives, including that of the driver, as well as to property. Consequently, an arrest would remove the hazard posed by the violator from the public roadways. Separate transport of prisoners is standard procedure in most departments.

32. *B.* Selection B is not true by any stretch of the imagination. If you knew that by breaking a particular traffic ordinance, you would, in fact, have to face a jury trial and inevitable incarceration, you would probably think twice about committing the infraction. However, if they simply face a monetary penalty for the same offense, most people will tend to push the limits of the law. Civil and criminal penalties do not evoke equal deterrence. In fact, A and C are quantitative benefits that result from streamlining the criminal justice system.

33. *C.* Only C fits the criteria established in the question to justify the use of a K-9 unit. Since containment has already been achieved in B and D, the use of a K-9 patrol would place both the handler and the dog at unnecessary risk. Selection A would be improper, since crowd control by itself does not imply a crime scene. An attempt to utilize K-9s to effect crowd control can result in indiscriminate injury to many and consequently become a civil liability to the officer and department involved.

34. *A.* Only A is completely true. A witness becomes more credible by pointing out a suspect from a photo montage of other, similar-looking individuals. Photos may include police officers or other innocent subjects. Selection B is absolutely false because the last thing the department would want to do is to seem suggestive. Evidence of this nature would be immediately dismissed by the courts. C and D are false presumptions.

35. *C.* While B may be true to some extent, C most comprehensively explains the supportive reasoning. The elimination of distractions is imperative in any successful interrogation. Selection D is absolutely false. All persons, regardless of what they may be accused of, should have their civil rights protected.

36. *A.* This question primarily hinges on the porosity of the material involved. It may not initially seem obvious, but B, C, and D are relatively porous. On the other hand, glass is a smooth yet solid surface that will allow for a high-quality print impression.

37. *B.* Both the medical examiner and firearms identification expert are considered to be expert witnesses who gave an opinion on matters they were qualified to testify about by virtue of their knowledge, special skill, or other abilities.

38. *D.* Both the revolver and the bullet can be considered real or physical evidence.

39. *C.* Since the witness in question was not aware of the murder and simply corroborated the fact that the defendant was seen fleeing the scene of the crime, the evidence can be considered circumstantial in that it indirectly ties the defendant to the murder. Selection A would be more in line if the witness involved actually saw the murder take place.

40. *D.* Effective communication between officers is paramount in coordinating any kind of concerted effort. If instructions are not completely understood, for whatever reason, an officer should request to have the information repeated.

41. *C.* Selections A and D would not be discernable differences that would make the suspect stand out in a crowd. Choice B would be of limited assistance; however, the jacket could be taken off. The key element here is the height and proportions of the suspect. This is well above the average height for a female.

42. *D.* Since the vehicle in question is wanted in connection with a felony, it is too dangerous for an individual officer to approach it. There would be no safe way of telling how many people are inside the van without the assistance of another one or two officers. Vans also present the special problem of having few windows to look through. Extreme caution should be exercised in this kind of situation.

43. *A.* Selection D may seem to be the correct answer, but considering the proximity of the officer to where the suspect was last seen, this kind of approach, when done carefully, is effective in minimizing detection. Brake lights can draw the same degree of attention that headlights can. Selection B is true to an extent; however, in this case it can be used.

44. *A.* Selections B, C, and D are all means of addressing crime symptomatically after the fact. Selection A can be an effective deterrent to crime before it occurs. Citizen block watches are examples of the kind of means that have been proven to reduce criminal activity in general.

45. *C.* Discretion is the better part of valor; the best choice here would be to release the prisoner. Since the crime is only a misdemeanor, it would not warrant the use of deadly force as prescribed in B unless the officer's life is directly threatened. In the case at hand, the suspect can be picked up at a later time under better circumstances. Selection D could potentially make the situation worse, and A may not be available in time to assist the officer. Officer Dunkin should consider his own safety first.

46. *C.* Armed men and busy intersections can cause a situation that places the public at significant risk. If an officer forces the issue, as dictated by A and D, an exchange of gunfire will be the likely result. The best thing to do initially would be to make a mental note of all physical descriptions, notify headquarters regarding the situation so that backup can be better coordinated, and then, as the primary officer on the scene, get statements from witnesses in the credit union and assess what happened.

47. *B.* Only B gives sufficient foundation to rescind an earlier order. The remaining reasons given do not justify such action. A, C, and D may appear controversial to the department as a whole, but not contradictory as B would have it.

48. *D.* Due to a police officer's time limitations and the multitude of other duties he or she must perform, many minor violations, such as the one cited in the question, can be overlooked. Under the circumstances described in the question, stopping the vehicle in violation would create more of a hazard than the violation itself presented. Therefore, the minor violation observed by Officer Nichols would be best ignored. It should be noted, however, that officers should make every attempt to stop those who commit intentional or hazardous violations.

49. *C.* Officers who employ this kind of search procedure can immediately recognize the fact that someone other than a police officer is attempting to leave the building. It alleviates any mistaken presumptions that can frustrate an ongoing investigation. Selections A and B are true to an extent; however, they do not reflect the primary reason for following such a procedure. Selection D is absolutely false. An officer must always be aware of everything in his or her surroundings, especially when conducting a building search. If an officer is cognizant only of what lies directly ahead, he or she is rendered vulnerable to attack from behind.

50. *A.* Understanding

51. *B.* Fulfillment

52. *C.* Honor

53. *A.* Arguable

54. *A.* Supporting

55. *B.* Elated

56. *B.* Uprightness

57. *B.* Strive

58. *A.* Glaring

59. *D.* Widespread

60. *A.* Gloomy

61. *B.* Querulous

62. *C.* Destitute

63. *B.* Immaterial

64. *B.* The word *any* is a key word; it may entail lethal force. After a warrant for arrest is served and the suspect flees, this may hold true. However, this case was not specifically addressed in the reading. Choices A, C, and D would be considered valid points of view.

65. *D.* As established in *Steagold v. U.S.* (1981), Mr. Livermore's presence in a third party's residence would require a search warrant in addition to an arrest warrant to effect an arrest.

66. *B.* You can figure out from the reading that if the porch of a person's home is considered to be a public domain (*U.S. v. Watson* [1976]) then a driveway would reasonably be considered a public domain as well. Therefore, an arrest warrant would not be required. In fact, Officer Anderson did save himself time and paperwork by arresting the suspect in the manner described. Selection D is proper; however, it fails to define the legality of the situation.

67. *D.* It was stressed early in the reading that if officers do not file a notice of infraction with the court within 48 hours, the court would dismiss the charges altogether. Since 72 hours had passed before Officer Davis filed the notice, the violation would be dismissed without prejudice by the court.

68. *C.* It is mentioned at the start of the reading that anyone who willfully refuses to sign an issuance can be cited additionally for failure to sign. That misdemeanor by itself warrants arrest and can mean incarceration for the violator.

69. *D.* A defendant receiving a notice of infraction by this means officially has 14 days to respond in some way to the issuance or face prosecution for a misdemeanor, as described in the reading.

70. *B.* Billy White should be charged with second degree malicious mischief, a Class C felony, because the damage estimate of $850 falls within the limits for that crime.

71. *D.* Relying on only the information contained in the reading, Mr. Blakemore would have to be charged with first degree malicious mischief, a Class B felony. Selection A would seem more appropriate for the crime committed; however, neither A nor B was addressed in the reading. Therefore they cannot be considered viable answers to this question.

72. *C.* If damage estimates had been in excess of $300, B would have been the correct answer. However, the damage estimate came in right at $300, thus justifying C. Selections A and D could have been initially eliminated purely on the basis that they are one and the same.

73. *C.* The opinion expressed in C best covers what the statement says. Selection A is neither directly said nor implied. Selection B is a blanket statement that is simply untrue and cannot be deduced from this reading alone. Duress, in fact, is an important aspect of any defense.

74. *B.* Since the person in question did not pose an imminent threat to anyone, including himself, the best thing Officer White could have done was to refer him to an appropriate social service organization. This is especially applicable if the individual is not known to be dangerous and has no prior arrests. The remaining selections are not true according to the guidelines presented.

75. *D.* Selection D addresses both reasons why the suspect was not properly processed.

76. *C.* Selection C is a clear and concise description of the event. Selections A, B, and D are awkward or confusing statements detailing the incident.

77. *A.* Selection A best describes what happened in a fairly concise manner. Selections B and D are confusing in that they make it seem as if the victim herself had been struck by the suspect's vehicle. Instead, there needs to be clarification that it was the vehicle she was driving that was struck. Selection C could be better arranged by mentioning the damage last.

78. *B.* Always do multiplication or division before doing any addition or subtraction unless any part of the equation is in parenthesis. In that case, work the parenthetical portion of the equation first, then do multiplication and division, and finally complete any addition or subtraction. Otherwise, you will end up with Choice A, which is incorrect.

$$\frac{9}{5} \times \frac{25}{1} = \frac{225}{5} = 45$$

45 + 32 = 77 degrees Fahrenheit

79. *C.* Since we are dealing with two different units of measure (yards and inches), it is necessary to convert one to the other. This can be done in one of two ways. The first way is to change inches to yards. Since we know that there are 36 inches in a yard, 16 inches is equal to 16/36 yard or, in reduced form, 4/9 yards. Or we can change yards into inches; we simply multiply $1^1/_3$ or

$$\frac{4}{3} \; x \; \frac{36 \text{ inches}}{1 \text{ yard}} = \frac{144}{3} = 48 \text{ inches}$$

For simplicity's sake, let's figure the ratio on the basis of inches:

$1^1/_3$ yards : 16 inches = 48 inches : 16 inches = 3 : 1 when reduced.

80. *D.* To figure the barrel's external diameter, the wall thickness must be counted twice to accurately represent a true cross section. (See diagram.)

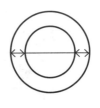

Therefore, $1.725 + 1.725 + 7 = 10.45$ mm outside diameter.

81. *B.* The 23rd Precinct had 39 fewer cases of domestic violence reported in 1992 than in 1991. To figure what percentage this difference corresponds to, we need to divide 39 by 252 and then multiply it by 100. Therefore,

$$\frac{39}{252} = 0.15476$$

$0.15476 \; x \; 100 = 15.476\%$ or 15.5% when rounded off.

82. *A.* 9th Precinct.
17th Precinct had four more cases of firearm-related domestic violence in 1992 than in 1991.

$4/14 \; x \; 100 = 28.57\%$ increase

23rd Precinct had 15 more cases of firearm related domestic violence in 1992 than in 1991.

$15/32 \; x \; 100 = 46.87\%$ increase

9th Precinct had two more cases of firearm related domestic violence in 1992 than in 1991.

$2/1 \; x \; 100 = 200\%$ increase

83. *D.* Since 14 fatalities were a result of domestic violence in Precinct 17 during 1991, we can figure the number of fatalities in 1992 by setting up the problem as shown (fatalities in 1993 = *X*):

$$\frac{X - \text{Fatalities in 1991}}{\text{Fatalities in 1991}} = 4.5$$

Therefore,

$$\frac{X - 14}{14} = 4.5$$

$X - 14 = 63$; $X = 63 + 14 = 77$ fatalities in 1993.

84. *A.* The square footage of a rectangle is found by multiplying its length by its width. In this case, 47.5 ft x 13.2 ft = 627 square feet

85. *B.* The best way to work this kind of problem is to use the equation below:

amount of 100% antifreeze (1.00X) + amount of 45% antifreeze solution (0.45 [14 – X]) = amount of pure antifreeze in 75% solution (.75 x 14).

$$1X + 6.3 - 4.5X = 10.5$$
$$1X - 0.45X + 6.3 = 10.5$$
$$0.55X = 4.2$$
$$X = 7.636, \text{ or } 7.64 \text{ quarts of } 100\% \text{ antifreeze}$$

To verify that this is indeed the appropriate amount, plug 7.64 into the equation designed for this problem and see if it holds true:

$$1.0 \times 7.64 + .45 (14 - 7.64) = 10.5$$
$$7.64 + 2.862 = 10.5$$
$$10.5 = 10.5$$

86. *B.* This question simply requires a direct proportion:

$$\frac{5 \text{ gallons}}{30 \text{ gallons}} = \frac{115 \text{ miles}}{X \text{ miles}}$$

Therefore,

$$5X = 3,450$$
$$X = 690 \text{ miles}$$

87. *D.* This is basically a two-part question involving an inverse proportion. First, it must be determined how many inmates are in the overcrowded correctional facility: 1.40 (i.e., 140%) x 240 (facility capacity) = 336 inmates. The second step involves setting up an inverse proportion to determine the solution. (It is an inverse rather than a direct proportion because the more inmates incarcerated, the shorter the time that provisions will last.) Therefore,

$$\frac{336 \text{ inmates}}{240 \text{ inmates}} = \frac{14 \text{ days}}{X \text{ days}}$$

$336\, X = 3360$
$X = 10 \text{ days}$

88. *B.* Since the widest extent of a circle is its diameter (i.e., radius x 2), that would represent the minimum width required to sufficiently cover the area described. Therefore, a 13-foot square tarpaulin would suffice.

89. *C.* We realize that the faster someone drives to a given destination, the shorter the time it will require to get there. Therefore, an inverse proportion is needed to solve the problem.

$$\frac{45 \text{ minutes}}{X \text{ minutes}} = \frac{35 \text{ mph}}{30 \text{ mph}}$$

$35X = 1350$
$X = 38.57 \text{ minutes}$

If you selected A, you failed to recognize the need for an inverse proportion and used a direct proportion instead.

90. *C.* The words "for example" are nonrestrictive modifiers that should be preceded and followed by commas.

91. *A.* When the relative or interrogative pronoun is the subject of the verb, the nominative form *who* is used, not *whom*, even when the subject is separated from its verb by other words.

92. *B.* *Proceedure* is misspelled. It should be spelled *procedure*.

93. *C.* "Uniform Crime Reports" requires capitalization.

94. *C.* The independent clause "he was immediately disqualified" should have been preceeded by a comma.

95. *D.* Grammatically correct.

96. *B.* *Commited* is misspelled. It should be spelled *committed*.

97. *A.* The antecedent, "police officers," fails to agree with the pronoun "you." It would be correctly written by using "they" in place of "you."

98. *B.* The word *insure* is an inappropriate homonym which means "to guarantee against loss or harm." *Ensure* means "to secure or guarantee." This is a subtle kind of misspelling that many people tend to overlook.

99. *A.* The sentence contains a misplaced participal phrase. A better way to say the same thing is, "Containing a glove pouch, handcuff case, mace holder, and pen holder, a police officer's belt stores much more than a gun."

100. *C.* Mr. George Peterson is the complainant in this case since he was the person who reported the incident to the authorities. Dennis Foster is the victim.

101. *D.* Box 16 reveals this information. Selection C reflects the date the report was made. Selection A is the victim's date of birth.

102. *B.* The phone number (618) 572-2147 is the home phone of Ms. Antonia Evansdale, the witness.

103. *D.* The true dollar figure should be $3,255.00. Selection A does not take into account that there were two TV sets valued at $95 each ($190 total) and two Dalquist speakers valued at $480 each ($960 total). Pay particular attention to quantities stated in property value summaries.

104. *B.* Box 85 would reveal this information. This case was investigated by Officer Charles Dirkson.

105. *A.* Mr. Foster was the victim in this case; he may or may not have been home at the time. The preliminary investigation report fails to clarify this matter. However, the witness, Ms. Evansdale, can be presumed to be the person who furnished the information concerning the suspects.

106. *C.* Selection A is true because the Weatherby rifle was listed as being worth $700. Selection B is true because the time of occurrence was given as between 1900 hours and 2315 hours, which is 7:00 and 11:15 p.m., respectively. Selection C is incorrect because (618) 572-2147 is Ms. Evansdale's home phone number; the number given is her work phone number. Selection D is true.

107. *C.* Selection A could potentially endanger Officer Duper because medical assistance is not rendered on the scene. Bleeding must be stopped. Selection B would unnecessarily place the public at risk of being struck by a stray bullet or ricochet. Selection D may seem appropriate; however, the best immediate action taken by Officer Gaston is to use the radio to summon medical help and then request backup to pursue the suspect.

108. *C.* Police officers should not accept gratuities for any reason. Not only may an innocent gesture be construed as illegal activity, but it may place the officer in a potentially compromising position that could prejudice his or her actions. Selection C would be the best alternative because the supervisor could contact the owner directly and explain the implications.

109. *D.* Off-duty Officer Bradley's best action would be to tell the host what he saw and allow him or her to handle it. The best thing he could do at that point would be to distance himself from a potentially compromising position. Whom a police officer associates with says a lot about his or her character.

110. *A.* Selection A best sums up what Officer Martin should do. Selection B would be incorrect because serious injuries were a result of the accident. If such things as bleeding and shock are not addressed immediately, the victim(s) involved could die. Life always supersedes property. Selection D makes a poor assumption. This decision could cause an unnecessary delay in medical assistance, thus resulting in the same problem as in B. Selection C detracts from a two-person unit's effectiveness. Partners should always back each other up on individual calls. Assistance for another incident can be summoned by radio.

111. *C.* Again, radioing for another unit to respond would make the best sense. If the young lady had mentioned that a family member was still in the house, it would be prudent for Officer Hastings to become involved even after another unit is radioed to investigate. Potentially life-threatening situations always take precedence over minor traffic accidents. Under the circumstances, though, Choice C would be best. Choices A and D are simply ridiculous.

112. *B.* The best action would be to get as many details as possible from the complainant and then forward the report to an appropriate supervisor. Thus, as would not happen if A were chosen, the complainant will feel the issue is being addressed immediately and the officer can have a chance to explain the circumstances involved. If corrective measures are deemed appropriate, only then will an officer be reprimanded. Selection C could only further exacerbate the problem instead of rectifying it. Selection D is incorrect because that responsibility lies with the supervisor, not dispatch.

113. *D.* Since Officer Hoptkins was eating lunch in another district, jurisdiction should be given due consideration. Under the circumstances, D would be appropriate. If it involved a more serious crime than what was reported, it might have been handled in a different manner. Selections A and C ignore jurisdictional consideration. Selection B is incorrect if Officer Hoptkins does as Selection D prescribes.

114. *D.* Although A may seem appropriate, D is actually correct. Circumstances dictate that a supervisory-level decision should be made about how to handle such a situation. Ignoring the incident, as suggested in B, would be incorrect. Selection C is incorrect because it potentially places both the public and the driver himself at unnecessary risk.

115. *A.* If Officer Milligan does what is described in either C or D, he places public safety at unnecessary risk. This is especially true for a high-speed chase in a residential area. Officer Milligan should slow down and use the radio to coordinate a search and should get assistance from other officers in stopping the suspect. Teamwork is important in such a situation. Selection B works contrary to that notion.

116. *D.* All of the descriptions are helpful; however, D serves as the most distinctive. Many valuable rings are made out of gold and diamonds; however, a ring shaped like a horse's head is relatively rare.

117. *D.* Selection D is correct. Rumors often distort or actually falsify people's character. You should get to know the officer firsthand before jumping to any conclusions. In other words, give the person a chance to demonstrate professionalism.

118. *D.* Selection D is the best method of demonstrating empathy for a person set on committing suicide. Obviously, people place themselves in this kind of position because of strong feelings of alienation. Further chastising the person for what he or she intends to do, as seen in B and C, is exactly the opposite. Instead, the disquieted person should be put at ease and made to feel understood. Selection A could abruptly terminate any such rapport and probably consummate the suicide.

119. *A.* Southeast. The compass perspective may seem a little confusing; however southeast, not east, is the correct answer.

120. *C.* East. Look at the compass legend provided in the previous answer for verification.

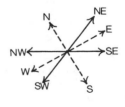

121. *B.* Selection B is correct. Selections A and D are wrong because Pine is a one-way street. Only a right turn is permitted to vehicles leaving Blue Spruce Court. Selection C is wrong because the officer is placed in a position that will require a right turn onto Ranston Avenue from 7th Street to investigate the 500 block of Ranston. This would run against one-way traffic on Ranston Avenue.

122. *C.* Sector C. Look at the jurisdictional boundaries below as described in the map's legend. The 500 block of Ranston Avenue falls within Sector C's jurisdiction. Choice B is fairly close, but it does not encompass the area of concern.

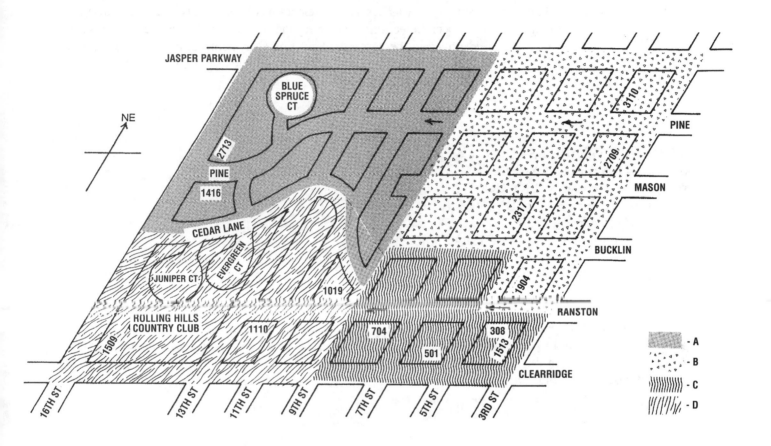

123. *D.* Selection D is correct. It describes the patrol vehicle going to Cedar Lane, along Cedar Lane to 9th Street, on 9th Street to Bucklin, on Bucklin to 3rd Street, and finally along 3rd Street to Jasper at the intersection where Officer Howard is needed. Selections A and C are wrong because the intersection of Jasper Parkway and 9th Street is still blocked (remember, from 10:17 a.m. to 2:32 p.m.). Additionally, the potential traffic congestion in the area would make it almost impossible to get to the destination prescribed. Selection B is wrong because you cannot travel in a southeasterly direction on 16th Street, nor can you travel northeast on Jasper Parkway.

124. *B.* Selection B is incorrect because part of the route (13th Street from Clearridge to Pine) is blocked due to road construction between 0905 and 1115 hours. Selection A is correct in stating that the officer at 704 Ranston Avenue could get to a call on Juniper most quickly by turning right from Ranston Avenue to 9th Street and then left onto Cedar Lane. Selection C is correct in stating that Sector C is basically southwest of Sector B. (If necessary, refer to the jurisdictional map provided in the answer to Question 122.) Selection D is correct in stating that if an officer leaves the precinct station on the corner of 9th Street and Mason Avenue and follows the directions given, he would end up at the intersection of 7th Street and Mason Avenue, placing the officer exactly one block southeast of his point of origin.

125. *D.* Selection D best represents what was described. Selection A is obviously wrong because the vehicle turns with the suspect. Selection B has everyone on foot headed east after the intersection, not west, as described in the narrative. Selection C is incorrect not only because of the directions shown to be taken by everyone involved, but because the officers have taken up incorrect positions according to the reading.

TEST RATINGS ARE AS FOLLOWS:
   120–125 correct, EXCELLENT
   113–119 correct, VERY GOOD
   106–112 correct, GOOD
   100–105 correct, FAIR
   99 or fewer correct, UNSATISFACTORY

Go back to each question you missed and determine if the question was just misinterpreted for one reason or another, or if your response reflects a weakness in subject matter. If it is a matter of misinterpretation, try reading the question more slowly while paying particular attention to key words such as *not, least, except, without,* etc. If, on the other hand, you determine a weakness in a certain area, do not despair. That is what this study guide is for: to identify any area of weakness before you take the actual exam. Reread the material on the area of concern in this study guide. If you still feel a need for supplemental material, your local library is an excellent source.

Practice Examination III

THE TIME ALLOWED for the entire examination is two and a half hours. Each question has four answers, letters A, B, C, and D. Choose the best answer and then, on the answer sheet provided on pages 283–284 (which you can remove from the study guide), find the corresponding question number and darken the circle corresponding to the answer you have selected.

Study the following narrative for five minutes. Do not exceed the time allowance. When your time is up, turn to questions 1–10 without making further reference to this reading.

At 1845 hours on February 11, 1997, State Patrol officers Denise Williams, badge number 1419, and Curt Hansen, badge number 8725, pulled up behind a disabled 1993 Ford Aerostar van parked on the shoulder of Brice Canyon Freeway. When Officer Williams approached the driver to inquire about the problem and offer roadside assistance, if needed, Officer Hansen ran a standard computer check on the van's license plate number AVL-653 for any existing wants and warrants. The driver of the van, Rick Porter, told Officer Williams that they had simply ran out of gas. He also insisted that their assistance was not necessary because another friend was already en route to a nearby filling station to get some gas. When the records search came up that the van was, in fact, reported to be stolen, both the driver and lone passenger in the front seat of the van, Sarah Conners, were placed under arrest for being in possession of a stolen vehicle. At the same time the suspects were being placed in the back seat of the patrol vehicle, a 1989 Ford Mustang GT, license number BOK-151, pulled up behind them. Assuming this was the friend the driver of the van made reference to, Officer Hansen approached the driver and requested to see his license and registration. While inspecting the documents, he asked the driver, Martin Brooks, if he was aware that the van belonging to his friend was stolen. He responded rather flippantly that it was news to him, but anyone who would even contemplate stealing an Aerostar deserved to go to jail anyway! There was a five-gallon gas can in plain view on the back seat as well as a small black nylon duffel bag on the front passenger seat. As a backup unit arrived to assist, Officer Hansen asked the driver to step out of the vehicle to allow for a pat-down search. Nothing of significance was found on his person. However, the duffel bag contained incriminating drug paraphernalia as well as five unwrapped bricks of marijuana. Brooks was placed under arrest for possession of controlled substances. Backup State Patrol officer Vernon Fuller, badge number 1458, took custodial responsibility of the suspect.

The subsequent search of the van turned up a brown-colored leather fanny pack beneath the front passenger seat containing $3,750.00 in cash and close to half a pound of suspected methamphetamines. Additionally, a cache of weapons were discovered beneath the driver's seat which included a Colt Python .357 Magnum revolver, Smith and Wesson Model 19 .38 special revolver, and a Series 80 Colt Mark IV .45 pistol with two spare seven-round clips. The driver did not have a concealed weapons permit so, in addition to narcotics trafficking and auto theft, he was also charged with illegal possession of concealed firearms. Both vehicles were impounded for state's evidence and the three suspects were transported to Evans County Adult Detention for intake and booking. The incident was assigned arrest report number 6781 and filed with Lieutenant Howard Pope, badge number 1580 (acting desk officer for District 3 of the State Patrol) at 2115 hours.

1. The rank of the acting desk officer referred to in the narrative is which of the following?
   A. Captain
   B. Sergeant
   C. Lieutenant
   D. Chief

2. The name of the patrol officer who took custodial responsibility of Martin Brooks was given to be?
   A. Sarah Conners
   B. Vernon Fuller
   C. Rick Porter
   D. Curt Hansen

3. Referring to question number 2, what was the officer's badge number?
   A. 1458
   B. 1518
   C. 1419
   D. 8752

4. What was the year, make/model, and license plate number of the car driven by Martin Brooks?
   A. 1993 Ford Taurus GL, AVL-635
   B. 1989 Ford Thunderbird LX, BKU-997
   C. 1993 Chevrolet Lumina, AVL-653
   D. 1989 Ford Mustang GT, BOK-151

5. According to the narrative, which of the following items was not found beneath the driver's seat in the van?
   A. Series 80 Colt Mark IV .45 revolver
   B. Two spare seven-round clips
   C. Colt Python .357 Magnum revolver
   D. Smith and Wesson Model 19 .38 special revolver

6. When and where did the described incident initially take place?
   A. 2115 hours, February 11, 1997 - Black Canyon Highway
   B. 1845 hours, February 11, 1996 - Brice Canyon Freeway
   C. 1845 hours, February 11, 1997 - Brice Canyon Freeway
   D. 1930 hours, February 1, 1996 - Canyon Falls Highway

7. What was the year, make/model, and license plate number of the vehicle found stranded on the roadside because of running out of gas?
   A. 1989 Ford Aerostar van, AVL-635
   B. 1993 Ford Aerostar van, AVL-653
   C. 1989 Ford Mustang GT, BKO-151
   D. 1991 Ford Probe GT, ALK-791

8. What was the badge number of the patrol officer that ran a standard computer check on the vehicle described in question number 7?

   A. 6871

   B. 8725

   C. 1419

   D. It was not given in the reading

9. What did Officer Hansen see in the back seat of Mr. Brooks' vehicle?

   A. A black nylon duffel bag

   B. A brown leather fanny pack

   C. Illegal contraband

   D. A five-gallon gas can

10. Rick Porter was charged with all of the following crimes except?

    A. Narcotics trafficking

    B. Illegal possession of concealed firearms

    C. Attempted felony elude of a police officer

    D. Auto theft

Assume you are a patrol officer who has fifteen minutes to spare prior to beginning a given patrol assignment. Before leaving headquarters you devote that time to studying the most recent composite list of wants and warrants posted on a squadron bulletin board. Four particular suspects garner your attention because they were last seen in the district you have been assigned to patrol. Keeping the fifteen-minute time frame in mind, study the information pertinent to the four individuals given and then proceed to answer questions 11–25 without further reference to the file.

SUSPECT 1

Name:	Enrico J. Fuentes
Alias:	Frederico L. Garcia
Date of Birth:	11-15-80
Height:	5'3"
Weight:	130 pounds
Hair:	Black
Eyes:	Brown
Sex:	Male
Race:	Hispanic
Scars or Marks:	Scar on right side of forehead extending to around the right eye. Additionally, a crescent-shaped scar is apparent on the left side of the lower lip.
Social Security No.	851-22-4309
Wants and Warrants:	First-degree rape of a child, first-degree kidnapping, and willful failure to return from furlough.
Criminal Record:	Third-degree child molestation, first-degree promoting prostitution, and indecent liberties. Automated Want and Warrant System (AWWS) number 183-52.

SUSPECT 2

Name:	Emily Jean Foster
Alias:	None
Date of Birth:	6-18-73
Height:	5'1"
Weight:	165 pounds
Hair:	Blonde
Eyes:	Green
Sex:	Female
Race:	Caucasian
Scars or Marks:	None
Social Security No.	697-33-4461
Wants and Warrants:	Vehicular homicide and eluding a pursuing police vehicle.
Criminal Record:	No prior.

SUSPECT 3

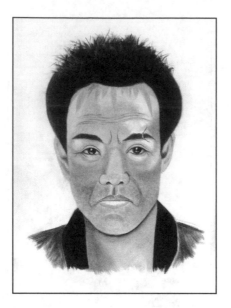

Name: Bruce Yamanaka

Alias: Ichiro Yanagimachi

Date of Birth: 2-6-73

Height: 5'4"

Weight: 155 pounds

Hair: Black

Eyes: Hazel

Sex: Male

Race: Asian American

Scars or Marks: Crescent-shaped scar above left eyebrow.

Social Security No. 580-36-7001

Wants and Warrants: Second-degree custodial interference, first-degree abandonment of a dependent person, and forgery.

Criminal Record: First-degree theft and second-degree possession of stolen property. NCIC File Number 428-10

SUSPECT 4

Name: Alisha Ann Sternquist

Alias: Catherine Middendorf,
Rene Benson

Date of Birth: 5-16-78

Height: 5'7"

Weight: 143 pounds

Hair: Black

Eyes: Brown

Sex: Female

Race: African American

Scars or Marks: None

Social
Security No. 014-38-7891

Wants and
Warrants: First-degree manslaughter.

Criminal Record: Second-degree arson, first-degree malicious mischief, criminal gang intimidation, and reckless endangerment. Considered armed and dangerous.
NCIC File Number 137-38

11. The individual pictured has past convictions for which of the following offenses?

   A. Second-degree theft
   B. First-degree child molestation
   C. Vehicular homicide
   D. This particular suspect did not have any prior convictions.

12. Which of the following sketches is representative of the individual who is wanted for first-degree kidnapping, first-degree rape of a child, and willful failure to return from furlough?

A 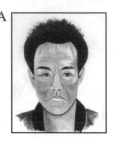   B 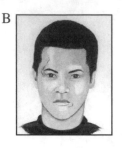   C 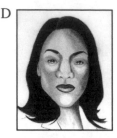   D

13. Which of the following four suspects utilized multiple aliases in the commission of his or her crimes?

   A. Suspects 1 and 3
   B. Suspect 3
   C. Suspect 4
   D. Suspects 2 and 4

14. What is the color of Emily Jean Foster's hair, according to the records provided.

   A. Blonde
   B. Brown
   C. Black
   D. Auburn

15. What kind of distinguishing scars or marks did suspect #3 have?

   A. Crescent-shaped scar on the left side of the lower lip
   B. Crescent-shaped scar above the right eyebrow.
   C. Scar on the right side of forehead extending to around the right eye
   D. Crescent-shaped scar above the left eyebrow.

16. According to the files provided, the suspect pictured below has a criminal record that includes all of the following except:

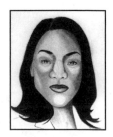

   A. Criminal gang intimidation
   B. First-degree theft
   C. First-degree malicious mischief
   D. Second-degree arson.

17. What is the social security number of the suspect identified as having June 18, 1973 as a DOB?

   A. 014-83-7891
   B. 697-33-4461
   C. 697-36-7001
   D. 041-38-4001

18. According to the NCIC file number 428-10, which of the following statements is false?

    A. Weight and height descriptions are 155 pounds and 5'4" respectively
    B. The individual in question is an Asian American male
    C. Hair and eye color descriptions arc black and hazel, respectively
    D. The person described in this file is wanted for Second-degree possession of stolen property and First-degree theft

19. Which of the following composite sketches is representative of the individual that has a case file number posted in the Automated Want and Warrant System?

    A  B 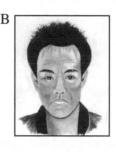 C 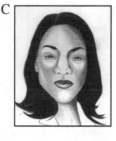 D

20. With regard to question number 19, the case file number assigned to this particular suspect is which of the following?

    A. 183-52
    B. 428-10
    C. 138-58
    D. None of the above

21. Which of the suspects is described as being armed and dangerous?

    A  B  C 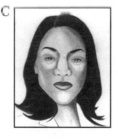 D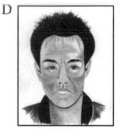

22. The suspect pictured below is described to weigh how much?

    A. 130 pounds
    B. 145 pounds
    C. 155 pounds
    D. 165 pounds

23. According to the case file provided, Suspect #3 went by what other name?

    A. Catherine Middendorf
    B. Ichiro Yanagimachi
    C. Enrico Fuentes
    D. Federico Garcia

24. The suspect shown in the picture at right has what kind of eye color?

    A. Hazel

    B. Blue

    C. Brown

    D. Green

25. Which of the four suspects utilized multiple aliases in the commission of his or her crime?

A 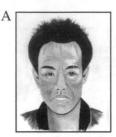   B 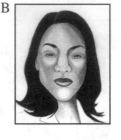   C    D

26. One of the reform bills various state legislatures have approved to toughen drunk driving laws involves changing the legal blood-alcohol threshold to .0008 from .001. Quantitatively speaking, this reflects what kind of modification?

    A. 20% increase

    B. .02% increase

    C. .02% decrease

    D. 20% decrease

27. For the purpose of this question, assume that a direct proportional correlation exists with regard to different individuals' ability to metabolize alcohol; variances are not an issue here. If a 130-pound woman could consume $3^1/_3$ glasses of wine per hour on an empty stomach and remain legally sober, how many glasses of wine could a 156-pound woman consume under the same circumstances and do likewise?

    A. 4

    B. $4^1/_4$

    C. $4^1/_2$

    D. $4^2/_3$

28. During a statewide emphasis patrol one weekend, troopers arrested 380 individuals for driving while under the influence (DUI). Ninety percent of those cases were attributed to alcohol while the remaining involved drug-impaired driving. According to a State Patrol Toxicologist, approximately 5 percent of the latter group of cases actually involved prescription or over-the-counter medication. On the basis of this information, how many people were cited for driving while being impaired by illegal drugs?

    A. 2   B. 5   C. 36   D. 38

29. Officer Nelson was given the assignment of transporting an inmate from Green Meadow Corrections to Silverlake's Adult Detention. According to a road map in Nelson's possession, the two locations are approximately $2^3/_4$ inches apart. If the map's scale stipulates that $^1/_4$ of an inch is equal to 20 miles, how many miles would this trip entail?

    A. 205 miles

    B. 220 miles

    C. 225 miles

    D. 230 miles

30. Assume two precinct stations have the same number of personnel. Station A has $1/8$ of its officers signed up on the overtime-desired roster, whereas Station B has $1/4$ of its officers desiring to work the overtime. Between the two stations, what is the average fraction of personnel preferring to work overtime?

    A. $1/6$

    B. $3/16$

    C. $1/3$

    D. $2/3$

31. A narcotics interdiction task force comprised three different agencies. One-third of the complement consisted of State Patrol officers from commercial vehicle inspection, one-half were affiliated with the Sheriff's Department, and five detectives from a municipal precinct were participating via temporary assignment. Given this information, how many personnel are involved in this task force?

    A. 30

    B. 32

    C. 36

    D. Not possible to determine

32. Officer Swenson received a radio dispatch to investigate a domestic dispute that was approximately 15 miles away. If Officer Swenson drove at a speed that averaged 70 mph as opposed to 50 mph, how much time would she save on her response?

    A. 2.35 minutes

    B. 3.75 minutes

    C. 4 minutes

    D. 5.16 minutes

33. Detective Gephart drove from Boston to a suburb in Washington, D.C., an approximate distance of 475 miles. She left Boston at 9:00 a.m. and arrived at her destination at 9:00 p.m. Assuming that she stopped along the way for an hour and fifteen minute lunch break and one fill up that took approximately fifteen minutes, what was her average rate of speed?

    A. 62.7 MPH

    B. 53.5 MPH

    C. 45.2 MPH

    D. 42.3 MPH

34. If a sheriff's deputy was out sick for 5 days during the first quarter of the year, which comprised a total of 60 work days, how could this be best expressed as a ratio of days worked to sick days?

    A. 60:5

    B. 12:1

    C. 11:1

    D. 12:5

35. The site of a gang-related murder was cordoned off by authorities to preserve evidence. If the area in question is square and one side to that boundary measured 22.25 feet in length, what would be the perimeter of this crime scene?

    A. 89 feet

    B. 80 feet

    C. 44.5 feet

    D. 40 feet

36. Referring to question number 35, what is the area of the described crime scene?
    A. 89 square feet
    B. 220.50 square feet
    C. 465.5685 square feet
    D. 495.0625 square feet

37. Assume departmental policy stipulates that, in the event of a biohazardous material spill, an area at least 15 feet in length from the point of the spill must be cordoned off out of concern for public safety. Under that kind of guideline, what would be the minimum length of rope or cautionary tape necessary to secure a perimeter?
    A. 60 feet
    B. 94.25 feet
    C. 99.75 feet
    D. 102 feet

38. According to what was stated in question number 37, the standardized area of isolating a biohazardous material spill from the general public involves how many square feet?
    A. 706.86 square feet
    B. 685.12 square feet
    C. 47.12 square feet
    D. 25.75 square feet

Questions 39 through 49 relate to grammar, punctuation, and spelling. Each question will provide a written statement that may or may not contain specific errors. From the choices provided, select the answer that represents an accurate assessment of the statement in question and then mark your answer sheet accordingly.

39. Officer Bill Blaine is as tall as, if not taller, than his partner.
    The statement, in terms of English usage,
    A. Is structurally incorrect
    B. Contains one or more misspellings
    C. Lacks necessary punctuation and/or capitalization
    D. Is correct in all aspects.

40. The requisite courses for the first quarter are basic physical science, english composition, and firearm safety.
    The statement, in terms of English usage,
    A. Is structurally incorrect
    B. Contains one or more misspellings
    C. Lacks necessary punctuation and/or capitalization
    D. Is correct in all aspects.

41. The laws of most states provide for a preliminary hearing to decide whether an accused person should be treated as a juvenile delinquent.
    The statement, in terms of English usage,
    A. Is structurally incorrect
    B. Contains one or more misspellings
    C. Lacks necessary punctuation and/or capitalization
    D. Is correct in all aspects.

42. Lieutenent Carmichael chose to have her acceptance speech on Friday, August 2, 2002, in order to reach a larger audience.
     The statement, in terms of English usage,
A. Is structurally incorrect
B. Contains one or more misspellings
C. Lacks necessary punctuation and/or capitalization
D. Is correct in all aspects.

43. Officer Phinney, together with some close friends and neighbors, are planning a neighborhood meeting that addresses crime prevention.
     The statement, in terms of English usage,
A. Is structurally incorrect
B. Contains one or more misspellings
C. Lacks necessary punctuation and/or capitalization
D. Is correct in all aspects.

44. Neither of the courses are acceptable for post graduate studies.
     The statement, in terms of English usage,
A. Is structurally incorrect
B. Contains one or more misspellings
C. Lacks necessary punctuation and/or capitalization
D. Is correct in all aspects.

45. Methamphetamine users frequently suffer from the allusion they are invincible.
     The statement, in terms of English usage,
A. Is structurally incorrect
B. Contains one or more misspellings
C. Lacks necessary punctuation and/or capitalization
D. Is correct in all aspects.

46. Detective Matson worked quick in gathering statements from potential witnesses.
     The statement, in terms of English usage,
A. Is structurally incorrect
B. Contains one or more misspellings
C. Lacks necessary punctuation and/or capitalization
D. Is correct in all aspects.

47. He looked differently after his return from Canada.
     The statement, in terms of English usage,
A. Is structurally incorrect
B. Contains one or more misspellings
C. Lacks necessary punctuation and/or capitalization
D. Is correct in all aspects.

48. The defendant claimed that she had borrowed her father's in-law car on several previous occasions.
     The statement, in terms of English usage,
A. Is structurally incorrect
B. Contains one or more misspellings
C. Lacks necessary punctuation and/or capitalization
D. Is correct in all aspects.

49. The titanium framework of this particular revolver is more stronger than other conventional models. The statement, in terms of English usage,

   A. Is structurally incorrect
   B. Contains one or more misspellings
   C. Lacks necessary punctuation and/or capitalization
   D. Is correct in all aspects.

Questions 50–60 pertain to spelling. Each question has four numerically identified columns, each comprising various word sets. One of the word sets given will contain an intentionally misspelled word. Select the column number that represents the misspelled word and mark your answer sheet accordingly.

50.

I.	II.	III.	IV.
subpoena	fraudulent	rhythmic	pedestrian
ultimatum	mustache	sterilyze	intoxicated
license	oxygen	terrorism	khaki
schedule	prohibitive	opportunity	homicide

   A. I
   B. II
   C. III
   D. IV

51.

I.	II.	III.	IV.
racial	embezzlement	menace	profanity
psychology	breathilyzer	inquiry	reference
noticeable	suicidal	evidence	ordinance
counterfeit	prostitution	microfiche	mileage

   A. I
   B. II
   C. III
   D. IV

52.

I.	II.	III.	IV.
resistance	nausea	procedure	headache
incorrigible	laboratory	seize	iliterate
felony	illegal	interrogate	physician
personnel	obstacle	gauge	lieutenant

   A. I
   B. II
   C. III
   D. IV

53.

I.	II.	III.	IV.
probationary	concealed	substantiate	proximity
persistent	admonition	bruise	preliminary
marijuana	vicious	anonymous	fornication
grievence	suspicion	unconscious	miscellaneous

A. I
B. II
C. III
D. IV

54.

I.	II.	III.	IV.
injured	detention	sobriety	questionaire
malicious	ammunition	tourniquet	forcibly
loiter	surveillance	skidded	hazardous
contraband	pursuit	incriminate	knife

A. I
B. II
C. III
D. IV

55.

I.	II.	III.	IV.
motorcycle	transferred	permanent	arraignment
opinion	tongue	municipol	commercial
strangulate	larceny	revoked	summons
voluntary	feminine	casualty	conscious

A. I
B. II
C. III
D. IV

56.

I.	II.	III.	IV.
submitting	ocurred	corroborate	promiscuous
rationalization	proceeded	disposition	intimidation
patience	bulletin	assistance	juvenile
interview	apparent	statute	misdemeanor

A. I
B. II
C. III
D. IV

57.

I.	II.	III.	IV.
fracture	vagrancy	robbery	extortion
Miranda	nerotic	inherent	complainant
semiautomatic	representation	government	credibility
sexual	punitive	obnoxious	admissible

A. I
B. II
C. III
D. IV

58.

I.	II.	III.	IV.
sacrifice	judgment	conspiracy	stationary
religious	forgery	subtle	occasion
official	boulevard	secretary	liquor
mitigate	apprehend	relivant	negotiable

A. I
B. II
C. III
D. IV

59.

I.	II.	III.	IV.
spontaneous	depression	emergency	metropolitan
prescription	criteria	vicinity	fugitive
indigent	attorney	translucent	individual
conviction	accident	regrettable	informent

A. I
B. II
C. III
D. IV

60.

I.	II.	III.	IV.
chauffeur	receipt	indecent	suffocate
trespassing	mischief	toxicology	forfeit
commited	scheme	behavior	liability
prejudiced	tattoo	alcohol	superintendent

A. I
B. II
C. III
D. IV

Questions 61–70 pertain to vocabulary proficiency. Each question will pose a statement that will have two key words deleted from its context. You must determine from the four selections given which pair of respective words best fits the meaning of the sentence as a whole.

61. The forensic expert's _____ testimony _____ the filed police report.
    A. Sanguine/Epitomized
    B. Incontrovertible/Corroborated
    C. Irrefutable/Instigated
    D. Perfunctory/Commemorated

62. Officer Peters' _____ demeanor is probably the reason he is able to _____ information from witnesses.
    A. Ambivalent/Elicit
    B. Cordial/Illicit
    C. Affable/Elicit
    D. Benevolent/Illicit

63. There is no _____ way to identify a potentially violent individual's _____ for committing murder.
    A. Unerring/Exigency
    B. Irreconcilable/Attenuation
    C. Ambiguous/Propensity
    D. Infallible/Predisposition

64. This _____ law has had a bottom line _____ of reducing consumer identity fraud complaints.
    A. Venerable/Affect
    B. Supercilious/Effect
    C. Contrived/Affect
    D. Inclusive/Effect

65. Detective Tyson thought it was an _____ idea to remain _____ in a marginally covered position during a gunfight.
    A. Insipid/Stationery
    B. Inane/Stationary
    C. Insolent/Stationery
    D. Inconspicuous/Stationary

66. Sergeant Henderson had a _____ that the _____ weather would prompt a rash of vehicular accidents.
    A. Penchant/Eminent
    B. Premonition/Inclement
    C. Premeditation/Inauspicious
    D. Pensiveness/Docile

67. Despite being _____ by the press, Officer Platt has been nothing but _____ toward the indigent.
    A. Vilified/Magnanimous
    B. Reproached/Meticulous
    C. Extolled/Resplendent
    D. Stigmatized/Indolent

68. Police Chief Nichols maintained the _____ position that the department will never _____ to the whims of political correctness.
    A. Malleable/Succumb
    B. Capricious/Subvert
    C. Staunch/Capitulate
    D. Tenuous/Recapitulate

69. According to Field Training Officer Johnson, most rookie officers initially seem to _____ between being incompetent one moment and then quite _____ the next.
    A. Vacillate/Adroit
    B. Embellish/Facetious
    C. Paradox/Propitious
    D. Repose/Surreptitious

70. Law enforcement officers are _____ by the increasing numbers of motorists _____ traffic laws.
    A. Disdained/Flaunting
    B. Chagrined/Flouting
    C. Loath/Subjugating
    D. Disenfranchised/Conforming

Questions 71 through 79 involve composite sketch cross comparison. Look at the original sketch of the subject on the left and then try to discern which of the four other sketches to the right (labeled a, b, c, d) provided is the same individual attempting to disguise his or her appearance. Unless otherwise stated, assume the individual in question has not undergone any surgery.

71.

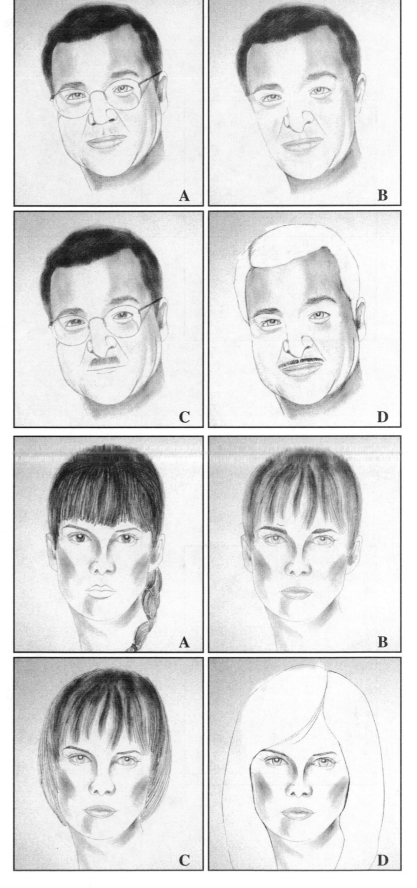

72.

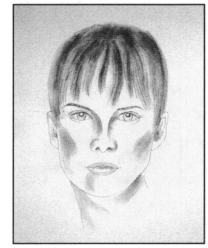

73.

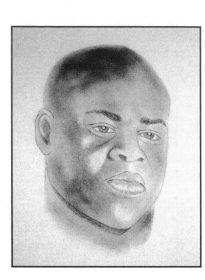

74.

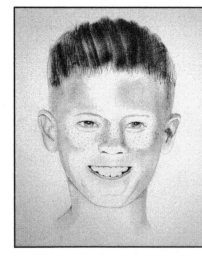

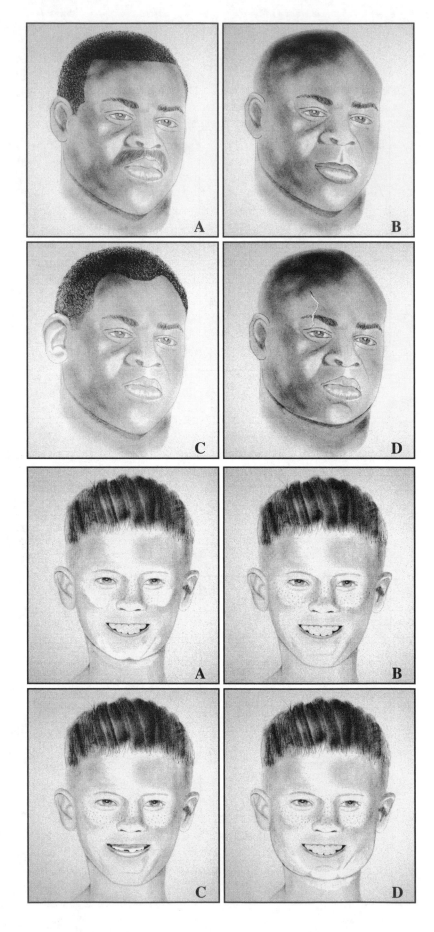

75.

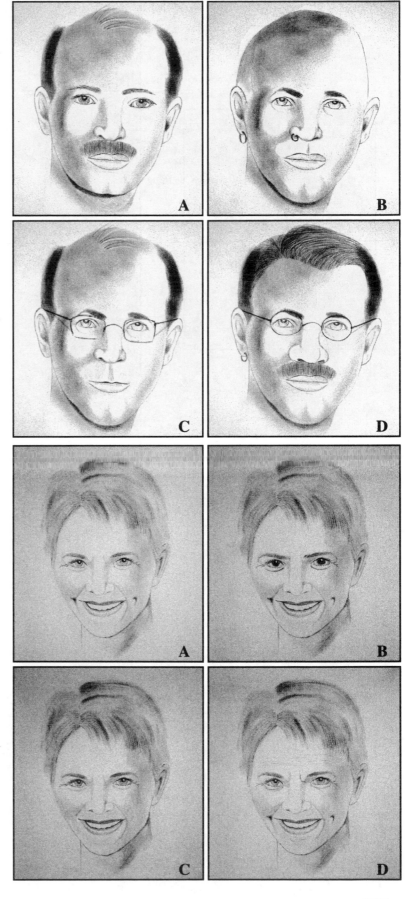

76.

77.

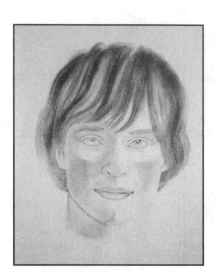

78.

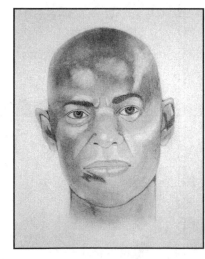

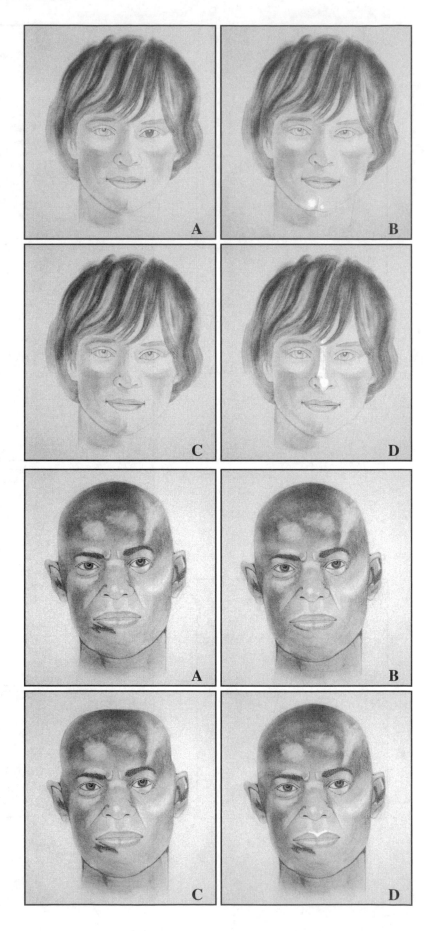

79.

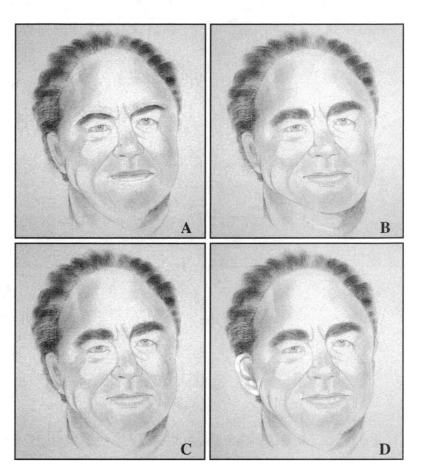

Answer questions 80 and 81 on the basis of the pie chart presented below.

2002 FISCAL BUDGET APPROPRIATIONS FOR JOHNSON COUNTY
DEPARTMENT OF PUBLIC SAFETY ARE AS FOLLOWS:

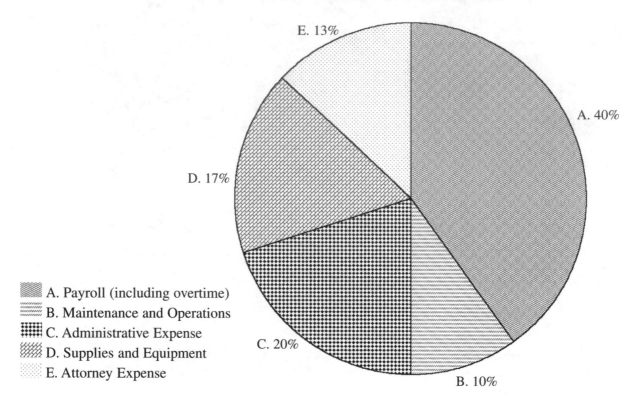

A. Payroll (including overtime)
B. Maintenance and Operations
C. Administrative Expense
D. Supplies and Equipment
E. Attorney Expense

80. Which of the following statements would be considered true with respect to Johnson County's budgetary appropriations?
   A. Both D and E represent the largest outlay of expense.
   B. Both A and B represent the largest outlay of expense.
   C. Supplies and Equipment represent the smallest of financial outlays.
   D. Both Administrative Expense and Payroll represent the largest outlay of expense.

81. All of the following statements are false except:
   A. Attorney expenses for the department is the third largest outlay, according to the chart provided.
   B. Supplies and Equipment in combination with Administrative expense constitute a larger percentage of the overall budget as opposed to Payroll.
   C. Administrative expense is second only to Payroll in terms of the overall budget.
   D. Maintenance and Operation comprises one quarter of the entire budget.

The line graph below represents a report compilation for a State Patrol district over a five-year period. Answer questions 82–84 based on the following data.

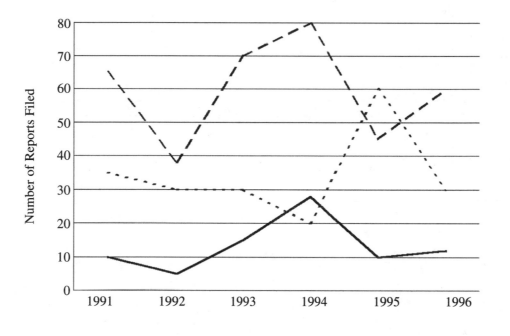

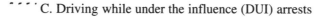 A. Auto accidents involving fatalities

B. Auto accidents involving injuries

C. Driving while under the influence (DUI) arrests

82. Which year clearly demonstrated that drunk driving emphasis patrols yielded tangible benefits with regard to public safety?
    A. 1992
    B. 1994
    C. 1995
    D. 1996

83. Public safety wise, which year was conclusively the worst?
    A. 1996
    B. 1994
    C. 1993
    D. 1992

84. Assuming that population figures within the State Patrol District remained roughly the same over the five year study, what year in particular most likely reflected either better than normal road conditions or the prospect that motorists exercised more caution while driving?
    A. 1992
    B. 1993
    C. 1995
    D. 1996

Answer questions 85 through 88 on the basis of the following data.

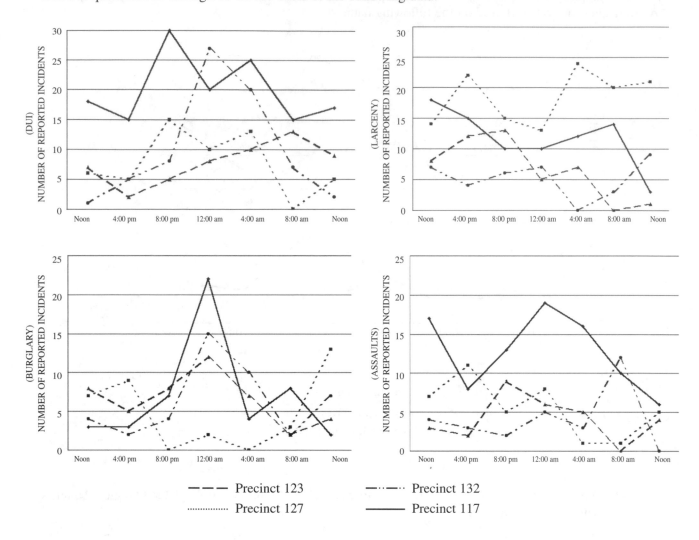

------ Precinct 123   —·—·— Precinct 132
············· Precinct 127   ———— Precinct 117

Precinct 123 encompasses the 500–4000 blocks of all alphabetically identified avenues and 4100–8000 blocks of all alphabetically identified streets.

Precinct 127 encompasses the 500–4000 blocks of all alphabetically identified streets and 4100–8000 blocks of all alphabetically identified avenues.

Precinct 132 encompasses the 500–4000 blocks of all numerically identified streets and 4100–8000 blocks of all numerically identified avenues.

Precinct 117 encompasses the 4100–8000 blocks of all numerically identified streets, 500–4000 blocks of all numerically identified avenues, and all other named streets not inclusive in other precinct jurisdictions.

85. If Police Chief Fitzgerald wanted to best address the incidence of DUIs reported in the downtown area (i.e., 1000 block) of 16th, 17th, and 18th streets, he would do which of the following?
   A. Assign additional 8 p.m. drunk driving emphasis patrols in Precinct 117
   B. Assign additional midnight drunk driving emphasis patrols in Precinct 132
   C. Assign additional midnight drunk driving emphasis patrols in Precinct 123
   D. Assign additional 4 a.m. drunk driving emphasis patrols in Precinct 132

86. Assume Police Chief Fitzgerald received complaints from City Hall that not enough was being done about the drunk drivers departing from various taverns located on the 3000 block of 140th Avenue. His most effective means to address this problem would be which of the following?
    A. Assign additional 8 a.m. DUI patrols in Precinct 123
    B. Assign additional midnight DUI patrols in Precinct 132
    C. Assign additional 8 a.m. DUI patrols in Precinct 117
    D. Assign additional 8 p.m. DUI patrols in Precinct 117

87. What would be the best appropriation of additional police patrols in countering the incidence of assault occurring around the 1500 block of D and E streets?
    A. Bolster the 8 p.m. shift in Precinct 123
    B. Bolster the 4 p.m. shift in Precinct 127
    C. Bolster the noon shift in Precinct 127
    D. Bolster the 8 a.m. shift in Precinct 123

88. Which of the following personnel directives would have the least probable effect of deterring assault in a low income housing project located on the 700 block of H Avenue? NOTE: Assignments outside of the jurisdiction in question cannot be considered as a viable option.
    A. Increase the number of patrol units working the 8 a.m. shift in Precinct 123
    B. Increase the number of patrol units working the noon shift in Precinct 132
    C. Increase the number of patrol units working the 4 a.m. shift in Precinct 127
    D. Increase the number of patrol units working the 8 p.m. shift in Precinct 123

Below is a bar graph that represents statewide issuances of speeding citations by the State Patrol during a given 24-hour period. Answer questions 89 through 91 on the basis of the following data.

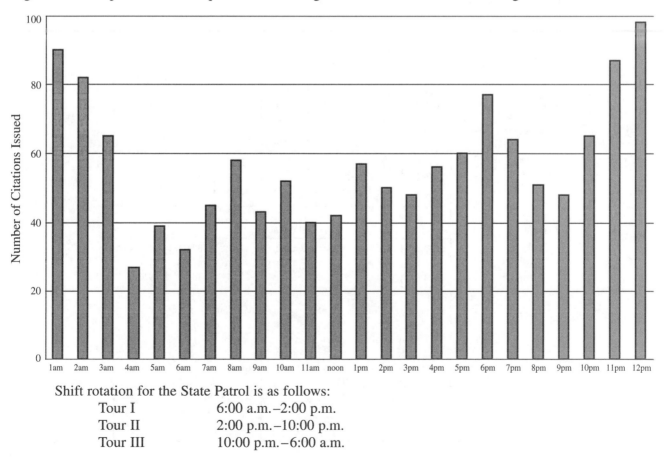

Shift rotation for the State Patrol is as follows:
    Tour I   6:00 a.m.–2:00 p.m.
    Tour II   2:00 p.m.–10:00 p.m.
    Tour III   10:00 p.m.–6:00 a.m.

89. According to the statistics provided, which of the following assumptions has merit?
    A. There are about twice as many speeding citations issued in the early afternoon hours as opposed to late morning hours.
    B. Perhaps for visibility reasons, motorists are much more cautious about speeding at night.
    C. "Rush hour" for the day would unequivocally be from noon to 1:00 p.m.
    D. Motorists tend to drive somewhat more conservatively during the late morning hours as opposed to late evening hours.

90. The lowest incidence of speeding occurred during which State Patrol shift rotation?
    A. Tour I
    B. Tour II
    C. Tour III
    D. A determination cannot be made from the data provided

91. Select the statement below that least accurately represents the information provided in the study.
    A. Tours I and II issued roughly the same number of speeding citations during their first hour of duty.
    B. Among the three shifts, Tour III issued the largest proportion of speeding tickets.
    C. There were significant increases in speeding incidents at about the halfway mark into each of the three shifts.
    D. The 10:00 p.m.–6:00 a.m. shift, without question, demonstrated the widest variance with respect to speeding ticket issuances.

Answer questions 92–98 on the basis of the information provided below.

Effective July 1, 1998 by order of Commander Jamison, Post Command District 18 assigned work schedules are as follows:

Personnel Roster/Badge No.

Wiggins - 521
Hershberger - 145
Brown - 976
Vanderpool - 329
Klinger - 131
Bateman - 670
Locke - 563
Santoya - 802
Tyson - 718
Unger - 314
Ryzek - 612
Pratt - 152
Powell - 417
Hudson - 410

SECTOR 14

M	T	W	TH	F	S	S
521-C	329-B	417-C	521-C	670-A	521-B	145-B
329-A	131-C	145-B	612-A	521-B	152-C	802-A
670-B	976-A	612-A	802-B	152-C	802-A	521-C

SECTOR 12

670-C	314-B	329-A	417-C	131-C	718-B	314-A
976-B	718-C	131-C	131-B	145-B	314-A	718-B
145-A	802-A	976-B	314-A	802-A	612-C	152-C

SECTOR 9

802-A	670-B	670-B	145-B	417-B	329-A	329-A
718-C	145-A	314-A	152-C	976-A	417-B	417-C
314-B	612-C	718-C	670-A	612-C	131-C	976-B

Annual Leave postings:

July 1–7	(976)
July 1–14	(131)
July 7–21	(612)
July 14–21	(314)
July 21–26	(329)
July 21–31	(145)

Vacation Relief:
(410)
(563)

Tours:
A – 6:30 am – 2:30 pm
B – 2:30 pm – 10:30 pm
C – 10:30 pm – 6:30 am

92. According to the duty roster, which patrol officer drew a part-time (i.e., less than forty hours) work assignment?
    A. Santoya
    B. Vanderpool
    C. Pratt
    D. Klinger

93. Assuming that Tour A was the preferred shift among police personnel, which of the following individuals received the best schedule presumably due to his or her seniority status?
    A. Brown
    B. Ryzek
    C. Powell
    D. Unger

94. Who was assigned to work the Monday 10:30 p.m.–6:30 a.m. shift in Sector 9?
    A. Tyson
    B. Santoya
    C. Unger
    D. Bateman

95. On the presumption that District 18 did not have a serious shortage of patrol personnel, who seems to be the subject of an apparent scheduling error?
    A. Locke
    B. Bateman
    C. Hudson
    D. Wiggins

96. If Independence Day fell on a Saturday, who would be working Tour C on July 6 in Sector 12?
    A. Hudson
    B. Tyson
    C. Vanderpool
    D. Hershberger

97. If Independence Day fell on a Friday, who would be working the Tour A detail on July 18th in Sector 14?
    A. Klinger
    B. Brown
    C. Ryzek
    D. Bateman

98. If July 22nd fell on a Thursday, who is scheduled to work Tour C detail in Sector 14 on July 13th?
    A. Klinger
    B. Pratt
    C. Locke
    D. Wiggins

Answer questions 99 through 106 on the basis of the following passage.

Mr. James Emery Hall was arrested November 13, 1996, by State Patrol Officer Lt. Pete Kendrick, badge number 1515, on charges of aggravated assault of an officer (NCIC Code 13501-A) and resisting arrest (NCIC Code 13721-B). Mr. Hall's erratic driving pattern on Interstate 199 prompted Officer Kendrick to pull him over to conduct a field sobriety check. Pursuant to Officer Kendrick's request to submit to a breathalyzer test, Mr. Hall became agitated and struck the officer in the face. There was a brief struggle, but Mr. Hall was subdued, handcuffed, and Mirandized (i.e., read his rights). During the course of the arrest, Mr. Hall (the suspect in question) maintained that his name was Jeffrey T. Beaumont. A computer-records search of what apparently was a forged ID indicated that no such person existed. However, his physical description—Caucasian, 6'2", approximately 215 pounds, black hair and brown eyes—matched that of a Mr. James Emery Hall, who was the legally registered owner of the vehicle pulled over. There was also an existing warrant out for his arrest for failure to appear in court over two unrelated misdemeanor charges. Lakeview Police Officer Harry M. Stevens, badge number 503, took custodial responsibility for transporting Mr. Hall to Lewis County Detention for booking and intake. Corrections Officer John Cornwall, badge number 181, received Mr. Hall at 0937 hours on the same day of his arrest and inventoried his personal effects for property storage. Mr. Hall was issued receipt number 1517 for his personal belongings. Mr. Hall was much more compliant during the booking and intake process than he was during his arrest. Not only was he cooperative with being fingerprinted, he additionally provided Officer Cornwall his true identity, including his Social Security number (555-22-0557), place of birth (Cedar Rapids, IA), and birth date (October 3, 1957). He remains in detention pending an arraignment hearing scheduled on November 19, 1996, in Lewis County Superior Court. Mr. Hall's case file reference number is 26-07A.

99. Assuming the Lewis County Deputy Prosecutor's office needed to review file information pertinent to the defendant (i.e., the person arrested), which of the following case file numbers would be used for proper reference?
    A. 62-71C
    B. 15-17A
    C. 26-07A
    D. 50-01E

100. The arresting officer in this particular incident was whom?
    A. Lewis County Sheriff Harry M. Stevens
    B. Lakeview Police officer James E. Hall
    C. State Patrol officer Sergeant John Cornwall
    D. State Patrol officer Pete Kendrick

101. According to the narrative, the defendant in question tried to use which of the following names as an alias?
    A. Jeffrey T. Beaumont
    B. James E. Hall
    C. Jeffrey M. Kendrick
    D. John A. Cornwall

102. Fingerprint Processing Reports have a standard entry for applicable NCIC codes detailing charges against the person arrested. Since the defendant in question was charged with resisting arrest and aggravated assault of an officer, the respective NCIC codes entered into such a report would be which of the following?
    A. 13501-A and 13721-B
    B. 1515-B and 0937-A
    C. 13503-A and 13215-C
    D. 13721-B and 13501-A

103. Pursuant to the defendant's release after posting the required bail, he was scheduled to appear when for an Arraignment Hearing in Lewis County Superior Court?
    A. 9-19-96
    B. 11-19-96
    C. 10-3-96
    D. None of the above

104. All of the following selections are accurate physical descriptions of the defendant except?
    A. Black hair
    B. Blue eyes
    C. Caucasian
    D. 6'2"

105. Who took custodial responsibility of transporting the defendant to Lewis County Detention for booking and intake?
    A. State Patrol officer John Cornwall
    B. Lakeview Police officer Harry M. Stevens
    C. County Sheriff Lieutenant Pete Kendrick
    D. Corrections officer James E. Hall

106. According to the narrative, what was the defendant's Social Security number?
    A. 222-55-0257
    B. 552-55-0227
    C. 555-22-0557
    D. 252-55-0227

107. Police Officer McMillan is the first officer to arrive at the scene of a smash-and-grab burglary. Four witnesses provided the following license plate numbers belonging to the vehicle used in the get away. On the presumption that witnesses can confuse various details, which of the following descriptions is most likely to be the license plate number in question?
    A. CRT 589
    B. ORI 589
    C. CBT 509
    D. CRT 581

108. Sheriff Albright receives a radio dispatch to investigate a drive-by shooting in a rural area that has seen a recent spate of gang-related activity. Upon her arrival, four witnesses to the event provided the following descriptions of the suspect vehicle involved.

    A. A hunter green colored BMW, two-door sedan, that has collision damage to the left rear quarter panel

    B. A black colored Mercedes, two-door sedan, that has collision damage to the right rear quarter panel

    C. A black colored BMW, two-door sedan, that has collision damage to the left rear quarter panel

    D. A black colored BMW, four-door sedan, that has collision damage to the right rear quarter panel.

    Which of these descriptions should Officer Albright consider the most likely to be correct?

109. Detective Blackmore was dispatched to a local college campus to investigate the rape of a female student. Four witnesses saw the incident and offered the following descriptions of the assailant.

    A. A white male, approximately 30 years of age, 6'2", 200 pounds, wearing a white sweatshirt and brown pants

    B. A white male, approximately 23 years of age, 6'1", 195 pounds, wearing a white T-shirt and beige pants

    C. A white male, approximately 20 years of age, 5'7", 195 pounds, wearing a white sweatshirt and brown pants

    D. A white male, approximately 21 years of age, 6 feet, 225 pounds, wearing a white T-shirt and tan pants.

    Which of the preceding descriptions would most likely be an accurate profile of the perpetrator in question?

Various crime definitions and applicable code index numbers are provided below. Review each of these terms before proceeding with questions 110 through 114.

Disorderly Conduct (01.52.33)—an individual that commits intentional disruption of any lawful assembly of people without the legal authority to act OR the intentional risk of assault fomented by using abusive language.

Riot/Second Degree (01.62.71)—an individual who conspires with four or more people to purposely and illegally threaten or actually utilize force against property or other individuals.

Riot/First Degree (01.62.17)—comparable to Riot/Second Degree with the exception that the use of force includes a deadly weapon.

Failure to Disperse (01.25.47)—an individual's acts of conduct among four or more people that constitutes substantial risk of injury to others or significant harm to public or private property.

Reckless Endangerment (01.47.33)—an individual's acts of conduct that create substantial risk of injury or death to another person.

Obstructing a Law Enforcement Officer (01.25.33)—any individual's actions that purposefully delay, hinder, or obstruct any officer in the discharge of his or her duties.

Resisting Arrest (01.52.17)—any conduct of an individual that intentionally prevents or attempts to prevent a law enforcement officer from executing his or her arrest.

110. As part of a gang initiation, Tom Morris drove past a rival gang member's house and shot out the living room windows with a .40-caliber pistol. There were four people inside the house at the time of the shooting. The residents were unnerved by the incident but, fortunately, no one was injured. Pursuant to Mr. Morris' apprehension and subsequent arrest, which of the following statute codes could Mr. Morris be charged with?

A. 01.62.17

B. 01.47.33

C. 01.52.33

D. None of the above

111. Police Officer McFarland was in close pursuit with a vehicle that was reported to have been stolen thirty minutes earlier. A high-speed chase ensued through several residential areas until a pedestrian inadvertently stepped out in front of McFarland's police cruiser. Officer McFarland managed to stop in time to avoid hitting the individual, but the suspect got away. An ID check of the pedestrian in question revealed a home address that coincidentally was the same block where the registered owner of the stolen vehicle lived. Under the circumstances, which of the following selections would be the best course of action for Officer McFarland to take?

A. Arrest the pedestrian for violating statute codes 01.25.33 and 01.47.33

B. Arrest the pedestrian for violating statute codes 01.52.17 and 01.25.33

C. Arrest the pedestrian for violating statute code 01.25.33

D. None of the above

112. Frank Santiago and Tyler "Shortie" Hopkins, both of whom belonged to the Crips gang, were among a large turnout of people in a downtown metropolitan area celebrating Mardi Gras. Tyler spotted two individuals in the crowd that were sporting insignia that identified them as belonging to a rival gang. Tyler wasted little time in convincing Frank and four other Crips members that the two were trespassing on their "turf" and needed to be made an example of. Frank got the pair's attention, not to mention ire, by shouting profane and derogatory remarks about the gang they belonged to. It was not long before a heated exchange of words turned into a full-scale brawl. Two Transit Police Officers happened to be in the vicinity at the time and they interceded to break up the fight, but not before "Shortie" Hopkins produced a switchblade knife and waved it around in a threatening manner toward the two he intended to intimidate.

Assuming Mr. Santiago was placed under arrest without further incident, what statute code or codes could he be charged with for his part in the altercation?

A. 01.62.71, 01.25.47, and 01.52.33

B. 01.47.33

C. 01.62.17, 01.52.33 and 01.25.47

D. 01.25.33, 01.52.33, and 01.52.17

113. On the presumption that Mr. Hopkins was anything but cooperative for his arrest, which of the following statute codes would apply in his case?

A. 01.25.33, 01.62.17, 01.25.47, and 01.52.33

B. 01.52.17, 01.25.47, 01.52.33, and 01.62.17

C. 01.62.17 and 01.52.33

D. 01.62.71 and 01.52.33

114. Detective Bret Morrison had a search warrant for the apartment of a tenant suspected of manufacturing a controlled substance for distribution. However, the apartment manager, Kay Wright, had known the suspect for years and doubted the merits of such an accusation. As a result, she refused to comply with Officer Morrison's request to search the apartment. Under the circumstances, Ms. Wright could be charged with which of the following statute codes?

    A. 01.47.33
    B. 01.52.17
    C. 01.25.33
    D. 01.52.33

115. Officer Bill Kenyon has prepared an incident report detailing a robbery of a convenience store. The following five sentences were taken out of the text of that report in no particular order.

    1. CENCOM received the robbery-in-progress call at 1715 hours
    2. The owner of the store, Kwon Trang, was laying on the floor unconscious with serious contusions to the left side of his face
    3. Statements from two witnesses indicated the pair of suspects left the area in a maroon colored Plymouth Voyager
    4. An undetermined amount of money was taken from the cash register
    5. At 1718 hours, I was dispatched to investigate a robbery at R&H Market on 4th Street and Yelm

    Which of the following alternatives represent the correct chronological order of events?

A.	1	5	2	3	4
B.	5	1	2	4	3
C.	2	1	5	3	4
D.	2	1	3	5	4

116. The following sentences are notes taken from an officer's activity log detailing the investigation of a domestic dispute. The sentences are not arranged in any particular order. Select the alternative that represents the facts as they would appear chronologically in the official activity log.

    1. Paramedics arrived at 2050 hours and bandaged Ms. Williams' ear before taking her to Saint Moreland Hospital
    2. I placed Ms. Henderson under arrest for second-degree assault
    3. Ms. Williams was clearly in an intoxicated state in addition to having blood running down the side of her neck from her left ear
    4. Ms. Henderson claimed she had to protect herself so she bit Ms. Williams' ear
    5. Mr. Cecil Cole, the complainant who lived next door in the same duplex, wanted the fighting between his neighbors stopped immediately

A.	5	2	3	4	1
B.	4	3	5	1	2
C.	5	3	4	1	2
D.	4	2	1	3	5

117. Police Officer Tricia Jones has prepared a report detailing a traffic accident that occurred at the intersection of 14th Avenue and Claymore Street. The following five sentences were taken out of the text of that report in no particular order.

    1. The pedestrian, Melissa Tate, was thrown approximately fifteen feet from the point of impact and remained motionless in the middle of the street.
    2. The driver of the van, Patricia Gordon, reeked of alcohol and later tested to have a blood alcohol level of .02 percent.

3. I conducted CPR on the victim until Fire District 17 paramedics arrived and took over her care.

4. Ms. Gordon was arrested and charged with involuntary manslaughter and driving while under the influence.

5. Witnesses said the driver of the van did not slow down or even attempt to swerve out of the way to avoid hitting the pedestrian in the crosswalk.

Which of the following alternatives represent the correct chronological order of events?

A. 1 3 2 4 5
B. 3 1 5 2 4
C. 4 3 2 5 1
D. 1 3 2 5 4

118. The following sentences are notes taken from Patrol Officer Dean Wells' activity log detailing the investigation of a disorderly conduct incident. The sentences are not arranged in any particular order. Select the alternative that represents the facts as they would appear chronologically in the official activity log.

1. The bartender claimed that four men determined to celebrate past the 2:00 a.m. closure time started to shout profanities at him when he quit serving drinks for the night

2. Two of the three men were clearly intoxicated

3. I received a dispatch at 0215 hours to investigate a disturbance at the Speedway Tavern located on Pike Street and 7th Avenue

4. After Mr. Younger ignored repeated requests to leave the premises, I placed him under arrest for disorderly conduct

5. The bartender's mere threat of contacting the authorities managed to dissuade one of the patrons from staying

A. 1 2 3 4 5
B. 3 1 5 2 4
C. 3 2 1 5 4
D. 2 1 3 5 4

119. If a patrol officer was driving northeast on a county road and, in getting to a particular destination, made two right turns followed by two left turns, and then another right turn, what direction would he or she then be headed? (Assume all turns were right-angle, 90-degree change of direction)

A. North
B. Southeast
C. Northeast
D. Southwest

120. Assume you are a patrol officer traveling southeast on a given highway when you clock an oncoming vehicle doing 35 miles per hour over the speed limit. If you make a U-turn to initiate a pursuit, which direction would you now be traveling?

A. Northeast
B. Northwest
C. Southwest
D. North

121. If the same motorist described in question number 120 attempts a right turn in an obvious bid to elude an inevitable citation, which direction would you now have to travel to effect an arrest?

    A. Northeast   B. Northwest   C. Southwest   D. North

Answer questions 122–125 on the basis of the map provided below.

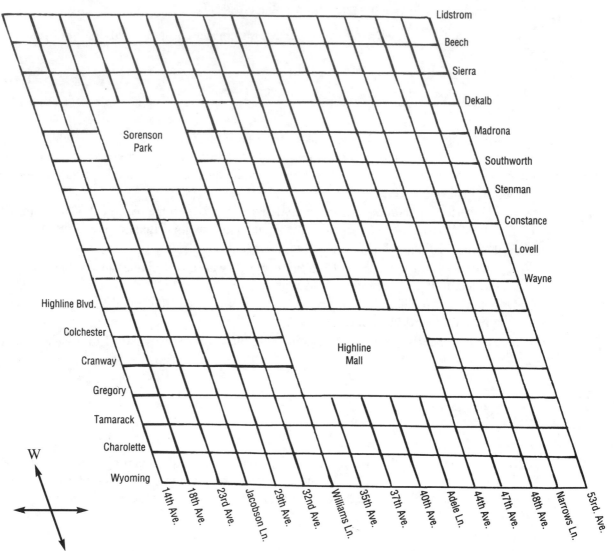

122. Assume that Constance, Highline, Gregory, and Charolette are one-way streets that direct traffic flow north; all odd-numbered avenues are one-way streets that direct traffic flow east; all other streets not referenced can be presumed to be two-way streets. Which of the alternative routes provided below would be considered legal means for a police officer working traffic enforcement at the intersection of Charolette and 35th Avenue to respond to a traffic accident that occurred on Constance and 29th Avenue?

    A. Go from 35th Avenue on Charolette to 32nd Avenue, turn right, go eight blocks before turning left and driving one block.

    B. Go east one block, south four blocks, west nine blocks, and then one block north.

    C. Go north on Charolette one block, turn left, go one block west, turn left again, go five blocks south, turn right, go seven blocks west, turn right again and go one block north.

    D. Go east four blocks and then eight blocks south.

123. Assume that Wayne, Constance, Tamarack, and Charolette are one-way streets that direct traffic flow north; all even-numbered avenues are one-way streets that direct traffic flow east; all other streets not referenced can be presumed to be two-way streets. Which of the alternative routes provided below would be considered legal means for a police officer working traffic enforcement at the intersection of Wyoming and 40th Avenue to respond to a traffic accident that occurred on Southworth and 14th Avenue?

   A. Go south on Wyoming nine blocks, turn right, and then proceed eleven blocks west.
   B. Go from Wyoming to Gregory on 40th Avenue, turn left, go seven blocks, turn right, go eight blocks west before turning left and proceeding two more blocks south.
   C. Go south on Wyoming seven blocks, turn right, go eleven blocks before turning right and proceeding two more blocks.
   D. Go south on Wyoming one block, turn right, go three blocks west, turn left, go six blocks south, turn right, go eight blocks west before turning left and proceeding south two more blocks.

124. If Patrol Officer Alex Kimbell is presently positioned at Dekalb and 29th Avenue and is dispatched to investigate a vehicular assault that allegedly took place at the northeast corner of the Highline Mall parking lot, which of the alternative routes provided below would afford him the quickest means to respond? (Assume all streets are two-way and have identical speed limits—all other factors remain constant.)

   A. Go ten blocks east on 28th Avenue before turning left and proceeding approximately six more blocks; the scene should be in view on the left.
   B. Go seven blocks north on Dekalb before turning left and proceeding approximately nine blocks; the scene should be in view on the right.
   C. Go ten blocks north on Dekalb, nine blocks east on Narrows Lane, and then three blocks south on Cranway; the scene should be in view directly ahead.
   D. Go two blocks north on Dekalb and then ten blocks east on Williams before turning left and proceeding approximately four more blocks; the scene should be in view on the left.

125. Assume that Sierra, Southworth, Wayne, Dekalb, and Colchester are one-way streets that direct traffic flow south; all even-numbered avenues are one-way streets that direct traffic flow west; all other streets not referenced can be presumed to be two-way streets. Other situations of concern involve a repaving project on 44th and 47th Avenues between Stenman and Wayne that will necessitate closure to thru traffic for the entire day; the intersection of Lovell and 48th Avenue will be closed between 10:30 a.m. and 1:45 p.m. for an underground natural gas line repair; and a tanker truck transporting anhydrous ammonia experiences a minor valve leak at the intersection of Madrona and 40th Avenue. As a safety precaution, a hazardous materials team working under the auspices of the local fire department cordon off all streets within a four-square block area surrounding the site. The chemical spill occurred at 8:45 a.m. and it's expected to take approximately five hours to clear and reopen to public transit. Under the given circumstances, if Patrol Officer Joe Blakemore was dispatched from his district post located at Beech and 35th Avenue at 1330 hours to investigate a traffic fatality that occurred at the intersection of Wayne and 48th Avenue, which of the routes given below would serve as a viable means of response?

   A. Go north on Beech to 48th Avenue, turn right and then drive eight blocks east.
   B. Go five blocks north on Beech, turn right, go eight blocks east before turning left and proceeding one more block.
   C. Go three blocks north on Beech, turn right, go nine blocks east, turn left, go three blocks north before turning west and proceeding one more block.
   D. Go eight blocks north on Beech, turn right, go eight blocks east before turning south and proceeding two more blocks.

NORMAN HALL'S POLICE EXAM PREPARATION BOOK

ANSWER SHEET FOR PRACTICE EXAM III

1. (A) (B) (C) (D)
2. (A) (B) (C) (D)
3. (A) (B) (C) (D)
4. (A) (B) (C) (D)
5. (A) (B) (C) (D)
6. (A) (B) (C) (D)
7. (A) (B) (C) (D)
8. (A) (B) (C) (D)
9. (A) (B) (C) (D)
10. (A) (B) (C) (D)
11. (A) (B) (C) (D)
12. (A) (B) (C) (D)
13. (A) (B) (C) (D)
14. (A) (B) (C) (D)
15. (A) (B) (C) (D)
16. (A) (B) (C) (D)
17. (A) (B) (C) (D)
18. (A) (B) (C) (D)
19. (A) (B) (C) (D)
20. (A) (B) (C) (D)
21. (A) (B) (C) (D)
22. (A) (B) (C) (D)
23. (A) (B) (C) (D)
24. (A) (B) (C) (D)
25. (A) (B) (C) (D)
26. (A) (B) (C) (D)
27. (A) (B) (C) (D)
28. (A) (B) (C) (D)
29. (A) (B) (C) (D)
30. (A) (B) (C) (D)
31. (A) (B) (C) (D)

32. (A) (B) (C) (D)
33. (A) (B) (C) (D)
34. (A) (B) (C) (D)
35. (A) (B) (C) (D)
36. (A) (B) (C) (D)
37. (A) (B) (C) (D)
38. (A) (B) (C) (D)
39. (A) (B) (C) (D)
40. (A) (B) (C) (D)
41. (A) (B) (C) (D)
42. (A) (B) (C) (D)
43. (A) (B) (C) (D)
44. (A) (B) (C) (D)
45. (A) (B) (C) (D)
46. (A) (B) (C) (D)
47. (A) (B) (C) (D)
48. (A) (B) (C) (D)
49. (A) (B) (C) (D)
50. (A) (B) (C) (D)
51. (A) (B) (C) (D)
52. (A) (B) (C) (D)
53. (A) (B) (C) (D)
54. (A) (B) (C) (D)
55. (A) (B) (C) (D)
56. (A) (B) (C) (D)
57. (A) (B) (C) (D)
58. (A) (B) (C) (D)
59. (A) (B) (C) (D)
60. (A) (B) (C) (D)
61. (A) (B) (C) (D)
62. (A) (B) (C) (D)

63. (A) (B) (C) (D)
64. (A) (B) (C) (D)
65. (A) (B) (C) (D)
66. (A) (B) (C) (D)
67. (A) (B) (C) (D)
68. (A) (B) (C) (D)
69. (A) (B) (C) (D)
70. (A) (B) (C) (D)
71. (A) (B) (C) (D)
72. (A) (B) (C) (D)
73. (A) (B) (C) (D)
74. (A) (B) (C) (D)
75. (A) (B) (C) (D)
76. (A) (B) (C) (D)
77. (A) (B) (C) (D)
78. (A) (B) (C) (D)
79. (A) (B) (C) (D)
80. (A) (B) (C) (D)
81. (A) (B) (C) (D)
82. (A) (B) (C) (D)
83. (A) (B) (C) (D)
84. (A) (B) (C) (D)
85. (A) (B) (C) (D)
86. (A) (B) (C) (D)
87. (A) (B) (C) (D)
88. (A) (B) (C) (D)
89. (A) (B) (C) (D)
90. (A) (B) (C) (D)
91. (A) (B) (C) (D)
92. (A) (B) (C) (D)
93. (A) (B) (C) (D)

94. Ⓐ Ⓑ Ⓒ Ⓓ
95. Ⓐ Ⓑ Ⓒ Ⓓ
96. Ⓐ Ⓑ Ⓒ Ⓓ
97. Ⓐ Ⓑ Ⓒ Ⓓ
98. Ⓐ Ⓑ Ⓒ Ⓓ
99. Ⓐ Ⓑ Ⓒ Ⓓ
100. Ⓐ Ⓑ Ⓒ Ⓓ
101. Ⓐ Ⓑ Ⓒ Ⓓ
102. Ⓐ Ⓑ Ⓒ Ⓓ
103. Ⓐ Ⓑ Ⓒ Ⓓ
104. Ⓐ Ⓑ Ⓒ Ⓓ

105. Ⓐ Ⓑ Ⓒ Ⓓ
106. Ⓐ Ⓑ Ⓒ Ⓓ
107. Ⓐ Ⓑ Ⓒ Ⓓ
108. Ⓐ Ⓑ Ⓒ Ⓓ
109. Ⓐ Ⓑ Ⓒ Ⓓ
110. Ⓐ Ⓑ Ⓒ Ⓓ
111. Ⓐ Ⓑ Ⓒ Ⓓ
112. Ⓐ Ⓑ Ⓒ Ⓓ
113. Ⓐ Ⓑ Ⓒ Ⓓ
114. Ⓐ Ⓑ Ⓒ Ⓓ
115. Ⓐ Ⓑ Ⓒ Ⓓ

116. Ⓐ Ⓑ Ⓒ Ⓓ
117. Ⓐ Ⓑ Ⓒ Ⓓ
118. Ⓐ Ⓑ Ⓒ Ⓓ
119. Ⓐ Ⓑ Ⓒ Ⓓ
120. Ⓐ Ⓑ Ⓒ Ⓓ
121. Ⓐ Ⓑ Ⓒ Ⓓ
122. Ⓐ Ⓑ Ⓒ Ⓓ
123. Ⓐ Ⓑ Ⓒ Ⓓ
124. Ⓐ Ⓑ Ⓒ Ⓓ
125. Ⓐ Ⓑ Ⓒ Ⓓ

ANSWERS TO PRACTICE EXAM III

Refer to the narratives for any clarification on questions 1–25.

1. *C.* Lieutenant

2. *B.* Vernon Fuller

3. *A.* 1458

4. *D.* 1989 Ford Mustang GT BOK-151

5. *A.* Series 80 Colt Mark IV .45 revolver

6. *C.* 1845 hours (i.e., 6:45 P.M.) February 11, 1997 - Brice Canyon Freeway

7. *B.* 1993 Ford Aerostar van, AVL-653

8. *B.* Officer Hansen, badge number 8725, ran the standard computer check on the van in question

9. *D.* Five-gallon gas can

10. *C.* Attempted felony elude of a police officer

11. *D.* No prior convictions were given

12. *B.* Suspect #1 - Enrico J. Fuente

13. *C.* Suspect #4 had multiple aliases

14. *A.* Blonde

15. *D.* Crescent-shaped scar above the left eyebrow

16. *B.* First-degree theft

17. *B.* 697-33-4461

18. *D.* First-degree theft and second-degree possession of stolen property represented Bruce Yamanaka's criminal record; wants and warrants included second-degree custodial interference, first-degree abandonment of a dependent person, and forgery.

19. *A.* Suspect #1

20. *A.* 183-52

21. *C.* Suspect #4

22. *D.* Emily Foster's weight was 165 pounds

23. *B.* Ichiro Yanagimachi

24. *C.* Brown

25. *B.* Alisha Ann Sternquist was also known as Catherine Middendorf and Rene Benson

26. *D.* Without even figuring the mathematics, selection A and B can be discarded as viable choices. It was given within the question that the legislative intent was to toughen drunk driving laws. That would involve lowering, not raising, the legal blood-alcohol threshold for suspected drunk drivers.

.001 - .0008 = .0002 represents the difference involved by lowering the blood-alcohol threshold as specified. To figure what percentage change this difference represents, we need to divide it by the original threshold limit (i.e., .001) and multiply by 100. Therefore,

$$\frac{.0002}{.001} \times 100 = 20\%$$

27. *A.* Since it was stated in the question that you are working a direct proportion, the equation would be set up accordingly.

$$\frac{3^1/_3 \ glasses}{130 \ pounds} = \frac{X \ glasses}{156 \ pounds} \; ; \; 130X = 519.95; \; X = 4.0$$

28. *C.* If 90 percent of the 380 drivers were arrested for drunk driving, that would mean the remaining cases involving drug-impaired driving would constitute 10 percent of the total caseload (100%–90% = 10%). Ten percent of 380 equates to 38 people caught driving while under the influence of drugs. Regardless of the potential for abuse, over-the-counter medication and prescription drugs are considered to be legal. Since it was given that approximately 5 percent of those affected utilized legal medication in some abusive capacity, that means 95 percent of the group used illegal drugs. Therefore, 95 percent of 38 people works out to be 36 individuals affected.

29. *B.* The map's scale provides that $^1/_4$ or .25 inch is the equivalent of 20 miles. $2^3/_4$ or 2.75 inches divided by .25 and then multiplied by 20 miles reveals that Officer Nelson is looking at a trip that is 220 miles long.

30. *B.* To determine the average fraction of personnel between the two officers desiring to work the available overtime, the following equation should be used.

$$(^1/_8 + ^1/_4) \div 2 = X$$

The lowest common denominator for both fractions would be expressed in eighths. Therefore,

$$(^1/_8 + ^2/_8) \div 2 = X$$
$$^3/_8 \times ^1/_2 = X$$
$$X = ^3/_{16}$$

31. *A.* Let $^1/_3X$ represent State Patrol, $^1/_2X$ represent Sheriff personnel, 5 being the number of detectives on duty, and X as the sum total of personnel working on the task force.

$$^1/_3X + ^1/_2X + 5 = X$$

By converting to the lowest common denominator, the equation would be restated as:

$$^2/_6X + ^3/_6X + 5 = X$$
or $$^5/_6 + 5 = X$$

Therefore,

$$5 = X \text{ (or } ^6/_6) - {}^5/_6$$
$$5 = {}^1/_6 X$$
$$X = 30$$

32. *D.*

$$\text{Time} = \frac{\text{Distance}}{\text{Rate}} \qquad T = \frac{15 \text{ miles}}{70 \text{ MPH}} = .214 \text{ hours}$$

$$T = \frac{15 \text{ miles}}{50 \text{ MPH}} = .3 \text{ hours}$$

The actual time saved: .3 hours - .214 hours = .086 hours
or .086 hours x 60 minutes = 5.16 minutes

33. *C.*

$$\text{Rate} = \frac{\text{Distance}}{\text{Time}}$$

$$X = \frac{475 \text{ miles}}{(12 \text{ hrs.} - 1.5 \text{ hrs})}$$

$$X = 45.238 \text{ MPH}$$

34. *C.* Since the officer in question actually worked 55 days in the quarter, the ratio of days worked to sick days would be 55:5, or 11:1 when reduced to simplest form.

35. *A.* The length and width of a square are equal. If the length of one side is 22.25 feet and there are four sides to the perimeter of a square, 22.25 x 4 = 89 feet.

36. *D.* The area of a square is equal to its length times width.

22.25 ft. x 22.25 ft. = 495.0625 square feet.

37. *B.* This question portrays a circular area with a 15 foot radius. The perimeter length or circumference of this area is determined by multiplying 3.1416 (π) x diameter (radius x 2). Therefore, the minimum length of rope or cautionary tape needed to secure the area is 3.1416 x 30 feet or 94.25 feet.

38. *A.* The radius of the cordoned area is 15 feet. The area of a circle is equal to πR^2.

(3.1416) (15^2) or (3.1416) (225) = 706.86 square feet.

39. *C.* The sentence structure will not read smoothly with the parenthetical element removed. A comma placed after the word *than* eliminates that problem.

40. *C.* Specific course titles should be capitalized because they are considered to be proper nouns.

41. *D.* The statement in question is correct in all aspects.

42. *B.* Lieutenant is misspelled.

43. *A.* The statement is structurally incorrect because the subject and verb are not in agreement. Officer Phinney is considered a singular subject which necessitates the use of the singular verb *is*.

44. *A.* This statement is structurally incorrect. Since the word neither is used as a pronoun in the sentence structure, it is always considered singular. Therefore, the word *is* should be substituted for the word *are*.

45. *B.* Allusion refers to a point of reference. Delusion, on the other hand, is an aberration of the mind.

46. *A.* The adverbial form *quickly* is needed to modify the verb *worked*.

47. *A.* The statement is structurally incorrect because a predicate adjective is needed to modify the subject pronoun *he*. The word *different* would render the statement grammatically correct.

48. *C.* A properly written compound possessive would add an apostrophe and S to the last word only (i.e., father-in-law's).

49. *A.* The sentence would structurally be improved by dropping the word *more* and using *stronger* as a single comparative.

50. *C.* STERILIZE

51. *B.* BREATHALYZER

52. *D.* ILLITERATE

53. *A.* GRIEVANCE

54. *D.* QUESTIONNAIRE

55. *C.* MUNICIPAL

56. *B.* OCCURRED

57. *B.* NEUROTIC

58. *C.* RELEVANT

59. *D.* INFORMANT

60. *A.* COMMITTED

61. *B.* Incontrovertible/Corroborated

62. *C.* Affable/Elicit

63. *D.* Infallible/Predisposition

64. *D.* Inclusive/Effect

65. *B.* Inane/Stationary

66. *B.* Premonition/Inclement

67. *A.* Vilified/Magnanimous

68. *C.* Staunch/Capitulate

69. *A.* Vacillate/Adroit

70. *B.* Chagrined/Flouting

71. *D.* Subject A has a different nose
Subject B has a thinner face and different ears
Subject C has different lips and eyes

72. *D.* Subject A has different lips and eyes
Subject B has a scar above the right eyebrow
Subject C has a wider nose

73. *A.* Subject B has different lips
Subject C has larger ears
Subject D has an obvious scar above the right eye and a different chin

74. *B.* Subject A has fewer freckles and a cleft chin
Subject C has larger lips and different teeth
Subject D has a rounder face and button chin

75. *B.* Subject A has different eyes
Subject C has different lips
Subject D has a different nose

76. *A.* Subject B has different eyes
Subject C does not have dimples
Subject D has more facial wrinkles

77. *C.* Subject A has different eyes
Subject B has a different chin
Subject D has a different nose

78. *A.* Subject B does not have a birthmark beneath the lower lip
Subject C has a different head shape
Subject D has different lips

79. *C.* Subject A has different lips and less prominent eyebrows
Subject B has a chin that is less fleshy
Subject D has different ears

80. *D.* Selection D (i.e., C and A according to the chart provided) account for the two largest shares (20% + 40%) of the total budget as opposed to either Selection A (17% + 13%) or selection B (40% + 10%). Selection C is incorrect because Maintenance and Operations (10%) represents the smallest financial outlay.

81. *C.* Administrative expense is the second largest outlay in the department's budget. Attorney expense, on the other hand, is the fourth, not third, greatest expense shown by the chart. Selection B is false because Administrative expense combined with Supplies and Equipment (20% + 17%) does not exceed that portion of the budget dedicated to payroll (40%). Selection D is false as well, because Maintenance and Operations comprises 10% or one-tenth of the budget, not one-quarter or 25%.

82. *C.* DUI arrests nearly doubled in 1995 while auto accidents involving fatalities dropped by more than 50% from the year before. A similar correlation exists for auto accidents involving injuries. The inverse relationship of A and B and C in 1995 is rather profound.

83. *B.* Auto accidents involving fatalities as well as injuries reached a pinnacle during 1994. No other year in the study fared as poorly with respect to the public safety issue.

84. *A.* In comparison to the other years in the study, 1992 was a banner year for public safety. Better road conditions and/or driving with extra caution are two such factors that would have a beneficial effect on motorist safety.

85. *B.* The 1000 block of 16th, 17th, and 18th streets falls within Precinct 132's jurisdiction. According to the graphed data, the highest incidence of DUI's occurred around midnight.

86. *D.* The 3000 block of 140th Avenue falls within Precinct 117's jurisdiction. The highest incidence of DUI's for this precinct occur around 8 p.m.

87. *B.* The 1500 block of D and E Streets fall within Precinct 127's jurisdiction. Since there is a higher incidence of assault reported around 4 p.m., selection B would be the best approach taken.

88. *A.* The 700 block of H avenue falls within Precinct 123's jurisdiction. According to the data provided, there were zero incidents of assault reported around 8 a.m. A larger police presence during that shift would make little difference.

89. *D.* Selection D is, in fact, true when the number of citations issued is compared. A is incorrect because the two time frames examined are comparable to each other. B is false because, judging by the data presented, it is clear that the exact opposite is true. Speeding incidents were distinctly up during the later evening hours. That apparently carried over into the early morning hours as well. The usual application of the phrase "rush hour" typically refers to traffic volume. However, in this study, it has relevance to the hour of day that the most speeding citations were issued. Eleven p.m. to midnight fits that definition, instead of noon to 1:00 p.m.

90. *A.* Tour I was responsible for issuing only 389 total citations. Tour II and Tour III were responsible for 471 and 522 citations, respectively.

91. *C.* The key word in this statement is "significant." While it is true that Tours II and III followed that pattern, the same cannot be said for Tour I. Ticket issuances averaged close to fifty throughout the entire shift.

92. *C.* Officer Pratt (Badge No. 152) is only scheduled to work on four days (i.e., 32 hours). All other personnel are either working full time or overtime.

93. *D.* Despite the fact that Officer Unger (Badge No. 314) drew a schedule that dictated overtime, four of the six work days did involve Tour A assignments. Officers Brown (Badge No. 976) and Ryzek (Badge No. 612) were assigned Tour A on a couple days for the week, however, from a comparative standpoint, Officer Unger fared substantially better.

94. *A.* Patrol Officer Tyson (Badge No. 718) was scheduled to work Tour C on Monday in Sector 9.

95. *B.* If the given work schedule was implemented without revision, Officer Bateman (Badge No. 670) would be working a double shift on Mondays (i.e., Tours B and C for 16 straight working hours). The fact that District 18 does not have a personnel shortage precludes the necessity of having any officers work that kind of overtime.

96. *B.* This kind of question first requires a determination of which day of the week July 6 falls on. Since Independence Day (i.e., July 4) is said to be on a Saturday, then the 6th would be the following Monday. According to the duty roster, Officer Tyson (Badge No. 718) is assigned C shift in Sector 9.

97 *D.* Because July 4th fell on Friday and July 18th is exactly two weeks following, it too is a Friday. Therefore, looking at the schedule for Friday, Officer Bateman (Badge No. 670) is shown to be assigned to A shift in Sector 14.

98. *C.*

S	M	T	W	T	F	S
		13	14	15	16	17
18	19	20	21	22		

By backtracking in calendar fashion as shown above, the day that July 13th falls on can easily be discerned. Since the 13th is a Tuesday, Tour C in Section 14 is normally assigned to Officer Klinger (Badge No. 131). However, that date coincides with his vacation leave. Therefore, Officer Locke (Badge No. 563) would serve as his relief. Patrol Officer Hudson (Badge No. 410) could serve in a similar capacity but his name was not provided within the question for consideration.

99. *C.* 26-07A

100. *D.* State Patrol Officer Lieutenant Pete Kendrick

101. *A.* Jeffrey T. Beaumont

102. *D.* 13721-B and 13501-A. Selection A is the correct chronology of NCIC codes given in the narrative, however, one has to pay particular attention to how a question is worded. In this case, the order of the charges against the defendant were revised, thus changing the respective order of the applicable NCIC codes.

103. *D.* Selection B is the correct date for the scheduled arraignment hearing, but the reading stipulated that the defendant remained in detention; he was not released after posting bail.

104. *B.* The subject was described as having brown eyes

105. *B.* Lakeview Police Officer Harry M. Stevens

106. *C.* 555-22-0557

107. *A.* Selection B should be eliminated due to the fact that three witnesses were in agreement that C was the first letter on the suspect's license plate. Selection C can be removed from consideration because the second letter and second number do not reconcile with the other three descriptions. Selection D can be ignored as well, because there was a preponderance of statements indicating that 9 was the last number to the license plate in question.

108. *C.* Selection A can be eliminated because three witnesses corroborated the fact that the suspect vehicle is black. Since three of the four witnesses were in agreement about the vehicle being a BMW, selection B can be dropped from further consideration. Selection D is of the lone belief that the suspect vehicle was a four-door sedan.

109. *B.* All of the statements offered to Detective Blackmore corroborate the fact that a Caucasian male is culpable for the rape. However, a general consensus of witness statements profile the suspect as being in his early twenties (eliminate choice A), approximately 6 feet tall (eliminate choice C) and weighs about 200 pounds (eliminate choice D).

110. *B.* 01.47.33 Reckless Endangerment

111. *D.* None of the above. The pedestrian in question lacked willful intent in obstructing Officer McFarland.

112. *A.* 01.62.71 Riot/Second Degree
01.25.47 Failure to Disperse
and 01.52.33 Disorderly Conduct

113. *B.* 01.52.17 Resisting Arrest
     01.25.47 Failure to Disperse
     01.52.33 Disorderly Conduct and 01.62.17 Riot/First Degree

114. *C.* 01.25.33 Obstructing a Law Enforcement Officer

115. *A.* The crime was reported at 1715 hours and responded to by Officer Kenyon at 1718 hours. On that premise alone, selections B, C and D can be eliminated.

116. *C.* Statement 5 defines the beginning of the incident, which eliminates choices B and D. Choice A can be dropped from consideration as well because Ms. Henderson would not be arrested for assault without the officer first seeing the extent of Ms. Williams' injuries.

117. *D.* Statement 4 defines the conclusion of the report, therefore, choices A and C can be eliminated. Choice B can be ignored because statement 1 must precede statement 3.

118. *B.* Statement 4 is the end result to the disturbance call Officer Wells responded to, therefore, selection A can be eliminated. Statement 3 is the beginning of the incident report, so selection D can be removed from consideration. Statement 1 clearly establishes what had taken place to prompt the bartender to call the police in the first place. Secondary observations such as statements 5 and 2 should follow; selection C can be eliminated on that premise.

119. *B.* Southeast

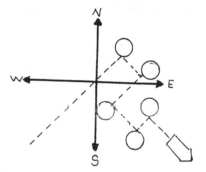

120. *B.* Northwest

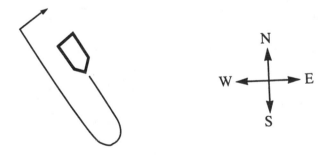

121. *A.* Northeast

122. *B.* Selection A is incorrect because the officer would be driving the wrong direction on a one-way street at two points: south on Charolette and south on Constance. Selection C is incorrect because turning left on 37th Avenue from Charolette runs counter to established traffic flow. Selection D, if followed accordingly, would place the officer at a point that is completely off the map.

123. *D.* Selection A is incorrect with respect to turning right on 14th Avenue from Wyoming; even-numbered streets were given to be one-way streets heading east, not west. Selection B is incorrect because 40th Avenue is a one-way street heading east; going from Wyoming to Gregory by way of 40th Avenue would run counter to traffic flow. Selection C would actually place the officer within the boundaries of Sorenson Park; a left turn instead of a right turn onto Southworth from 23rd Avenue is required to reach the scene of the accident given.

124. *D.* Selection A is wrong because Sorenson Park interrupts an easterly heading on 29th Avenue. Selection B is incorrect because turning left from Dekalb onto 44th Avenue would be a westward heading; maintaining this course for approximately nine blocks would place Officer Kimbell at a point off the map. Both choices C and D are viable routes of getting to the place of concern. However, selection D stands out as being the shortest or quickest means of responding.

125. *D.* Selection A is wrong for two reasons: a right turn onto 48th Avenue from Beech Street would have Officer Blakemore going the wrong direction on a one-way street, in addition to the fact that at 1330 hours (i.e., 1:30 p.m.) the intersection of Lovell and 48th Avenue is closed due to a gas line repair. So, even if 48th Avenue was a two-way street, the utility repair would deny any such approach. Selection B is wrong for two reasons as well: an easterly heading on 47th Avenue would come to an abrupt halt at the Stenman intersection because of the ongoing repaving project specified earlier. Additionally, were it even possible to get through that, a northern heading on Wayne Street would run counter to one-way traffic flow. Selection C is incorrect because the four-square-block perimeter set up around the chemical spill that had taken place precludes vehicular transit on Adele Street between Dekalb and Southworth. Had it been any later than 1:45 p.m., this would not have been a factor to consider and the route given would have, indeed, served as a viable means of approach.

TEST RATINGS ARE AS FOLLOWS:
    120–125 correct, EXCELLENT
    113–119 correct, VERY GOOD
    106–112 correct, GOOD
    100–105 correct, FAIR
    99 or fewer correct, UNSATISFACTORY

Go back to each question you missed and determine if the question was just misinterpreted for one reason or another, or if your response reflects a weakness in subject matter. If it is a matter of misinterpretation, try reading the question slower while paying particular attention to key words such as *not, least, except* or *without*. If, on the other hand, you determine a weakness in a certain area, do not despair, because that is what this study guide is for: to identify any area of weakness before you take the actual exam. Reread the material on the area of concern in this study guide. If you still feel a need for supplemental material, your local library is an excellent source.

Physical Fitness

WITH THE PHYSICAL DEMANDS that law enforcement may entail, it is not hard to understand why police departments require employees to be in top physical shape. In-station tasks require little exertion; however, when police officers are called to active duty, the switch from a sedentary pace to substantial physical exertion is stressful. This is particularly true for someone who is out of shape. The job may demand running, climbing, jumping, twisting, pulling, and lifting. The difficulty is also compounded by the fact that work may be performed under extreme temperatures and/or in poor-quality air. A police officer must be physically able to respond to these conditions while always being careful of his or her own safety. This is the primary reason police departments place an emphasis on physical fitness exams.

As mentioned in the introduction, physical fitness exams can be quite varied. What one department considers suitable may be considered inadequate by another. The point of the matter is that all physical ability tests are designed specifically to measure strength, stamina, and flexibility. How these capabilities are determined lies solely with the department you have applied to, since there is no nationally recognized standard. Try to ascertain in advance what will be expected by the department you are interested in. Then, practice these events in trial runs as best you can prior to that actual exam. It is better to learn of potential weaknesses beforehand, rather than fall short during a timed event and perform poorly, or, worse, fail the test altogether. There should be no reason to let this job opportunity slip away simply because of physical unpreparedness. Approach this part of the screening process in the same manner as you did the written exam. By practicing the workout schedule suggested below, not only will you get in better shape, but you will be able to approach the physical fitness exam with the same degree of confidence and sense of ease as you did the written exam.

Before charging into any fitness workout, however, it is suggested that you visit your family doctor and get a complete medical evaluation. This will be a precondition to your employment with the police department, in order to determine if any disease or physical condition may impair your ability to perform. (For further reference, see the chapter on Medical Evaluation at the beginning of this guide.) If, in fact, you do have a condition that potentially warrants rejection from employment consideration, consult your doctor. He or she may be able to prescribe treatment through a change of diet, specialized workout, medication, or surgery to correct the problem.

Inform your physician of your intentions concerning any kind of physical workout. No two people are the same; workout schedules vary. The guidelines provided in this book are just that: guidelines. Your doctor is better able to tailor a training program that will benefit you. Keep your doctor's advice in mind while you prepare for the exam.

Prior to actually taking the physical abilities test, you will be asked either to sign a liability waiver or to fill out some form of medical questionnaire. The latter involves a wide range of questions relating to your present state of health. This kind of information will allow examiners to make an educated decision as to whether such an exam poses a health risk to a test candidate. Be truthful in filling out such a questionnaire, because this is one more element that is cross-checked in a routine background investigation. Falsifying any information is grounds enough to disqualify an applicant.

Despite the variation seen in physical fitness exams, it can be generally assumed that three kinds of physical attributes are being scrutinized during these exams: flexibility, cardiovascular fitness, and muscular strength and endurance. Each of these areas uses different groups of muscles, and the exercises suggested below for each will improve them. However, it is important to realize that prior to any exercise there are preliminaries that can help to prevent injury.

RELAXATION AND WARM-UP ROUTINE

The first thing to do before starting any rigorous exercise is a relaxation and warm-up routine, which involves the head roll, paced breathing, and shoulder shrugs.

For the head roll, you can either stand, sit, or kneel. Allow your head to go limp and roll it around your neck two or three times in one direction and then two or three times in the other direction. It helps to close your eyes during this exercise to prevent any dizziness or loss of balance. Try to conduct this exercise slowly and smoothly.

Paced breathing involves lying on your back and placing your hands on your stomach. Concentrate on your breathing by paying close attention to how far your chest rises during each inhalation. Breathe evenly and slowly, and relax for about one minute during this exercise.

The third relaxation exercise is shoulder shrugs. Again, lie on your back. Simply pull your shoulders upward and maintain that position for a few seconds before allowing your shoulders to return slowly to their original position. Try to coordinate your breathing so that you inhale while pulling your shoulders up and exhale when your shoulders drop. Perform this exercise for approximately one minute.

FLEXIBILITY EXERCISES

Stretching exercises are important, too, because they prepare tendons and ligaments for further stretching and increase the flow of fluid around various joints. The whole concept is based on smooth, even, and slow motion. This kind of exercise is not intended to be conducted in fast or jerky movements.

The back stretch or swivel is the first flexibility exercise to do. Stand, and with your arms at your sides, try to lean as far forward as possible. Then lean as far backward as you can. Repeat these exercises at least four times in both directions. Now, to limber up your back for bending sideways, remain standing, turn your head to the right, and slide your right hand down the length of your right leg as far as possible. Do this exercise at least four times on the right side, then four times on the left side.

To stretch the quadriceps (thigh muscles), stand and lean against a wall using your left hand as support. Reach behind with your right hand and lift your right leg up so that you can grasp your toes. Slowly pull your heel closer to your buttocks until the thigh feels stretched. Maintain this position for approximately five seconds. Repeat this exercise four times with the right leg before doing the same with the left leg.

To stretch the calf muscles in your leg, remain standing within arm's length of the wall. While facing the wall, keep your feet flat on the ground (do not allow your heels to lift), and allow yourself to lean forward for a few seconds. Push off against the wall to return to the starting position. Repeat this exercise three or four times with each leg.

Now, while sitting on the floor with your legs spread apart and the back of your legs flat on the floor (your knees should not lift), slide both hands as far down the leg as possible. Hold this position for a few seconds before sitting erect again. Repeat this exercise three to four times, and then do the same for the other leg. This exercise stretches both back and hamstring muscles.

Remain in the sitting position and cross your legs, putting the soles of your feet together. Now, lean forward as far as possible and hold this position for a few seconds before sitting erect again. Repeat this exercise three or four times. This exercise stretches the groin muscles.

To stretch the hips, remain in the sitting position with your legs straight. Now, take your right leg and cross it over the left leg. Take the knee of the right leg and slowly bring it up to your chest. Hold that position for three to four seconds, and then repeat this exercise twice more. Do the same with the left leg.

The final exercise involves stretching chest, shoulder, and back muscles. While kneeling, place your palms on the floor, then slowly slide both hands forward until your elbows touch the floor. Keep your head and back straight during this exercise. Return to your starting position and repeat this exercise three or four times.

Remember, the whole point of these exercises is to stretch various muscles. If you force a muscle to extend too far, pulling or tearing can occur, defeating the purpose of stretching and, possibly, incurring injury. Stretch various muscles only to the point of mild sensation, hold for a few seconds, then relax. This procedure has the effect of increasing flexibility and loosening muscles for other exercises.

The last preliminary needed before any exercise is a cardiorespiratory warmup. This simply involves conducting an exercise that is not too stressful, such as brisk walking or slow jogging for a few minutes. This allows the heart rate to increase gradually and prepares the heart for vigorous exercise. To prevent potential injury, a warmup routine should always be done before any stressful exercise.

CARDIOVASCULAR FITNESS

Cardiovascular fitness has to do with your heart and lung capacity. As both of these organs become more fit, your body's ability to transport oxygen to its cells improves. Another beneficial result is that the heart beats less quickly but pumps with greater strength—or, in other words, works more efficiently. There is also a corresponding increase in the peripheral circulatory system, thereby making it easier for various cells to absorb oxygen.

The best way to achieve cardiovascular endurance is to employ what physiologists call aerobic exercise. This may come in one of four forms: running, swimming, bicycling, or walking. When any of these forms of exercise is conducted fairly rigorously for approximately 25 minutes three times a week, cardiovascular endurance will improve. The key point here is to exercise at a moderate intensity, nonstop for the full 25 minutes. Less time makes the exercise much less useful. That is why sports such as baseball, tennis, or basketball do not suffice. These sports require tremendous energy output some of the time; however, there are breaks in between. To be effective, the exercise has to be conducted for 25 *consecutive* minutes, stopping only to check your pulse.

To calibrate your progress using aerobics, physiologists have come up with a pulse-rated system. Your pulse measures the number of times your heart beats per minute. As your cardiovascular endurance improves, your heart beats less quickly when subjected to stress. To measure your pulse, simply apply one or two of your fingers (not your thumb) to the front of your neck next to the larynx and feel for the carotid artery. The pulse should be fairly obvious there. Be careful not to press too hard on this artery because unconsciousness may result, particularly after exercise. Count the number of times your heart beats within 10 seconds, and then multiply that number by 6. This will provide you with an accurate assessment of your pulse. When performing a rigorous exercise for 25 minutes, stop after the first 10 minutes to take a brief pulse (10 seconds), and immediately resume the exercise.

Intermix the four events of running, swimming, bicycling, and walking in your training. This helps to alleviate boredom and perpetuates the desire to continue training. When your 25 minutes of exercise is completed, it is necessary to follow it with a cooldown period. Walk or jog slowly for 5 to 10 minutes. The general idea is to permit your body to return to its normal condition gradually. This cooldown can be followed by a few stretching exercises as well.

MUSCULAR STRENGTH AND ENDURANCE

Strength development can be accomplished by weight training and calisthenics. Both improve muscular endurance through repetitive movement but do so in different ways. Calisthenics essentially uses exercises that employ your own body weight to serve as resistance. On the other hand, weight training involves lifting progressively heavier weights or resistances in the form of barbells or variable-resistance weight-training equipment.

Calisthenics

Calisthenics, like cardiovascular endurance exercises, need to be proceeded by relaxation, stretching, and warmup exercises. A daily routine of push-ups, sit-ups, pull-ups, leg lifts, and squats should be conducted over a period of 15 to 25 minutes. Start out doing 15 repetitions of each exercise, and then work your way up to 30. Don't expect this to occur overnight. Regularity is the key. Your persistence will reward you with greater strength within three to four weeks. Descriptions of each exercise are given below:

Push-ups

Lie on your abdomen on the floor, and place your hands, palm down, beneath your chest. As you extend your arms and push off from the floor, be sure to keep your back and knees straight. Once your arms are fully extended, lower yourself to the floor slowly and repeat the exercise.

Sit-ups

Lie on your back on the floor and either place your feet beneath a sofa or other heavy object, or have someone restrain your feet from lifting. Your knees should be straight and flat. With your hands locked behind your head, sit up and attempt to touch your knees with your elbows without lifting your knees. Do not try to force yourself to extend beyond what is comfortable. Stretch as far as possible, and then return to the starting position to repeat.

Pull-ups

Use a chinning bar that is just a few inches higher than your highest reach when you are standing up and your arms are extended overhead, Using an overhand grip on the bar, raise yourself to the point where you bring your chin level with the bar. Try not to kick or swing while raising yourself. Lower yourself slowly to the starting position and repeat.

Leg Lifts

Lie on the floor on your right side with your legs kept straight and in line with one another. Use your left arm to gain support from the floor to prevent rollover. Lift your left leg as far as possible before returning to the starting position. Repeat this exercise a minimum of 15 times before changing sides and doing the same exercise with the other leg.

Squats

In the standing position, extend your arms forward and then squat until your thighs are parallel to the ground. Return to the standing position and repeat the exercise.

Weight Training

Weight training, when done correctly, significantly increases muscular strength and endurance. However, three things should always be kept in mind before starting any kind of weight-training routine. Supervision by either a professional weight training assistant or someone to act as a safety person during your lifts is essential. This is particularly true while bench-pressing barbells. The second consideration is always to begin light and progressively increase the weight you lift as you become stronger. Starting heavy is an open invitation to injuring muscle tissue instead of building it. The third consideration is to conduct a weight training routine only three times per week at the maximum. Keep the number of repetitions to only three sets of ten. Doing more will tend to increase bulk rather than strength. If the repetitions seem fairly easy initially, increase the weight load by 5 or 10 pounds at a time. Continue this progressive addition of weight as your strength improves. Below are exercises that concentrate on developing muscles needed most for police officer fitness exams: chest, shoulder, arm, and back.

Bench Press

For safety reasons, it is better to use bench press equipment rather than free weights. Whichever is available, lie on your back and grip the bar with both hands at shoulder width. Begin with light weights, as mentioned earlier, and lift or press the bar in a direction directly perpendicular to the chest by extending your arms. Try not to lock your elbows when fully extended. Slowly lower the bar to your chest and repeat the exercise.

Arm Curls

While standing, preferably with your back to a wall, allow your arms to be fully extended downward. Grasp the barbell with an underhand grip, with hands spaced shoulder width. Raise the barbell to your chest without allowing your elbows to move from your side. Lower the barbell to the starting position and repeat.

Half Squats

This is similar to squat calisthenics. The difference is that a barbell rests on the back of your neck while it is supported by both hands at shoulder width. As the weight is steadied on your shoulders, conduct squat repetitions as described under calisthenics.

Bent-over Rows

Begin in the standing position with the weight bar on the floor directly in front of you. While keeping your legs straight, lean over the barbell in such a way that your back becomes parallel to the floor. With an overhand grip, grasp the weight bar with both hands spaced shoulder width and lift the weight to your chest. Try to keep your back straight (i.e., parallel to the floor) and your head up while attempting the lift. Return the weight to the floor and repeat the exercise.

The Oral Board

ONCE YOU HAVE REACHED THIS POINT in the selection process, you will want to bear a few things in mind about the oral board. You will be notified by mail of the time and place of the interview. Pay particular attention to the date and become familiar in advance with the location of the interview. One sure way to disqualify yourself from serious consideration is to show up late for the interview. There really are no excuses for this.

Appearance is also important. Most people are told not to judge others by outward appearance; however, interviewers gain a distinct impression from the manner in which a candidate dresses. If an applicant is not well groomed (e.g., unshaven, hair uncombed) interviewers perceive that candidate, before so much as asking one question, as uncaring and somewhat sloppy. Even though the candidate may be the most hardworking and concerned person among those being interviewed, he or she will, in all likelihood, be passed over for another with a better appearance. First impressions are just as important as how you respond to questions asked by the interviewers. Therefore, be well groomed for the occasion and dress neatly. For men, this would entail a nice shirt (tie is optional), slacks, and a pair of dress shoes. For women, an attractive blouse, dress pants (or suit or skirt), and shoes (or a conservative dress) would be appropriate.

Also avoid smoking or chewing gum prior to or during an oral board. Habits like these can create a poor appearance. The whole idea is to put your best foot forward to indicate you are the most enthusiastic and best-qualified candidate for the job. Contrary to what some applicants may think, outward appearance is very important. For the limited amount of time an interview board spends with a test applicant, all things become relevant, including the smallest of details.

The interview itself is normally conducted by a board of three to five people. Most interview panels consist of Police Department officials or civil service personnel. Occasionally, people outside the police department and civil service are brought in to avoid potential bias on the board.

Ideally, those conducting the interview and the applicant being interviewed are complete strangers to one another. This way, a candidate who is not hired cannot discredit the selection process on the basis of bias or favoritism. Board members are also made aware that race, sex, color, creed, and political background have no bearing on these proceedings. Each interviewer has a rating sheet listing specific qualifications. The series of questions provides the interviewers with enough insight to accurately gauge the applicant's potential capabilities. Usually the beginning of the interview will focus attention on your job application form. Such things as your educational background, past employment history, and references are examined. It would behoove you to review everything you listed on your application form and have supportive reasoning for any career changes. If you can somehow demonstrate that the direction you took was based on the underlying aspiration to work in law enforcement, so much the better. However, do not deceive the panel regarding past choices. Chances are that if you do, you may contradict yourself at one point or another, and this will become immediately evident to the interviewers. The best policy here is to answer all questions honestly, even if some past decisions were not necessarily the best ones. If you feel that you have made a questionable career move or have had a falling out with one or more past employers, explain why. If you can also show that something was learned or gained from the experience, point that out as well. Interviewers will appreciate your honesty and sincerity. A history of switching jobs or changing careers all too frequently without just cause is usually reason enough not to be hired.

While you are being interviewed in these areas of concern, interviewers will be assessing your communications skills and how well you respond to the questioning. It is well understood that oral boards are stressful to applicants. However, if an applicant appears excessively fidgety or worried or perspires profusely, and such nervousness encumbers the applicant's ability to answer questions, it can detract from what otherwise would have been a good interview. Advance preparation for the interview should help in this regard. Knowing (in general) the kinds of questions interviewers most likely will ask enhances your confidence. Beside further expounding on information given on the application form, questions such as the following are equally important:

- Why do you want to become a police officer?
- Why should you be hired over other similarly qualified applicants?
- Now that we know your strong points, what are your weaknesses?
- If you had to do everything over, what would you do differently?
- Do you have any regrets for anything in the past?
- What, if anything, do you feel are major accomplishments or achievements in your life?
- Is there any reason you did not actively participate in athletics in school?
- How do you feel you can help the community by working in the police department?

These and a myriad of other questions are thought provoking. If you are prepared for such questioning, you will be better able to answer these questions in a satisfactory manner, rather than pausing at length to think of something. Simply answering "yes" or "no" is not sufficient. Supportive reasoning, even if it is brief, is what interviewers want to hear.

Concern during an interview will also focus on what your interests or hobbies are, as well as attitudes toward particular job requirements. For instance,

- Why do you like to hunt, swim, bike, camp, etc?
- Couldn't you have used your leisure time to better purpose?
- Do you do any extracurricular reading, and if so, what?
- Do you keep current with local events by reading the paper?
- How do you feel about working irregular hours in the police department?
- Do you respond to criticism in a positive manner?
- Have you ever displayed temper with co-workers at past jobs?
- What do you think of drugs and alcohol, both in the work place and at home?
- Are you afraid of anything such as dying, heights, or speaking in front of large groups of people?
- How do you feel about using lethal force against another person when necessary?

Having prepared answers to these questions and others of similar nature will definitely give you an edge over those who aren't prepared. Try to think of as many questions about your life as possible and prepare some reasoning to support your answers. You may be caught off guard by a few questions, but overall your preparation will pay off.

One other form the interview may take may concern your reaction to hypothetical circumstances or emergencies. It is not expected that you will have advanced knowledge of any specialized law-enforcement training. However, this kind of question can give interviewers insight into how well you can quickly reason and solve a problem. You may be given certain conditions to work within, and then be expected to show how you would bring the situation under control.

These kinds of questions are obviously more difficult to prepare for, but two things are important to keep in mind. First, the safety of both police personnel and the victim or member of the public involved is a primary consideration. Second, nearly everything police personnel do should be part of a team effort. Consider these two things during any questioning. Interviewers will describe some situation and may very well throw in some constraints that may make the situation worse. Whatever is given, think the question through as best you can, and decide how you would handle the circumstances. Immediate answers to questions of this nature without much forethought are bound to be incomplete and show poor judgment. Interviewers will observe how well you can assimilate information and identify specific problem areas. Your initiative and leadership beyond what is minimally necessary are other factors assessed.

If your interview is more in line with this kind of questioning, answer to the best of your ability and see the exercise through to the end. Whatever you do, don't become exasperated with the situation given and give up. Remember, the interviewers know that they are placing you in a very stressful position. Reacting in an appropriate and confident manner bodes well for your employment consideration.

When the interview is winding to a close, one of the panel members will ask you if you have any questions or concerns regarding the police department. If you feel that you have other positive qualities that were not discussed during the interview, now is the time to mention them briefly. If you have some specific concerns regarding the police department, this is the appropriate time to ask. Since there are other candidates to be interviewed, do not protract your own interview beyond a few minutes after the interviewers ask you for any further comments. Rambling on about something longer than necessary is viewed with disdain. Be brief with your questions if you have any, then thank each interviewer for his or her time and consideration.

Don't loiter after the interview to see how well you did. It will be another week or two before all things are considered and decisions are made with regard to hiring.

If you later learn you did not fare as well as expected in the interview, don't become upset and write the experience off as though the examiners made the mistake. Rather, find out where your weaknesses were and learn from the experience. That way, on a follow-up interview to another exam, you will not make the same mistakes. It can also be said that a candidate who goes through the testing and selection process more than once is very determined. That attribute is looked upon favorably by any police department because it shows that the applicant is truly dedicated to becoming a police officer. More often than not, these are candidates that departments seek to hire. There may be a few disappointments along the way to being hired; however, hard work and persistence are two key virtues that are prerequisites to a fulfilling career in law enforcement.

REFUND POLICY

IN THE UNLIKELY EVENT that you use this book but score less than 80 percent on the police officer examination, your money will be refunded. This guarantee specifically applies to the written exam, not the physical fitness, psychological, or medical exams. If a test applicant scores above 80 percent on the written test, but fails the aforementioned portions of the exam, he or she will not be eligible for a refund.

The following conditions must be met before any refund will be made. All exercises in this guide must be completed to demonstrate that the applicant did make a real attempt to practice and prepare to score 80 percent or better. Any refund must be claimed within ninety days of the date of purchase shown on your sales receipt. Anything submitted beyond this ninety-day period will be subject to the publisher's discretion. Refunds are only available for copies of the book purchased through retail bookstores. The refund amount is limited to the purchase price and may not exceed the cover price of the book.

If you mail this study guide back for a refund, please include your sales receipt, validated test results,* and a self-addressed, stamped envelope. Requests for refunds should be addressed to Adams Media Corporation, Police Officer Exams Division, 57 Littlefield Street, Avon, MA 02322. Please allow approximately four weeks for processing.

---

* On occasion, exam results are not mailed to the test applicant. Test scores may be posted at either the Police Department or the place of examination. If this is the case for you, procure a copy of your test score from the personnel office and be sure your name and address are indicated (Social Security numbers are insufficient to claim a refund).

Other titles by Norman Hall

Money-back guarantee! No other exam books make this offer because no other exam books are as comprehensive and up-to-date!

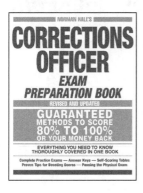

Corrections Officer Exam Preparation Book

Test expert Norman Hall shows readers guaranteed methods for scoring 80% to 100% on the corrections officer test. Hall analyzes every aspect of the most current version of the test and shows readers what they need to qualify, from memory tests to basic mathematics. Norman Hall covers everything you'll need to know to be hired, including:

- Written exams
- Physical abilitites test
- Oral boards
- Psychological examinations
- And more!

Careers, trade paperback, 8½" x 11", $14.95, 1-59337-389-9

State Trooper & Highway Patrol Exam Preparation Book

Guaranteed methods for scoring 80% to 100% on the state trooper and highway patrol officer qualification tests. Hall analyzes every aspect of the most current versions of the tests—from reading comprehension to simple math to physical fitness—and shows readers what they need to qualify, including:

- Memory
- Reading comprehension
- Reasoning and judgment
- Map reading
- Report writing
- Grammar, vocabulary, and spelling

Careers, trade paperback, 8½" x 11", $14.95, 1-58062-077-9

Available wherever books are sold.

HOW TO ORDER: If you cannot find these titles at your favorite retail outlet, you may order them directly from the publisher. BY PHONE: Call 1-800-258-0929. We accept Visa, Mastercard, and American Express. $4.95 will be added to your total order for shipping and handling. BY MAIL: Write out the full titles of the books you'd like to order and send payment, including $4.95 for shipping and handling, to: KP Books, Attention: Adams Media Orders, 700 East State Street, Iola, WI 54990. 30-day money-back guarantee.